MW01107503

JOURNAL
FOR
PENELOPE

by

ERNESTINE
HUNT
COTTON

VANTAGE PRESS
New York

FIRST EDITION

Copyright © 2005 by Martha Cotton

Published by Vantage Press, Inc.
419 Park Ave. South, New York, NY 10016

Manufactured in the United States of America
ISBN: 0-533-15042-6

Library of Congress Catalog Card No.: 2004096819

0 9 8 7 6 5 4 3 2 1

Dedicated to
Lieutenant Peter Nelson Dean, R.N., F.A.A.
with Love and Gratitude and Pride

"Greater Love hath no man
Than that he lay down his life for another."

FOREWORD

Dear Little Penelope,

At the beginning of World War II your Nana (grandmother) Cotton decided to keep a diary, or rather a book of notes. Because Nana felt that one day her family, and perhaps some friends, might be interested in reading of the many varied events that undoubtedly, in one way or another, would affect our (the Cottons) lives during that period of modern history to be known as World War II.

One day, of course, you will read in your history books the whole story of those tragic war years of 1939-1945. Historians will have put all the important events into a chronological and informative sequence. You will also read many other books, stories and articles about that short, full, turbulent slice of history wherein you spent your first five years. And there will always be personal stories told to you by your immediate family--Mummie, your four grandparents (English and American), and your Aunt and two uncles. But, in spite of all this, Nana wished to make some sort of <u>written</u> personal record for <u>us</u> to keep as a testament of Life as it was lived <u>in England by Americans</u> (your Mummie's people) from the Declaration of War, September 3rd, 1939 to V.J. Day, August 14th, 1945-- almost six years. And so Nana wrote this book.

This is not a "story book." Yet it does tell a story. For, as you read the different episodes that Nana found of particular interest in that frightening time of World War II--and found time to record for future family reference--you will feel that this book might well have commenced as so many "story books" do commence--"Once upon a time there was a brave young man, and he lived in a small but beautiful country set like a green jewel in the sea." As you know, the Country is

England and the young man was your Daddy, Lieutenant Peter Nelson Dean, R.N., F.A.A. (Royal Navy, Fleet Air Arm.)

But, dear little Penelope, although this books is titled "Journal for Penelope" and is dedicated "to Lieut. Peter Nelson Dean, R.N., F.A.A." the book, as a whole, is representative of the lives of many thousands of families who lived in England throughout the War, sharing the harsh conditions and dangers of that War, as well as the little happinesses and laughter-making episodes that somehow always balance tragedy.

And so the title might well read--"Journal for Children of World War II," and the dedication might be--"Dedicated to those Men who fought and died that these Children might live--in Peace, Security and Freedom." Because Life (or living)--as you will one day understand--is not a uniquely personal and singular ex'stence. Life is a large multiple experience shared with a large number of people--the World in fact. If you, Penelope, and others of your generation can realize this, then whatever contributions you make to the future of the world will be worthwhile. And, eventually, that lasting Peace, which the present and past generations have failed to realize, will be yours.

May it come true.
Nana

Prelude to War

In August, 1939, we, the Cotton family, which consists of my husband (Dick), our two daughters, (Alix & Martha), our son (Gerry) and myself (Peg)--were all spending the summer at Swanage, Dorset, on the South Coast of England. We had rented the lower floor of a villa on the grounds of the Grosvenor Hotel, where we took our meals. The arrangement made for leisure, health and fun. And Swanage, being but 2 1/2 hours' run by car from London--where we were living at Regency Lodge, St. Johns Wood--afforded Dick week-end relaxation.-

(We were living in London because of the Depression in the United States. An excellent position in London had been offered Dick shortly before the Christmas of 1934 and he had left Boston at once. I followed in February of 1935 with our three children. Both Dick and I felt that the more remunerative job plus the experience of living in another country would be fine for all of us.

"I have decided to use Boston, Massachusetts as our "home town" in the States, because no one in England has ever heard of Newtonville, Mass., a suburb just a few miles outside Boston. We were always having to explain!)

Alix, our elder daughter, had become engaged to Lieut. Peter Nelson Dean, R.N., who that same August was on leave, recuperating from appendicitis. Peter, his brother (Tony) and his mother (Dorothy--Mrs. Arthur Dean), were visiting us at Swanage. Our "suite" was crowded to say the least. But the weather was so lovely that we lived out of doors most of the time. With the friendly sea at the foot of the lawn, a blaze of

1

flowers in the gardens all about, and blue skies overhead, all seemed well with the world.

Suddenly the shadow of War began to loom upon the horizon of our peaceful world--far across the Channel, away off in Poland, in fact. Remembering the outcome of the "Crisis," a year ago, War seemed improbable. Why, here was the comfortable hotel! The swimming pool! The tennis courts! Crowds of happy and laughing people! The singing ocean still rose and fell in white crescendo and diminuendo upon the beach! And the hourly steamer from Bournemouth unfailingly chug-chugged in and out of the picturesque harbor! Everything seemed normal.

Or was it? For we did feel "something"--a vague sense of impending change and unpleasantness--but no solid frightening threat. A shadow is so ephemeral!

However, one by one, our daughters' dancing partners, tennis opponents, swimming companions--all those young men who had helped to make the Summer a happy one--began to disappear from the scene. "Word has come," they said, "Must leave at once." Young wives were left to finish out their holiday alone, with the children, or to pack and return home. "Tom--or Bill--or Jack--is in the Reserve." We began to feel deserted, and by September 1st a bit scared. Supposing there really was a war!

On August 30th, a young man who had been Gerry's tutor at York House--a Prep. school in London--came over from Bournemouth to spend the day with us. He was anxious about the Great Evacuation, as all teachers had been notified to "stand by." We laughed, and said, "You don't really mean you'll have to go up to London for that!" But the young man had been very serious and patient, and had explained the wonderful

2

scheme to us. Still, it didn't make sense--the Evacuation of children because of threatened air raids!--until the announcement over the radio the very next evening, Thursday, August 31st. The girls, Dorothy, Peter, Tony, and I were in the Hotel Lounge, along with many hotel guests, when Dorothy looked at me raised her eyebrows, and said,

"So it's come to that!"

Everyone began to exclaim, incredulity sharpening the voices,

"Evacuation tomorrow!"

"The Government must feel pretty certain!"

"Pooh! It's just a dress rehearsal."

"No, things are bad--very."

Foreboding settled on us all, and I decided to send at once for Gerry who was visiting his school pal, Hugh Silk, in Bognor Regis, ninety miles away. We must all be together in this Crisis!

Friday, September 1st, was a lovely day--blue skies, a bay like lapis lazuli, the flowers riotous with color, their perfume so mingled with sunshine as to be felt like a warm caressing breath. A benediction of a day.

Yes?

Before noon German bombs had fallen upon Poland.

Dorothy and I were gloomily discussing the probabilities of war when Peter, followed by Alix, burst into our villa. "Mum!" he shouted, "The Germans have bombed Poland!"

Dorothy jumped to her feet.

"It's come!" she said, "That means war!"

Her eyes filled and she bit her lip.

"I can't bear it!   I can't bear it!--All that horror and deprivation again!" Her fingers gripped a chair and her

3

knuckles turned white.

"Don't, Mum!" said Peter, putting his arms about her.

"Tony!" she whispered. "He's just eighteen. Oh, they shan't take you both!"

"Hush, Mum. We'll be all right."

I saw Dorothy's emotions slowly set into a controlled calm.

Dorothy's husband served in the R.N.V.R. (Royal Navy Volunteer Reserve.) during the last war. He was in action at the Battle of Jutland. She herself was a V.A.D. (Member of Volunteer Aid Detachment.) in the hospital at Folkestone where she saw German bombs dig a crater in the street outside during an air-raid. Peter was born during the war, and Dorothy never forgets that there were but two scuttles of coal left at the time--and later one a day, so that she froze until evening when the precious coal was used for a few hours' warmth and comfort. She remembers the constant heartbreaks--as when she went to a Scottish port to spend a few hours with her husband only to find his ship gone--and weeks before it's return, with no surety of that. We will never forget the casualty lists.

Yet, after that one momentary outburst, "I suppose, dear, you'll be getting notice to report back?"

"I suppose so," said Peter.

"I'll help you pack," said Dorothy.

"And so will I," said Alix.

And that was that.

Immediately after lunch Alix & Peter set off in the car for Bognor Regis to fetch Gerry. Although they bypassed the highways wherever possible, and did not stop at the Silk's cottage for more than a cup of tea, the hundred and eighteen miles over and back took until 9 o'clock that night. The roads had been teeming with all sorts of transport, evacuating hundreds of children from London! Alix, Peter and Gerry arrived back at the Grosvenor Hotel in Swanage simultaneously with my husband who had driven down from London with two of our friends, Mr. and Mrs. Frank Heaver, for the week-end.

"I've booked passage for you and the children," was my husband's greeting.

"Are you going, Dick?" I asked.

"No, I can't quit the factory--the work's too vital."

"Then I'm staying. We'll all stay on the same side of the Atlantic. Besides, I don't want to miss anything!"

"Are you crazy?", etc., etc.,

But we are all in England and plan to stay.

That evening of September 1st, we had a taste of what was later to become an accepted condition--a "black-out." For some time preparations to handle night traffic had been in readiness-- and there had even been a trial "black-out" in London one night the preceding week. I happened to be in town at Regency Lodge for a few days, with two friends from the States--Mrs. Van der Groen and her daughter Nora--who, after a summer in Holland, were on their way back to America. The trial black-out, with the city streets blanketed in unlighted night, fascinated us. We decided to sample it.

It had been fun, cruising in a taxi in the dark, with a minimum of lights--along the Finchley Road, Wellington Road, Baker Street, on down to Oxford and Regent Streets, Piccadilly Circus, Piccadilly, Park Lane and home again to St. John's Wood. But now, with German Bombs falling on Poland, and a feeling of unknown but impending disaster vibrating in the air,

5

it was not so amusing.

After dinner at the hotel that night of September 1st, we had to stumble along the flower bordered paths and gravel walks back to the villa in complete darkness. Our pretty suite had become a dim and blue lit cave! Hotel employees had either draped the lights with odd bits of dark, or black, cloth-- or had put in blue bulbs. We couldn't read or play cards. We just sat and talked and wondered if there really was going to be a war, or if there'd be another reprieve as in the last September.

Twice we were interrupted by bangings on the outer door. The Air Raid Warden warned us that light was showing. So we tucked the window drapes and curtains more closely to the walls, as the only window properly blacked out was that in the bath, where heavy black paper had been pasted over the panes of glass and where one must stifle after dark as no windows could be open while there was a light in the room.

The Grosvenor Hotel, within, had seemed a blaze of glory by comparison. Although the number of lights was drastically cut down and those near the heavily curtained windows were unlit or well dimmed, one could still read, play cards, and enjoy an illusion of normality. Dancing went on in the ballroom, but uncomfortably so because of the lack of air. Ping Pong, billiards, and darts continued in the game room. So we stumbled back to the Hotel for the rest of the evening.

By noon the next day, Saturday September 2nd, all the torches (flashlights) in the village were sold--also all the extra batteries. Sandbags were being filled and piled about the fire-alarms and police-call boxes. The air raid siren scared the wits out of the populace in long-drawn shrieks as it was tested. Tension and expectancy possessed us. But we all went swimming, and then lay on the warm sands and looked up

6

at the peaceful blue above us and tried to imagine a German bomber suddenly zooming down from it. The thought seemed too utterly trivial and fantastic! We couldn't be bothered. There wasn't a war. There was just the ocean, the sand, and a bit of warm sun.

But later, as we sat at tea in the open bay window of our sitting room, watching the youngsters on the croquet lawn and the little Bournemouth steamer swinging out from the dock for the five o'clock trip, we were startled by the sharp and persistent blasts of the steamer's siren--toot, too-Ot, toot, too-Ot, toot--the usual procedure being but two short hoots.

Every one on its deck waved and shouted. People on shore waved in answer, saluted and jumped up and down. The siren screeched some more. And the little steamer puffed off across the bay, majestic and a bit arrogant, we thought.

"Why all the fuss?" We puzzled Americans asked.

"She's been called up for patrol duty--did this in the last war--those whistles were a farewell salute."

Only a tiny pleasure craft, but sturdy enough for dangerous duty--ready for it, cocky and gay. A silly thing to catch one's breath over? Maybe. But it brought the word "war" back into our mental vocabulary.

That evening there was a terrific thunderstorm, a fit accompaniment to any Witch's Sabbath that might be brewing. The young people had gone to the cinema in the town. The rest of us, Dorothy, the Heavers, Dick and I were in our sitting-room, having coffee, and listening to the fierce cannonade of thunder, the heavy downpour of rain and the wild gusts of wind that beat upon the villa. Because of this din we were slow to notice a frantic pounding on the entry door.

7

"Do you hear that?"

Cries of "Help! Help!" accompanied the beatings on the glass door panel.

"Someone's in an awful hurry!"

"They'll break the glass!"

Dick opened the door to a terrified young woman, hatless, coatless, and barefoot, completely drenched--the water in the driveway up to her ankles.

"Oh, please, can you come and help us? My mother and the baby--they'll drown! Oh, do come quick! Over there!"

She pointed back up the driveway to a stone cottage at the foot of the hill which rose behind our grounds. Water was simply sluicing down the hill slopes--washing out gullies, and uprooting fragile garden plants. The bright lightening lit up the macabre scene. Gone were all thoughts of black-out. Elsie (Mrs. Heaver), Dorothy and I stood in the open doorway and watched Dick and Frank (Mr. Heaver) follow the young woman back through the storm to the cottage. Through a lighted window of the kitchen we could see an elderly woman holding a baby.

The men tried the door. It was jammed--the kitchen table against it, the flood water waist high. Impatiently the young woman rushed to the window and shattered its panes with her fists.

"Mother, I've got help for you--we're here--we're here!" she shrieked hysterically.

Frank reached through the broken panes and unlatched the window. He then climbed into the seething room--the only way to describe it. We could see everything plainly. The stormy heavens swung frequent sweeping flashes, like a gigantic lantern above the scene.

The little kitchen seemed alive. Chairs bobbed in the rushing flood water--the dust-bin, apparently empty, was lifted ceiling-ward--and even the linoleum, torn loose, curled above the water.

Enthralled, we three women watched Frank hand the baby through the window to the young woman and then, with great difficulty, because of the deep and swirling water, maneuver the elderly woman up on to the table where Dick could reach her and lift her out. The poor soul was in such an exhausted state that the men had to carry her to the villa. And the young woman was so heedless of anything but safety for the baby in her arms that she ran and stumbled over the sharp stones and rubble, cutting her feet so badly that our hall carpet and my bedroom rug became well spotted with blood.

Dorothy, as a former V.A.D., took charge of the young woman and her cut feet. Elsie commandeered the baby. And I undressed Grandma and wrapped her in blankets, getting a bit of gin down her throat with the aid of her daughter's, "Go on, Mother,--that isn't "drinking!" You've been nearly drowned, you know."

By the time the storm ceased, and a doctor arrived, and the bewildered husband managed to get back from the village-- where he had been attending an A.R.P. (Air Raid Precautions) meeting--our three "patients" were fairly comfortable. The hotel management arranged room for them all, and the grateful husband herded them off to bed.

Eleven p.m. Tea-time. Elsie departed to the kitchen to put the kettle on, Dorothy got a basin of water and began washing up the blood stains. I wrung out the wet cloths, and generally tidied the rooms. The men turned on the wireless for the late news. And the young people returned from the cinema,

9

goggled-eyed at the confusion, full of stories about the storm havoc in the town. We grouped around the table for tea.

"Chamberlain speaks to the Nation at 11:15 tomorrow morning."

"Yes, Britain's ultimatum to Germany expires at 11 a.m."

"Do you thing it's really war this time?"

"Looks like it."

"So far as I'm concerned it's already begun!" Dorothy had appeared in the doorway, basin in hand. "Be with you in a minute. This particular job takes me back to the Folkestone Hospital." And she left to empty the basin and wash her hands.

We all looked at each other.

And I'm sure we all thought the same thing.

Why yes. If there's a War things are going to be very different, aren't they? And not at all nice. --No.--But dreadful,--dreadful!

We sipped our tea in silence.

On the following day, Sunday, September 3rd, the sun pouring in at the windows awakened us to a day of bloom and beauty. But also, alas, to a day of sad decision. Everyone, save the very young, awaited Chamberlain's speech with trepidation. And at eleven o'clock groups of friends and families settled by the various radios. Our little group, as usual, met in our sitting-room where Dick sat beside the radio, like a master of ceremonies, and where an undercurrent of excitement possessed the disjointed conversation.

11:15 a.m.

Time seemed to pause for one fateful second. The world seemed static, and all within it.

The better the day, the better the deed--the better the day--. No. It wasn't going to work this time.

10

Chamberlain's voice poured into the room. And the timbre of his voice told us everything.

"I am speaking to you from the Cabinet room at 10 Downing Street. This morning the British Ambassador in Berlin handed the German Government an official note stating that, unless we heard from them by 11 o'clock that they were prepared at once to withdraw their troops from Poland, a state of war would exist between us. I have to tell you now that no such undertaking has been received and that, consequently, this country is at war with Germany . . . " and on to the end of that memorable speech.

No one spoke. No one exclaimed. The men's faces set in grim determination. The women closed their eyes a moment, each hiding her secret thoughts and worries at such a dreaded pronouncement.

"This country is at war with Germany."

A kind of horror crept over me. Would there be tremendous Air Raids at once? Certainly there was preparation for these--and there was the evacuation of the children! The psychological effect was such that I automatically and unconsciously slid down a bit in my chair, seeking a vague protection. And at the end of the speech I went to the window and looked fearfully across the bay as though flocks of German bombers might appear at any moment.

Now what?

Plans, of course.

Peter, alone, knew what to do. Dorothy and Alix helped him pack and he left that afternoon to report back for duty. Then, after some discussion, Dorothy and Tony drove off to Winchester--as Tony had decided to help with the Harvest there outside the city, replacing some chap already called up, and where he remained, until he returned to school some weeks later. Dorothy, after a spell of night duty in a Winchester A.R.P. (Air Raid Precautions) depot, went to London and joined a First Aid Unit in a Casualty Station under the Savoy Hotel. But sleeping on a mattress on the stone floor there gave her such rheumatism that she was forced to give up and is now running a canteen in a Service Men's Club in Chelsea from 5:00 to 11:00 p.m. 5 days a week.

Our rooms were engaged for a week longer so we felt that we had a breathing spell in which to find a school for Gerry--who, for the past year, had been at "La Chataigneraie" near Geneva, Switzerland, but who must now enter an English Public School because of travel difficulties in war-time. We decided to pack family luggage into the car when it came time to leave next week-end, and trek inland across lovely Dorsetshire via Wiltshire and Buckinghamshire, into Oxfordshire and there locate a house away from London and Air Raids, but near enough for Dick to spend week-ends with us.

The Heavers had just sold their house in Wimbledon and had taken a flat in London near us, in St. Johns Wood. But they decided to move in just the same and so planned driving up to London the next day, Monday September 4th, with Dick. I was to stay on at Swanage with the children and try to contact a school somewhere in a so-called safety zone.

After tea the hotel Manager asked us to move into the Hotel as the villas were so difficult to black out and there were now available rooms in the main building. So we spent a couple of busy hours transporting our clothes, luggage and what-not. Our new rooms looked like jumble-sales upon completion of the job. And I was not too pleased to find us all ensconced on the top floor of the Hotel--very handy for bombs! In no mood to straighten the confusion we dressed for dinner and went down to the Bar.

The place was crowded--young and old chattering sixteen to the dozen and having "one more for luck, Old Boy." Youngsters of 18 to 20 were making plans to join the Air Force, Navy or Army. A few older, solemn faces were in conclave over "How to Win the War." Perched on a stool at the bar counter was a morose looking chap of forty-odd. He engaged Dick and Frank in conversation.

It seemed that he, the sad looking individual, had come up from the town to the Hotel with the express purpose of drowning his sorrows. The Great Evacuation was likely to finish him off! Some time ago the authorities had investigated his household and, finding that there were two quite unused bedrooms, had awarded four Evacuees to him and his wife as their quota in the enormous and humanitarian scheme. All well and good. They would do their bit. True, he'd fought in the last war, but if he had to play nursemaid in this he'd not shirk his duty. "God and Country, Old Chap, you know." So he had another, this time on Dick, and continued, all of us now interested listeners.

Saturday afternoon the evacuees had arrived--quite as expected. But there seemed to have been a slight mistake somewhere, for not four evacuee children, but seven children and two women were deposited by the London bus before his doorstep, and, despite his and his wife's frantic protestations, were left there, expectant and hopeful of sanctuary. The "quota" immediately swarmed into the house--plus nine food parcels, nine changes of underwear and nine gas masks. And all that evening the seven children had roared with fright at the

13

thunderstorm, and there hadn't been enough bedding--let alone beds--and, the Good God Save us!--Yes, he'd have another-- but that wasn't all! A woman and two babies--two babies mind you!--had but just appeared at 6 o'clock today.

"And now, my friends, what is the solution?"

Tears filled his eyes.

"It is too much--too much."

We all agreed. But we all were also hungry. So we left the Old Man who had so many children he didn't know what to do, and went in to dinner.

That evening, as I made ready for bed, I felt committed to an unknown adventure and one that I prayed would have a happy ending. As I pulled aside the thick black curtains to open the windows, I watched a pale and nervous moon slide in and out the ominous cloudbanks. Would an enemy plane, death laden, find ambush in those soft and silken outposts of Heaven?

It was a long time before I fell asleep that night.

A State of War Exists

The next morning, Monday, September 4th, I awoke very early--to find Dick already dressed and packing a bag. Heavens above! I had said last night that I was going up to London after all--raids or no raids.

I have no doubt but that my second cocktail the evening before had given me the courage to make the decision for I was frankly afraid--afraid to have Dick return to London, afraid to leave the children at Swanage, up under the roof at nights, and without their gas masks--afraid of bombs, shells, gas, whatever Hitler was about to fling upon England--for at that time London

14

was expected to be the immediate objective of the German Luftwaffe.

Dick and Frank had argued loud and long to get me to change my mind. But if Elsie went up to town, I didn't see why I shouldn't. And there were all the clothes in the flat to be packed, the silver to be stored and the precious personal knick-knacks to be hidden in cupboards, etc.

So, the sooner I got to London the better. The place might be bombed that very night!

Very well, I could take a train back to Swanage as soon as the packing was finished, said Dick. But I could see that he was most annoyed at my, "Don't you dare to go without me!" as he went down to breakfast, bag in hand.

I tore into my clothes--never took so little notice of make-up--grabbed a few needed articles of clothing and crammed them into my migrator. The room looked simply awful! Wardrobe trunks stood open, trailing frocks and undies; there was a bag of laundry in one corner, a pile of newly washed clothes on a chair, boxes of books, magazines and games cluttered the floor along with several lots of cereal, soap, sugar, and even cosmetics and medicines that we had bought upon the advice of English friends who had been through the last war. there were coats, hats, and shoes in a skyscraper on the couch. I shall never forget that scene. How it crowded and pushed me about, and how incongruous it all appeared because of the beautiful calm day outside, the familiar cry of seagulls.

Alix and Gerry were still asleep, so I tiptoed in to the youngsters in turn and gave them a kiss and said a tiny prayer, for I was certain that Dick, the Heavers and I were walking into a death trap and that, with Portsmouth on one side and Weymouth on the other, both Naval Bases, Swanage didn't

15

seem to be exactly a safety area for the children.

Martha, my younger daughter, was downstairs ahead of me and prodding the headwaiter into making me some toast, as early breakfast had been prepared for only three. The wretches hadn't taken me seriously!

"Martha, run out to the car and tell them I'm coming at once."

Clutching the buttered toast, wrapped in a serviette, I flew after her--just in time to meet the newsboy with the early editions.

"Passenger steamer torpedoed!--S.S. Athenia attacked by Submarine! Americans lost!"

Shades of the Lusitania! I could read the men's thoughts as I scrambled into the car. Waving to Martha, we drove off through the entrance gates, I thanked my lucky stars that the children and I weren't booked for an Atlantic crossing.

The suddenness of the German sea attack seemed almost unbelievable--and then again, just what we must expect, of course. The horrors of war! The lovely morning became overcast with dark premonitions, and indeed the usually familiar scenes along the 125 mile route to London had a strange and foreboding aspect. All road and traffic signs wore wooden "bonnets"--shades, hastily improvised from boxes. The 'phone kiosks and police-call-box shelters were banked with sand bags. There was an extra sandbag atop each fire-alarm pedestal, giving it a slightly tipsy look.

The postman on his cycle, the housewife with her market basket, the children playing in the streets and fields, each wore a small square cardboard box on homemade shoulder straps of string or tape. Gas masks! How foolish they seemed amidst the sunshine and the rural scenes.

A plane passed overhead.

Again I had the sensation of shrinking.

"The air-raids will be on moonlight nights, won't they?" I asked. Frank was a pilot during the last war.

"Won't make any difference this time," he said, "Moon or no moon, instrument flying's changed all that."

My stomach curled up like a caterpillar.

Long lines of Army lorries, impatient soldiers on motor cycles, and now and then a heavy mounted gun, held us up at times. But what impressed us the most was the sight of taxicabs filled with people, the cab roofs piled high with luggage and bundles of various description. The strangely familiar, high-built, blue and black vehicles whizzed past at frequent intervals--going in the opposite direction. They puzzled us a bit, these ultra citified conveyances now in the depths of the country.

"I have it!" said Dick.

"Those are London cabs. People are getting out of town as fast as they can. You see!" He turned to me. "I told you not to come!"

"Well, I can do the same thing--take a taxi--if I have to!" But I didn't feel as cocky as I sounded.

The nearer we got to London the more prevalent became the signs of war. "Air Raid Shelter" in large black letters appeared on walls and fences, a black arrow pointing the way. Groups of people could be seen digging in the Parks and the green Squares, the women along with the men. Civilians in tin hats and wearing service gas masks patrolled the streets as War Reserve Police or Special Point Duty Constables. And everywhere there were the glaring news posters, "S.S. ATHENIA Torpedoed--Americans lost."

17

At last, on the outskirts of London we sighted the balloon barrage. Hundreds of monstrous silvery gray fish, grotesque blown-up toys, floated thousands of feet above the factories and homes of the Largest-City-in-the-World and now, surely, one of the busiest.

We edged our way through the thickening traffic. Hospitals were still evacuating patients. All kinds of Volunteer or Auxiliary Services were in evidence.

Car after car, with an official sticker on its windshield, uniformed figures within, hooted its way past. Driving through Hyde Park we saw anti-aircraft guns, and wide deep craters whence great loads of sand were being carted for the millions of sandbags that make the padded fortifications about entrances and ground floor windows of shops, banks, hotels, hospitals, and Air Raid Shelters. The quaint old Squares of London Town--their green island refuges encircled by iron fences or high hedges--now harbored large canvas reservoirs of water, like outsize fish ponds, or partially deflated barrage balloons swaying at their shortened chains like tethered elephants.

We drove into the courtyard of Regency Lodge, our block of flats in St. John's Wood--a residential section of London, where we lived--to find several removal vans and their crews busy there. Tenants were leaving. And ever since, almost every day, there has been a removal van in the courtyard. For tenants go--and come--and go--in fluctuation with the rumors of raids--no raids--raids--and so on ad infinitum. For this is an unpredictable war.

Dick left me at Regency Lodge and drove out to the factory, dropping the Heavers at their flat in Northways, nearby. Poor Elsie was up to her neck with new curtains, carpet laying, and the many odd jobs required when one moves. The van men had thought it very funny to be moving people in to London. "Everyone else is going' out, ma'am,--and fast!" they had told her.

'Phoning for a plumber or a carpenter, Elsie always got the same reply, "Sorry, ma'am, our man's called-up. But we'll send some one along as soon as we can."

I once said to Elsie, "too bad you and Frank can't enjoy your new home. This dark war!"

"But we are enjoying it," she answered.

And they continue to do so--with an Air Raid Shelter in the hall below, barrage balloons overhead, and well fitted blackout arrangements at the windows.

However, on that Monday of September 4th, most of these war-time "amenities" were in their infancy. I had to see to blacking-out our flat at once. So Lily, my daily maid, and I went over the rooms, measuring windows and counting lights. The yardage necessary for lining draperies and the number of black shades needed for the lights was appalling. I must evolve a cheaper scheme, and then go shopping.

Lily got out the gas masks--as I must now carry mine--and we used ordinary heavy white twine to make shoulder straps. This is an incident strangely significant--Lily and I at the dining table, threading twine through five cardboard boxes containing gas masks, and Lily telling me of her little girl who had been evacuated to the country on Saturday.

"Where is she?" I asked.

"I don't know, Madam--not 'til I get a card telling me. But I'm sure she's in a safe place."

Such faith!

I thought how terribly hard it would be for me to send one of my brood off to an unknown destination--into the care of strangers.

"By and by I can go to see her," continued Lily. "I'm to pay eight and six ($2.10) a week. But she'll be safe. Here, Madam, let me tighten the string a bit on your gas mask--it slips on your shoulder."

So casual!

I picked up my handbag and went off to catch the No. 13 Bus, as I was meeting Elsie at Frank's office on the Strand for lunch.

From the top of the bus, where I prefer to ride, I surveyed familiar scenes that were the same--yet different. I could <u>feel</u> the change due to war, a certain subdued atmosphere with a pulsing undercurrent. And certainly one feature made the greatest difference of all. The gas masks. With every man, woman and child wearing or carrying those funny little boxes, all London seemed setting out on a gigantic picnic. You've no idea how odd it looked--all those gas masks, like little lunch boxes.

The shopping districts had a Sunday or Bank Holiday appearance--there were so few people about, so many already out of London. Yet, when I went into Selfridges on Oxford Street to buy black-out material, that particular department was crowded, and <u>pale blue</u> stuff was all that I could get, that is, that the salesgirl would guarantee as lightproof. Enough for just the kitchen window cost me one pound ($5.00). I wondered how the really poor were going to manage complete black-outs, and have since noticed the many <u>painted</u> windows, black or dark blue. No doubt an economy--but how dismal those houses must be, like caves. I also bought eight shillings worth ($2.00) of adhesive tape and was disconcerted later to find out that the whole lot only did for the one large bay window in our bedroom, criss-cross on every pane in the approved fashion, as a preventive from shattered glass due to explosions. Later on some of the larger shops displayed most artistic and unique designs in gummed tape on their windows, and cellophane has been extensively used for the same purpose.

The prevalence of uniforms set me to thinking of the last war, and how exciting and romantic it had all seemed back in the States when far from the actual scenes. Now I was going to be in a war--I and my family. But neither excitement nor glamour seemed likely--rather a steadiness of purpose and duty, no doubt a harsh endurance. And what of those air raids?

One hardly dared to think! I had noticed how simply the young men set about joining various units, how casually they spoke of "getting commissions"--their eyes, only, betraying a realization of what war could mean.

When Dick returned to the flat that afternoon shortly before dinner, he brought a thick roll of black paper (similar to what we call tarpaper in the States) and enough gummed tape to "do" all the windows. We set to work at once. the windows in the kitchen and the bathrooms were first criss-crossed with the gummed tape. We then completely covered the bathroom windows with black paper--which still remains, necessitating a light by day as well as night. In the kitchen we pasted six to eight inch wide strips of black paper down each side, across the top and bottom and down the middle of the one big window there. Lily and I had already run-up the pale blue light-proof curtains and hung them there at tea-time. With the curtains drawn, and improvised black paper shades about the ceiling and wall lights, we felt efficiently blacked-out so far as the kitchen and baths were concerned, but I'm sure poor Lily found the arrangements anything but efficient for cooking. Shadows

21

fell everywhere, into the soup and vegetables cooking on the stove, across the grill, so that Lily had to strike a match to note the progress of things cooking. Weeks later I made some extra heavy black sateen curtains and embellished them with appliquéed cretonne roses. These curtains now permit us to have every light ablaze in the kitchen and to snap our fingers at Hitler, air-raids and wardens--and to get on with a proper job of cooking. But in the early weeks of the war before I lined all the drapes with black in order to have sufficient lights on, it was almost as gloomy, after dark, inside our flat as outside in the blackout, and we received several sharp and embarrassing "warnings" from Air-Raid wardens about mere threads and tiny gleams of light. One must be so careful not to provide a guide of any sort to Hitler's Hell-Bearers.

We had to fill bathtubs, basins, and pitchers with water in case the water mains should be blown up by German bombs or terrible fires should break out from the thousands of incendiary bombs dropped upon us. There was little comfort to be had from a first-aid kit, a torch, a gas mask on one's bedside table, a heavy coat and boots ready to one's hand. For, in the early weeks of war, no one expected Hitler to stay his hand, and nightly we and our friends held arguments and guessing contests as to just what the fiend was going to do next. Would it be an Air-Raid?

That first week of war was hectic. I packed clothes indiscriminately, feeling that everything possible must be taken out to the country. Dick had brought some large wooden packing cases from the factory. So Lily and I cleaned all the china and glass ornaments from the shelves and window ledges, wrapped them well in quantities of tissue and newspaper and packed them in these cases.

22

All of the silver--save that necessary for daily use--was also packed in this way, as we preferred to take it along with us rather than to store it in a Bank. The Bank might be bombed.

I lingered a bit over the little personal ornaments brought from home in the States. Memories crowded thickly. And as I wrapped up an old shell, upon which is carved the Lord's Prayer, and tucked it inside a bowl made by and bought from Anton Lang, himself, years ago--two dearly loved treasures of my Mother's--I wondered if this act of hiding the Lord's Prayer within the little bowl from Oberammergau could be an omen, and that the things of the Spirit and the Mind were not to be hidden under a regime of darkness and brutality. My heart is indeed troubled over many things, i.e. of taxis tomorrow, and the drive back to the children. but each morning I would answer Dick's question, "Well, are you going back to-day?" with, "No, I'm staying until Friday when you go back." You see, if Dick was going to stay in London, I figured that I could find the courage to do so, too. Yet I was really afraid, and the closing in of those uncertain nights used to get me down a bit. One night we were roused from sleep shortly after midnight to collect our "gear" and descend to the Air Raid shelter in the basement.

AIR RAID WARNING!

And then that strange, unreal scene--like a bad dream. The crowded basement shelter. Everyone carrying those funny little boxes. The women in various stages of undress, some wrapped in comforters and half asleep, some looking real perky with pastel fish-net snoods over their hair and wearing gay

23

house-wraps. Most of the men in slacks and pullovers, though some wore dressing gowns over pajamas, and many sported caps because of the drafts. And, let me say, there is something incongruous and a bit comic in the combination of pajamas, bath robe, and tweed cap--no matter whether one expects bombs or not.

I see it all again--and wonder when we must repeat this mad performance, men and women, most of them strangers to each other, hurrying from their separate and particular flats, down into one common room of refuge, the large basement, where they sit side by side, still strangers, though sharing a common emotion--that of fearful apprehension--and waiting, waiting thus, still strangers. While above and outside, the empty city streets--patrolled only by wardens, A.R.P. and A.F.S. (Auxiliary Fire Service) squads--wait also for hell-fire, destruction, the end of a sane world.

Everything was turned completely upside down--like an hour glass--so that the sands of time seemed to run in the opposite direction, back to uncertainty and fear, back to war and the killing of men.

Everywhere one was reminded that calamity and death might now descend upon us.

There were buckets of sand, longhandled shovels for incendiary bombs and pick-axes ornamenting doorsteps and hallways. The lovely parks and gardens were being turned into huge rabbit warrens as hundreds of underground shelters were hastily dug. There was an enormous excavation for sand in Regents Park, and the story got about that this was to become a common grave for thousands of casualties and that some factory had already turned out thousands of cardboard coffins, for just such an emergency. (I learned later that part of this story was true--the manufacture of thousands ot cardboard coffins.) I don't believe that now--but at the time it made me quite ill. One does not happily contemplate being a corpse.

The weather was so lovely--true September summer with sun and soft air. How ironic!

Walking up the Finchley Road for my morning marketing, I felt like the old woman in the nursery rhyme, "Lawks-a-mercy, can this be I?" Those barrage balloons so far above me, dotting the blue sky like monstrous silver bees, put strange notions into my mind.

"Why do those bees swarm over your head?"

"To keep off the Germans, Sir," she said.

Doesn't make sense, does it? But neither did a lot of other things.

Housewives, their babies parked nearby in prams, (Perambulators, Baby carriages) were to be seen lending a hand to young men and women, even girls and boys, busily engaged in filling burlap bags with sand from lorries by the curb. These workers were ordinary citizens, not laborers. The young men were stacking the filled bags in tiers to form emergency shelters for those people caught in the streets during an air raid. I saw passers-by take off their coats and join in the work for ten or fifteen minutes--and then go on about their business. The hundreds of emergency shelters that went up in this way at the beginning of the war were later reconstructed into small fortresses reinforced with concrete and labeled, "This shelter to hold ......persons"." They look forbidding, but are now as familiar as the sand bagged pillar boxes (mail boxes) and fire alarms. But at the time, in that first week of war, to see ordinary people in hurry and fear bent over this extraordinary task of self-preservation--well, it somehow was almost unbelievable!

And so were the fruit and provision vans with "Ambulance" roughly painted in large white letters above such inscriptions as "W.B. Flasher, Fruiterer, St. John's Wood." Young women in slacks and jumpers were at the wheels, tin hats and gas masks slung across their shoulders, while two to four iron cots bounced about inside the vans as alibi for that daubed sign "Ambulance." I'm sure if I were rushed to the hospital in any such conveyance I'd never last the trip. For, in spite of the fact that most of these so-called ambulances are now freshly painted and lettered, the cots within still bounce and rattle.

A familiar large garage, like many others, has been turned into a depot for those hybred vehicles. The young women drivers could be seen each day busily learning to make it up the steep curved drive while wearing their gas masks. This is very difficult in daylight, but try doing it in a blackout! However, for weeks, all over London these girls practiced quick getaways at their various depots while wearing decontamination suits and gas masks, and covered every route to every assigned hospital until each route was learned by heart--so that finally the word "Guy's" or "Westminster," or "St. Thomas's" would simply start up a certain set of reflexes and the ambulances would roll out and off, into the day, or blackout, on to their destinations, piloted by grotesque figures who looked and acted more like robots than bits of feminine humanity. They do a proper war job--even though it reverted to knitting and boredom for some months. But rather boredom than bombs! (The anticipated raids, the civilian casualties, etc. did not materialize for quite some months. This state of fevered preparation plus nagging frustration became known as the Phoney War. The British called it the Bore War or the Funny War.)

The blackout is a most annoying wartime precaution, although we have learned to take it in our stride. But for weeks it was frightening and depressing. How dependent one is on light--and how helpless one can feel without it. At the very beginning of the war we were not allowed torches (flashlights) on the streets. And when I look back on those early nocturnal excursions I wonder how we ever got about. For get about we did, with the aid of hooded wee red, yellow, or green crosses (mere slits instead of full lights) at traffic points, and elusive white painted patches and stripes on curbs, trees and lamp standards. This groping about, with other shadowy figures, in a ghostly world, seems like a fantastic game of Blindman's Bluff. Voices tinkle in the blackout. Soft laughter comes from out the void. Silence possesses the night.

But later, with blue tissue over the glass, when torches were finally permitted, their tiny lights flitting through the dark reminded me of fireflies. Memories of summers on Cape Cod would cross my mind. And then a jolt from some passing stranger, or "Mind the curb!" from Dick, or the roar of London buses, or a clipped English accent in the dark, would snatch me into the present, into the blackout, into the war. I still have those nostalgic moments when out at night. The blackout breeds a bitter magic.

But out of the alarms and discomforts of war, there gradually emerged one pleasant change--a new relationship among the English people. Not only was there the strange companionship of people huddled in air raid shelters, and the

27

feverish camaraderie of those in the streets filling sandbags, but there appeared a neighborliness amongst the populace such as we had never dreamed possible here in England, where friends of long standing make dates for tea, rather than pay impromptu calls. Uncertainty and fear, the closing of cinemas, the restrictions of the blackout kept people at home but it also drove them into other homes seeking companionship and cheer. The tight little homes of England expanded. The Jones had evening tea with the Smiths, and the Browns and the Whites dropped in to join them. The great guessing contest--as to whether there were going to be air-raids or not, and when-- was on.

No one thought of anything else, consciously or unconsciously. Our lives were patterned to this threat of death from the air. And so, on Friday, September 8th, Dick and I left London and drove down to Swanage to collect the children and to start out across the softly beautiful English countryside to find a refuge from bombs.

A last weekend in that charming old seaside town of Swanage where stands John Wesley's modest stone cottage, and upon whose outskirts rise sentinel and ruins of Corfe Castle, once a strong-hold of the Wessex Kings, later stormed and battered by Cromwell. Below the castle now stretched a large encampment as of old, but no plumed knights in coats of mail, no prancing steeds were there, unless mayhap their ghosts. Instead, there were hundreds of khaki-clad soldiers of the King who swarmed about the country roads on noisy motor-bikes or rumbling lorries and busied themselves in modern war manoeuvre.

We found the Grosvenor Hotel full of uniforms,

particularly at tea and dinner. Officers and their staffs were quartered in the villas on the Hotel grounds. The inevitable buckets of sand and long handled shovels, for incendiary bombs, cluttered the entrances and halls. Wide beams from searchlights on the Isle of Wight across the bay swept the heavens at night. You couldn't forget the war if you wanted to.

We all had a last swim Sunday morning and after mid-day dinner set out for Henley-on-Thames, our first objective. Our way led through the New Forest, pale green and shadowy, where dozens of wild ponies roam at will and crop the roadside grass. Later, newspaper articles told of the danger of these little beasts, both to themselves and motorists, in the black-out, and suggested painting the ponies with white stripes! But on this particular day we saw more interesting things than wild ponies. Hidden behind hedges and beneath low growing trees, camouflaged by shelters of branches, were hundreds of soldiers, lorries and equipment--waiting for nightfall and its protective darkness. Temporary signs reading "Southampton" or "To the Docks" at roadside intersections completed the story. Britain's first Expeditionary Force would embark that night for France.

"Tough luck to be going out so soon," said my husband.
"Yes."
"Not so much chance of coming back."

Oh, the pity of it! The sacrifice of Youth again--again. Apprehension stole across the children's faces. Save for Gerry's questions we drove almost in silence until tea time.

Stopping before one of these picturesque English country Pubs with its thatched roof and rambling garden, we were surprised to have the landlord, in a most deprecating manner, apologize that, due to the military having taken over his place,

29

he could not serve us tea.

"It is, Madame, as you know, the war."

Too true. In spite of the peace and beauty all about us we felt an unseen threat which harried us to the point of pushing on, past all inviting inns and pubs until we reached "The Catherine Wheel" at Henley-on-Thames, shortly before dinner time.

The whitewashed exterior looked inviting; it was the only hostelry in the town with accommodations for us and we were hungry, so we booked rooms and ordered our luggage in.

Now, should you want to experience the romantic lodging of ancient, low and beamed ceilings, to search for your bedroom in narrow corridors with steps up and down in the most unexpected places and dark corners, to stand outside a bathroom door in hopeful anticipation of being its next occupant, only to discover, after a wait of some fifteen minutes, that said bath has two doors and has been catering to the other half of your second floor--whereupon you rush down three sections of crooked stairs, along a hall (under the bathroom) and up a fourth stairway, so on the cant as to resemble a ship's companion-way in a storm, to find the second door not only locked but guarded by a "bathroom anticipator" with whom you make a deal that she, like those others, will leave the second door locked when leaving, permitting you to enter from this side after her exit, and so drape yourself against the wall, towels nonchalantly disposed, and do Patience-on-a-Monument for another fifteen minutes--should you desire these "amenities" in a country pub, plus doubtful food, china with a past, and beds that require sleeping on the eiderdown (put beneath the lower sheet) rather than under it--why, then, my friends, visit "The Catherine Wheel." We spent three uncomfortable weeks

30

there before locating a house which suited both our pocket book and the size of our family.

Interlude at Henley-On-Thames

Henley-on-Thames, thirty-five miles from London, is famous for its rowing and sculling competitions held on the river there. Before the war, crews from many countries met in annual regattas at Henley-on-Thames. The big white tents set up as individual Headquarters and where tea was served, the regalia of the crews, colorful blazers, caps, and scarves of the Public School boys, the attendant gaiety and movement gave the river bank a gala Country Fair aspect. On race days, the milling crowds throbbing with excitement were the pulse of a sporting Nation and its friends. Now the sporting atmosphere was gone, but the sportsmanship remained. English men and women were rallying to every kind of service for their country.

Gerry and the girls were all for getting into some war work at once. So Monday morning, (Sept. 11th) Gerry went off to the City Hall to join the sandbaggers, and Alix and Martha enrolled in the Hospital Auxiliary to make bandages, splints, etc. The next thing was to find a house.

Easier said than done, even this early in the war. The Evacuation of Children had filled up the extra accommodation in the town and villages about. And those householders who felt free to rent seemed bent on making not a little, but a great deal of money. Buses in the country are few and far between, also they do not stray from the beaten path. So I hired a car-- Dick using ours to commute to and from London--and set out with an assorted list of "prospects" obtained from a local

31

Letting Office.

Such picturesqueness as would lure me into the most disappointing places! Enchanting gardens, low-browed thatched roofs, a plush-like sweep of green, a gardener's lodge in feudal stone, an ornamental pond; each attribute a gem, each whole an impossible conglomeration of tiny, dark low-ceilinged rooms or drafty barn-like halls and drawing-rooms, and all quite unheated save by fire places or totally inadequate electric fires. And the sculleries, the boot rooms, the airing cupboards and such "oddments" of these country houses seemed only so much make-weight to my American mind. At the end of a week my search had narrowed down to two possibilities; a cottage in the village of Wargrave, and a large rambling old house called "Longlands" in Henley proper. The latter we had not even considered as it already harbored three Evacuees who, the Letting Clerk informed us, "went with the house."

The prospectus of the cottage in Wargrave read like a fairy tale: "old-world garden, poplar-lined drive, tennis court, central heating, the owner will leave personal treasures as ornaments." The girls and I set out with expectation. It was a warm and sunny day, but the road along the river was shadowed darkly by tall trees and a dampness could be felt as it had rained the night before. The nearer we got to Wargrave the lower sank our spirits.

"Ugh! This place gives me the creeps," said Alix, "I don't think I could live in such a place."

And Martha and I quite understood. We hadn't liked the name either. But we decided to have a look, just in case we might be missing something.

At last, at the end of a lonely road <u>beyond</u> the village of

Wargrave, we came upon the cottage, surrounded by its guardian fence of wattle. The gate door swung open at a touch and we faced, at the end of a curving moss-grown walk, a house straight out of a book. You know, the Witch's house in "Hansel and Gretel." It was like that. Two high pointed gables, one at each end, windows with tiny leaded panes, a hooded shelter over the door step. And all so wee and huddled, with a wavy roof--and even smoke coming out of the chimney--that we looked for a big black cat and expected a cadaverous hooked-nose creature to answer our knock on the moldy door.

We surveyed the "old-world garden" as we waited; riotous gone-to-seed plants, select weeds, uncut grass, a stagnant canal beyond with a very weeping willow mourning above it. Someone needed a new pair of glasses! Or else, whoever wrote the prospectus had never seen this. Or the "poplar-lined drive" which had turned into a path and two poplar trees. Or the "tennis court" that had become a hayfield with a girdle of torn net across its middle. All under the Witch's spell of course.

And then the door opened and the fattest woman I have ever seen (outside of a circus) boomed at us in a military voice, "Is it about the house? And if it is, come in!"

From then on we never got a chance to do much of anything but listen and look. We were completely fascinated as to how such a huge woman navigated such wee rooms filled with huge furniture to meet her needs, and with brass pots, jardinieres and jugs cropping up over the floors like rocks in a Vermont pasture. And they felt the same, too, against our toes.

On the walls were African shields and javelins, almost overlapping they were so numerous;--the "personal treasures to

33

be left as ornaments." And we gave up counting the low teakwood tables when eleven had been accounted for in two rooms, each room the size of a self-respecting American bath.

Our guide had a disconcerting habit of confusing her subject matter. As the girls and I felt our way up the corkscrew staircase in complete gloom--there being no window in the hall below, or above--she rumbled on.

"We are very proud of these stairs. The carpenter was so certain we couldn't manage any in this space when we remodeled. The blond one is quite a Dresden type, isn't she? Now mine are both dark like the other. This is the bath. But I can't open the door as my elder daughter's sitting in there....with the dog, (seeing Alix's face!), he's ferocious." Which was quite unnecessary as tremendous growls had already been heard downstairs. "Yes, it's nice to have a variety. Mine are the same coloring. Here is the master's bedroom. Do you like the beautiful view? If you want separate ones, a cot can be put up at night."

I think the kitchen intrigued us the most. Set in the middle of the tiny box-like house, it was comparable to the last and wee-est of the nest of boxes, like those toys of our childhood. Not a single window. An ever-burning electric light bulb hung, like an effulgent spider, above a sink piled with soiled dishes.

"My maid is a refugee. She's after bread at the moment. That's her room," pointing to an open door. Straight off the kitchen, it appeared to be a remodeled cowshed, nothing else.

As we left I mentioned the central heating.

"Why, that's in the hall," said our hostess

"Here."

I looked. The girls looked.

"Here!" with an edge to it. Her large hand indicated a telephone directory. The book completely covered the top of the single radiator in the place.

No wonder we had failed to see any signs of the modern miracle we had somehow expected in this outlandish domicile.

"I say we have a look at the place with the Evacuees," said Martha as we drove away. "It can't be any worse."

"Longlands" proved to be situated in the very heart of Henley-on-Thames, its tall front windows with cream colored shutters and flower boxes overlooking the pavement of the High Street. The shining brass knocker and the Doctor's plate on the front door looked respectable and inviting. We rang the Day Bell with assurance. Evacuees or not, this looked the kind of house in which we could be at home.

Square, three stories high, of red brick, with a fanlight over the entrance, it resembled houses to be found in the historic quarters of Boston, Mass.

A very rosy-cheeked and smiling maid opened the door to us and Madam was bathing the baby, but if we would wait . . .

We would.

The maid showed us into a small square drawing-room of light paper and white woodwork, inviting chintz-covered furniture, and polished brass fire-irons winking in the five o'clock sun.

The girls and I beamed at each other. Our satisfied gaze took in the vista beyond the open folding doors at one end--a second room, in tan and brown, obviously a study, with a view of the garden through its two tall windows. Fireplaces in each room meant no central heating, but there was a certain homelike atmosphere about the place that beckoned us. Bobbing about the room, trying out the chairs, peering from the

35

windows, the girls chattered.

"Right on the High Street. Handy to everything."

"And really in the country, too. Lovely walks by the river."

"Daddy can go fishing."

"Gerry can have his bike."

"Look! Here's an old chair like we had in the nursery at home."

Mrs. Lansdell entered to find us very much at home. We liked her at once--young, dark, charming. Her husband, the doctor, had been called up. She was going to give up the house "for the duration" and stay with friends near-by. The evacuee problem had been a terrible drawback to renting the place. But, if the new tenants required all the rooms, the authorities might consider moving the children elsewhere when she left.

We saw these youngsters, three boys under ten years of age, in the enormous kitchen where the cook was supervising their supper at a table 4 by 10 feet. Six round eyes above three tilted porridge bowls stared at us in curiosity. The children looked dirty, but content.

"I don't know where they are half the time," said Mrs. Lansdell. "After school they run wild." She sighed. "They never say anything, but they don't appear to be homesick. I have them all in one big room on the top floor."

The youngest child slipped down from the table. And, as a matter of course, the pleasant-faced cook took him by the hand and led him away.

"Mary puts them to bed," said Mrs. Lansdell.

I indicated some boy's underwear drying before the stove.

"Yes, Mary washes their clothes."

It seemed to me that Mary was a jewel, with a heart of gold, and patriotic to the core--taking on three unknown children in addition to her usual duties. I was not mistaken. Later I took over Mary and Jean, the parlor maid, with the house and enjoyed their willing and perfect service for several months. Had circumstances permitted I would still have them with me.

The house was not convenient. It was not in perfect repair. But it was homelike. There was a runner of matting in the lower hall and the black painted floor was worn white in places. But there was a jug of Michaelmas daisies on an old carved chest, and the brass stair rods shone. You could see light through wide cracks in the front door, and the door leading into the garden had a good sized hole in one of its glass panels, the result of a ball game by the evacuees. But the door itself looked so quaint with it's amber, green and violet glass squares traced with grape vines in gilt, that we quite overlooked the hole until the cold winds and fogs of winter set in. The now familiar bucket of sand, long handled shovel and pickax stood by the stairs.

The house, being square, had a square room in each corner, and a narrowed hall divided both the upper and lower floors down the center. Opposite the drawing room on the ground floor was the dining room. Here red velvet drapes from ceiling to floor, a large fire-lace with pewter mugs marching along its mantle piece, a grandfather's clock and furniture of Mary and William period in black mahogany, all looked so English as to be almost American--if you know what I mean.

Woman like, I began envisioning my own linen on the table's large mirrored surface. My silver candelabra and bowls on the huge buffet running the entire length of one wall. I rather liked what I saw in my mind, and made note of a butler's pantry through to the kitchen. The food would not have to travel the usual long drafty halls of an English country house.

Upstairs the house seemed a bit bare, save for the master's bedroom, where a beige carpet and white fur rug lent a bit of softness, and deep rose drapes and silken bedspread and pillows to match gave an illusion of comfort. For a tiny electric heater was all that promised warmth in the icy months to come. But by now I was ready, or resigned, to take my bedroom cold in the approved English fashion.

On the same floor there were three other bedrooms, two of them with fireplaces which "drew", praise be, and a dressing room and bath. While on the top floor there was accommodation for Mary-Jean, the parlor maid, coming in by the day--and a large room with barred windows where the three little evacuees slept.

Except for the master bedroom, the floors were covered with linoleum, waxed and polished until it shone like finest wood, and thin faded rugs. The furnishings were very scanty, the young doctor and his wife having but recently bought the house, but we decided to move in at once. Longlands pulled at our hearts; it was a home. The three main rooms on the ground floor were adequately and attractively furnished. In fact, there was so much we liked about the place that we quite overlooked the uncomfortable factors that were to cause us later to decide that we preferred our warm and convenient flat in London, in spite of Air Raid threats.

"Longlands", like a kite, had a tail--a long ell running back from the main square of the house and forming one side of the walled-in flower and kitchen gardens: (Edith Cavell's house was beyond the wall at the foot of the gardens--on the next street. Edith Cavell was a Nursing Sister in World War I. Stationed at a hospital in Belgium she helped many wounded English soldiers to escape. For this the Germans executed her before a firing squad.) In this ell was the huge stone floored kitchen, a scullery, a coal-room, and an unnamed portion that might have been a stable at one time.

In the kitchen Mary reigned supreme, an excellent cook, willing to try my American recipes and most successful with them, to our mutual delight. Mary was also clean and cheerful.

She must have walked miles each day just fetching water from the scullery with which to boil vegetables on the gas "cooker" 'way at the opposite end of that twenty-three foot kitchen. The table--the size of a billiard table, and plumb in the middle of the room--had to be walked around dozens of times a day. There was a small stove to stoke and clean as this provided the only heat. But Mary and Jean assured me they preferred the cold--and truly they seemed to thrive on it. In their spare time they liked to sit, knitting, one on either side of the stove, in a pair of old wicker chairs. And to reach the saucepans hanging on the wall Mary had to climb up on one of these chairs several times a day. It appears that English cooking often involves a lot of foot work. A high and open-shelved dresser accommodated the china, and the dust. The only modern notes in that sprawling kitchen were the "Fridge" and the radio, which latter tinkled and talked all day.

After we had moved in, I used to like to visit there a few moments each day and chat with the two maids of their home life and future plans, the War, the current daily news. For the homely atmosphere in that old English kitchen bred a feeling of contentment, and work well done, and common happiness.

The world has had too much. The pampered ones have risen, full of greed and might, or dawdled, overstuffed with confidence. And now Mankind must suffer for its blindness.

As you see, we rented "Longlands." The little evacuees departed for new quarters. And we prepared to move in October first.

In the meantime we endured Life at "The Catherine Wheel."

There were blackout curtains to be made for two of the bedrooms at "Longlands", and I wanted to lay in what provisions I could, especially sugar, for we wanted to make some jam. So Alix, Martha, and I went the rounds of the various shops, purchasing assorted lots of groceries, as we only could get sugar if we bought other commodities at the same time, because we were not standing customers. Once more my bed-room looked like a rummage sale. Open cases of clothes, a pile of laundry, odd bags of groceries, were heaped about the floor. I used to navigate these "islands" in the dark with caution when opening the drapes and windows before getting into bed.

The so-called drapes were merely coarse black burlap like material ruffled on tape, and it was quite a job to "work" the folds back along this tape each night. Then I would lean on the sill of the open window and look up and down the deserted and darkened street below. Now and then a lone car, with shuttered lights, would whir up over the bridge at the left from the direction of London, and flee like a ghost along the High Street between the darkened houses.

I did a lot of high-pressure praying from that low window under the roof. Whether fair or wet, the Heavens starred or black, I seemed to feel in the soft night air a benediction. It was more comfort to me than my gas mask, torch and first-aid kit--for these are the symbols of man's weakness. But the miracle of sky and star and cloud mean God.

Upon the recommendation of friends we decided upon a school for Gerry. Bryanston School in Blandford, Dorsetshire. Once the country seat of the Duke of Portland, Bryanston is set in several hundred acres of lovely countryside. Its curriculum is varied and of high standard. Its methods and ideals new and broad. Gerry settled in there very well later. But at the time he needed a complete new outfit, all his other gear being in Switzerland--suits, overcoat, ski clothes, books and bicycle-- everything. Their return was quite impossible due to the war.

There was no question of our return to the States. Dick had offered to remain in England "for the duration" to keep the factory at fullest production. For the factory was now turning out a very particular gadget used in quantity by the R.A.F., and planes were to become the life-blood of the nation.

Gerry was very keen to see the Anti-Aircraft guns, the trenches, and the balloon barrage in London. So, the week before Bryanston opened, he and I returned to our flat at Regency Lodge in St. John's Wood, London.

We did the required shopping and took in a few cinemas, most of Gerry;s spare time being spent in "inspection" of the various defenses throughout the city. And at the following week end Dick and I saw Gerry off on the School Special from Waterloo, then drove out to Henley-on-Thames, where we shifted our many trunks, cases, and provisions from "The Catherine Wheel: "to" Longlands". This would be our refuge.

41

But the girls, having spent two weeks in the country, clamored to return to London and their friends for "just a few days."

Now I have never liked living with other people's things and miss my own possessions about me when in hotels, pensions or pubs, so it sounded good to me, too. Dick sportingly gave in to our arguments and we were all back in London early Monday morning, Sept. 25th--presumably for a few days. But Peter appeared on an unexpected leave, and the next thing I knew, we were planning for his and Alix's wedding to be held in less than two weeks time. "Longlands" didn't see us again for nearly a month.

Alix's Wedding

The last week of September, 1939, and the first week of October, were full to the brim with friends, impromptu teas, shopping, fittings; a spate of gorgeous days culminating in a bit of true Indian Summer on Saturday, October 7th, Alix's wedding day.

We had planned so differently. An engagement party that Autumn, a wedding in the Spring, but the war had changed all that. Young people were simply tumbling in and out of the Registry Offices. Church weddings bloomed hurriedly in a forcing atmosphere of War, Love and Patriotism. It was all very disturbing and understandable.

Only a few months before, my husband had returned from a trip to the States, bringing with him his mother's wedding gown of heavy ivory satin and pearl-beaded passementerie. This we had planned to have remodeled for Alix. Now such pageantry seemed out of place. We decided on an informal affair--but a church ceremony, followed by a reception in our flat.

With costumes to be made for Alix, Martha and myself, (Impossible to buy ready-made frocks here that fit without alterations! No extensive category of sizes as in the states, alas.) A small trousseau to assemble, and the catering, flowers, etc., to be ordered, I would sink onto the divan in the drawing room at tea time each day with a deep sigh, my tongue literally hanging out for a rejuvenating cup of tea. At such times I was seldom alone. Women love a wedding. Any of my friends and those of my daughters were no exception. We talked Wedding and War, War and Wedding, day after day. Conversation was a pot pourri of frocks, foreign affairs, foibles, A.R.P. work English wedding customs, and the proper way to endure an Air Raid.

Among my friends was a vivacious Frenchwoman who used to make us laugh with her very complete preparedness for raids and her detailed advice on the subject. The French are realists. Ziki left nothing to chance, and she was as witty as she was wise. The very first day I returned from Henley Ziki rushed in, keyed up with excitement over the air-raid warnings we had had to sit through. "Een company with the strangest pipple you ever saw. One man, what I could tell you of heem! He was afraid! We had to give heem brandy!" Her eyes rolled Heavenward. "Now I will tell you what you must do, Phi". (One of my nicknames.) "The Jairmans will come vairy airly in the morning--about three o'clock--to break our rest--to ruin our morale. That they will nevair do!" with a toss of her head. "so, have your rest airly. And get up at two o'clock." Her enthusiasm was sincere. "I sleep from ten to two. Then I dress and stay up until seven. After that"--her hands making a wide arc, "one can go back to bed, and sleep and sleep."

I am afraid that no one else followed this nocturnal schedule. But Ziki kept it faithfully those first few weeks of the war. Until the fact finally dawned upon the English public that the Germans had other fish to fry in their incendiary bombs for the time being. But during the early months of comparative calm, Ziki would lay out the same paraphernalia each evening on a small table in her front hall; torch, gas mask, first-aid kit, brandy, and a night light burning like a votive offering to Peace--"May it endure this night, Oh, God",--And she carried a capacious knitting bag everywhere, wherein an endless number of like articles--even to the brandy flask--accompanied her knitting.   Fond of music and an excellent pianist, temperamental and effusive, Ziki, nevertheless, was one of the most practical people I ever knew. She kept both feet on the ground always.

Unfortunately that is something that I never do. I hop, skip and jump from one thing to another, and during those two weeks preceding Alix's wedding I more or less floated.

But it was a happy time for all of us. Love and joy are infectious and Alix simply radiated both. True, the nights were very worrying and I used to wonder if we would "get through things" before "real trouble started." And the nearer it got to the seventh of October, the more I worried over whether a bomb was going to ruin all our plans--and the lovely presents displayed in the dining room. People had been so kind and generous.   We counted the presents, our friends, and our blessings--and felt very nice, indeed, inspite of the war.

Saturday, October 7th, 1939.

A perfect day. A day made to order for a blond bride with blue eyes. Sunshine and a late summer sky, a soft and sentimental haze in the warm air. No one would need a coat. Our light wool costumes would be perfection, my fuschia, Martha's amethyst and Alix's soft pale blue. We hurried through the morning with many willing helpers, two former maids having called up to offer their services. My kitchen teemed like an ant-hill.

Judy Beverly (a young American friend from Springfield, Mass., married to an English Naval officer) (Judy and Stan Beverley of Eaton Place, London. Lt. Stanley C. Beverley, R.N.) and Martha arranged tiny sandwiches on silver salvers, and snacks in divided plates. The little silver bells on the three-tiered wedding cake trembled in the excitement.

The wedding was to take place in St. Paul's Church on Avenue Road, above Regents Park, only a few doors from our home. Dr. Malet, the vicar, was a dear, helpful and interested, and as disappointed as we that there could be no choir since the boys all had been evacuated to the country.

Now October 8th was Harvest Sunday--a day of Thanksgiving, when all churches in England are decorated with field flowers and the "fruits of harvest" are displayed for blessing. So I was a bit perturbed that these rural offerings might make the church look cluttered, as the women parishioners were to do the Harvest decorating on the morning of Saturday, October 7th, the day of the wedding.

I slipped over to St. Paul's to see to things for myself about noon, and to supervise our own particular share of the flower decorations. I expected to find, as the Parish contribution,

45

merely jugs of autumn leaves, perhaps some chrysanthemums, and surely baskets of tomatoes, potatoes and marrow along the chancel rails. Well, it couldn't be helped, and we must make the best of it. It was an English custom, this Harvest Sunday. People would understand about the vegetables.

My fears proved groundless. The ladies of the Church decorating committee had created a charming and lovely setting. The choir stalls and chancel rails were outlined with continuous garlands of mauve Michaelmas daises and fuchsia colored asters; the pulpit and carved archways were etched in trailing sprays of green; the fretwork entrance to the little inner chapel at one side of the nave was hung with graceful vines and heavy clusters of purple grapes--a dignified and lush effect. As for the vegetables; they were tastefully and unobtrusively ranged in their alternate reds and greens and browns upon the floor against the chancel wall. There remained only our flowers--Easter lilies, and gladioli, salmon, pale pink and cream--to be added to the scene. One of the ladies kindly offered to help, and we set to work.

The lilies (Flowers are so plentiful and cheap here.) were concentrated on the long altar--in a row of seven golden vases against a background of green leaves and tall, white candles. The long pastel spikes of gladioli were bunched in earthen jugs set on the stone floor against the dark walnut of the chancel rail and down the aisle. The simple artistry achieved was far more satisfying than the usual professional decorations. Alix's wedding would be beautiful.

We all lunched at the Heaver's, Elsie's thoughtful contribution to the day's success. And by three-thirty the Cottons were arrayed in their wedding finery and an assortment of nerves. The flat bloomed with Easter lilies, gladioli, and big

46

shaggy pink and white chrysanthemums. From the kitchen below could be heard the tinkle of ice as Curtis (the chauffeur) packed the champagne. The photographer arrived.

The service was to be at four-thirty. Firstly, because English law prohibited such after six p.m. and secondly, because the blackout must be considered.

The marriage of a daughter is an unforgettable occasion, a milestone in one's own married life, a memory to cherish and to mull over with fondness and delight. Alix's wedding was no exception. In spite of the war, the 100-odd gas masks accompanying the guests, and Pete's orders to report back to Naval Air Base on the very next day, nothing could detract from Alix's loveliness as she came down the aisle of that old English church on her father's arm--a Dresden china figure in her pale blue costume, tiny ermine hat and muff, (These had belonged to her Grandmother Cotton.) and corsage of pale pink roses and lilies-of-the-valley.

Awaiting her stood Pete and his Best Man, Rob D'Almaine, Lieutenant on a submarine. Resplendent in their Naval uniforms, they seemed young heroes of a new Crusade. May God protect them both!

The many lighted candles shed a benediction upon all-- flowers, friends and married couple. An illusion of Peace on Earth prevailed. Until after the gay and friendly reception at our flat and the riotous send-off in the usual shower of confetti and rose leaves. Then, to my own dismay, as the last of the guests departed I dissolved into tears. But I believe it was the War, and not the Wedding that got me down.

Winter Comes
Cold weather set in early that winter of 1939-1940.

47

How grateful we were, the first evening that we returned to "Longlands" after Alix's wedding, to have Jean, of her own initiative, bring in a tray of sherry and cocktails. It was not our custom at all, and reserved usually for guests, but we soon came to depend on this seven o'clock "warmer-up" or we should have quite frozen those damp and chilly evenings in spite of the stove in the study where we used to spend most of our time when indoors. The sliding door between the study and the drawing-room had to be closed, and strips of carpet folded along its base, else icy drafts snaked about our feet and stabbed across our shoulders. We used to dash across the arctic hall at dinner time, and take turns sitting at the side of the table nearer the open fire in the dining-room.

We loved the "scenery," though; the candles on the dark polished table with its pale lemon organdy mats, and late garden flowers, the crackling fire, the red, white and green lights in ships' lanterns above the mantel. The Doctor evidently loved the sea. But not even a well cooked dinner and the promise of "hot-bottles" in one's bed later, could conjure up real comfort. We either rushed through freezing halls, or huddled before blazing fires, most of our stay at "Longlands".

Not only was there the cold to contend with, but it was a day's journey to the one bathroom! And then one had to queue up outside it in the morning with the rest of the family, as the bathroom was also the only place in which to wash.

Why comforts and necessities should be tacked onto so many English houses like afterthoughts is inexplainable. But, at "Longlands", to reach the bath one had to traverse a long cold hallway, go down a half flight of stairs and up another, through a door, and then across a square back hall. The bath, itself--W.C. (Toilet) being separate--occupied an enormous room with rafters overhead and white-washed stone walls and was situated above the ell. A second door in the bathroom made entrance into a space beneath the roof where the hot water pipes came up from the kitchen boiler. This door was kept open to afford a bit of warmth. But this warmth was so infinitesimal as to be practically non-existent. To have a bath necessitated running the hot water for some time, thus getting a good cloud of hot steam into the room--and then hustling around, both in and out of the tub, with chattering teeth and shaking limbs. The "Order of the Bath" would not have been inappropriate as Decoration after such campaigns.

But the countryside, as always, enchanted us. The winding paths along the river were perfect walks in the autumn sun, or in the lacey rain. The yellow, orange and brown of turning leaves and the steel blue of November skies compensated a bit for the fact that we were there, not to behold this beauty, but to escape a threatened death from these self-same skies. Strange thought. And some strange sights, too.

Taking a motor launch up the river one fine afternoon, we passed the palatial estate of the Duke of Hamilton, the white mansion overlooking a terraced sweep of green down to the river's edge. Here, seated upon rustic benches, was a motley lot of women, knitting, chattering, dozing--gas masks dangling from their arms, a general air of resignation about them. They were so incongruous against that dignified background that we inquired about them upon our return to the village.

"Evacuees," said the rental boatman laconically. "'Omesick fer the streets of Lunnon, more'n likely." He spat into the river. "But wait 'till they hev ter go back. Spoiled they'll be--an' proper. There's a sign o' folks, now languishing' in genteel surroundin's as'll make a clamor later abart their precious

49

council 'ouses and slum 'omes. Yes, sir." He spat again. "And then wot's the answer goin' ter be?"

Too true. Evacuation may solve some present problems but it is also certainly laying up problems for the future. At "The Catherine Wheel" we had met an elderly gentleman who had opened his fine country house to fifteen evacuees. Their boorish ways and total lack of consideration for other people's property, even to the extent of deliberately breaking ornaments and defacing pictures, had quite shocked the old man into several heart attacks, and finally departure from his home. And the wife of the Vicar of Henley, after Christian forbearance and strong willpower for three dreadful weeks, finally had to ask the local committee to remove her lot of evacuees;--a Mother and five children who knew no sanitary laws and acted like beasts of the fields throughout her charming home, so that the poor lady was obliged to have all her carpets cleaned, and some of the bedding and mattresses burned. Education of the people, or lack of it, is at fault here, of course. The future must bring many changes indeed. But on the whole, this gigantic effort of the British Government to save its women and children must be acclaimed as humane and successful. The majority of evacuees and their hostesses are living and working together for a common cause--the welfare and victory of Britain. They must not fail.

In December, although we feared the raids, they had not commenced. Our thoughts were mostly taken up with plans for Christmas. Dick and I were charmed with the idea of a real country Christmas in an old English house. Alix and Pete, with luck, should be able to join us. For Pete, now with the Fleet Air Arm, was training at Salisbury Plain. He and Alix were in digs at Fighldene near by. Dorothy and Tony could come, and Gerry could invite a school pal to share the holidays. Martha and I would gather greens and holly from the fields and lanes and make the house as festive as possible. We'd have a decorated tree and lots of presents and sing carols.

Alack! The only thing that materialized in the country was the holly--masses of it. English holly is gorgeous. It grows on trees as well as hedges and bushes. The leaves are thick, and shine as though polished. The clusters of berries are light scarlet, almost orange, and bunched like tiny grapes. Branches of this gay foliage are to be had for the cutting in country lanes. We gathered armfuls of it in the damp chill gray days that England offers in December.

But because of the severe weather we soon gave up spending more than week-ends at "Longlands". The rest of the week we stored up warmth in our London flat, Jean and Mary coming in to town alternate weeks to "do" for us. Jean loved the visits and took to city life. But Mary always pined a bit for her beau, the butcher's boy in Henley, and said, "I'm a yokel at heart, Madame."

Jean, who had her own little home and cared for her husband and mother-in-law as well as coming to me by the day, had a little evacuee, a four year old girl who was the apple of her eye. Jean used to knit her pretty jumpers, and gave her a birthday party, and told me with pride, "Baby says she wants me for her Mother now--and we'd like to keep her, Madame." Another evacuee problem to be solved sometime, I suppose.

Two weeks before the twenty-fifth of December, 1939, the family unanimously voted to stay in London for Christmas. That brought up the question of a thorough black-out in the flat as we had so far managed with only black shades on the lights, and a minimum of these. The effect was terribly gloomy.

We couldn't have a lighted tree without black-out curtains. And Christmas without a tree was unthinkable. So we had all the drapes throughout the flat lined with heavy black sateen to the tune of 9 pounds ($45.00). Nine pounds for a Christmas tree! Extravagant? No. That shining tree was a symbol of many things--custom, security, Peace on Earth, good will toward men. And we could now move more freely through every room after dark, provided the drapes were closely drawn. We simply basked in the now permissible flood of light. In fact, we switched on practically every light in the place to begin with, it seemed so darned exhilarating.

The weather was dreadful--one of England's coldest winters, with a lot of fog. It snowed a bit now and then, but the snow never remained long on the ground.

After arrival in London February 1935, we so missed the sun and snow of American winters near Boston, Massachusetts, that we had spent a few weeks each Christmas season in Switzerland or Germany for winter sports. The winter before the war, 1938-1939, we were at Garmisch-Partenkirchen in the Bavarian Alps for the holidays. Since reminiscences of that visit are rather revealing in certain ways, let me tell you a bit about it.

Christmas in Germany - 1938

We left London on the morning of Thursday, December 22nd, 1938, Pete going with us for his Christmas leave. This was before Alix and Pete were married, of course. We expected to arrive in cologne at ten that night, where Dick's German agent, Herr Kohler, was most anxious to entertain us

52

at late supper in one of the cafes. We planned to remain overnight in Cologne, visit the famous cathedral in the morning, and finish our trip to Garmisch by the next morning. But the weather demon had other plans. It snowed hard as we crossed the English channel. Very gratifying to us Americans. Snow was what we were in search of.

But the cold! The bitter biting cold of that spell of severe weather that swept over the Continent for a week upset our plans a bit. From Aachen, on the Belgian-German frontier where we went through the Customs, this intense cold slowed down our train. By then it was night, and we simply crawled through the flat black countryside. Peering from the windows of our compartment, we were astonished to see lighted Christmas trees at every station, every crossroad, and even in the squares of tiny villages. This welcome sight amazed us. For we had been told that German Youth worshipped Wotan, the God of Light, and that they had just held festivals in his honor, Yet these bright Christmas trees were a bit like our own American celebration, much of which had originated in this country. Surely the simple and good people of Germany were not all crushed beneath the Nazi Heel.

But later we decided that the Christmas trees and the Festival of Light must have been deliberately synchronized by the Nazis. Many, many people in Germany still loved Christmas and all that it stood for, and the trees were a concession to them. But these lighted trees also blended with the flaming torches and bonfires of the Hitler Youth in their pagan celebrations. Hitler was very neatly presenting Christ and Wotan in a double bill with equal lighting effects. And the public reacted in its own way and according to its lights-- literally. That was all.

However, at the time, we were thrilled, and as the train crept through the night, every island of sparkling light in the passing dark outside was a welcoming "Tannenbaum" in "that fair land" of which the Germans used to sing so robustly. We too burst into song. Gerry had brought along a small booklet of Christmas carols, a relic from home, printed by the Boston Transcript. We sang it through from beginning to end several times. And the spirit of Christmas settled into the train compartment with us. We needed it, for the cold and the dragging speed of the train began to tell on us. Ten o'clock came and went. So did eleven. We were hungry. Gerry was sleepy. Midnight found us huddled against each other, napping. It was one a.m. before we pulled into the big station at Cologne. Our hotel was just across the square--so we stumbled along on foot after the porters through the snowy starlit night.

In spite of the hour there were torches flaming atop the garlanded poles before the cathedral. At the time they looked Christmasy to me, and I felt a genuine glow of kindliness and peace as I drifted off to sleep later, beneath the plump linen-covered "duchent". ("duchent"--an eiderdown, or puff.) atop our bed.

The scene from our bedroom window the following morning warmed the cockles of my sentimental heart. Dick was not so impressed. "More cold," he said, "with more snow." Indeed yes. Snow on the ground, on the buildings, sparkling in the sun! Evergreens, twisted about poles and strung in garlands across the street, with gaily painted Christmas greetings in German hanging below. Quaint gabled shops and houses on one side of the square, beautiful Cologne Cathedral on the other.

Cologne Cathedral on the banks of the Rhine! there was magic in the words. But when we all visited the cathedral immediately after breakfast, although we found the Gothic arches, the serried stone pillars, the beautiful stained-glass windows all duly imposing, we also felt a puzzling lack. The Cathedral seemed so empty. Not just empty of people, but empty of the inspiration and satisfaction to the soul that one expects within the house of God.

Perhaps it was because there was no creche that Christmas-tide, with its infant Christ-child, by the alter. Perhaps it was because the vast nave was so cold and dark. But, also, perhaps Pete had the right answer to our disappointment.

"Ugh!" he said with a shiver,
"the church is dead, probably purged!"

"S-sh!" said Alix, looking over her shoulder.

We hurried out into the friendly sunshine. Herr Kohler appeared, and we took a quick turn about the town.

The lovely woolen pullovers and jackets of picturesque design in the shops fascinated me. I had decided on a handsome navy and white ski-pullover for Gerry when Herr Kohler jogged my elbow.

"Lift it up," he whispered.

I did so. The pullover weighed a ton--heavy as lead, unwieldly.

Herr Kohler held the wool against my face. The garment smelt of lead and oil.

"It will shrink to nothing if wet," he continued in a guarded undertone. "Ersazt!"

To placate the clerk I bought gay woolen ties for the men, and several bottles of "4711" cologne. It was very funny later, on Christmas Eve in Garmisch when we exchanged gifts about our little tree, to count the flasks of "Koln Wasser." Everyone had several. "When in Koln, Buy Koln" had been a most productive motto.

My, how cold it was! Bitter! Our train was almost two hours late in leaving Koln (Cologne) that afternoon. To see the lovely white and ice-bound scenery along the Rhine we had continually to scrape the frost from the carriage windows. The Robber-Barons' castles on their crags, the terraced, snow-covered vineyards, the red-roofed hamlets, the Mouse Tower at Bingen, seen thus, seemed like those kaleidoscopic pictures that I--as a child--used to peek at through the glazed openings of sugared eggs "Made in Germany." Remember them?

We had a good lunch on the train, with the best of beer. Supper, too, was excellent. There seemed no lack of butter or meat. But we could get no milk. Herr Kohler, who was making part of the train trip with us, ate everything in sight.

"While I have the chance," he said cryptically.

Later he confided that his wife had not been able to buy even one egg to bake a Christmas cake. And this was before the war. Sugar was almost negligible, butter a thing of the past, meat very scarce and unpalatable. Those who could aford to, ate in public places where a decent bill-of-fare proclaimed plenty to the outer world. We found this so everywhere. The good food was concentrated in two places; 1. Restaurants and hotels, 2. The Army. The German man-in-the-street and his hausefrau could jolly well whistle for it otherwise--that is if they felt like whistling. (Quite some time later--after we were back in London and the War was on--a cry for help came from the Kohlers. In a bid for escape from Germany they had managed to reach the Belgian border and were in a certain railroad station there, where they planned to stay that day--but must leave by nightfall. Would Mr. Cotton cable them £50. ($250.00) at once? The cable had been sent to the factory. But Dick was in the States. So Mr. Anderson, in charge at the time, 'phoned me. Could I suggest what Mr. Cotton might do-- after all, the £50. would come from Mr. Cotton's pocket. I said I would take full responsibility and to cable the £50. at once. We never head from the Kohlers again. They had been caught, of course.)

Again at nightfall the lighted Christmas trees, in all their electric glory, stood sentinel at every station and crossroad, and even far out upon the darkened country landscape as we rumbled on toward Munich.·

"Oh, isn't that a beauty!"

"Look! There's one, way over. Must be a town there."

We saw veritable mountains of packages awaiting shipment on every station platform.

"Did you ever see so many presents in your life?"

"Never, all at once!"

Hundreds. No, thousands, All sizes, square, round, oblong; some of them quite recognizable as sleds or doll carriages. The German people might lack butter, but they certainly weren't going to lack Christmas presents.

We had expected to reach Munich in time to get a train to Garmisch-Partenkirchen that night. But the late start from Koln, plus the severe cold, upset our plans again. Puff, puff-- squeak, squeak--rumble, rumble. The engine grew breathless, the wheels protested, the train sulked. When at last we came to a clanking stop in the dingy Munich Bahnhof, there were only a few sleepy porters to pull our luggage out through the carriage windows. It was 2 a.m.

We followed the porters out into the Station Square. The

Platz was deserted, shadowed and pale beneath one swinging street light. But on the facade of a large shop across the way a gigantic sign proclaimed "Froliche Weinacht" and two seven foot wooden angels flourished gilded trumpets. The early hours of the day before Christmas! Germany with her folklore and homefolk! Munich, even though asleep!

There were no taxis. But we didn't mind the walk in the cold. That night we slept beneath even higher "duchents"-- eight to ten inches thick--in a clean and comfortable hotel in the very center of the town, and awoke to bright sunshine, a hot and hearty breakfast, a morning of shopping in fascinating Yule-decked streets.

Alix and Pete went off on their own, hand in hand, like two children. We were all happy and eager. Dick and Gerry got bogged down at once in a toy shop; the electric trains held them rooted. So Martha and I wondered on into some of the older streets. We saw the old carved stone Town Hall, the jail, the ancient gabled houses and shuttered buildings, the arcaded streets. The Brown House never entered our heads! Hitler had nothing in common with these milling crowds of Christmas shoppers, this evergreen-trimmed town, this Day-Before-Christmas-in-Germany.

The three o'clock train to Garmisch was packed--people, luggage, skis jammed the corridors. Three strangers, and even four, goodnaturedly shared seats meant for two. Up, up-- through a paradise of snow and sunshine. Then into lavender light as the mountain tops rose close about us. Garmisch! We had arrived.

To one who remembers old fashioned New England winters with their deep snow drifts, sleigh rides and tinkling bells, this sugar coated Germany, musical with shouts, laughter, and welcoming sleigh bells, seemed all I'd ever dreamed it would be. Our hotel, halfway up a mountain side on a small ice-bound lake, stood in the shadow of the Zugspitz, Germany's highest mountain. It was evening, and the lighted windows had sprays of holly and evergreen on every ledge. In our room (Dick's and mine) stood a small tree dripping with silver icicles, brave with tiny red candles. A large porcelain stove glowed hospitably in one corner. In spite of having to feed this monster with awkward blocks of wood I became quite attached to its presence, not so much because of its comforting warmth, but because it reminded me of "The Nurnberg Stove", and the little boy who loved it so--one of my favorite stories as a child.

In the dining room we found each table decorated with a crown of evergreen alight with small red candles. These table decorations were similar to the crowns worn by Norwegian and Swedish maidens at the Festival of St. Catherine. The Invasion of Norway a year and some months later brought those pretty little symbols of "Peace-on-Earth, Good-Will-toward-Men" sharply to mind. It then occurred to me that, if Hitler used every similarity of custom and creed as excuse for Lebensraum-poaching, there would not be many corners of the earth exempt, save by Armed Defense.

But at that Christmas season of 1938 the little lighted crowns meant only that the Spirit of Christmas was with us there in Germany. Oh, how friendly it all seemed. Dick, Pete, the children and I exchanged gifts around our little tree, and with "Froliche Weinachts" all went happily to bed--this time beneath duchents which rose, like fresh loaves, in billows now 14 inches high. It took us three nights to master the things-- they were so elusive! We learned to sleep immobilized, to use

59

a wartime expression. I'd like to see a movie of Robert Benchley trying to sleep under a duchent!

The hotel was full of families. The atmosphere was "sehr gemutlich," so friendly and so courteous were the people.

There was a charming Bavarian family with numerous children from 21 down to 8 years of age. Although we knew very little German, and they knew practically no English at all, we became very friendly. Their table was next to ours in the dining salon, and smiles, nods and gestures are a happy medium of expression. Somehow we learned that Herr B -'s grandmother had been one-eighth Jewish so that the Nazis had "taken over" the family business, paying a sum barely sufficient to keep the family in mediocre comfort. Herr B - had an unforgetting and unforgiving glint in his eyes which belied his smiling charm.

Then there were the people from Berlin whose son was most attentive to Martha. We liked the young man very much-- blond, rosy complexioned, good looking. He spoke English so well that we felt most at ease with him. He and Martha, Pete and Alix used to skate, ski and rodel together. We have a snapshot of Joachim and Pete together on a rodel (sled). Pete is steering, with Joachim behind him, arms around Pete's waist. To think of these two as enemies and fighting to the death against one another is a crime against one's reason, let alone one's heart. Joachim hated the thought of his coming military service, and that his hair must be cropped close. "Like a prisoner!"

Months after our return to London--in fact, right up until War was declared--Joachim and Martha corresponded, Joachim always closing his letters with, "Until my service is ended, then I am coming to London." I wonder if he ever did--

as a prisoner of war, or to be shot down in aerial combat. He was never a Nazi, inwardly.

The Canadian Hockey Team was in Garmisch. So we attended some of the games in the Olympic Stadium beyond the village. Crowds from miles around packed the benches, with a section reserved for the German soldiers, those pampered darlings of the Nazi regime. Big and sturdy, full of the people's butter and eggs, they dominated the scene. There were Army Barracks on the valley floor below our Hotel, and every day companies of Nazi uniformed skiers poured across the snow-covered meadows and swarmed up the mountain sides. They had an arrogance about them that made me want to push them over whenever they crowded me to one side of the lanes or roads. So different from the smiling, rushing Bavarian youngsters who shouted cheerily in warning and called "Bitte" or "Danke" as they touched their caps in passing.

At the hockey games, exhibition skating filled the intermissions. The German players and skaters, before commencing their show, would automatically stand at attention, roll their eyes upward and snap out a Nazi salute with "Heil Hitler"--then swing into their turn. These salutes became almost meaningless to us. As a greeting of Hail and Farewell, in shops, cafes, and on the streets arms went up and down like semaphores. "Heil Hitler?"

Deep in the fir woods about a quarter mile beyond the Hotel, stood a small cafe built of logs. This was the mecca of skiers and rodelers coming down from the mountain top, for chocolate, or beer, at five o'clock. I used to walk over there, after Dick had returned to London, and meet the children, when we would simply wallow in steaming chocolate topped with great blobs of "schlag." A harpist sat in the corner strumming

61

local ballads and folk songs in which the Germans used to join noisily, drumming on the table tops with their steins and swaying in time to the lilt. How could such people object to an enforced mere raising of the arm and a mere two words, "Heil Hitler?" For I never saw this salute given with any expression. The waitresses would "Heil Hitler" you upon your entrance, and "Heil Hitler" you when they picked up your tip and wiped off the table. It was just another arm exercise.

On the cafe door was a 12-inch circle of metal, black and yellow, with "Juden Unerwunnscht" (Jews not wanted) printed in large letters about the rim, the swastika rampant in the center. Gerry acquired this sign--no matter how--as a souvenir. Later, when at Aachen on our homeward trip, Martha took it out of his case and sat upon it while the Customs Inspectors went through our luggage. The sign now ornaments the mantelpiece in Gerry's bedroom.

These waspish signs were on nearly every cafe, restaurant, hotel, and shop door throughout Germany. There were times when I wished that I could grow--just temporarily-- a most Hebraic nose, and barge into one of these places, demanding the best the proprietors had to offer. Should they refuse and point to the sign, I would then say, very loudly, "I am an American! Touch me if you dare!"

Those signs were ever a challenge to me, and I am not Jewish. If--If, I say--the Nazis invade England, and one of them should get as far as our house, I hope I have the pleasure of shie-ing that black and yellow metal platter out of the window and neatly clipping Herr Nazi's head off.

New Year's Eve at Garmisch was fun. Extra tables were set up in the tea-dance salon, and this and the dining room were thrown open together. The usual gala dinner was served amidst the usual festive decorations, and much Rhine wine and Champagne were drunk. There was a floor show of local talent, and dancing for everyone. All seemed happy and gay. The dancers were either fast and furious German waltzes or very mannered foxtrots. No jazz was allowed--by Hitler's decree. No modern pieces--by Hitler's decree. Old, well-known tunes and spiels monotonously followed each other in rotation.

At the first bars of music, German youths, appraising the modestly arrayed "madchens" would sedately walk over to their choice and bow. "Darf inch diesen tanz haben?" Then the couple--just as sedately and almost without speaking--would go through the dance. And afterwards the young man would escort his partner to her parents. "Danke sehr, meine Fraulein." Another bow, and the young man would return to his own table, where he would sit sipping beer or wine until the next dance. And so it went. No introductions were necessary. And my daughters discovered that none were expected, tho' they always introduced themselves and managed, in most cases, to get a bit of animation in exchange. Every afternoon and evening, no matter who attended the dances--people from nearby hotels, villagers, or guests--it was the man's prerogative to choose whom he liked, whether he knew her or not, whether he was ever likely to meet her again or no. The system had a strange impermanence.

New Year's Eve the little green crowns with red candles still decorated the tables and the Christmas holly and sparkling tree were still in bloom, just as they were kept at home in America until after New Year's Day. Five minutes to midnight all the electric lights in the tea salon and dining room went out, leaving the soft flickering candlelight. Dancers left the floor.

63

Families and parties assembled. I watched, as filled wineglasses were lifted in readiness, and saw eyes, like lodestars, drawn to answering eyes.

Silence fell

The enchantment of timelessness hung over the scene.

"Bong-bong-bong-bong-and on."

Twelve strokes.

"Frohliche Neu jahr!" And the clink of meeting glasses.

My husband kissed me.

The children kissed each other.

Everyone about us exchanged kisses--solemn kisses like pledges.

People we knew by name, by smile, or by greeting, came over to drink our health and shake our hands.

"Froliche Neu jahr!"

"Froliche Neu jahr!"

One Sunday there was a very scanty menu set before us.

"Fish or soup." That was all. We asked the waiter why.

"This is our One-Dish Sunday, Madame," he replied. "We have one every month."

We chose the fish. When this was served and we saw the soup on neighboring tables we felt decidedly "done," for the fish was a mere slab of something like boiled cod with white sauce, but the soup was a small tureen full of meat and vegetables in thin gravy. We filled up on bread and butter and tramped down to the village for a hockey match.

At tea time we were famished! We could get hot coffee in the grandstand, but that was all. By the time we climbed back up the mountain path to the Hotel our tummies felt like empty drums wherein Mexican jumping beans held carnival. With visions of "Kuchen mit schlag" (Cake with whipped cream) and hot chocolate we hurried into the tea lounge. Tea and dry biscuits were what we got! The Germans are a thorough race.

The hotel Bier Stube was a popular resort with the youngsters, and people coming up from the village for skating and ski-ing filled it daily at lunch and tea. "Goulash und bier," dark Munich, was a favorite combination. We began to grow fat on German food. Guns might be piling up in the background but the Public Eating Front seemed undiminished.

A Beer Festival was to be held in the Bier Stube. Bavarian costume was expected and Bavarian dances would be the order. All hotel guests were invited. Dick, alas, was in London, but the girls and I donned our gayest Innsbruck jumpers and Gerry put on a New Mexican gold jacket which, with it's Indian symbols, was wilder than the brightest of his ski pullovers. We went to the Spiel, and found Carnival and Bedlam already there.

The background of low ceiling, carved casement windows, painted furniture and polished table tops set off the gay colored costumes of the women; their full skirts, bodices, and puffed sleeves; the short trousers, embroidered braces and peasant shirts of the men. Three fiddlers exercised a spell of folk music, and the "schulplattler" was noisily clattered by young and old in breathless laughter.

There was a new dance introduced that night. Hitler did not like the Lambeth Walk, introduced in England but popular throughout the world. It was verboten, both dance and tune. I forget the name of the dance demonstrated, but we all voted it far more inelegant than the Lambeth Walk! In the course of the dance the men went down on one knee and the girl sat upon the

65

other. They then swayed from side to side, bobbed cheek to cheek, in time to the music, and the last "step", instead of the thumbs up and "oi!" of the Lambeth Walk, was a resounding whack administered by the young man upon the usual whackable portion of anatomy belonging to his partner.

The audience shouted in glee. And I thought I detected a childlike maliciousness in the way the dance was applauded and in the eagerness with which everyone hurried onto the floor to learn it. I could imagine the following being said--or at least thought. "So! The Lambeth Walk is low, Mein Fuhrer? Nun! Sehen Sie! We have created a new German dance--an Aryan reel--a lyric manifestation of our noble race's higher passions. Heil Hitler!"

Steins 10 to 15 inches high, foaming with the ice cold dark brown brew of Munich, were passed--and passed again. Such draughts put the heart of a lion into one. Grandparents sidled and pranced, youngsters whirled and leapt. The little carnival hats, perched like confetti, slipped into crazier attitudes. Perspiration became as frank as an American "ad." Finally the smoke and warmth began to lull our senses, even to dull them a bit. The children were tired. I was an absolute wreck, due to the waltzing-mice technique of my dancing partners. A last wild reel, accompanied by deafening shouts, wound up the evening.

"Guten Nacht!"

The Beer Festival was finished--and so were we.

Of course we drove over to Oberammergau, it was so near. It is an enchanting spot. And we were properly impressed by the theater, costumes and props of the Passion Play. It didn't take much imagination to picture the play set out beneath a summer's sky. But one wonders now when the world will ever see its moving pageantry again. Commercialized though it may have been to a degree, there was still sincerity and much inspiration to be found in the production.

There were camps and soldiers to be seen even in this vicinity--with reason, no doubt, as the district is fairly inaccessible, high up in the mountains and beyond the ways of ordinary traffic.

There was a charming pale blue building in the main street of a tiny mountain village just before Oberammergau. This was a school. Laughing children were painted on its walls, and large blue and pink letters proclaimed "Froebel Kinder Garten." There were gay geraniums in the windows, framed by ruffled white curtains.

Surely happy children must go in and out of that school, I thought. I recalled that my first piano lessons were at the "Froebel School of Music" in Boston, Massachusetts.

Driving back to Garmisch we passed a picturesque, whitewashed church with the onion spire native to the region. The church stood on the outskirts of the town, and a funeral cortege was just leaving the grounds. In fact we waited for its progress through the gate and down the road. The coffin was drawn upon a sledge, and there were simple green wreaths and boughs piled above it. Later, in 1940, when reading "Escape", I place the locale of the story (in my mind) in this picturesque Bavarian village of Garmisch. And the funeral scene within the book became identified with the setting and the people in the little Drama of Sorrow there before us that January day of 1939.

During our visit in Garmisch there came a day when the Spectre-Behind-the-Scenes of Nazified Germany stalked in upon our winter stage of fun and frolic. Hess and his entourage arrived at our Hotel on his way to see Hitler at Berchtesgaden. The three days Hess remained at the hotel were an interlude of studied caution and watchful waiting on the part of the Hotel guests, and the Personnel leapt and dashed about in concentrated service, with furrowed brows. Airplanes continuously droned overhead.

Hess and his party sat at the table next to ours in the dining room, and near us in the dancing salon each evening. We had ample opportunity to observe these Nazis and to digest our observations. They were not agreeable. Rudolph Hess, himself, is tall and broad shouldered with dark wavy hair and heavy black eyebrows jutting above sunken eyes in a pallid, square-jawed face. His eyes are blue and cold like twin sword points at an enemy's throat, they have such a menacing glint. His mouth is a steel trap, nothing else. I never saw him smile. Accompanying him were two men and two women. The men were nimble satellites revolving about their lord and master-- the women, young and like Amazons over six feet tall. With no make-up and frizzled mouse-colored hair they appeared, in their long black velvet evening frocks, like shop girls out with traveling salesmen--all third class.

A body guard of four thugs followed everywhere, sitting at neighboring tables in dining room and dance salon. These thugs made us chuckle among ourselves--they were such replicas of the gangsters seen in American crime films. Complete as to firearms and ape-like features, one of the thugs even possessed that finishing cachet of gangsterdom--a flattened, broken nose.

We used to sit in our particular cozy corner in the dance-salon after dinner, sipping coffee or chocolate, and observing these representatives of Nazi Kulture--Hess and Company. (One evening Hess sent an Aide to ask Alix for a dance. She refused. From then on--until Hess left--we felt not only marked people but as pariahs in an alien world.) And we realized that only Force, Evil Force, could have imposed the will of such as these upon a kind and decent people, and that, if all the Masters of Nazi Germany were like this Death's Head, Hess--and we had cause to believe they were--then God help Germany and her Good People. For we knew there were good people in that persecuted country--and that even among the Nazis there must be some with faith in a better regime, but they were few, I fear.

In that human harvest that Hitler was reaping for himself, should you sift the wheat from the chaff, you would discover a preponderance of chaff. It was this worthless chaff that was even then being disseminated, by a hurricane of Evil, throughout Germany--and even into the World. Naught but bareness and suffocation can come of it for Humanity.

Of December, 1939, into May, 1940.
London, May 23rd. 1940

First, I wish to write a bit of our 1939 Christmas here, in London--for which we had made a most expensive black-out in order to have a lighted Christmas tree. Only one year since our visit to Germany for the holidays of Christmas 1938 and New Year 1939! But now Germany and Britain are at war, and we Americans, living in London, share the conditions of that war. This past December 1939 the war was only fourteen weeks old, yet already it lay, heavy upon us. A frightening shadow weighted with doom. However, since Pete had a weeks' leave, Martha three days from the Clinic in Wellbeck Street (Martha is completing her speech therapy course), and Dick the usual two days (Christmas and Boxing Day, Dec. 26th), we arranged a family get-together. Gerry, of course, was home from Bryanston and we invited Dorothy and Tony to join us. We would forget the war a bit. We could afford to then; no air-raids on London yet, the Army entrenched in France. We had a breathing spell.

The Finnish War was on, and one felt as though Archangels wrestled in the Northern snows with the rapacious Russian Beasts. Always the white hooded-coats of the Finns seemed celestial robes. That valiant army, so outnumbered, was superhuman--it had the prayers and admiration of the world, our world.

Two days before Christmas, Bob d'Almaine (who had been Pete's Best Man), and his young Swedish wife, Margareta, spent Bob's short leave with us. Bob is a Lieutenant on a submarine, and because London is nearer than his home in Oxfordshire he almost always stays with us. We are always pleased to have any of the boys accept our hospitality--it makes us feel that we are somehow helping a bit.

While Bob and Margareta were with us the Christmas tree was brought in and set up in a corner of the living-room. Its dark green needles scented the place. Margareta sniffed the air.

"M-mm! 'Tis just like home."

She wrinkled her nose and smiled. But deep in her eyes I saw a bit of home-longing. Her first Christmas away from home and likely to be spent with Bob at his Base.

"Oh, but we shall be together! And we shall have our

gifts, and think har-rd (she deeply rolls her R's) of those we love, and wish them a Merry Christmas."

Two of her brothers were fighting with the Finns, her sister nursing among the wounded. Baron Mannerheim is a family friend and the boys were serving under him.

"Oh, but he is gr-rand!" said Margareta. (As events during the war years progressed and continually changed, so did one's ideas and comprehensions of these events progress and change. Throughout my journal this may be observed--that my reactions and opinions altered, or remained firmly the same. According to the scope of my knowledge and my acceptance or rejection of such.)

This past Christmas of 1939 the streets of London were deserted. A thin coating of ice beneath the chill layer of fog proved treacherous. Dorothy and Tony were marooned in Hampstead. No taxi would venture forth for them, and walking was out of the question. So they missed our carol-singing.

Gerry and Dick had strung the tree with lights, and then everyone took a hand at decorating it. Not realizing the scarcity of ornaments I had left their purchase until too late. We had to depend on old ones, tinsel and all. But they made a brave show, and one box of shredded, tinfoil icicles proved magic-plus. The threat hanging over us seemed very far away. Lighted red candles, set about the room, were festive and sentimental. We grouped about the piano and sang Christmas carols with cheer and fervency. At midnight, in a circle, we toasted those at home, "Love and Merry Christmas,"--saluted the boys defending us, and went to bed.

My prayers were a beseeching and a questioning. "Dear God, please end this war as soon as Justice may be done.

71

And give the Finns strength--and a victory. Dear God, why are we in such peril? Give us a sign that You are there--and here-- and everywhere." I can not reconcile the birth of that only begotten Son and our celebration of that Birth-with the dark horrors now overtaking the world.

But Christmas Day was lovely, homey and gay. Turkey and cranberry sauce and mince pie and ice-cream! And friends warming our hearts in the late afternoon and evening! And the last of the red candles lighting us for more carols! There seemed no black-out, no war, no nagging fear within the house that day or night--until the guests had left and all my dears had said goodnight. I went the rounds in thankfulness and love, and felt protected by a calm and brooding strength. Complacent I. When stretched in bed, the whole black swarm of worries, fears, and panoply of War beset me. Christmas had been but a spangled interlude. But oh, how sweet. One could thank God for that.

On December 28th, the Finns had a victory for which I'd prayed. Lake Kianta. How wonderful and right it seemed. We kept expecting miracles to happen. When America refused Finland's annual payment of her War Debt I had the wild idea that America would succor that proud courageous people further. Wishful thinking!

New Year's Eve we had a gay family party at the Mayfair. Pete had reported back to duty that morning, but Alix went along with us, and Dorothy and Tony. There were fourteen of us including friends, at the long table. Gerry had his first dinner jacket, his first caviare, his first champagne. Favors, confetti--singing, dancing--blue and khaki uniforms-- gay frocks and black "tails." The usual New Year's Eve potpourri with a dash of War--a soupcon, as it were, for at the moment we were only touched by war preparations and alarms.

At midnight six Scots Guards blew a fanfare on trumpets--and everyone linked hands to sing Auld Lang Syne. The war was so new that the excitement running in one's veins was as the heady wine of adventure, romance, and crusade. Personal casualty lists had not yet curdled our souls and tied our hearts into knots.

I met a Miss Saltonstall that night at the Mayfair. She came from Boston, Mass.--said she was a cousin of the Governor. She was young, dark, vivacious, and wore a white frock. I shall probably never see her again--or recognize her if I do--but in that crucible of New Year's Eve excitement and wartime atmosphere the flame of friendship flared easily and high. I saw her later in the lobby--at dawn--and called, "Bon Voyage--my regards to Boston." She was sailing in a day or two.

"See you there sometime," she answered, and waved a streamered horn.

Maybe.

The middle of January the usual flue epidemic sent me to bed. And unusual cold weather and severe storms caused a shortage of coals in London. Transportation was

73

snowed up. The Poor suffered terribly and everyone else endured discomfort. For days we had no heat in the flat, save a tiny electric heater which we shifted about in a desperate attempt to keep from freezing. It seemed colder indoors than out. There was no hot water. It was awful.

We all drank gallons of hot tea those marrow-freezing days. And when Frank Heaver managed to get two small bags of coal for us from a dealer in Wimbledon we huddled about the open fire in gratitude and relief. After several such bitter experiences how much more did my vitals contract in painful sympathy with the Finns--and even the marauding Russians--as they perished by the hundreds that frightful winter, frozen into their own monuments, grotesquely pitiful.

On March 2nd we knew that the Finns were being licked! The Big Bully had given his fine little neighbor two black eyes--Koursto and Viipuri--and was planning the Knockout blow.

The honest creeds, the Sportsmanship, the Help-Thy-Neighbour doctrine upon which all decent peoples have been nourished seem a poor ration in these days of Pirates and Gangsters. Or does such a diet promote a "delayed action" with a "kick" in it? We must wait and see.

By March 13th I felt as though the votive flame burning before an alter to Courage and Righteousness had flickered out. The cathedral woods of Finland stood cold and dark. Was this the first shadow of a Long Night closing down upon threatened

74

Europe?

One evening during the Norwegian Campaign, Bob returned to us for a short leave, Margareta with him. We were a full house, as Pete had just returned from the South of France where he had been practicing take-offs and landings on an Aircraft Carrier. So the two boys had a great reunion.

Bob was keyed up, nervy and elated. His sub had bagged four German boats--two freighters, one destroyer, and one troopship (Bob was "Mentioned in despatches" for this). Twenty-one-inch torpedoes, carrying 800 lbs. of explosive, were used. Bob was at the periscope each time--and Bob gave the orders. That bucked him no end. Pete was thrilled with vicarious experience.

"What'd it feel like?--Killing those Jerrys."

"Sickening," said Bob. "Of course I was excited when the first ship hove in sight and I knew that we could bag her."

"Yes?" said Pete.

"But when that torpedo struck and Hell tore loose--I felt awful. Had to go and be sick!" Bob looked a bit shamefaced.

But Pete nodded knowingly and sucked hard on his pipe.

"First time I'd killed anyone," continued Bob, "And seemed like there were hundreds--hundreds." He gazed meditatively at the rug and shifted his heavy Navy boots. "The last ship we sank I never turned a hair." He flung up his head and shook back a blond lock, a most characteristic gesture. "It was a good job."

"Very," said Pete.

"To your successes," said my husband, and raised his glass.

We drank the toast in whiskey and soda--a British drink for a British deed. But I felt sad and a bit muddled in mind and heart. Every Jerry that perished was a son, a brother, a husband or a father. I don't feel the same way now, I've seen too much of their dirty work. But at the time it all seemed such a waste--and still does for that matter--and I realized that something rather heat-breaking was happening to the English lads who must fight and kill, even though in duty and honor. Bob would never be the same. I saw it in his eyes.

Margareta kept her chin up, and she felt and spoke her pride. But now she looked at her man with the shutters of her mind wide open.   Margareta is Swedish, and in Sweden German is the first language in school, as French is in America. If that means anything. (English is now the "first" language in Swedish schools.)

The tenth of May, Germany invaded Holland.

"Now they've done it!" was the consensus of opinion. In spite of the pillage of Denmark and Norway, this invasion of the Dutch Queen's tiny tranquil country seemed real War at last. The shadow of Death spread its gray chill across the Channel.

Dick had been ordered a week's rest by the doctor. Concentrated business (the running of a factory making necessary "gadgets" (De-icing pumps for the R.A.F.). Planes on leaflet raids over Germany and Austria had been lost because of the icing-up of the planes' wings at very high altitudes.) for the R.A.F. plus War and all its attendant difficulties, plus government delays, do not mix into a tonic. So we had planned a visit to the Grosvenor Hotel at Swanage in Dorsetshire for this same date, May 10th. It was a lovely Spring day, and as we drove deeper into the countryside of

76

Southern England high hedges of flowering May rose in drifts of white scented bloom along the winding lanes. England--in her best green frock with ruffles of flowery lace, and rustic perfume stirring with every swish of her grass skirts in the warm breeze.

All the Peace. All this Loveliness. It brought a lump into one's throat. Yet khakied soldiers, army lorries, and motor cycles were weaving through it all--with partial blockades of wire and old motorcars and formidable cement pylons thrusting across the map of nature's tapestry. It seemed incongruous. It was. And stranger still seemed the crowded boats that slowly moved into Poole Harbor, across the Bay from Swanage--for days after our arrival at the Grosvenor Hotel. For these craft bore Dutch Refugees, and among them was the Dutch Royal family.

Standing on the flowered terrace of the Grosvenor Hotel above the sea, watching each ship as it passed, we wondered if our friends, the Reurs, were among those now homeless people fleeing for their lives. We had all come a long way from those secure and happy days spent outside Boston, Massachusetts, as good friends and neighbors when Jan Reurs was a Director of the Holland-America line and Consul of the Netherlands in Boston as well. What of the Reurs' hospitable home there with its long beds of tulips imported from Holland? What of the chalet-type house in Le Vesinet, a suburb of Paris, where the Reurs later lived for several years? But most particularly, what of the new home in Rotterdam (their home-town) where they had returned a year ago? The new home was furnished and decorated and ready for a house-warming the very month that War was declared. Had a succession of charming and secure domiciles terminated in ruins and flight--if not death? One square mile of Rotterdam now lay in smoking ruins. Vividly we remembered Mrs. Reurs' prophecies of the past few years.

"There will be war!--I know it."

And she had not wanted to live in Europe.

"It is not safe.--Wait and see."

And now there was war. And perhaps the Reurs family were dead in the midst of the still smoking holocaust that once was the heart of Rotterdam.. But also, perhaps they had escaped. So we drove over to the refugee camp established on Brown's Island to make inquiries. There was no one by the name of Reurs. (And for months we had no word of them-- until a card, through the Red Cross at   Geneva,   reached   a mutual friend in Boston, Mass., who then wrote to me. Reurs family were "safe and well and now living in the Hague." that was all, but enough, considering the times one lived in. For by then we had experienced the evacuation of Dunkirk and gone through the Battle of Britain. To be alive was almost all that mattered.)

While we were at the Grosvenor Hotel in Swanage, on May 10th 1940, Mr. Churchill succeeded Mr. Chamberlain. We heard the news over the radio at dinner, and the transcript of the "change over" made in the House of Commons. Mr. Chamberlain's voice broke once or twice. It was truly a sad occasion. One felt sympathy and sorrow at a career now ended.

But we had hoped for this change for a long, long, time. The Ship of State should now drive full speed ahead, billows of efficiency and accomplishment in its wake. Too long had the full stop of appeasement, followed by the half speed of muddle, shown upon its indicator. Cheers for the new Captain at the helm.

By May 18th the radio had become a Curse and a Revelation with its news. Brussels had fallen. And I felt an urge to "say my say" once again to the folks at home. Already in the months past, I had sent several cables to Senator Pepper, urging the United State's entry into the War. And away back, at the time of the Czecho-Slovakian crisis, I had cabled President Roosevelt, himself; and to my immense surprise had received a reply through the American Embassy in London. (I have the letter.)

Now, sitting in the conservatory of the Grosvenor Hotel at Swanage, the blue sea of the channel before me, I felt on the very rim of the War amphitheater. Couldn't I do something? So I decided to write a letter to the New York Herald Tribune. Here are some portions of that letter. The paper did not publish it. I am afraid that I would not make a journalist; my feelings run rampant, my reason freezes into cynicism. But I meant what I said, every word of it.

Swanage, Dorset, England May 18th 1940
"Brussels has fallen. I have not seen a smiling face all morning. My heart is sick along with untold numbers of others. A gallant little country, in her turn, is fighting for Freedom and the Right. The grim French and stubborn English are once more standing along with Belgium in a bulwark of Might and Right. The forces of Evil must be conquered, else

79

'Lights Out Over Europe' becomes the epitome of moral and spiritual darkness. What inheritance is that for a just and proud people--or for any nation--and its generations to come?

I am an American--one hundred percent. But I and my husband and three children (we are from Boston, Massachusetts) have lived in London for the past five years, and I very much want to express the opinion that now is the time for English speaking people to stick together and fight together.

On Wednesday of last week, May 8th, a young British Naval Officer, Lieutenant on a submarine, returned from his spell of active duty to rejoin his wife who was with us in London, as she often is during these anxious times. Her husband arrived at our home in the late evening. We sat until nearly 2 a.m. talking, arguing, and wondering. And inevitably appeared the question of America's entrance into the War. "She must come in!" said the young Lieutenant. 'She can't simply sit by and let us and the French fight this Nazi horde-- these beasts and their treachery. Why, it's not in the nature of the American people!' He had been to the States. 'The American public will rise to a moral cause. They are an idealistic nation. Oh, why don't they join us as brothers-in-arms!"

President Roosevelt in his speech of May 16th said, "We have learned our lesson," and now America must be prepared to protect herself. But before America is threatened England and France must be conquered. Should this happen you would indeed have a Dark Continent over here--and although America might sit in well-armed safety, self sufficient and isolated, is that an ideal ambition? What of the beautiful things in life--the gorgeous art works of Europe, the lovely natural beauties of each country, the individual architecture? What of the things of the Soul, the great catthedrals, the inspiring music festivals, the literature of other nations? Shall the altars of the Mind become stone cold and the great Universities despoiled of their Humanity? What of the Heart-- the goodness and happiness and spiritual content of each people? Should these things be "blacked-out" in Europe and England, what of America's heritage of Freedom, Honor and Humanity? Must the bells of Liberty toll, 'Too late, too late,' and the generations to come in America cry, 'Why didn't we help our brothers in Democracy and Christ?'. . . . . "

> May 23rd.
> "Regency Lodge"
> St. John's Wood
> London

(Letter continued upon return to flat in London.)

" . . . . Tonight it is May 23rd--the enemy is in Boulogne. Can you imagine, even so little, what that mans to England? It has become a matter of days--or even hours, perhaps,--before the Nazi winged hordes of Death may hurl fire and destruction upon another Democratic and Christian nation. My husband, younger daughter and I sit in our home stripped of its pictures and ornaments, the silver hidden, three bags (one apiece) packed and ready should we be ordered out.

But the entry of America--my country, your country, our country, the country the World now looks to--her entry into this gigantic and dreadful war might stop the final deadly thrust. I shall pray tonight, as I do every night, that My People rise to this tremendous moral issue--as the young British Naval Lieutenant is so confident they will--and stand side by side with the people of Britain and France in this dread fight for the Right and all that I, as an American, was taught to believe in.

It is now more than a War. It is a struggle for the survival of Christianity and Mankind on this side of the Atlantic. (Does all that read like hysteria? Perhaps. But one felt so much in those early months of War. Hovering threats of calamity are doubly hard to endure--one shrinks from an unknown horror. Later, when all those potent threats of Death and Destruction became a reality, everyone met them with far more equanimity than one could ever have believed possible-- the apprehension had been so great. A hardening process set in--crystallization of courage and fortitude.)

On the next afternoon, May 24th, Ziki Witcomb came to tea. It was a lovely spring day, yet London shivered. The shattering vibrations of mechanized warfare--Panzers, Stukas, etc.--seemed as though transmitted across the Channel. The air was electric with stories of Germany Blitzkreig versus poorly equipped companies of English soldiers. The French were being accused of cowardice and treason. Failure to destroy the Meuse Bridges looked very nasty indeed.

A young British officer, spending a leave with us, used strong and condemnatory language about the fact and claimed that the French were running from the Germans. This was more than Ziki could stand. She rose precipitately, her face scarlet.

"How dare you call my people cowards!"

She glared at the young officer, who, much taken aback, mumbled, "Well, are the French standing their ground?"

"And would you?" demanded Ziki. Both hands dramatically raised in clenched fists, she brought them down in sweeping arcs over the young man's head. He ducked.

"You see!" she exclaimed. "Bah!" Do not speak to me of courage!" And she flounced back to her chair.

"Madame," the young officer remonstrated, "You have only to consider the evidence--the undestroyed bridges. Call it stupidity, or treason--as you like. The facts remain. The bridges stand, and the French flee."

"And what of the English?" asked Ziki in such measured tones that, knowing her, we waited in fascinated apprehension.

"They'll fight to the last man. You can count on that. I've got a brother there now, and I can't see him running in the wrong direction!"

"Has he ever seen a Panzaire before? Has he ever had an iron monster assault him from the skies? These dive bombers--these Stukahs! Can one push them away with bare hands?" She was up in a flash to illustrate her point.

The young man recoiled within his chair.

"See! You are soft--and you have no sense."

"But, Madame, you are a woman!" spluttered the officer. "I can't retaliate."

"So!" exploded Ziki. Bending her body back she raised terrified eyes to the ceiling and beat upon her breast with clenched fists. "There are Panzairs! There are Stukahs! They rush at me! They swoop down!" She crouched. "I have a gun!" She made the appropriate gestures. "I might even have a tank! But what are these against those iron monsters of the

Jairmans? For years they make those juggernauts of Death!
Can flesh and blood stand up to them?" Again she bent
threateningly above the young officer. "It is just common
sense I ask of you! Me, I am French--I am a realist." She
dusted her hands together, and sat down.

A strained silence fell for some seconds. Then
someone spoke. "How about some more tea?" And the war
receded for the time being.

But in the light of the following events we all felt
that was partially justified. The young officer's brother was
wounded in the retreat to Dunkirk, and after hospitalization
came to us for convalescence. We learned enough to agree
with Ziki that flesh and blood could not stand up to "Panzairs
and Stukahs." For the young British officer had gone into
battle without even a revolver--until he took one from a brother
officer after he was killed. There were nowhere near enough
English planes to beat off a German air attack.

"God! We never even saw an English plane!--
Where in Hell was the R.A.F.?" .... (Planes of the R.A.F.
were kept in England, ready for feared invasion by sea or air.
But planes of the Fleet Air Arm--Pete's among them--were of
that fabulous and grotesque armada which rescued over
300,000 British soldiers from the shores of Dunkirk.)

A roaring lion, a stout hearted lion, is helpless against a swarm of vultures. He has no choice but to retreat-- and arm himself adequately for the next battle.

There were two miracles that month of May, 1940-- the Retreat from Dunkirk and the abiding Faith of the British Army, which, inadequately armed through Governmental failure and muddle, yet rose above recriminations and pledged itself anew. I have never met one man back from that ignominious Hell who didn't say "Wait 'till we get the arms-- just wait!"

Sunday Evening, May 26th, 1940

Today Dick and I drove to Chandlers Ford, outside Southhampton, to spend the day with Alix and Pete. Pete is practicing dive bombing there while awaiting fresh orders. Dorothy and Martha went with us.

There is something frightening going on across the Channel. Some miles the other side of Winchester, we met and were halted by a long column of lorries and buses filled with soldiers. Used as we were to such military sights, the first lot did not impress us. But after thirty or more lorries had rumbled past, we began to wonder and then to concentrate. These soldiers were not as usual--they neither smiled nor sang. There was a fatalistic mood about the procession as it went on and on. We counted over one hundred vehicles and stared at the jumbled lot of soldiers, blankets, and equipment in uncomprehending dismay. The men looked half dead. Some were asleep. All were dirty. Their sun-baked, swollen-eyed faces had a pathetic little boy quality.

Our hearts were wrung as enlightenment slowly crept upon us. And Dick exclaimed, "Those boys are coming back from France! The English must be retreating--clear into England. What in God's name can be happening?"

Alix and Pete could tell us nothing. They were as stricken as we. Pete says they must be evacuating the British Expeditionary Force from Belgium and France. It is hard to believe, and terrifying.

Alix and Pete are well--and so happy! The Inn where they are living is comfortable and Chandlers Ford a pretty place.

For two days after this Alix stood by the roadside, helping serve coffee to a steady, slow-moving stream of returning soldiers. Alix said there were no complaints from them, though some looked ill. Some even had a joke now and then. All were grateful for the coffee.

"But they looked so, Mother! It was very sad."

And indeed it was.

As the British Expeditionary Force tumbled back into England, the decision to keep Dick's factory in London "until the bombs dropped" tumbled also. Very tired and exasperated after a long day spent between the factory and the Air Ministry, Dick announced at dinner one night that factory personnel were all to be moved North at once. I must drive up to the immediate neighborhood of the site chosen and try to find a house. This didn't appeal to me; Lancashire is a dismal county, and the vicinity of Liverpool seemed unwise. But orders are orders. We left early the next morning, Martha and

I, with Elsie Heaver for company and Hartley Davies (a very good friend), as Good Angel, for he chauffeured us. I'm no good at this left side of the road driving!

For seven hours, steadily, we drove with little inspiration from a war-like countryside, passing through the bleak pottery district with its towering, smoking chimneys, dismal slag heaps and black rows of sordid, slum cottages. In all our search through that flat, unappetizing, Northern landscape, we found but one pretty spot, Knutsford, and one house--and that with an option on it. Everything else was stuffed to the gills with "the Military," or wives of such.

Putting up at a hard-bedded pub for the night we returned to London the next day, arriving home for late tea, tired and very grimy. The War news was more dismal than ever. A very special Hell seemed concentrated at Dunkirk. And then Pete walked in to tell us all about it.

To walk--or to fly--through the Valley of the Shadow of Death, Man must strip his Mortality of human fears and phobias. That he does it, over and over again, and overcomes the most awful calamities with spirit and courage is always a shining miracle to me. The boys and men who continually pass through this war's dark adventures never fail to stir my heart. I am a sentimental woman. And as such, I watched and listened to Pete as he recounted his share in the Evacuation from Dunkirk.

The world knows in detail of that epic performance. But, because Pete had battled in the skies there and there shot down his first Nazi, I felt singularly affected. And were we all proud of him! Pete, himself, was most matter-of-fact and calm, although when he appeared so unexpectedly that late afternoon, he'd been up since three a.m.--literally up, in a plane-scrapping

Nazi dive-bombers.

"Weren't you scared?" asked Alix.

"No!" said Pete. "I wondered about that a bit when I set off. But the sight of those Nazi planes roaring up and down over the beaches and deliberately machine-gunning women and children--why it turned my blood to ice. I couldn't hate those Jerries enough! And then, too, things happen so fast in the air! I just got on with the job. --Got a Nazi, too!"

Dick and Hartley looked a bit envious--as though shooting Nazis was a gilt-edged privilege. But I know a lot of people who feel that way now.

"It was the most amazing sight I've ever seen," continued Pete. "The countryside blazing like one enormous bonfire! The sea full of ships of all kinds and sizes-- troopships, destroyers, launches--even dinghys and rowboats strung out on hawsers behind larger ships. It did look crazy, that channel fleet!" He smiled faintly and took a long pull at his pipe. "And every one of the ships crowded to the gunwales with soldiers! The Channel was alive! Such a sight! And all the time Stukas attacking and bombs dropping and machine guns raking everything. What a Hell!" He shook his head, as though it were unbelievable even then to him. "What a Hell! -- ---------But what a wonderful job the Navy's doing! I'll never forget it. I'm glad I had a part in it."

Pete's been to War. Pete's been into battle. Pete's killed a Nazi. Pete's in it at last. Tick, tick went my mind as I listened. Tick, tick, what next?

"I've come for some gear," he said, "Must drive up to the cottage and get my tropical kit. I'm off tomorrow."

Where, he couldn't say--only that he would be on the "Illustrious," England's newest aircraft carrier.

So Alix and Pete drove out to Letchworth, Dorothy's home, after dinner for Pete's white uniforms--and spent the next morning at Gieves in Piccadilly, purchasing sun helmets, shorts, etc. The youngsters were as happy as clams over pete's coming "cruise". Alix didn't know that Pete was to test Navy planes for dive-bombing.

The next day, May 31st, Gerry returned from school for a. week's holiday. I went down to Waterloo Station to meet him. His train was due at 11:23 a.m. and arrived at 3:10 p.m. Such a wait! and Gerry was just as tired as I when at last his train pulled in. He'd had no lunch, no tea--as the school train had been shunted onto a siding to allow the troop trains Right of Way.

As I waited in Waterloo, I watched train after train of returning B.E.F. (British Expeditionary Force.) unload--and saw the walking wounded and the stretcher cases, lines of them! My heart felt like a swollen Reservoir of Tears.

Since Pete was leaving from Waterloo that afternoon, I had planned to see him off. So, at 2 o'clock, I rushed the length of the station--from Platform No. 10 (Gerry's train) to Platform No. 3 (Pete's train)--and anxiously scanned the faces of Naval Officers and Personnel, kit-laden, pouring through the gates marked "Plymouth and Devonport." But no Pete. Since there were several such trains between two and three o'clock I more or less shuttled back and forth between platforms No. 3 and No. 10 getting very tired and hot, and exceedingly downhearted at the apparently endless stream of worn and wounded whose waiting relatives swarmed throughout the station. But although anxiety stretched tired faces into taunt masks, when the long awaited lad finally appeared there was always a smile for him. And the lad, wounded or no, could summon a grin--and a joke as well, sometimes--for his Ma or his girl.

My apparently continuous curiosity concerning the comings and goings of Service Men aroused the interest of two Bobbies. They accosted me in no uncertain terms, and demanded to know what I was doing and why. My explanation--that I was awaiting my son's return from school--held water only in so far as there really was a train due in sometime from Blandford. But there is a big Army Camp there as well as Bryanston School. As for the story--that I also wished to say good-bye to my son-in-law as he left for Active Service--that seemed a bit thick. The two Constables shadowed me for the rest of my wait. I felt like a fool, with two blue-trousered chaperons trailing me as I continued my trek between platforms No.3 and No.10. Not until the Blandford train came in, and Gerry truly materialized, did the two Bobbies leave me--and with a rather deprecating smile. So I smiled, too.

"Now I know what a spy feels like," I thought.

But the family roared with laughter when I told them later. Mother as a spy was super ridiculous.

As it happened, Pete didn't sail until June 9th, having frequent short visits with Alix before then. Halcyon days for them both. I am so grateful for that.

"Don't say good-by," said Pete as he finally left. "Say Au'voir." And he gave Alix a bottle of her favorite perfume, "Je Reviens."

The scent still lingers in the little blue vial on her dresser. "Je Reviens."

First Summer of the War

June 10th, 1940.

The Air Ministry made another "decision"--Dick's factory would remain in London "until the bombs dropped" after all!

Mussolini declared War as from midnight.

President Roosevelt made a speech in which he spoke of people who "stab in the back."

The Allied troops were out of Norway.

King Haakon was now in London

And the loss of the Aircraft Carrier "Glorious" and four other English vessels was announced.

A busy day for those who wait and listen and accept. A busier one for those who work and fight and endure. And disappointment and heartbreak threading it all together.

As usual, I had expected too much too soon from America. Scorn and sharp words do not stay a hand upraised to strike. The Italian mongrel could well growl, "Sticks and stones may break my bones but words will never hurt me." Why couldn't America at least put a few stones into the sling shot of the British David? The German Goliath might crumble them.

On June 13th, I wrote in my diary, "Such a strange day! The air has been thick with yellow dust, or smoke--like a dry fog. People's faces looked saffron in the weird light, and a sultriness has lain heavy upon London. A feeling of doom broods over the place tonight. My skin prickles with it."

At the time I had two refugee maids from Vienna. They were in alternate states of hysteria, fright or tears during May and June. Sophie, the cook, had a nervous habit of grasping her top-knot of dark hair and pumping it up and down like an accordion while she wailed.

"Madame! The Chermans haff only to chump the Channel. Then we shall be dead! To flee all the way from Wien (Vienna) for this!"

Her top-knot would bounce under pressure and her black eyes snap and she would stamp up and down the kitchen and bang the pans about.

"But Yess, Madame!" Jennie, the parlormaid, would hissingly interrupt. "Yess! Mien bruder vass made to valk tee streets of Wien mit a placert on his chest. 'Ich bin Jude.' Und tee Nazis kicked him to make him yell, 'Ich bin Jude!' 'Louter!' tay vould shout at him, 'Louter.'"

Jennie would then look down her long nose and wipe away the tears with her apron. Her brother is now in a Concentration Camp--if alive. She doesn't know.

"I can neffer forget, Madame--neffer. Und if tee Chermans come to London tay vill keel me. Yess, I know!"

Our soups and vegetables must have been well salted with tears those tragic days.

But Sophie and Jennie were not the only ones who feared. The disintegration of France became an unbelievable horror as we watched its treacherous and rotten progress.

On Sunday, June 16th--the weekend preceding France's capitulation--I attended morning service in beautiful Exeter Cathedral, South Devon.

Dick had driven down to Exeter (from London) on Saturday to look for a factory site, and Martha and I had gone along, as usual, to house hunt. Hartley was with us--good company, good friend, and again Good Angel at the wheel. Saturday evening we sat in the tiny parlor of the Royal Clarence, an old Posting Inn within the Cathedral Close, and desultorily played cards. The radio--at six, nine and midnight--chanted the melancholy tale of France's downfall. Each announcement seemed more improbable than the last.

"It can't be!"

"France will never give in!"

"While they fight there's hope!"

But when at last we went to bed, the fate of France seemed already sealed--into a vault of Nazism, only to be resurrected when a mundane Gabriel, Democracy, sounds the trumpet of Universal Peace and Freedom. Symbolism creeps automatically into one's speech nowadays--events are so cataclysmic and farflung.

That Sunday morning of June 16th, 1940, was bright with sun, warm with humanity. A community of English gentlefolk had gathered to pray for an Ally's preservation. Exeter Cathedral was crowded. The little wooden prayer seats were set thick as grass blades within the stone nave and along the walls. Prayer rose like incense. The faces of men, women, and children had an ecstatic intensity that looked hypnotic. And when, at Service, the Congregation rose to sing the

"Marseillaise" and "God Save the King," the added gleam of tears lent, not depression, but shining Faith to every countenance.

England would fight on. Her women would continue to give their sons. Her men their lives.

Noblesse oblige.

Back in London the next evening, June 17th, we had dinner with friends in Kensington. Kathleen Marlow, our hostess, played for us--a lovely treat, for she is a Concert Pianist. There was bright moon-light outside. Every chimney pot arched itself like a black cat in silhouette against a lightened sky. The blacked-out city crouched secretively beneath the ever impending threat of air-raids.

This evening is listed among my unforgettable evenings of the War. For I made a trite discovery that somehow seemed very important at the time--that the things of the Soul and the Spirit and the Mind can never die and are always a source of inspiration. And thus, so long as a people can call upon such inner resources, so long do they feel invincible. For, under the spell of Kathleen's music, we sat immovable for hours--and I am certain that all of us, not I alone, felt strengthened with its beauty and ready for any future. From then on I never wanted to leave London--raids or no.

The Marlow's studio has since lost its skylight and windows. The walls are shrapnel-scarred. The wee garden is blackened from incendiaries. But the ghosts of lovely melodies still inhabit the place. I'm sure that they rise anew whenever the sirens scream and drum defiance to the Nazi hymn of hate.

When for security reasons the road signs, station names,

94

and those of every city, town and village were removed, or blotted out, England became a "No-Name-Land." So travel by road or rail has become quite an adventure. One finds only such signs as "To the West" or "To the North," etc.

People turn suspicious of inquiring motorists, and one more or less gropes about England, particularly if driving in strange parts. If you have a good road map with the name of every tiny village--as well as town and city--you have only to ask, "Is this the road to Otters--St. Giles?" or, "Do we come next to "Bury-in-the-Wold?" thus intimating a knowledge of the district. But without these little stepping stones to guide one, a plain enquiry for some important town or city brings dark looks, and a searching glance at the rear seat as though Fifth Columnists lurk under the robe.

Dick's business takes him about the country quite a bit and his American accent is often only recognized as "Different from English." We--as I often drive with him--have had some amusing adventures and some aggravating ones. At the very beginning of the War we had occasion to drive to Deal, neighboring town to Dover, on the South East Coast. There had been some short, but sharp, raids on coastal shipping there. Ships had been sunk, and shrapnel had broken windows along the waterfront. But the bombing on land hadn't started yet.

The Heavers went along with us. And because it was our first trip into a Defense Area and entailed driving after black-out in unfamiliar countryside, I recall the adventure vividly and distinctly.

As I write this particular episode in my journal--while on another trip with Dick--I am sitting above the sea, "Somewhere on the South Coast," with barbed wire and land mines forbidding me the shore, sand-bagged machine gun nests to the right and left, the Military swarming about everywhere. Two nights ago bright flashes at sea, with ominous rumbles, meant attack on a Convoy. At times machine-gun fire rattles in the distance.

But I now pay no attention to such reminders of war. I have seen too much. However, that early trip to Deal still holds a certain fascination for me. Probably because it was the first such trip, and an unknown quantity at the time. It really seemed exciting then--like a game played in the dark.

We did not leave London until early dusk, so we had to nose our way long the roads. It was black when we reached Canterbury. The narrow streets, with their hump-backed houses, were a maze. The flat country beyond, of salt marshes and infrequent villages, became an unchartered desert. We had to refer to the map continually. So Elsie and I, in the back of the car, would crouch under the robe and by the light of a glow-worm-powered torch--as no torches were permitted out in the black-out at that date--we would read out the place-names to Dick and Frank. Whenever we came to a crossroad Frank hopped out and figured the proper direction according to Elsie's map-reading. Sometimes he got it right. But we did a lot of weaving that night.

At times high hedges crowded us, or wind-twisted trees shook like witches' claws. And fantastic shapes--hay-ricks and cottages--loomed like crouching beasts along our way. It was a night for hob-goblins. The wind was high. And the sea smelt of secret dark adventure.

Finally, when we were at an utter standstill where four roads met a friendly farmer rumbled up in a two-wheeled cart and pleasantly answered Dick's, "Would you please direct us to Deal?" with a cheery, "Just follow me, Sir." His nag was tired, so we had to crawl--but we'd been doing that most of the time because of the black-out.

Visibility was poor in spite of the stars. The white line, now painted down the centre of all roads, became an elusive thread that seemed to spin out into infinity. I sat on the edge of the back seat and peered ahead into the night, my neck stuck out like a dying clam's.

When, at long last, we stumbled through the darkened entrance of the hotel at Deal, and pushed back the flapping black-out curtains at the entrance to the lounge, the clock dial shining beneath a dimmed electric light bulb read only 7:30 p.m. We were absolutely amazed! It had seemed like the middle of the night, and that we had been driving hours and hours and hours.

The next morning the sun revealed a dozen or so ships of assorted nations riding at anchor on this night. Naval launches bustled in and out among them. Cargoes and papers must be checked and cleared. England was policing sea traffic. Masts and funnels of sunken ships stuck up here and there like sinister fingers. These, and the shrapnel scars on pier and buildings, were the only bit of War we saw. No "Dog-fight" materialized in the night that we were there. But this, my first night into a Defense Area, sharply brought the war into close, clear focus, where it had been blurred before.

The claws of the yellow Nazi Tiger had scratched the British Lion. I had seen the scars. There was going to be the Fight of All Time when they both got going. I felt the frightfulness and bloodiness of the battles to come with premonitive urgency.

June 20, I went to Exeter for the day, to look again for a

97

house away from probable bombing areas. Elsie Heaver went with me. We left London on the 9 a.m. train and arrived in Exeter at 4 p.m. Hardly according to plan. Our train was the usual extra-long, over-burdened one of wartime. So, at several stations, it had been necessary to stop twice--moving up the coaches at the rear, as the station platform could not accommodate them all at once. At noon, shortly before reaching Yeovil, the Restaurant Car Steward appeared at our compartment with seating tickets and suggested that we get out at Yeovil and wait for the restaurant Car to be moved up, as otherwise we would find it difficult, if not impossible, to reach it because all the train corridors were jam-packed with soldiers and their gear. This advice sounded sensible. So, at Yeovil, Elsie and I, two Naval Officers, and a middle-aged couple, all occupants of our compartment, hopped out on the platform and walked back toward the Restaurant Car--expecting it to eventually pull up before us, as it was then several cars beyond the platforms' end. The Steward was with us, and we confidently waited.

At last the Guard blew his whistle. The heavy train fell back, bumpers clanking and rattling, then jerkily pulled up and began to lunge forward, slowly. We kept our eyes on the Restaurant Car and moved to the platforms' edge.

But the Restaurant Car slid past us.

We began to run.

The Steward shouted, "It's all right, Ladies and Gentlemen. The train will stop further up the platform."

But the train went faster. So did we. Our cries mingled with the Steward's assurances--and they made no symphony. To our consternation and chargrin the train, our lunch, our coats and magazines, simply slid away and away, chuggingly and inexorably, off to Exeter and Plymouth.

"The Head Steward told me the train would move up at Yeovil!--It was assured, Ladies and Gentlemen!" expostulated the unlucky Steward as the Navy showed every sign of beating him up. The Officers' luggage, caps and greatcoats had gone on to Plymouth. So had our small oddments. There was nothing for it but to practice patience-on-a-monument and await the following Local.

Later, with only an hour in Exeter, Elsie and I managed to find one house that might do--provided one overlooked a few little things like lack of heat, a kitchen with no window, and having the bath on the stair-landing. No particular prize for our trouble.

Trains are a bit unaccountable nowadays. We waited almost two hours at Exeter Central for the 5:15 p.m. from Exeter back to London. It didn't come in until 7 o'clock--but with good reason, the debarkation at Plymouth of troops from France. More weary and wounded boys come home again. Making our way at once to the Restaurant Car, for we had missed both lunch and tea, Elsie and I were grateful for the bacon and eggs, bread and tea that were served at dinner that evening. But we would gladly have done without, had our meal meant depriving any of those Men and Officers who looked so dead-beat and in need of good hot food. Their faces scarlet and swollen from exposure, their eyes slits from lack of rest, some chaps with minor wounds, they fell asleep wherever they dropped. A young--very young--Lieutenant slept happily and heavily on my shoulder most of the trip back to town.

Moving through space after dark, with no shadowy vision

of passing landmarks, the black-out curtains close drawn, a small blue light bulb for illumination, one simply relaxes and leaves it all to wheels and fate. If you are going through to the terminal it will all come out right anyway. If unfamiliar with the route and you must alight somewhere along it, there's very little you can do about that either--unless you memorize the station names, for all have been removed. But pronunciation of names by the English is sometimes weird and wonderful--and that of English trainmen even more so. They have a distant way of simply ignoring letters and syllables. They are not on speaking acquaintance with certain words, as it were.

For instance, it is after black-out and you wish to alight at "Cirencester." If you hear "Sissester" bawled out along some station platform you pay no attention. When, at some following stop, a loud "Surenchester" is tossed verbally at you thru' your open compartment door, you then poke your head out and look up and down the shadowy platform. "Ladies" is the only sign you can dimly make out. Inquiry reveals that you are at "South Warrenchester" and that you should have gotten out at "Sissester!" But, had you done so, the station might have borne only the sign "Gentlemen"--which is monotonously vague, as all stations are now named "Ladies" or "Gentlemen", or "Ladies-Gentlemen," in high British hyphenated style. So there seem but two answers to the riddle of travel in No-Name-Land. I. Travel in day light. II. Carry a large card with your station's name on it. You can then flash this at the Station-Master. And if he says, "Yes," you get out! One of Gerry's trips back to school in Blandford, Dorsetshire, after the Christmas holidays, he got out in the black-out at Salisbury, Wiltshire. It necessitated a taxi-ride of some length and price.

Wednesday, June 9th, I wrote in my diary--"Another fine day. Breezy. Bad air-raid at East Coast town. Twelve killed. Raids also in South West. I watch all these notices with fear and apprehension. South and South West mean Dorset to me." Gerry's school is in that county.

As a matter of fact one of those South West raids of June 9th was in Dorset and the bombs were dropped not far from Gerry's school. But Gerry had not even bothered to tell me about it--until June 20th when he wrote.

"By the way, Mother, I forgot to mention we had an air-raid warning a short while ago. The siren woke us all at 12:30 and we all got up, put on our wrappers and slippers, took our gas masks and torches, and went down into the shelter. We were there until the "All Clear" at 3:30 a.m. I played draughts (checkers) most of the time. Some of the boys read. We weren't sleepy at all. Three bombs were dropped about 2 miles away. I cycled over to see the craters the next day. Don't worry, Mother, it was just exciting."

That was "early-on," as the English say, and only an introduction to air-raids. But it terrified me just the same. Manston Aerodrome, in back of Weymouth, began getting a pasting at that time--and it isn't far from Blandford. A few miles are nothing to a plane. Gerry and his schoolmates were kept pretty busy, night and day, dashing for the shelter. There was a dog-fight right over their cricket ground one afternoon. The boys watched in fascination and saw the German plane spiral down, smoke trailing, into a nearby wood. Some of the youngsters later salvaged bits of the wreckage and enterprizingly sold them in the village for 2/6 (65 cents) apiece.

101

The electric atmosphere of war began to key up people. The scattered raids were sharp reminders of things to come, unknown and terrifying. Alix's doctor (the baby due in July) suggested we engage a specialist and hospital accommodation outside London--quite a way outside. So on Sunday afternoon, June 23rd, I saw Alix and Dorothy off from Waterloo for Exeter. Plans for moving Dick's factory to Exeter were still in the air, and Exeter is the town of SouthWest Devon for shops, Hospitals, Specialists, etc. If we must leave London, Exeter seemed a fortunate choice.

But thousands of other people apparently had the same idea. A 'phone call that evening from Dorothy reported that there was positively no room in any Hospital or Nursing Home, and the Specialist recommended by Dr. Nixon had been called-up. She and Alix would stop overnight at the Railway Hotel, the only place with available rooms. Irreverently, "There was no room at the Inn," popped into my head.

Consultation with Dick over matters resulted in my going down to Exeter the next day and chasing from one Real Estate Office to the other--vainly. Finally, in desperation, I hired a car and drove forty odd miles to Bideford on the North West Coast, near Westward Ho! There was one house to be had there--a great ark of a place, with innumerable French doors and windows and a huge glass-house (green-house) to be blacked-out. The grounds were gorgeous--two tennis courts, flower and vegetable gardens--and an unused well, which I made mental note to board over for the safety of my future grandchild. This well, and the tiny inadequate fireplaces for high ceilinged rooms and draughty halls, did not intrigue me. But the house was all there was to rent. "Absolutely all, Madame," said the agent. So I took an option on it, and returned to Exeter.

But that very night bombs were dropped slightly North of Bideford, (at Instow)--and there was an air-raid warning in London. That settled my mind good and proper. We'd stay in London! There didn't seem much <u>choice</u> of location with Nazi planes doing hundreds of miles an hour and jettisoning bombs nonchalantly, wherever handy, in a bid for escape from the R.A.F. You could not put your finger on one spot in England and say, "that will be safe,"--as time and events were to prove. And we did have a shelter of sorts in London, and friends to share any fears and calamities. I never regretted the decision. When hot, heartbreaking History was being forged by planes, bombs and intrepid young pilots and stout-hearted citizenry in the Battle of Britain, we--Americans from Boston, Massachusetts,--felt proud to have shared it all. We wear the experience in our hearts as a campaign ribbon, and when things look black we recall those dreadful, but inspiring days and nights and know that the English people are unbeatable. Victory will come.

While I looked for a home, Dick tried frantically to get the factory moved away from London. But the Higher-Ups seemed near-sighted, and were stubborn about the matter. Dick was in a proper state. For, not only is the factory full of expensive, vital and irreplaceable (save from the States) machinery and tools, it is also a main artery pumping life blood to the R.A.F.--literally, for the factory produces a certain type of mechanical pump, built into the planes.

In the evenings, at home in the flat, Dick would hold forth on this problem of moving the factory to anyone who would listen. 'Most everyone did, and 'most everyone agreed, but no one had the right answers. Dick tried every approach to the authorities, but felt that he needed the ear, both ears, of the Boss, Lord Beaverbrook, Minister of Aircraft Production.

And then Dr. Nixon (Alix's doctor) came to dinner. As usual "the problem" and its attendant worries, cropped up. Dr. Nixon was highly interested. Also, he had a solution! He most kindly offered to introduce Dick to Lord Walmer who, in turn, would pass Dick on to Lord Beaverbrook. The introductions materialized, and were of great assistance. I've always felt that Dr. Nixon should be decorated for this!--just as his brother-in-law, Capt. Vian (Later Rear Admiral Sir Philip Vian, R.N., and decorations.) of the Cossack, was decorated for the Almark episode. For Dick's first interview with Lord Beaverbrook bucked him no end (as the English say), and he's never been let down by Lord Beaverbrook since. The Beaver--as many affectionately call him--is indeed "an industrious builder," a builder of planes. And God, and the English people, know how much they counted when the Luftwaffe started strafing!

July, 1940

This month will ever stand alone in my memories. And could I depict its progress and events in color, I would shade the month of July from rhododendron pink thru' Heavenly blue, with bits of starry gold, into a wine-red that smelt of carnations and then faded out at last in mauve and gray.

July 1st I had guests for tea. Nothing unusual in that. But

the conversation was, for it turned into an intense debate on whether I should return to the States, or not, on the S.S. Washington sailing the 6th.   Among my guests were a charming Canadian woman, Mrs. Martens, whose five children were all "in the war" (the boys in the Services, the girls in War Work), Mrs. Quarles, the Norwegian wife of a Dutch diplomat, Lt. Geoffry Wilkes, the young C.O. of an Anti-Aircraft Battery, and Ziki Witcomb, who was definitely--"oh, but definitely!"--sailing on the S.S. Washington on the 6th, and had her tickets and visas already rubber-banded together in her handbag.   Why didn't I go home and take the children she wanted to know.

"Thees is the last ship, Phi", (one of my nicknames), she said. "After thees you must stay with the bombs!"

And that started it--the debate, I mean.

For days, if not weeks, I had been literally haunted by that question. "Should I take the children home?" and I simply couldn't make a decision, for my heart was divided into bits among my family. Dick would stay. That was settled. And I felt that I couldn't leave him. Martha didn't want to go home. She had had one year of Medical and was now within a few months of completing a course in Speech Therapy for Nervous and Shell-Shocked cases.

"Mother, you can't ask me to give up a real service at such a time as this. Why, I can help here!"

And I knew she wasn't thinking just of the Canteen shift she and I share. Martha is splendid among the sick, and would be so among the wounded. Gerry would do as I decided, being of two minds, anyway. He'd like to go home and see the Gang, but he'd also like to stay here and see the Show. Well, I had a similar feeling myself--that is, I didn't want to miss anything.

105

But I had one very important reason for staying in England. My eldest daughter was going to have a baby, and I couldn't see myself putting the Atlantic Ocean between her and me, her Mother.

My head buzzed with indecision and worry. There was Ziki, with her "Panzairs, Stukahs, and bombs" as potent arguments, and her ticket to get away from it all. There was Geoff who, as the Army, felt obliged to tell me I was crazy to stay. There was Mrs. Martens, who was very, very sure she was going to stay and look after her family.

"Why, they've got to have a home to come home to when on leave!"

And she still keeps that home, in London, raids or no.

And there was Mrs. Quarles, both her own and her husband's countries under the German heel, so strongly opposed to my separating the family that she stuttered in her insistence.

"No m-matter vaht happens, Mrs. C-Cotton, k-keep you familie toget-her--all in vun countree."

Poor dear, she knew well what she was talking about. She had had two sons at school in Holland, and since the German invasion, had received news of but one--a mere bit of information thru' Diplomatic channels that the younger son, ten years old, was "safe, with friends", Whom she didn't know. No word at all of the elder, fifteen. They (she and her husband) supposed he was trying to get to England somehow.

"He is yust the kind of bhoy who vould do such a ting. Ve can only vait and pray."

The tho't of this boy and his unknown adventure, or fate, kept me awake nights as I continually saw Gerry in like plight. But then Alix and her baby would slide across my mental screen and I could only lie in sleeplessness and indecision.

So the next day, July 2nd, I went downtown and had new passport pictures taken, then went on to the American Embassy where I got my exit permit and visa and was thumbprinted. Just in case, I thought.

Walking through to Oxford Street from Grosvenor Square, I ran into a friend I hadn't seen for some time. She lived out of town.

"What on earth are you doing here, Peg!" she asked. "I thought you had all left long ago. Or are you sailing on the Washington?"

"I don't think so," I answered. "Alix is having a baby this month. I can't bear to leave her."

"Oh, but she married an Englishman. Surely his Mother can be with her?"

"But that isn't the same," I said. "And there's a War. You never can tell," giving the usual dubious reasons for doing as one sees fit.

For I don't think I ever really thought of going home. But, until I saw Ziki's trunks and cases leave in the U.S. Line's van and wished her Bon Voyage, my indecision rose and fell sharply like a fever graph. And, for perhaps one frightened moment, I felt starkly deserted as Ziki drove off in a taxi, out of Regency Lodge courtyard, for the last time the morning of July 5th.

"But you can't go now, anyway, you idiot!" said I to myself and went back to the flat almost jauntily--to learn later that the German radio claimed H.M.S. Illustrious, Pete's ship, had been hit by a torpedo. There was no confirmation by the Admiralty. But the report was another reminder of what War could mean. Frightfulness, Destruction, and Death.

And only the day before, on the Fourth of July, the British Fleet had gone into action against the French Fleet, destroying some units and capturing others. Unprecedented and tragic, it had seemed like Brother against Brother. One wept for both sides in such a contest. It couldn't have been easy to fire upon an erstwhile ally.

That month of July, 1940,--as I have written--remains as a parti-colored page in the calendar of my memory, like a prism, reflecting the experiences of joy and grief muted to the emotions.

July 1st to July 13th. Excitement--indecision--and decision to go--or not to go--back to the States. Pink parties of chatter and tea. The flare-up of cyclamen in my mind at the Radio announcement of July 5th, "the Germans claim to have torpedoed H.M.S. Illustrious." The rhododendron pink of happiness that bloomed like an aura about Alix. The sharp scarlet of pain for her--the purple of fear for us--as we waited, Dick and I, the night of July 12th to 13th, for Dr. Nixon's 'phone call.

2:30 A.M.

"You have a granddaughter."

Purple was the right color then, too--Royal Purple. We, my husband and I, now grandparents, felt very grand indeed.

July 13th to July 18th. Days of Heavenly blue--the color of Alix' eyes and those of Penelope Marianne Dean, our new and shining Penny. Pete would be home in a few days on leave. The golden hours of contentment and pride and expectation illuminated that short interlude of Heaven-on-Earth for Alix as stars in a Peace-time sky.

July 18th was Hartley Davies' birthday. He was to come in to the flat for a drink--sherry and biscuits--with Dick and me before taking Martha out for the evening to celebrate On return from my daily visit to the hospital, about 6 p.m., I put fresh flowers (from a barrow in Baker Street) about the drawing-room and set out a tray of glasses with a sherry decanter. On impulse I poured myself a half glass and walked over to Pete's photo atop a low cabinet, where a vase of dark red carnations stood beside it--his favorite flower and color. (His little Bible, that his granny Dean had given him as a child and which was always in his cabin, along with his Naval books and his beloved Beethoven records, were bound in the same deep red.) And, still under some inner compulsion, I lifted my glass. "To you, Pete. A safe return."

Two days later, as I came out of my bedroom ready to go to the Hospital, I saw the yellow envelope of a telegram lying on the polished floor between the front door sill and the red and blue hall rug. My heart turned over, and I stared again. There was no envelope! My fool mind was at it again. I shook off the hallucination and went out.

But the next morning, as I was sorting linen in the airing cupboard, Hilda, my Daily, handed me a telegram. I knew what it was. I didn't have to open it. But when I did open it, the reading didn't make sense--"The Admiralty regrets -------," How could the Admiralty regret? And I couldn't believe it--for minutes, it seemed--as tho' I were paralyzed in my mind and heart. And I could not say anything except, "How can I tell her! How can I tell her!", over and over and over. And then I read the date again on the telegram and it was July 18th. And I remembered my toast to dear Pete in the early evening of that day. And the heady spice of deep red carnations filtered into my stunned senses.

For three days I moved in a coma, as it were, for Dr. Nixon

forbade us to tell Alix the news at once. And I shall never, never forget those three days. For Dick and I had at once gone to the Hospital, with two dozen fragrant wine-red carnations as a slight expression of our love and grief, only to be forbidden to mention the fateful telegram. And to walk into Alix' room, with all those flowers, and to smile and be cheerful and laugh with her, was the most heartbreaking thing I ever had to do. And for three days it went on--the stream of happy friends, the pride and joy of Alix. And all the time those wine carnations beside Pete's picture on Alix's bedside table scented the room with nostalgic memories, and my heart felt like a graven headstone, and my courage shrank to nothing--for I was going to destroy all this joy and beauty of life with a few tragic words.

Gerry was a great comfort to Alix at this time for, when she learned the truth, Gerry spent hours every day at the hospital and he and Alix would talk of Pete and what he had been and what he had done and what fine and lovely memories he had left for us.

Last week of July, 1940. Lovely summer days

But the bright sunshine only served to make the days emptier--like a naked light in a stripped room. I would take Alix up to Hampstead Heath, in a taxi, or to Hyde Park, where we'd sit in deck chairs on the grass by the Serpentine and watch the people swimming, or paddling about in little boats. And we would say nothing, nothing--for there was nothing to say. One could only feel. And the mauve and gray silk frock that Alix wore colored the tenor of those days in which a young couple's dream became distilled in lavender and tears--but secretly, within the heart, for Alix never wept to us. Grief is a private thing.

Introduction to the Battle of Britain

This particular part of my journal seems best left in Diary form. The immediacy of events thus being projected. Or are they? For, when re-reading the account, I am struck with the apparent slow pace of things, it may be that I was slightly dazed, or stunned, throughout this phase of the war!

Things happened fast--as we moved fast. But, always, there was so much waiting--a deadly waiting! And worry--and prayer--and somber thinking--and much argument. For people congregated together during the raids, and there was a lot of talk. This helped to pass the time and was definitely a morale-booster.

During this epoch of the war--the first terrible air-raids on London--a certain neighborliness bloomed among the inhabitants of London's flats, villas, and houses, where formerly a narrow self-sufficiency had proclaimed that, indeed, an Englishman's home is his castle, and that some of these castles had moats with raised draw-bridges! I wouldn't like to say, exactly, that good came out of these evil onslaughts from the skies, but the raids did produce a gathering together of people of all sorts, sharing like conditions and like emotions. And out of this enforced intimacy came a new relationship among Londoners. Neighborliness seems the best word to describe this relationship--a spontaneous sympathy, sharing and understanding between people who, under former conditions, might never have met.

That, in itself, seems good to me. Though only a madman can claim that the end justified the means. It was all a horrible nightmare and a ghastly experience, those raids--and need never have been, I believe. For it was Man's Selfishness and Cupidity and Lust for Power that produced the war. And the war produced the raids.

But, forever and ever, I shall never forget that I am here to write this Journal because a certain number, heartbreakingly great, of gallant young men, inadequately equipped, fought and died in the skies above London during the Battle of Britain. To them, and Pete, my endless gratitude.

The Battle of Britain

August 15th, 1940
London

Our flat in St. John's Wood, is a part of London, (much as Back Bay is a part of Boston--similarly placed within the city).

Things have started here, I'm afraid. Had the sirens at noon. I was in the kitchen getting lunch. What a shattering sound that Siren is! One seems to splinter inwardly at its impact on the nerves. I have the strange, but very definite, illusion of observing myself objectively as I ran from one bedroom to another, collecting gas masks, first aid kits, etc. It just didn't seem real--all that rushing about. Then all of us, including Nurse with Baby in her basket, congregating in the basement with the rest of the flat-dwellers. And doing it all over again at tea-time.

Dear God, what a madness has descended on the world!

Martha was at the Clinic in Welbeck Street. She says the patients were simply scared out of their wits by the siren. It was like herding the zoo to get them downstairs. Such a gabbling! Poor things! Tomorrow is Martha's day at the <u>Clinic in Croydon</u> (South of London). I don't like it. The Jerries are after Croydon Aerodrome.

Alas, what we have long feared appears about to catch up with us. I must admit that I am very apprehensive.

August 16th, 1940

Just as I thought last night! Martha got into a spot of bother today at Croydon. She skipped her tea there to catch the 5 o'clock back to London. Waiting on the station platform, she and a dozen or so other people were startled by the siren's sudden screech. Before anyone could take cover the planes roared over--Jerries, harried by the R.A.F. Everyone flopped down behind the benches on the station platform, or flattened against the room supports. Over swooped the planes again in a frightening roar and rattle. The 5 o'clock train appeared, and Martha dove for an open compartment. Just as the train pulled out of Croydon the Guard came along and ordered the windows closed and the blinds down. "Get down on the floor! Don't you know there's an air-raid?"

"How could I help knowing!" said Martha scornfully. She and one man shared the compartment. "We felt like fools-- down on that floor!"

113

The train slackened to a crawl, because a few days ago a passenger train narrowly escaped being wrecked in a raid when a bomb fell onto the track ahead of the engine as it was pulling out of Southhampton terminal. Had the train been speeding it would have plunged into the bomb crater. Geoff (Lieut. Wilks), a friend of Martha's, happened to be in this very raid, and was running down the High Street to catch a train up to London to have dinner with us, when a bomb exploded so near him that the concussion rolled him over and over. He was quite disheveled and covered with dust. But he caught his train and was in time for dinner with us.

Martha had no such luck. Her train was late. That awful creeping--simply creeping along. Martha says it gets on your nerves, it's so deadly. She peeked under the edge of the blinds and saw lots of planes, and fire and smoke about Croydon.

Tonight over the wireless, we learned that not one of the 12 German planes which attacked Croydon Aerodrome this afternoon returned home. Every one was shot down.

Bravo, R.A.F.!

Sunday, August 19th.

Dear God, what a way to spend the Sabbath! Have people in for tea--and then get the Sirens and have to huddle downstairs and wait for something to happen! It didn't. But, of course, it will one day.

Vivian was with us. Vivian (Lt. Vivian Bowyer, R.N.V.R.)(Later Lt. Commander Bowyer, R.N.V.R., D.S.O.) is in command of a minesweeper, so waiting for bombs does

not impress him. He gets bombs and machine-gunning daily.
What a life!

August 25th.

I had planned to compile a day-to-day, or night-to-night,
account of London's air-raids. How fatuous! If this is but the
beginning, or warming-up, as Dick says, I shall have neither
time nor the mental stability to write concurrent accounts.
However, I shall try to note down important episodes--those
that touch us as a family, for this Journal is a family record.

We have learned that when the wireless fades the Sirens are
imminent. This gives us an edge on getting down to our own
lower floor. We've given up the large basement shelter for 2
reasons; 1) We have neither privacy nor comforts there as we
have on our own lower floor; 2) The basement shelter being on
the same level, affords no greater protection. We have (at
Regency Lodge) what is called a maisonette--that is, a flat of
two floors, the ground and first floor levels.

I try to persuade myself that, being on the lowest floor of
this block of flats, one is fairly safe. But Dick has no such
illusions. Instead, he's quite sure that a bomb (a direct hit) will
come down thru' the 6 floors of Regency Lodge like a knife
thru' cheese! That is his expression and opinion. And one of
the reasons Ziki Witcomb sailed on the S.S. Washington.
However, here we are, in London--and likely to stay.
Because we Americans are classed as Aliens and carry cards to
this effect, we must be under our own roof by midnight. That

precludes any nightly escape into the outlying country districts as some people are doing, sleeping in their cars with pillows and rugs. But at least they sleep! I try to here. But, after the Siren goes, my apprehension is terrific. And the sound of planes overhead, with gunfire now and then, doesn't help matters. I am in a perpetual state of expectancy. When will the bombs fall on us?

Up to now, the outskirts of London have been getting it, but last night the bombs fell in London, itself. The guns on Primrose Hill shook us and Primrose Hill is only a few streets away. The Jerries were "in" all right! Dick went out into the courtyard to have a look and placed the bomb fires in "The City," the historic Financial District of London so well-known to all the world. Touché in the duel between the Luftwaffe and the R.A.F. over London.

This morning we drove to "The City" to see for ourselves, and discovered the smoking shell of a wax factory and the damaged exterior of an old church in the close vicinity of Dick's first London Office, near the Bank of England. We stood on the pavement before the street barricade and gazed, like everyone else in the small crowd there, and thought like everyone else, probably, that this, at last, is the beginning of Hitler's Blitzkrieg on London, and on its people, and on us. The faces of the men, women and children wore a closed look, like poker faces. If I am any judge of character, or have what men choose to call intuition, the British are "set"--and there'll be no moving them.

What a lot of time is wasted nowadays--an hour here, or an hour there, sitting in some "blooming" shelter. I spent a long spell thus, the other day, under John Lewis' shop in Oxford Street. I was buying some cretonne when the Banshee Howl drove me, along with everyone else, into the sub-basement. Such an extensive layout of rooms and corridors, a regular maze of them--like the catacombs! I walked and walked. The shop of John Lewis, Ltd., is in two large sections, each building covering a good-sized block, and the two buildings are connected underground. There, in the shelter below Oxford Street were hundred of people, mostly women shoppers, crowded on wooden benches set back to back in close rows across the basement rooms. I found a place among them and settled down to read. Almost everyone carries a book nowadays as well as a gasmask. Certain of the store staff, men and women, wore arm-bands reading, "Head of Personnel," "Shelter Warden," or "First Aid." Salesgirls circulated thru' the rooms selling candy, biscuits, soft drinks, small sixpenny books, embroidery patterns and silks, and even offering free wools in navy, khaki and Air-Force blue, complete with needles and directions.

"Won't you please knit for the Forces at John Lewis' expense?"

Music was furnished by gramophone and, every so often, an attendant sprayed the air with disinfectant. An hour and a half spent thus is not too bad. But still, it is an aggravation and a waste of time. And when the "Raiders Overhead" signal comes thru', it gives one a very nasty feeling.

I got a "perm" a few days ago. One less thing to bother with if one's hair is manageable. Of course the Sirens went while I was still crowned with wet hair-pinned snails! The attendant escorted me down 3 flights of stairs, as the lifts do not run during raids. I felt anything but nonchalant. However, I had plenty of company--lots of other women in various states of presentableness, or, rather, <u>unpresentableness</u>. I can see that inhibitions will soon be "Gone with the Wind"--or the bombs!

I have let my two maids go. Now that we are sheltering in our own flat we need the maids' room. The maids' room, one bath, dining room and kitchen comprise the lower floor of our flat. Alix, Nurse and little Penny now sleep in the maids' room. Penny's basket and stand are behind the headboard of Nurse's bed in a corner. We have pushed the wardrobe up before the window. And when the sirens go, the bedroom door is opened. According to Government pamphlets, this is supposed to mitigate any blast! I never thought to live under such conditions.

Our dining-room, with mattresses all over the floor, now has the air of a very select, or posh, flop-house, these bombing nights. The dining-table, chairs piled on top of it, is up against the windows. I try to think of this arrangement as some sort of real protection against bombs, as I am more terrified by what I am <u>told</u> than by what we have so far experienced. Of how a batch of people were crowded in a public shelter, and all killed from the blast alone. A sort of vicious and deadly vacuum having rushed into the shelter and pulled the people apart-- eviscerated them. Horrible!

Morning, noon and night--not omitting a short and aggravating raid at tea-time now and then--the meddling, bombing ways of the Nazis tear our ordered lives to shreds. Gunfire laces the atmosphere. The bombs, like variables approaching a limit, creep ever nearer--to cancel that theory eventually, for that they will arrive, we have no doubt. The R.A.F. are wonderful. But no one knows better than Dick how few are the young pilots--and, oh, so inadequately equipped.

Now that I have no maids, I am lucky to have Hilda back again as Daily. Good Old Hildy, as the girls say. But she decided to take Alan, her youngest, to her Mother's farm in Norfolk--definitely, a safer area than here. So, at the moment, I have a substitute Daily--Mary, a Welsh girl, who seems quite impervious to the Sirens. Anti-aircraft guns, or bombs. She pays absolutely no attention to them! She even comes and goes in the raids--a procedure the Government pamphlets strongly deplore. "Take cover," is shouted at people out in the streets by Wardens and Bobbies. And sometimes you see a large placard, "Take cover," pendant on the stout chest of a cycling Bobby as he patrols the streets during a raid.

"Take cover" reminds me of an amusing incident. Two of the Martens boys had been out of town the day before War was declared and, returning very late that Saturday night, had slept well into Sunday, the 3rd of September. The boys had neither read the newspapers nor heard Chamberlain's announcement on the wireless--"A state of war exists." they were dressing when the Sirens went, that first utterly fantastic air-raid warning of the war.

They didn't know what it was!

But it sounded awful.

So one of the boys, Terry, dashed downstairs and out into the deserted street to investigate--just in time to see one of the aforesaid Bobbies cycling along, the placard, "Take cover," very prominent and ominous.

"Hey!" shouted Terry.

"Take cover!" bawls the Bobby.

"What's up?" yells Terry.

And the Bobby nearly fell off his cycle.

"Don't you know war was declared this morning?--and here come the Jerrys a'ready!"

We now know that it was a false alarm--due to one friendly plane coming over from France. But the Martens brothers will long remember it--and laugh over it, as we do.

September 5th, 1940

We all went over to the Heaver's last night. Elsie and Frank have been so thrilled with the sight of flares drifting down from German planes, and the fairly distant flashes of exploding bombs, that they invited us over for a show. The Heavers' flat is on the 3rd floor of "Northways," on the next street to us, so they have quite a view all 'round--West over Maida Vale, South over St. John's Wood to Baker Street and Regents Park, and North to Hampstead and Hendon.

The Sirens hooted during a broadcast. So Frank turned out the lights, and parted the heavy drapes at the large bay-window in the dining-room. We could hear a bomber almost overhead. That insidious hum! Immediately the searchlights shot up from all directions. We could not see the plane, caught within the woven pattern of light, but soon, directly beneath the crossed beams, now to the West--red flashes shot up from the ground, one after the other, and died down. A stick of bombs had fallen.

Below us, in the Finchley Road, darkened cars moved cautiously. A bus was parked across the way, its passengers and crew in the cement shelter at the curb.

Another plane!

Once more tentacles of light were groping in the sky. They fastened on their prey--this time to hold and follow it toward a Northwest suburb.

We waited breathlessly.

Suddenly a fan of red light shot upwards from beneath the plane. A faint and muffled thud was heard. More red flashes. And more thuds, in quick succession. Six in all. Two sticks of bombs had found a mark of sorts.

My stomach revolts at such sights. It is really my heart, I know. It drops into my stomach like a stone. Then churns around there,--in fear, I suppose, or a combination of fear and apprehension for my family and pity for those families beneath the bombs.

There were no more "fireworks" for quite a while. So we had evening tea with Elsie and Frank and came home, wearing our tin hats because the Anti-Aircraft guns were intermittently firing. You can never tell about shrapnel! What goes up must come down. (In a later raid we got a piece of shrapnel in one wall.)

To think I used to feel such comfort from the sky!--A Brooding protection, almost a definite promise of safety thro' the night.

Martha is out of her job at the Welbeck Clinic. The Clinic "went" the other night! The Jerrys are using Land Mines in the air-raids. Life size packages, these monstrous High Explosives are dropped now and then. And, when they fall, it is like a miniature End-of-the-World! These Land Mines explode <u>above</u> the ground, and blast buildings and people over wide areas.

Because of one of these Land Mines, Martha had to <u>walk</u> most of the way to the Clinic the other morning--the streets being impassable to traffic, with litter and rubble scattered about. Martha's soles were cut to ribbons with shattered glass-- and her soul torn to bits with the sight of people being excavated. When she arrived at the Clinic, the Out Patient Department was quite gutted by an oil bomb. Rescue work had ended, but drugs and instruments were being salvaged. So Martha stayed to help. One nurse was killed. There were no casualties among the patients. What a miracle! And what a horror!

Of course, Martha cannot get her Degree now. There'll be no more lectures. She is deeply disappointed. But I am thankful for her help here. One can not <u>plan</u> a thing these days! You just live, strictly in the present.

But this living--in a world that bursts and splinters into air-raids <u>at all hours</u>--is most difficult. One dashes out between raids to get something to eat, which means standing in tedious queues. So many things are in short supply due to disruption of Transport.

122

Nurse can only wheel Penny around the block. No more lovely outings in Regents Park at the foot of our road. Just as soon as Penny is christened--on the 11th--I shall send her and Alix and Nurse out into the country. The strain on Alix is too much here. And it is a bit thick having Nurse so frightened during raids that she lies in her bed moaning, "Oh, we shall all be murdered in our beds!--the next bomb will kill us!"
Quite demoralizing.

Sunday, September 8th, 1940.

Only a few days have passed! But it seems like eons! So many things have happened. Or rather, so many Sirens have screeched. So many planes have threatened us. So many bombs have fallen. So many Incidents. (When and where bombs fall and create havoc and death, this is called an "Incident." Good old British understatement.) have occured. So many casualties have resulted from all this Hell.

Last night we had an awful raid! The dirty work commenced about 5 o'clock in the afternoon. Dick and I had driven out to Letchworth to fetch Alix, Penny and Nurse who were having a short visit with Dorothy at her cottage. We were all placidly at tea in the garden there when the wireless announced that London was having another air-raid. Well, raid or no raid, we must return to London--and the sooner we got under cover there the better. So we started off at once.

123

As we topped the rise at Hendon, on the way home, we spied an enormous dark cloud in the South East horizon. It rose ominously in an otherwise cloudless sky. Instinctively we all knew what it was. And the direction indicated the Docks. Driving into London was like driving into a fortress. And it sounded like one as evening fell.

After dinner we went up stairs to a friend's flat on the 6th floor in order to see the Big Fire, for the Nazis have really hit a few things in Dockland at last. We didn't dare step out onto the balcony as a raid was on, but we had a marvelous view from behind the French doors. In the clear night air Central London lay silhouetted before us against a slate blue sky. And, to the left, a pulsing curtain of orange and scarlet, shot with flame, hung like the monstrous backdrop of a nightmare presentation.

"Hell on Earth"
by
Hitler and Goering
Act I

"London's burning--London's burning," buzzed senselessly in my head, and I kept thinking of how my mother had been in the Great Chicago Fire when a little girl--and of how she used to tell us about it when we were children, my brothers and me.

The fire still burns today. And at noon a broadcast gave nearly 460 dead and over 1,000 injured. That is Calamity-and Tragedy--and Death! Stories of heroism fill the papers, and stories of suffering and heartbreak.

I have set all this down to preserve the facts and the atmosphere. Should we live to re-read it after the war--and when will that be? I've no doubt but what it will all seem quite

mad.
  Well, it is.

September 9th, 1940
Afternoon.

    I have been very worried over Mary. She didn't appear here for work yesterday nor this morning. And when she left on Saturday the Sirens had gone and the A.A. fire had already started. She simply will ignore these raids, bombs and all! So of course, I tho't that at last they had caught up with her. I was just going 'round to her address, between raids this afternoon, when the Telegraph Boy appeared. The message was from Ogmore Vale, South Wales, and it read, "Had the bombs Sunday night. Dug Father out and came to Sister's. Sorry, Madame. Mary.". (Later I had a note from Mary with more details, and learned that Father, when "Dug out" was quite alive and "now missing the excitements of London" but "still and all," they were staying in Wales. It seemed a good idea.)
    Well, I'm thankful she's safe. But Martha and I shall miss her very much. I believe that "keeping busy" is supposed to be a panacea for most evils. Well, you could have a hundred arms and legs, like a centipede, and keep all of them busy nowadays--and the raids would still get in your hair.
    I think that one of the most unpleasant features of life-beneath-the-raids is the unkempt feeling one gets. You can't feel neat and tidy, in spite of baths and clean clothes, while

125

hurriedly shuttling from one shop to another, or dodging at odd moments into a horrible little curbside shelter that looks like a Public Convenience or frantically pushing through one household task after another in a desperate effort to accomplish something before the darn Siren blasts your shaky insides into jelly, and you must go downstairs and sit and wait for bombs!

It seems that The Cotton Family, are sitting plum in the center of a target that the Jerries hope to bomb into bits! Regency Lodge to the North, and our most important life-lines in Britain's Transport System. One rail-road goes underground directly before Regency Lodge.

The Jerries bombed those same rail-roads from Zeppelins in the last war. An English friend of mine has told me of how she and her parents used to huddle in the cellar with big domed meat covers, stuffed with pillows, on their heads! And now people are huddling in cellars again.

What price Progress and Civilization!

Mr. Malet, our Vicar, has a theory that Regency Lodge and Northways, with their large flat white roofs, form a London landmark for these roads. And so the Jerries will be loathe to destroy our block of flats. I hope Mr. Malet is right. But Dick doesn't lean to this theory.

At this point in the Battle of Britain, I decided to <u>write a record of our experiences while a raid, or series of raids, was in progress</u>. As future family reference, this account, compiled concurrently with falling bombs and roaring guns, might be enlightening and, perhaps, in time to come, historic. So I deliberately chose the dates September 10th and 11th. Penny was to be christened on the 11th and a written record of the

126

ceremony and attendant events might one day hold a certain intrinsic value for her and her children.

Penny can say, "Your great-grandmother wrote this in an actual air-raid during the Battle of Britain, September 1940, in World War II. You see, I was a real war baby. And my Daddy was killed in that War. War is a dreadful thing. Never let it happen again. Read--and see why."

Account Written During Process of Raids.

Tuesday, September 10th, 1940

3 o'clock in the morning, to be exact. The most terrific air raid London has yet experienced is still going on. Somehow, until now, we managed a bit of sleep upstairs in our beds, in spite of the guns. But suddenly the bombs began falling quite near. One extra big crash! and cr-u-ump! shook our bed. Alix came into the bedroom, torch in hand.

"Mother!" that last bomb must have been awfully near," she said. "I got up to look at Penny--the explosion woke her. There's no light. Guess a main cable's been hit."

I made Dick, Martha and Gerry get up, and we all started downstairs with Alix. The bombing was certainly close. A whistling bomb whizzed down somewhere to the right of us.

The building shook.

We half fell, half stumbled down the stairway in the dark.

By the tiny glow of Alix's torch, we settled into our chairs in the lower hall, resigned to

127

sitting out the raid.

<u>3:30 a.m.</u>

And here we still sit- and wait - and wonder--and do a bit of praying. The uneven throbbing of a German bomber can be heard now and then. The night is riven with Anti-Aircraft fire. Martha has brought in two lighted candles from the dining-room, and placed them on a table by the gas masks, helmets, etc.

"So shines a good deed in a naughty world," I murmur irrelevantly.

"How are we going to cook?" asks Martha. "The stove is electric". "Get a primus (tiny oil stove)," says Alix.

"But I'm going to bake the cake tomorrow! Or is it today?" Martha wails.

She chopped candied fruit yesterday for Penny's Christening Cake. The Christening is set for the 11th, at 4:30 p.m. We hope the raiders leave us a free hour then.

<u>4:00 a.m.</u>

The bombs are quite frightening now--they are so near. But the electric light has come on. It lends a slight feeling of security in a shaken (literally) world. Martha has put the kettle on. The family discusses the war. I write.

CRASH!   CRASH!   CRASH!
    Cru-u-ump!   Cru-u-ump! Cru-u-ump!
Three bombs, one after the other, whistling down.

<u>It is 4:20 a.m.</u>

I have just looked at my watch. Dick, peering from the window in the blacked-out kitchen, reports smoke rising beyond the church across the street. There goes the hysterical

128

clang of an ambulance whizzing past.

"Oh, the poor people!"

"How many are hurt, do you suppose?"

We are all a bit sick in our middles.

5:00 a.m.

The "All Clear" has sounded. We have come up-stairs into the drawing-room. Release from tension, fear, and the aches and pains of tired limbs begging for rest.

Dick is 'phoning the factory. All seems O.K. there-- but they've had some near ones.

Alix has pulled open the drawing-room drapes, as black-out ends shortly after 5:00 a.m. "Mother, in this awful gray light everything looks as if it were recovering from a long illness."

I wish it were.

"'Tis in the wan hours of the night, before the dawn, that people are weakest, they say," I remind her.

"It is like my coming out of the anesthetic," says Alix. So pale--so ethereal-- so quiet is the atmosphere. The dark shapes of the houses, the church, and the feathery outlines of trees in the ashen light sat in sad reproach. Smoke filters the scene.

What will the sun rise upon in London town today? We dare not think. Our hearts are full for those poor souls who have suffered from tonight's Hell. Such experiences are so devastating to one's soul! The children, too, are beginning to wonder.

Why? Why all this destruction and death? It is now past 6 o'clock.

Daylight.

The rising sun has tinged a low cloud with gilt and pink. Two men cycle past to work. A bus rumbles along. But ominous thick veils of smoke rise over scattered localities. The Hun has left his mark. And the hatred and determination of a thus befouled Nation will rise and grow and strangle this enemy so surely as this planet still pulses with the breath of Life and Hope.

And, please God, America will help.

One's prayers bubble up and out of one's heart, now-a-days, in a continual stream--like the gush from a drinking fountain. And these prayers are as assuaging as the cool waters, for they permit us to go on.

Still Tuesday, September 10th

10 o'clock in the evening, to be precise.

I am alone in the drawing-room.

The day of September 10th is over.

> "Now the day is over,
> Night is drawing nigh,
> Shadows of the evening
> Steal across the sky."

More than shadows steal across the London sky tonight. Winged death is on the prowl.

The sirens went, early this evening--and then we got the "All Clear." But I can sense a "storm of raiders" coming up. The implacable beat of their wings, high in the sky and far away, penetrates to me here, alone. The family has retired. It is very much worthwhile to try and get some sleep before the vortex of the threatened "storm" moves in upon us. But I feel keyed up. I shall try to read a while.

And so into Wednesday September 11th

<u>1 o'clock in the morning</u>

The expected raid, a bad one, has been going on for some time. The blast of guns and startling thump of bombs spasmodically shakes the night about us.

Like an idiot I tried to finish my book and was still curled up on the sofa beneath the long window in the drawing-room, when a terrific crash! and boom! threw me forward. It was as though a planet, rushing through the Heavens, had torn loose from its beaten path and plunged down, with gigantic weight and fury, into the resistant earth. There had been no Siren!

I flew in to Dick. Still half asleep, he refused to move. And neither Martha nor Gerry had wakened fully. So I went downstairs. And am now here with Alix, Nurse and Baby in the lower hall. Alix has put Penny's basket on a chair beside her, and has curled up in a chair in an eiderdown to try to read awhile. Nurse has made a bed on the floor in a little alcove by the linen cupboard. I have my notebook and am recording the progress of this raid.

Cru-u-mp! --   Crash! --   Boom!
The flat rocks.

<u>Not quite 2:00 a.m.</u>

Dick, Martha and Gerry have joined us. They were almost thrown from their beds.

<u>2:30 a.m.</u>

Dick and Gerry are asleep on mattresses in the dining-room. Martha, like me, is wrapped in blankets and slung between two chairs. "Lucky I frosted the cake after dinner," says Martha. She had made a lovely two-tiered fruit cake for the Christening, after hoarding the eggs. The frosting is a great success in spite of having to use granulated sugar. Nurse is dozing on the

131

floor, rolled up like an Indian in Gerry's bright red Scout blankets. Alix has gone back to bed in the maids' room. And little Penny still sleeps, contented and rosy as a cherub, in her basket here beside me. One plump little army is upflung beside her moist and curling dark brown hair.   Innocence and confidence personified.

And what have we to offer her?

A nightmare of the world, where one must live in constant fear!

It is hard to believe that today, September 11th, 1940, my two months old grand-daughter, Penelope Marianne Dean, is to be christened at half-past four in the afternoon. What has such a Christian ceremony to do with these Pagan and Blasphemous air-raids!!!

4:00 a.m.

It has been quiet for a while.

The candles still flicker.

How we are going to cook breakfast, or even make a cup of tea, remains to be solved in the morning.

In the meantime, I ponder on the hundreds--no, thousands--of people enduring discomfort and fear this night. How dreadful to spend hours in one of those cold public mausoleums in the streets, or in a tiny, garden air-raid shelter, or to soothe a frightened child in the darkness and cold, amid the noises of destruction and death, or to lie in terror and helplessness on a mattress beneath a Hospital bed, for Nurses so shift each patient every night. And my heart aches for those who have suffered and are suffering--and for those who have died--and for those these Dead have left behind. And I pray for Security and Peace and Brotherly Love--for none of these is good without the others. And when we plan another World

132

again it must be built on these everlasting bricks, and not on the shifting sand of Politics and Privilege and Power.

4:30 a.m.

The "All Clear," has sounded.

I haven't slept a wink. but, with a grand-daughter to christen this afternoon, I must get some rest. And so, "Goodnight." Or should I say, "Good Morning?"

Penelope Marianne is Christened

September 11th, 1940
late Evening

I am writing, with the tea trolley as desk, in the lower hall. The rest of the gang are asleep--apparently. There has been, and still is, an almost continuous roar of guns. The flat shivers and trembles with the impact of solid sound upon its walls. The top of the trolley vibrates beneath my arms.

Well, it seems that, indeed, one can get used to anything! Besides, what else can one do save carry-on?

Penny was to be christened this afternoon at 4:30. But at that hour the Jerries and the R.A.F staged a dog-fight right over Regency Lodge. Shrapnel fell in the court-yard. Endeavoring to do as everyone else does--carry on as normally as possible--I continued to arrange the flowers, and chatted with the family and Dorothy and Tony, who had joined us about four o'clock, just before the Siren went. But a horribly insistent urge kept me glancing side-wise through the windows. I thought something was coming in at any moment!

I'm quite sure everyone else felt the same way, but no one said so. Alix quietly held Penny, dressed in her Great-Grand-Mother's Christening robe of lace and hand embroidery. (Penny's Great-Grand-Father was Bishop of the Barbados.) I think the events now-a-days are almost numbing to one's sensibilities, as one seems able to appear quite granite-like at times.

Well, the "All Clear" finally went, shortly before 5 o'clock. So Dick drove us around to the church--St. Paul's Church, Avenue Road, a block from our flat, the same little church in which Alix and dear Pete were married almost a year ago, on October 7th, 1939.

We were all grouped about the baptismal font, and Mr. Malet, the Vicar, had just given Baby her name. "Penelope Marianne" and had baptized her for the third time, "And of the Holy Ghost" when the Sirens went, and the Devil was upon us again.

"Shall I proceed?" asked Mr. Malet, "Or do you care to go down to the shelter?"

We elected to finish the ceremony. Then rushed Penny home in the car--the men following on foot, keeping under the trees as the A.A. guns were in action.

Alas, none of the God-Parents could attend the Christening, and only one friend, Hartley Davies, appeared--because of the darned raids. However, we (the family) and Dorothy, Tony, Hartley and Mr. Malet assembled here afterwards in the flat, and drank dear little Penny's health in sherry and had a piece of Martha's fine fruit cake, iced, and decorated with pink and white ribbons. Elsie and Frank almost got to the Christening. But the 4 o'clock raid drove them into a roadside shelter, and the A.A. fire kept them under cover until too late. A shame!

At 7 this evening we drove Alix, Nurse and Penny to Kings Cross Station, where we put them on the train for

Letchworth. Nurse has a friend there who has agreed to have them for a while. "Twill be a temporary refuge for them until we can make definite plans.

Tony returned to Oxford, where he is a student, but Dorothy and Hartley remained for dinner. We all talked late into the evening. And then the Sirens went. So we induced Hartley to stay, offering him a mattress on the dining-room floor, with the rest of the family. How quickly one accepts the extraordinary as ordinary! We often have friends sleeping on the floor with us now of nights.

Dorothy (who has a little flat in Kensington) is sleeping on a Lilo--one of those cushioned affairs that can be inflated and deflated. She brought the Lilo with her, intending to spend the night here, anyway, as she said the guns in Hyde Park kept her awake nights. Well, she seems to have moved from the frying pan into the fire.

The A.A. guns all around us here in St. John's Wood have been going ever since the Sirens screeched! My God, what a din! It is like being in a fortress with guns roaring from every wall. A Hell of sound let loose! Just let the Jerries try to get through that barrage of flying steel!

Gunfire, one's own, has a reassuring sound. 'Tis the bombs that are so frightening. Houses all about us have been hit. Hundreds of windows in the neighborhood are gone-- blown splintered into houses--often with maiming or death-dealing result. Many people have been rendered homeless. Mr. Malet has spent sleepless nights and most of his strength, finding accommodation for bombed-out families. Part of his flock are housed in the Church Hall. There is a large space at the head of our road where once two houses stood. It (the space) gapes like that left by a missing tooth--painful and ugly.

Well, in spite of, or, rather, in defiance of, these hideous raids, Penny has been christened. And I have made my record of the event. I'll now try to get some sleep, like the rest of the gang here. As I have said before, one can apparently get used to anything, and I am now so weary that the guns may well become a lullaby. Here's hoping.

It is Dick's and my wedding anniversary. But what a way to celebrate it! By way of something special we had a "Molotov Bread-basket" dropped above our flat last night during the usual air-raid. We could smell smoke and burning wood. Gerry went upstairs and peeked out of my bed-room window.

There's a big fire near here!" he called.

So Dick and Hartley (we had quite a bit of company through last night--Hartley, Frank, Elsie, and Elsie's mother) went out to investigate. The rest of us went upstairs and had a peep from under the blinds in my room. There certainly was a big fire near us. It looked very red and very hot. And when Dick and Hartley came in they reported a ring of fires 'round us. This was very worrying, as the Jerries could do some fancy bombing by their light. But Providence was on our side. It began to rain. And this, with the good work of the A.F.S. (Auxiliary Fire Service), put out the beacons in short order. However, two houses on the next street were smashed to heaps of broken bricks and rubble before the "All Clear," and we have not yet heard the fate of the people living in them. No one felt like sleep last night. So we had tea--and talked. Just after midnight Dick said to me, "do you know what day it is now?"

I certainly did.

"I've got a little something here for you," he continued, and strange as it may seem he handed me a small, square, red leather box. "Guess!" he said with a big grin.

"Well--it's a ring from the look of the box."

A ring indeed. A lovely ring.

Its bright facets conjured up mental pictures of twinkling stars, of lighted street lamps, of myriad lights from countless homes, of the benediction of illuminated stained glass windows in Churches at Evensong.

I facetiously call the ring my "blitz bauble." But it will ever be a symbol to me. And I was never so surprised in my life. Fancy getting an anniversary present in an air-raid!

The R.A.F. shot down 185 German planes last night. (This was an exaggerated figure. But the defeat of the Luftwaffe was assured.)

We are winning the Battle of Britain!

Our A.A. guns brought down a plane at Victoria right in the streets of London! Martha and I were having tea here at the flat, and Gerry was at the cinema in Leicester Square, when the Sirens wailed. As the A.A. guns went into action I placed them (by the sound) in the vicinity of Piccadilly. That meant Gerry. So I was very worried, in spite of the "All Clear," until he showed up.

Gerry had been in the street, returning home, when the German plane appeared. And as the plane dove for the house tops, Gerry dove for the Underground.

"I can't see why you worry, Mother," he said. " I can take care of myself."

So it seems. But what a muddle one's mind gets into now-a-days--accepting these strafings, and the strange realization that one's children accept them also!

But the downing of that plane, in the streets of, mid-London, has made a deep impression on me. Somehow, it seems more significant than getting bombs on the next street. "The enemy within the gates," I suppose.

September 18th, 1940
Evening

The Public are permitted to sleep in the Underground, on the station platforms there. Men, women and children, laden with rolls of bedding, bags of clothes, food and thermos flasks, queue up as early as 2 o'clock in the afternoon for this dubious privilege. I watch these queues from our windows in sad fascination. What have we civilized people come to that we hide in the ground to cower beneath the skies, in fear of Death from bombs and guns?

I recall the "Prophecies of Nostradamus," which Ziki had loaned me some months ago. Although written in French, I managed to glean the salient points of the book. One of the prophecies was, "and the peoples of the Aisles (British Isles?) shall hide in the Earth from the Terror in the Air above." Old Nostradamus seems to have got something there. Could he have meant these air-raids?

Also, he wrote of the coming of an Anti-Christ, whom he named "Hister." That is close enough to Hitler to give one

138

the creeps! I recall one day shortly before the war when Dick and I had dinner with Dr. and Mrs. Zimmerman in their London flat. Dr. Zimmerman is Dupont's representative in Europe. After dinner the four of us went walking in Kew Gardens. While the men were deep in talk of more mundane matters Mrs. Zimmerman and I discussed the eerie prophecy of this looming Anti-Christ. Could it be Hitler? It was a beautiful warm Sunday afternoon and the world seemed really at peace-- then.

But now, in a fantastic effort toward self-preservation, our windows are painted with anti-blast varnish which gives the outer world a dizzy look. Trees seem to wriggle like seaweed under water, people swim by, traffic is blurred. Today workmen came to build a protective brick wall outside the maid's room and dining-room windows--stout barriers, three feet away from the flat, and ten feet high. This may well mitigate the blast from bombs and save some windows--and us lying on mattresses nearby. The effect will not be cheering by day, but at night we shall lean mentally on these bulwarks with a slight bit of confidence.

This afternoon I went downtown to buy some fleece-lined boots. The very thought of winter is chilling. Martha went with me. On the way, I stopped to cash a check at Lloyds Bank in Baker Street. Time Bombs are sprinkled in that neighborhood like plums in a Christmas pudding. These bombs-dropped by Nazi planes and now buried, unexploded in the ground--go off with no warning whatsoever! One did so while Martha and I were in the Bank. We were almost thrown off our feet.

Because of these Time Bombs and the raid to flats and shops--with the ever-present threat of walls and debris falling into the street--our usual bus, No. 13, now detours windingly through the streets, past various ruins, bomb craters, and forbidding signs reading, "Keep Out--Time Bomb." Our Doctor's house and surgery are now a heap of rubble and splintered wood, with bits of chromium tubing sprouting here and there. The blitzed homes--their rooms ripped open and exposed, with entrails of plumbing and forsaken bits of furniture--look like Salvador Dali in a weeping mood.

It is one thing to read of the vandalism and desecration of London in the newspapers, or to hear of it over the wireless. It is quite another to live in it, and to go shopping in the midst of it all. Today Martha and I went to Lilley and Skinner's Shoe shop on Oxford Street. We found the large shop of John Lewis, Ltd. (whose commodious air-raid shelter I had sampled a while ago) now a charred and smoking shell--two shells, as both buildings of the big shop were showered with incendiaries last night. Firemen still fought the smoldering blaze.

Curious throngs pressed against the ropes and barriers about the danger area--but only a handful compared to the crowds that a good fire in the heart of the shopping district would have attracted in Peacetime. London is at War. And her people are soldiers. They have a job to do and Hellfire isn't going to stop them. There is a nonchalance and a casualness in their daily lives that belie the nights of fear and suffering. It is the good old British custom of savoir-faire, even beneath the Sword of Damocles.

Everywhere in the shops there were people. What if the ruins of one shop still smoked, and the shops still standing might get it this very night? Doris needs shoes. Tom needs woolens. Mother will buy them while she has the chance. So "Business as Usual" served me in Lilley and Skinner's. The

140

Duchess of Kent came in as I completed my purchase. Perfectly groomed, charming, she discussed an order with a salesgirl, then left--as though the sun, shining without, beamed upon a familiar and well-ordered world. I felt like a puppet in a play. God grant the title doesn't read, "The End of the World."

Quentin Reynolds wrote, in one of his reports on the Battle of Britain, "Courage is contagious." There is no doubt of that. One feels a quiet strength at times, which is certainly not born of the fears within oneself. But the phrase, "They can take it"--or, "We can take it,"--irks me. For <u>why</u> must we "Take it?" Because of Greed and Selfishness, Blunder and Muddle. I can see nothing praiseworthy in enduring the hideous result (the War and these Air-raids) of Man's Cupidity and Stupidity.

The axioms, "The Innocent Suffer" and "The Sins of the Father's, etc.," come to mind. But these axioms apply only to the very young, and, perhaps, to the very old. Certainly the intermediate generations, and I belong to one--must accept some blame for what the journalists choose to speak of as Appeasement, Isolationism and Complacency--and what the Germans call Decadence. It all adds up.

I suppose that this "We can take it" is really a tardy awakening to Man's real strength. It is a spiritual strength. And, in my opinion, it seems rather sad that human nature must continually fall, to rise again--even though it be to new heights.

And I can't feel that it's the Lord's will either.

Listen to this.

Mr. Baker's father lost both his hands in a raid last night.

Now Mr. Baker's father is a law-abiding citizen, a lover

141

of his country, and has worked all his life for considerably less than a lot of people I know think either adequate or decent. Yet Mr. Baker's father has been content.

And how has Mr. Baker's father been rewarded?

Some nights ago, in a raid, Mr. Baker Senior, lost his home--but kept his life. So he and his wife moved in with their son and daughter-in-law. When the Sirens went last night the women sheltered under the stairs--the men remained in bed. A nearby bomb blew in the windows with devastating force. Young Mr. Baker ducked under the bedclothes. Mr. Baker Sr. put his hands up--to shield his face. Flying glass cut both hands off at the wrist!

And, in spite of the raids' resultant horrors, young Mr. Baker reported to Dick at the factory this morning at the usual hour.

"They can take it!"

Solve that one if you can--the why and wherefore.

But I still try to believe in God.

October, 1940

All of a sudden, on less than 24 hours notice, Dick's factory was ordered out of London. And high time. I'll never forget the night that many factories in the Acton area of London "went"--leaving but a handful, among them Dick's. Providence had seemed to intervene again. For Dick's factory--one of only two factories making the so vital pumps for the R.A.F.--survived a night of shattering raids, a night in which the Jerries had, for once, put a crimp in Britain's war effort.

The morning following that raid I drove out with Dick to Acton, London, N.W. 10--and was quite stunned by the sight there. Where once many factories had stood, now there were only a pitiful few. Their squat rectangular shapes seemed more unlovely than ever, rising from acres of still smoking ruins. But they looked mighty good to Dick. British Rola, Ltd. was still a going concern.

For some time, in a preparation for the eventual removal of the factory from London, work had been going on at Bideford, North Devon--the site finally chosen. There a large garage and attendant out-buildings were being converted into efficient premises for British Rola, Ltd. A new office building had been erected. So, when the expected order came, Mr. Maynard, the Works Manager, was ready for "the move." But you can't transplant personnel, machines and all the impedimenta of a busy factory overnight. Neither can you stop the output of a factory contributing to the war effort. The factory must carry-on in spite of, and along with, its removal. So, since Dick must first arrange billets for all his personnel, and we had to find a house ourselves, Dick and I, Martha and Gerry went off to Bideford at once. Alix and Penny were still at Letchworth.

It is quite a drive from London to Bideford on the West Coast of England, 225 miles of narrow, winding roads, and our car was packed. Elsie and Frank Heaver decided to come along in their car; a weekend free of raids would do them good, and Frank was to move his London business into Dick's office building, anyway. So Gerry and Mr. Maynard set out in the Heaver's car. Hartley Davies, good friend that he is, went with us to share the driving with Dick. Martha and I were wedged in the back of the car, along with the overflow of luggage from the boot. Mitzi, my dachshund, sat upon my lap.

We thus set off on a Friday morning at 10 o'clock, with

mixed feelings; exuberance at escaping from sleepless, bomb-ridden nights for a while, and sorrow at leaving London. For the Largest-City-in-the-World has a fascination peculiar to itself. Dirty, foggy, so tradition-bound as to be almost retrogressive--and now bombed--London was still London. We looked back with regret as we turned into the Great West Road and headed out under the fringe of barrage balloons for the long drive ahead.

In less than twenty-five miles the Heavers' car broke down. "Impossible to put it on the road until tomorrow, Sir!" We were aghast. With resignation Elsie and Frank agreed to follow on later.

But Gerry, Mr. Maynard, and Mr. Maynard's luggage had to be transferred to our car. Martha moved in front, between Dick and Hartley, Gerry and Mr. Maynard in back with me. The assortment of bags and cases were now so closely stacked on the floor and piled on to our laps, that we could hardly move a finger, let alone a toe.

I never had a more uncomfortable drive. It went on for hours and hours. We stopped once to eat, prying ourselves out with difficulty, and then refitting ourselves into the car with even more difficulty as the bags and boxes seemed to have propagated in our absence. No matter how we stacked and maneuvered them, there were two left over! Finally I sat on one case--and Gerry managed the other, with Mitzi, on his lap.

Somerset is very lovely and Devon is very beautiful with their hedge-bordered winding roads, their thatched cottages, gardens, and "homely" villages. But so far as I was concerned, we were back on that flat, unchartered road to Deal at the beginning of the War--for there were no signs, no feeling of "place", and soon no feeling at all! I prayed over my legs, wondering if they were still there to pray over. When, in the early evening the car climbed steep little Bridge Street to the New Inn above the Torridge River at Bideford, N. Devon, simultaneous groans arose from us all. Now that we had arrived we could afford to make noises about our discomfort. There was relief in sight.

We stayed three weeks at the Inn--or, rather, it was our headquarters for that time. And the sway-backed iron and brass beds, the cans of luke warm water for washing brought up each morning with our tea, and the evil-smelling oil stoves for heat, all seemed celestial appurtenances. There were no sirens, no A.A. Fire, no bombs. We had arrived in Heaven-- from Hell--by way of Purgatory.

We liked Bideford at once. I think the fact that Market Day initiated us into the town's busy and friendly atmosphere had something to do with it. The bustle and chatter of people in the large covered Market Place across from the Inn; the tubs and buckets of gay flowers; the stalls with fresh bread; the panniers of garden produce; the baskets of eggs; the nude chickens, composed with folded legs, on clean white cloths; and the fur-coated rabbits, sleeping with open eyes.

After a morning of climbing the narrow streets, which run like fever graphs up and down the hillside upon which Bideford is built, I wondered if the Devon cows on their steeply sloping pastures were made like those legendary cows of the Swiss Alps--their legs longer on one side than the other. I certainly tho't I could do with a like set of legs myself.

On the High Street the window of an Iron- Monger (Hardware store) intrigued me. "-----hens---Brains" read the lettered sign upon the glass. Inquiry, later, revealed that "Stephens & Brains" had been the original! In time the sign came to read "-----he-s - B-ains." We hope it does not degenerate into a "----he-s - B--in-" as certain commodities there become ever scarcer during this War. When anyone wants nails, paint, clothes-pegs, tin openers, spills, basins, cookers, etc. we say, "Go to Hen's-Brains."

The night the factory personnel arrived in Bideford was probably the busiest night of the War for certain women, and men, of the town. The W.V.S. (Women's Volunteer Services) bore the brunt of the work. They fed hundreds of people and did a marvelous job. For not only the factory workers traveled down from London, but their families came, also. The train was so crowded, like most wartime trains, that the people were standing jam-packed in the corridors and iı. solid wedges of humanity in the luggage vans. Poor Mrs. Maynard was completely exhausted. She had not only stood the entire 6 hours of the trip,--those wartime British trains crowded and often hours late--but had held the large and restless black family cat all the way. And think of the Mothers with babies! And the poor youngsters being evacuated down here from the bombed areas!

The train was very late. There had been no Restaurant Car. So hunger was added to the traveler's weariness. When Dick returned to the Inn at about three o'clock in the morning he was quite worn out but enthusiastic about the welcome that his workers and their families had received.

"The town has been darned nice," he said. "The women simply marvelous. No one went hungry. Those W.V.S. workers--I take my hat off to them! They managed beans, eggs, bread and butter, cake, tea, etc. And the men helped in

146

getting the folks to billets. We've come to the right place all right . . ."

He still thinks so.

And so do I.

Well, we found a house--Martha and I--at Instow, 3 miles from Bideford, on a bay at the mouths of the Torridge and Taw rivers which empty into the Bristol Channel. Situated on a hill, with a lawn and rock garden in front, several walled fruit and vegetable gardens on the slope in back, "Springfield" overlooks a 3-mile open view of Devon countryside, with the Torridge river at the right, the twisting, turning road from Barnstable to Bideford spinning out along its edge.

After a compact and modern flat in London, Springfield seemed a bit too large and very inconvenient with its nine bedrooms, fireplaces for heat, and decidedly English "offices" (baths and W.C.'s, Staff room, etc.). But it was the better of the only two houses available. And Dick said, "It's the best built English house I've been in. Look at those walls." So we took it. When I interviewed Smale, the gardener, (who went with the house), I asked him where he lived. he pointed down the hill and said, "where the bombs dropped."

I tho't we'd come to a safety area, and said so Whereupon Smale replied,"them war an accident--like. Them warn't meant for us. Should of gone on Bristol."

And then I remembered June 24th--when I had been in Exeter with Alix and Dorothy and the "bombs, dropped north of a West Coast town (Bideford)" that night.

Well, here we were--because of the factory, because of the War--and here we were likely to stay a while by the look of things.

147

So Martha and I took window measurements, as we couldn't move in without blackout, and decided to go up to London with Dick the next day.

I think that no matter where else I may live, England will always tug at my heart, for several reasons. Both Dick's and my ancestors were among the Mayflower's and Sparhawk's passengers, so we always felt "at home" among the English, and being New Englanders we felt we understood, a bit, the English reticence and shyness--something so many Americans believe to be silent criticism and snobbishness. Aside from our love of the English people, which I must confess had to grow and develop, there was our love of the beautiful Island itself. We simply fell in love with that. The vivid green of grass and trees, the palpitating color of flowers and shrubs, the lush look of growing things, especially in the Spring and Summer. 'Tis the wetness of course produces this, and that we don't like. But often the cause is less attractive than the effect, and according to psychology, "Nothing exists but by comparison," anyway. (I learned that at Wellesley.)

Speaking of adverse features, and wet ones at that, the fogs in London, particularly the "pea-soupers," always thrilled us. They were so almost unbelievably really like what we'd read about, that a good fog and its resultant fantastic incidents seemed like a bit of Dickens come to life, and who doesn't like Dickens? The year that we arrived in England, February, 1935, London had some of her thickest fogs in a decade. I shall never forget them. They are among my interesting memories. The 1934-1935 Winter season offered quite the best fogs--or the worst, should one say?

Of course we all suffered from colds and flu, and Gerry had a bout of bronchitis. Coming from central heated--and I mean heated--American homes, we felt very much the lack of such heat in our first London home--a flat at Hamilton Terrace, St. Johns Wood. (St. John's Wood, London is comparable, location-wise, to Back Bay, Boston.) The only heat there was an open fire in the drawing-room which, of course, had to be built afresh every morning. The bed rooms had electric fires, quite inadequate ones, and the dining-room, kitchen, and hall had absolutely no heat at all. The chill in the rooms was always felt, save when one sat right beside the fire. But when there was a fog the chill became visible! It took on body--that of a white, gray, or saffron colored wraith--and slipped past the window frames and under the door sills to haunt the house. I have not only seen these London fogs inside my home, but I have bitten into them and swallowed them. They are gritty in the mouth and rasping in the throat. No wonder the old fashioned novels speak of the Heroines' "vapors." I'm sure they suffered from "fogitis!"

One afternoon that winter of 1934-1935, while coming home from shopping in Oxford. Street--where the lights had been on all day because of the fog--my taxi ran into a particularly thick stretch of "clouds" on Abby road. I had already felt as one with the angels for some time floating on air as it were, and I had begun to wonder what method, other than sight, my taxi driver employed;--a sense of touch (the near misses in the traffic and the kerb-bumps), or a sense of smell (the petrol-driven buses, the bakers' vans, the lorries or beer casks)--when we hit something, rose as a hunter at a fence, and sailed neatly between some iron palings and a lamp-post that, for one shaken second, I tho't was going to pierce the cab. The

149

driver never stopped. He never spoke. He completed the blind arc back into the hidden traffic. And I was shortly wafted to 63 Hamilton Terrace. It is no exaggeration when I say that I had to feel my way across the pavement to the front gate, and then to the door. Yet the taxi-driver had landed me on the right street at the right house--and the fog so thick one couldn't find the kerb without a torch.

As I was telling Gerry about my ride--the drawing-room like a fishbowl full of cold smoke--Martha came in, a bit white about the gills, and sank into a chair.

"I've been in an accident!" she said.

I could well believe it.

Martha had taken a bus home from Selfridges, and in Portman Square the bus had run up across the pavement and into the front of Daniel Neals' large shop. Everyone in the bus was thrown to the floor, or into the back of the seat ahead, and altho' but one passenger was injured, all had been bruised. However, the bus had continued the trip. And later, when the fog patches got too thick, along by Regents Park, the conductor had gotten out of the bus, pinned a large white handkerchief on his chest, and with a lighted torch in each hand walked ahead of the bus to guide the driver and warn off other traffic. It was all very dramatic. When Martha got out at the top of Hall road (our bus stop) she was quite helpless, until a man came along going towards Hamilton Terrace. She followed him and soon located the high brick wall that ran along to our corner. She then fumbled her way to the house.

Unless you have, yourself, experienced some of these eerie London fogs you are apt to be skeptical. But, sometimes, the fogs are so thick that flares must be lit at the crossroads, where several Bobbies stand in extra watchfulness. And the

Bobbies, as well as the Conductors, guide the buses and cars in the streets with torches. People slide in and out of clouds like mundane cherubim. These London fogs were no doubt excellent training for navigating the blackout later. For bus drivers, taxi-men, and chauffeurs of all kind seem to have cats' eyes nowadays." (This type of fog--a "pea-souper"--is now, practically non-existent in London. New buildings have central hating, and there is a Law prohibiting the use of any coal save that which has been rendered almost smokeless.)

We return to London From Bideford to pack household goods for removal.

October, 1940 (continued)

The Heavers and the Cottons. The Cottons and the Heavers. Once more the four of us were off to London and the raids, this time with knowledge and appreciation. Experience had made us wise--or so we thought. We didn't feel the apprehension we had felt that morning of September 4th, 1939, when we drove up to London from Swanage, Dorset into the unknown, a city of War. In a very slight way you might compare us to soldiers returning to the Front as we set out from Bideford for London. We could do without the bombs, the incendiaries and the shrapnel, but, if they had to be endured in order to finish the job, well, we'd have to put up with the bombs, the incendiaries and the shrapnel, and get on with the job. Carry-on, as the British say.

Martha went with us. Gerry was back at Bryanston School for the Winter Term. And Alix and Penny were now at Oxford with Dorothy, staying with a friend of hers. Making a home in the country was our present job, Martha's and mine, while Dick got the factory moved. So back to the raids we went.

We did a fool thing at once. We took down all the blackout in the flat, every curtain and drape, because we were taking them back in the car with us in a few days. And then, of course, we couldn't sleep in the flat! So we all, including the Heavers, decided to drive outside London and have dinner and a good night's sleep at some country inn. All that we got was the dinner--at the George and Crown in Stevenage, Hertfordshire.

There was absolutely no accommodation to be had, anywhere! You couldn't hire even a haystack in one of the fields. But wherever possible cars were parked in these fields--cars full of families, huddled in rugs and fortified with thermos of hot tea. We had heard about these nocturnal excursions. Now we were to share them. For we couldn't induce the proprietors of the "George and Crown" to let us sleep on the floor of the lounge there, altho' we assured them that we would leave very early in the morning. We strongly suspected that some of the people who sat there until 10 p.m., closing time, as we did, had their eyes on the cushioned benches along the walls and might well get to occupy them--later. However, we couldn't stay to find out; the lounge had closed. We paid our bill and went out into the star-lit dark, 'though the sirens had already started.

Why should I recall the fact that we had potted shrimps that night for dinner, or how marvelous they tasted? But that "bit" stays with me as strongly as the ensuing "bits" which made up those three nights spent in the car outside London during the last of the Battle of Britain. And I think I was more impressed with the fact that we actually slept thus than by the discomfort

152

of those nights.

Dick ran the car into the parking lot by a shack where lorry drivers obtained petrol and tea thru' the night on their long treks between the North and the South. The lot stood on a ridge facing London on one side and, in the distance on the other side, Cambridge. The "fireworks" had started, but we felt well out of it and settled ourselves in the car with rugs and cushions; Dick and I in the front, Martha between Elsie and Frank in the rear. We were all so weary that we fell asleep almost at once.

A sudden shudder of the car woke me. And an insistent glare, stripping the countryside of its protective dark, quite frightened me. Flares were drifting down to the back of us. I felt like a mushroom under glass, or a fish in a fishbowl, sitting there behind the windows of the car with all this threatening illumination about me. I woke Dick, much to his disgust.

"They're no where near us," he mumbled, still half asleep.

"But I felt the car shake!"

"Something dropped of course, in a field!" he snorted, and went to sleep again.

The glare died down, and I watched the "fireworks" over London until I dozed off.

In the morning, Martha complained, principally, of the snores. "Three different keys," she said, "And all going at once." Elsie complained of, or rather, commented on, the lorry drivers' language as they came and went at all hours. The men complained about their "beds." "Damned uncomfortable!" they expostulated in the gray light before dawn. No one mentioned the raids, except me.

For three nights we dined at the "George and Crown", sat in the lounge until closing time, and then drove out to our night's lodging place. And for three mornings we would

153

untangle ourselves from rugs and our cramped positions, consume large mugs of dubious tea offered by the proprietor of the shack, and then drive back to London, watching the sun come up, and guessing at what localities had "gotten it" during the night, from the columns of smoke rising here and there. After baths and breakfast at the flat Dick would go out to the factory, and Martha and I would pitch into the packing.

We were among the lucky ones, we still had light and water. But the Heavers came to us for baths and washing, taking large jugs of water back to their flat for tea and cooking. Poor Judy Beverley was boiling potatoes and vegetables in the central-heating plant (furnace) in the basement of their block of flats. And since she and Stan lived on the third floor, it wasn't too wonderful. But a lot of people were cooking in the streets in the worst hit districts.

Hilda, my Daily--"good old Hildy"--came every day to help me with the packing. Every single thing, save light fixtures and furniture, had to be packed, ready for the lorries. It wasn't easy. Hilda and I concentrated on the kitchen and the dining-room on the ground floor and Martha carried-on with the clothes cupboards and dresser drawers upstairs. It was a bit "hot and noisy" in the daytime, as well as night, at that period, so we always felt an urgency beyond that of mere hurry.

True to her type, Hilda minded the raids the last of us. The only sign she gave of her nervousness was her repetition of a phrase. Whenever the guns started their defensive barking Hilda would look at the window and then at me and say, "Something funny going on, Madam," and continue to stack tins, or what have you, into boxes.

During one such noisy interval, I went upstairs to see how Martha was making out. She was very methodically lifting frocks from the built-in wardrobe in my room and then laying them in precise pattern in a large case.

"Seems to be a bit of a raid," I said chattily, thinking Martha might want company.

"_Seems_ to be?" exclaimed Martha. "With guns _and_ bombs!" and went on with her folding and packing.

So I returned to the Kitchen and Hilda.

A fresh explosion made us both jump.

"Something funny going on, Madam!"

I must mention a strange coincidence! On the morning that we drove back to London from Bideford to pack and move our possessions that very morning--as on September 4th, 1939, when we left Swanage for London--the sinking of a ship headlined the morning papers. This time a ship of _children_ being evacuated to the States and Canada had been torpedoed.

In the conglomeration of printed horror two items fastened in my mind: the four children of a couple in Croyden, their entire young family, had been lost; and a young divinity student, volunteer shepherd of a certain number of these children, had given his life in the rescue work. "Greater love hath no man,"--read the news account. Repeatedly the young man had dived to retrieve one small life after another, only, in the very last attempt at rescue--to lose his own life, so full of promise.

Martha wondered if the young man were Michael Renne, whom she and Alix had known in London and who had been to tea with us at Regency Lodge.

"It's just the kind of thing that he would do," mourned Martha.

155

A few days later the newspapers printed the Divinity student's picture and gave some details of his life--his parent's name, his home address--and revealed that the young man, as did the shepherd with his ninety-and-nine sheep, had felt the loss of one of the little children so keenly that he must search and search. And so, diving over and over again for the one child still unaccounted for, had found the task too great. His heart had failed.

Michael Renne--for it was indeed the young friend of my daughters--is one of this War's heroes whose name will not be inscribed upon a War Office casualty list, a hero who has been awarded no decoration, but whose "gallantry beyond the line of duty" will live on in the lives of those he saved and in the hearts of those he loved, and who loved him. "Greater love hath no man."

November, 1940
"Springfield"
Instow N. Devon.

Our new address. We seem so far from things, with London about 3 hours away by train. And this business of going three miles to shop! That is, for things other than meat and groceries. Instow is such a small place. But we like being by the sea, and find compensations in our long view, the fine vegetable garden--no more wilted lettuces and shriveled spinach--and the feeling of sanctuary after the London raids.

The house needed a most thorough cleaning. Beards hung from the ceilings, and the red plush chairs in the dining

156

room threw smoke-screens when sat upon. But cleaning women seem very scarce. Smale (the gardener) fetched us a soldier's wife, but she was as untidy as the house. So the dirt remained static until Smale, again being helpful, produced two women from the village--friends and neighbors of his. They are pleasant, clean and efficient, but their names amuse us. Mrs. Pidler and Mrs. Waters. Imagine that combination! The Heavers laughed like anything when we told them.

I have decided to call Mrs. Pidler, Mrs. Pedler. She doesn't seem to mind. But Mrs. Pidler and Mrs. Waters! No, I couldn't go on saying, "Mrs. Pidler, would you and Mrs. Waters do thus and so"--all day long.

This house is an ark of a place, with only two bedrooms of nine really good sized and having H.&C. basins. There are steps for two levels on each upper floor--no one knows why!-- and the Bath and W.C. (offices!) on the 2nd floor are separate and rather tacky. The W.C. is most annoying. Altho' the tank is labeled "Super Silent" it is anything but silent, while the "super" apparently refers to the super long time intervals between said tank's performance.

The buses here intrigue us. They have an intimate quality in their dealings with those who ride in them and with the country homes whose doors they pass day by day on half-hourly schedules. The buses not only stop wherever one desires, even at one's own gate should it be on the route, but deliver parcels and articles of all sorts. One can call up a shop in Bideford, or Barnstable, and ask for 2 lbs. of sole to be put on the 10 a.m. bus, or a coal scuttle and two brooms to come out by the 4 o'clock. Even live stock is thus delivered. I have seen sedate hens and garrulous ducks, in crates, riding in state on the rear platform with the conductress. And boxes of eggs

157

are tenderly placed on the shelf beneath the stairs to the upper deck. Baskets of apples wobble under foot, the conductress good naturedly retrieving those apples that now and then spill out. Often the buses are met at the designated stop and the articles collected, but often, also, the conductress obligingly hops off with the parcel and delivers it to the door. Sometimes there will be an expectant figure waiting at the door or window, and then the bus merely slows down while the conductress heaves the box, or parcel, over the hedge into the garden. The tuppence or five-pence, etc. as the case may be, which the Bus Co. collects, is added to one's bill at the shop. Efficiency--country style.

We are beginning to feel fairly settled. Dick has installed stoves before the fireplaces in three of the downstairs rooms--drawing-room, dining-room, and study. The stoves are a constant care, but at least the fires need not be built anew each day and there is heat in the house, in spots. The blackout is finished at last and up at the 42 windows. Thank goodness 8 of the lot were already equipped with wooden plaques which we fit in with hasps at night. Our furniture has arrived from London, and we are trying to feel at home in a country quiet that is sometimes oppressive, open spaces that seem empty in spite of the scenic beauty and, so far, a lack of those friendly sorties into our home that meant so much to us in London. Frankly, I believe we miss the raids!

Dorothy, Alix, and little Penny are now here. Tony drove them down from Oxford. All look well and Penny is as good as gold. Not one of my three ever slept at night as she does. Wonderful! Dorothy is going to live with us for a while. She will have some of her things sent down from London.

"The people here don't know there's a War." So say

most of those coming here from the blitzed cities. Quite true in many ways. There's a small Sailing Club with a bar--the Marine Hotel, a glorified pub with family atmosphere--a beach where dogs and children (English order of priority!) are aired, and there are Evacuees.

Those people with Evacuees know there's a War. Also those people who, dependent on pensions, must live on those pensions. And, of course, most sadly, those people who have suffered personal loss in this War.

But we understand what visitors mean when they say, "The people here don't know there's a War!" You can sleep here at night in a bed. You can buy fruit and fresh eggs and chickens and more milk (this was before the rationing was put into effect). Such perishable articles have been almost non-existent in the cities, due to transport upsets because of the raids. One can go about here easier in the blackout with little fear of the sirens driving one to hasty shelter. There are cocktail and sherry parties. At that hour in London one is thinking of getting under something!

To be perfectly honest I feel a bit selfish, living here with friends still in London. I miss the city's life, though one of turmoil and danger; it's fighting people; it's feeling of being at the center of things.

Dick rushes up to London quite a bit. Sometimes I go with him. Leaving in the late afternoon, we drive as far as Exeter. It is a charming ride along the river Torridge, but so winding as to make me quite seasick. I suck soda mints and hang out of the car window for air.

159

One of the villages we pass thru'--St. Cyr--is so picturesque as to seem like a stage-set. As we swing around the last bend in the road before St. Cyr we always exclaim, "There it is! Just the same!" The cottages are all a faint pink like the under side of a mushroom. There is a stream, with a "water-splash," in the tiny square. And the undulating, thatched roofs overhang the very road on either side. The cottages blink as we rush by, and their eyebrows brush the car top.

Dick once inquired as to why all the cottages were tinted the same terra cotta pink.

"It be camouflage, Sur, fur any Nazi plane 'at cooms. Hur couldn't find us noo."

Well, the earth of S. Devon is a rose red, with shades of rust and blush in the furrowed fields.

"Mebbe so, Sur!" As they say hereabouts.

This night trip to London is otherwise most unpleasant. There are no sleeping compartments nowadays. And there's a wait of hours at Exeter. We have dinner at the Rougemont Hotel, go to a cinema, and then return to the Rougemont Hotel to sit in the lobby, reading ourselves into blindness by the rationed light and shriveling up with the cold as the rationed fire dies. Tea, and sometimes whiskey and soda, keep us awake until 1:30 a.m. when the taxi calls for us. It is a young woman who takes our bags--the women taxi drivers and women porters insist on this like men--and drives us at a good clip in spite of the blackout to "Exeter--St. David's" station. Here we wait on the platform for the 1:50 a.m. train from Plymouth to London. It is always late.

One night, or morning rather, it never arrived until after 4 o'clock. Dick and Frank had the long cold wait that night. I

160

was at "Springfield" where, with the rest of the family, I stood on the lawn and watched the glare, shot with sudden intense flashes, like an insidious Aurora Borealis in the South--as the Nazis blitzed Plymouth. No wonder the Plymouth-London train was late. But like most things here in this war, it still carried-on.

The trains are crowded with Troops and Navy personnel. Compartments and corridors are full up. Dick and I sleep on these night trips to town like everyone else, huddled on our neighbors' shoulders, our feet numbed by the floor drafts and our heads fuzzy with bad air. One night I had a bit of luck and shared a whole long seat with a Naval Officer. We slept feet to head quite cozily. And another night I had the warmest trip of all. A commercial traveler, in jaunty and friendly fashion, passed around a shaving mug of whiskey. A good swig from that put me to sleep for the whole trip. It was wonderful.

Doreen has come down on a short leave. She is in the L.A.A.S. (London Auxiliary Ambulance Service) and has been through all the blitzes. Doreen is Mrs. Shepherd, mother of young Capt. Gordon Shepherd, British Intelligence, a friend of Martha's.

Poor Doreen. She's not sleeping at all well. She keeps seeing particularly ghastly incidents, one especially; a 16 year old boy with his face stuck full of glass splinters, like a pincushion, and one big splinter thro' an eye.

"He never even whimpered when we lifted him into the

161

ambulance. Just twisted his mouth into a sort of a smile."

I know Doreen is thinking of Gordon and what may lie ahead for him. For Gordon's father is still alive, but totally helpless, from injuries received in the last war (World War I).

Had the sirens last night, and later we saw a line of fire back of the hill beyond Bideford. This a.m. when Doreen and I went in to market, everyone was talking about it. A Nazi raider had dropped incendiaries over Frithelstock, a tiny village about 3 miles outside Bideford. Some people think a shepherd's lantern attracted the plane. Others speak of a dummy air field there as a lure. Market gossip of course. But the incendiaries were a fact.

The end of December there was snow, sleet, and hail. Unprecedented weather for Devon. The first big snowflakes whirling down about the house started a babble of excitement and appreciation for the family. To New Englanders a snowstorm was inspiration. But the Devonians and other English loathed the stuff and said so. The snow was a welcome sight to us Americans in spite of the cold it brought along.

The girls dug out their ski-suits from the cedar chest, and went out on the snow-covered lawn to build a snow figure. They decorated it with an old hat and a broom and used two lumps of coal for eyes. My two maids, young farm girls, had never seen such a sight. They hovered by the dining-room windows, peeking around the drapes and giggling.

"Ooh! Luk at 'ur!" they whispered. "Luk!"

The snow went to my head a bit. I, too, put on my ski-suit, and went in to market thus attired. In spite of this wintry weather, the icy pavements and the falling snow, the Bidefordians stared at me as though I were some creature quite out of its element! They, the Bidefordians, looked as odd to me, and decidedly more out of their element. They seemed so inadequately clothed and shod for such harsh weather, while the proverbial umbrellas seemed to present a stolid British criticism of such unseemliness--snow, instead of rain, in Devon.

The Vicar of Appledore and his new, very young wife had been invited for tea that same afternoon, but we didn't expect them because of the weather. The buses were not running to schedule and the hill leading to our house was slippery with ice. So all of us were clumping about outdoors in our ski boots when the Vicar and his wife appeared in the drive--she in her Red Cross uniform, and he rosy-cheeked and puffing, furled umbrella tightly clutched in exertion, his gaitered legs making uneven, but steady, progress up the icy incline.

The Vicar, over 70 and old in the Service of the Lord, had recently married for the second time, to the slightly scandalized disappointment of his congregation. His wife was not only young in years but her ideas were according. She joined the Red Cross and was away from the Vicarage most of the time. Now, she being on furlough, we were to meet her.

I am afraid that our hobble-de-hoy welcome and the resultant noisy tea by the drawing-room fire were just what our guests expected of Americans. But they seemed to enjoy the visit, as did we.

We were all amused and impressed by the Vicar's account of the trip over. Apppledore is 10 miles from Instow.

163

The Vicar had carefully 'phoned the main Bus Office to make sure that, if the Appledore bus reached Biddeford in the present storm, he and his wife would find a Barnstable bus, via Instow, running on schedule. The Vicar was so promised, and he and his wife set out to keep their tea-date with us, leaving very early to allow for hold-ups.

There <u>was</u> a hold-up--a lengthy one. No bus was waiting at the Main Office. And there was to be none. The storm was too severe, the roads quite unsafe. "We can not cope!" said the Manager there.

The Vicar was irate. A promise was a promise. And he so informed the Staff in the Bus Office. Why should he and his wife make the trip from Appledore into town for nothing-- and in such weather! They were promised a bus to Instow, and they were going to have one.

At the end of the lengthy argument, coupled with that obdurate quality which, from its very matter-of-factness, makes it impervious and which the Vicar seems to possess to an immoderate degree, for he never once smiled in the telling--in the end the Bus Co. gave in and produced a bus, complete with driver and conductress. And the Vicar and his wife were chauffeured here in state, lone passengers in that Southern Transport bus.

We still laugh about it. But such perseverance and effort to keep a mere friendly engagement gave us to think, as the French say. For it was truly a friendly gesture, that trip in such inclement weather. And we felt that the Vicar's congregation must have good reason to be so fond of him, as popular opinion here quotes. He would never offer his flock "a stone for bread," neither would he fail in his undertakings to them.

There are those hereabout who say, "He's a bit odd, you know, The Vicar of Appledore." But, "they love him in Appledore!" comes out in the same breath. "He's very popular in his church."

There is no pattern for integrity and faith. Besides, one has always heard "the Lord works in a mysterious way." Because the Vicar of Appledore goes off the deep end and marries a girl 30 odd years his junior, or because he eats buns from a paper bag while standing in a bus queue, or because he has "pixiesh" ways about him--all this does not preclude that the Vicar is not an able Servant of the Lord. It only makes him human. The Church of England can do with a little humanity, the common kind that flourishes on the little things in life.

A very odd thing happened in the same month, December. With Gerry due home from Bryanston for the Christmas holiday, I decided to go through and assemble his heavy underwear. As I sorted the woollies on the shelves of his wardrobe I found a parcel wrapped in an undersuit. The parcel was about 7" by 9", done up in quite fresh brown paper (which is practically non-existent nowadays) and tied with twine.

For a moment I was nonplused. Then I had the bright idea that it must be a Christmas gift for me from Dick. For my husband has often hidden such before. But never in such a queer place, I thought.

I decided to put the parcel along with the several that already were on Dick's side of the long shelf at the top of the big clothes cupboard in our bedroom--and await developments.

Nothing happened--nothing was said. And in my busyness, I soon forgot the episode--until Christmas morning.

After our traditional exchange of gifts about the tree (which Smale had cut for us), I suddenly remembered the brown paper parcel. Although I had already received a lovely gift from Dick, I asked him where my other present was. He looked blank.

"The one in brown paper on the shelf in our clothes cupboard!" I said.

"That's not mine," said Dick. "Thought it was yours!"

So I ran up and got the parcel. Back in the drawing-room I untied the string and opened-out the brown paper. There lay a flat, gray, rather worn shield-shaped leather jeweler's box, tooled in tarnished gilt. Puzzled I unclasped the lid of the box and opened it. In stupefied astonishment, we all gazed upon it's contents.

A lavaliere of small diamonds, sapphires and rubies with a pear-shaped pearl pendant--lay spread upon white satin. The satin was yellowed with age and for the same reason the jeweler's name, in faded gilt, was quite indecipherable. But we could make out the word Wien (Vienna). Undoubtedly, the necklace was an heirloom, brought to England by some refugee from the Continent. This is common practice nowadays. The English jewelers are stocked with such offerings, as many refugees have been forced to flee without their money. In order to live--here, in England--such hopeless and helpless people must sell family treasures.

I wore the necklace just once--at Christmas dinner. Dick took it up to London on his next trip there.

We have no idea where it came from!

But we feel quite sure that the necklace was placed in

166

Gerry's wardrobe in London, as the wardrobe was brought here just as it was at the time of removal--full of underwear, shirts and pullovers--and no one, so far as I know, had touched the contents while it was in Gerry's room at the flat and he was at Bryanston. Certainly no one here had opened the wardrobe as it was still locked when I went to check Gerry's winter clothes shortly before his arrival here for the Christmas holidays.

Of course, we have several theories concerning this strange business. The most realistic, we feel, is that a thief (having stolen the necklace) was running from the Police in the blackout during a raid. That he had leapt through an open window into Gerry's room, which was on the first floor and opened onto the courtyard of Regency Lodge--and in haste and fear had disposed of the parcel containing the necklace. In a raid we'd have been sheltering on our lower floor and because of the guns would have heard nothing of this. Just a guess, of course. We'll just have to wait.

But fancy finding a diamond necklace wrapped in a suit of your son's winter underwear! (The mystery was never solved. I did write a story about this.)

The Oxford and Bucks Light Infantry are stationed at Westward-Ho!, and among the Officers are some ten or a dozen young men who like to drop in for a chat, a game of bridge, a sing-song, and the inevitable whiskey and soda. One evening just before Christmas we popped corn to the great edification of the Englishmen. They had never seen it done before, and their remarks were as boyish as their expressions, providing the adage (or feminine belief) that "men are just big boys, anyway." When the girls stirred the popped corn into treacle and then rolled the sticky mess into balls on a floured board, there were many willing helpers. Uniforms became dusty with flour, and the kitchen full of laughter. (I have had several of these same young officers write me at the following Christmas seasons -- from the far off Middle East stations, Africa, etc. -- that they have never forgotten their Christmas when they popped corn and that they wished they might be with us again at "Springfield". It is the kind of sentiment I like -- a love of "homely" things.)

January 1st, 1941
Afternoon.

New Year's Day.

We drove over to the Officer's Mess this morning for "elevenses" of sherry, and last night we spent a lovely evening there--all of us; the family, Dorothy and Tony. Very good dinner. Formal dress. It was fun stepping out in our best bibs and tuckers. The dancing got very gay, and at midnight the usual circles of friends formed and sang "Auld Lang Syne."

Happy New Year!

Was there such a hope within each heart there?

Human nature is a child-like phenomenon. One doesn't really forget the War, but diversions such as this New year's Eve celebration lay its specter, fleetingly, for a few hours.

Each individual sorrow and tragedy still burns--within, like the Eternal Flame, never to die out from one's remembering. But a measure of joy and laughter must leaven this Wartime living. Sanity requires a balance.

I wonder how far ahead the end to all this lies--this dreadful War. Dick says 3 more years at least! And when is America coming in? For, of course, we will--eventually.

February, 1941

Rain, streaming rain! The view from the front windows is almost obscured. The days are gray all day long. This eternal curtain of rain! It is like living under Niagara Falls. No wonder the Farmers' Almanac calls this month "February--Filldyke!" But the Devonshire folk, with typical British understatement, call these downpours "Devonshire Drizzles," and refuse to stay indoors. A rainstorm to bother these hardy people would probably have to be a Biblical Flood. And then, I suppose, they'd simply dig out an ark from somewhere, dust it off, and get on with salvaging their crops and cattle.

March, 1941.

I had another birthday in the middle of this month. But the less said of that the better--altho' the family always treat me marvelously; presents, a cake with candles. I love flourishes.

But Father Time never forgets the extra wrinkle, which is far too generous of him. I can never prevail upon him to take it back. He snorts, and mumbles in his beard something about not looking a gift-horse in the mouth.

Either because we have a "house in the country" (Always a magnet to town dwellers and now a sanctuary from bombs), or because we like to have a lot of friends come to see us, or because, being the kind of family we are, we can't bear an hour that doesn't seethe with people and babble--at any rate, "Springfield," with its 9 bedrooms is usually full nowadays. Sometimes, overnight, the sofa and wing chairs in the drawing-room are occupied as well, and once several officers slept on the floor there, wrapped up in blankets like papooses.

With the early blackout of the winter months one's overnight guests often arrive and leave in the dark. A young airman from the nearby Drome, on one such visit here, nearly broke a leg because of this! Our drive is a tortuous affair, and close by the first turning is a walk down into the rock garden. This garden is banked at the further end along the road, and upon the bank stands a high red fence covered with rambler-rose vines. The young Airman, in his rush to catch the first morning bus, chose the path instead of the drive in the still hovering dark. Becoming lost in the garden, and time being short, he decided to climb over the fence--having no idea just what particular fence it was. He soon found out! And was lucky to get off with a badly sprained ankle. It's a terrific drop to the road below the fence.

We now make a point of mapping out exits and entrances to "Springfield." I had a sedate Instow inhabitant become quite mazed among the graveled intricacies one evening after a small cocktail party. We have become accustomed to seeing people off in the blackout with a series of shouted directions.

"No,--not that one! The drive's in the middle."

"Yes,--to the right! Just keep going."

"Oh dear!--you're in the crocuses. Turn left!--and step down."

Torches (wartime dimmed, with blue tissue on the glass) are feeble things and the orientation of some people is even feebler. No matter how often we start people off in the dark in the right direction, with a little pat and a brisk admonition to just go straight ahead--as in playing "Pin the tail on the donkey"--some people will end up in the strangest places!

Everyone has been giving a pint of blood--except me. When I climbed up on the table at the improvised clinic in the Recreation Hall on the Front the Doctor took a look at my eyes and my nails and shook his head. Having already been "typed" some weeks ago, I felt disappointed, and somehow slightly humiliated as I climbed down from the table and went out past the half dozen mattresses spread upon the floor. Here, resting and sipping tea, were various donors--young matrons, retired Colonels, farmers, etc., a catholic assortment, the huskiest among them feeling the worst. One strapping farmer fainted.

Alix has had headaches ever since. As has young Mrs. John Durnford-Slater. Neither should have spared the blood, it seems, altho' Martha has given 2 pints. One would think a test for anemia should be given as well as the typing of one's blood. The whole business appears rather casual to me, a Doctor's daughter. A mobile Blood Bank Unit tours the districts, and local V.A.D's assist the young Doctor in some cleared and sheet-hung public room. But, when one considers the method and the place of the <u>disbursement</u> of these pints of blood--to begrimed and wounded men yet on the battlefield--one ceases to make comparisons. There just aren't any.

April 1941.
Spring in England! April in Devonshire! This <u>could</u> have been the part of England that inspired Wordsworth's poem on the daffodils.
"Beside the lake, beneath the trees,
Fluttering and dancing in the breeze."
How true. One sees the lovely golden cups everywhere. The woods are aglow with pools of yellow light that move in the soft stir of air. Each garden, our garden, is bright with nodding shafts of earthly sun that spatter the paths and plots. And I spend unstinted time capturing this garden sunshine and distributing it about the house in big blobs of yellow that illuminate a whole room. The friendly gaiety of a bowl of daffodils can do just that--illuminate a place.
To share an English spring is to share a bit of Heaven. It is lovely-gracious--tender--this colorful and scented season. No wonder the fighting Englishmen defend it to their last breath--.
"This Blessed plot, this earth, this realm, this England."

172

Whitsun week-end, 1941.

Over the long Easter week-end at Whitsun, Kay and Bill Williams and their wee Vanessa were with us. Also Hartley Davies. The weather was perfect. The kind of weather we often miss here in England! Warm and sunny with blue skies, nearly outdoor weather--provided one wore a cardigan. We basked and chatted and drank tea; and listened to the damn radio--the twice-damned radio, for one could be set on one's heels by it's wartime pronouncements.

But all went well that week-end. It was one of those spuriously calm interludes in this horrible war that, momentarily and seductively lulls one into a dream of normalcy and peace.

May 1941.

The afternoon of May 23rd the girls and I went to tea at the Durnford-Slater's. Madame Durnford-Slater has her two daughters-in-law and three grandchildren staying with her for the duration. The tea table was a noisy and crowded one, but gracious and hospitable. It is nice to be neighbors of such friendly people. Commander Robin Durnford-Slater was on leave, so I asked him and his wife, Sally, to come up the following day at 6:30 p.m. and have drinks and a chat with us all at "Springfield."

At 6 p.m. the next day, May 24th, the radio gave out the shocking news of the sinking of H.M.S. Hood. One salvo from the guns of the Bismarck straight into the ammunition stores, one terrific explosion ripping the Hood apart, and then one sole survivor. But these details and the matter of the sole survivor were not learned until much later. (And much later still we were to have that sole survivor as guest.) The radio announcement of that early evening simply stated that there were some survivors, and employed the usual phrase "the next of kin have been informed."

The 'phone rang. Commander Durnford-Slater wished to say that the sinking of H.M.S. Hood has been a very harsh and very intimate blow. Sally's brother was one of its Officers. Sally was most upset, not knowing whether he was a survivor or not. But Sally would like to come up with Commander Durnford-Slater just the same, it would occupy her mind a bit. But would we please excuse her if she seemed rather poor company.

So the young Durnford-Slaters came up for drinks. And Robin and Dick discussed the war. And Sally, the girls and I discussed the War. For what else was there at the time, but War--and the results of War, the sinking of the Hood, for instance.

After Sally and Robin left, I stood at the bay window in the drawing-room and looked long into the gray distance. And, while the twilight dimmed the countryside, long deep thoughts took hold of me--and I felt the following lines come out of the sad English land and sea-scape there before me.

On the Sinking of H.M.S. Hood
May 24th, 1941
(Dedicated to the Royal Navy and her Sons.)

"Dark velvet trees are marching over the hillside.
The metal disk of setting sun
Slips into a tearful sea,
And translucent twilight, following close,
Wraps the soft scene in cellophane
And delivers it to me--
A bit of beauty for my soul,
Balm for my heart--
For the Hood and her Men are gone
Into Eternity.
Without, in the twilight world of glass,
Move unseen Heroes,
Clad in Honor, brave in Glory,
Newcomers to that Band
Of Immortal Youth one is indebted to
For very life. Do not be sorry;
Find work to do; and charity to serve;
And put Love into your living with mankind.
'Twill make a better end than tears
To Heroes' story.

To you, whose Men these sailors were,
To you, who wait in vain
For happy home-returns and love,
I say, "Take courage.
Look into the World that spins about you.

175

Look above.
And let some part of that
Which is truly God-given--
As Light, or Peace--
Into your heart's core move.

There is a Heaven, a Future, and a God--
Each warrior His son.
Be certain that he lives--your Man--
In pleasant company,
His best task done.
Feel not alone.
And do not weep. But sing
Praises for those who knew no fear,
Who loved the ocean, storm and battle,
Who fought the good fight--and won!"
                                    Amen

                                    June 5th, 1941.
    Bob is missing.   Robert D'Alaime, Lieutenant in the
Royal Navy, Peter's pal, Best Man at Peter's and Alix's
wedding. I had a note from Margareta, his wife, some days
ago. She was numbed by the news, but ready to hope, god
grant there is hope. My prayers get longer every night.

                                    176

June 6th, 1941.

Today June 6th, Bob is officially declared lost. "The submarine, "Undaunted", with its entire crew, is long overdue and must be considered lost." There are now Margareta and little blond Karin Elizabeth, eight months old. We want them to come to us for as long as they care to stay. Margareta's family is in Stockholm. How doubly hard the separation must be now for Margareta's mother. It is hard to have a daughter far away from you in joy and happiness. It is almost unendurable to have a daughter far away in sorrow and heartbreak. And there is Bob's Mother. He was her only child. She called him Rob and Robbie. What can one say? What can one do? How utterly helpless, useless and futile one is in these tragedies of the heart. For the heart is a private place, belonging to one person alone--the Lover and the Beloved, for they are as One.

I think of what it would have meant to Alix and Penny, alone here after Peter's loss, had we all gone to the States a year ago this May when that last American ship sailed. And I think of Margareta, and her constant cheerfulness and endurance in that primitive cottage in a tiny village in the Scottish Highlands where she and Karin have lived for months, and where Rob went on leave. He and Margareta would hike for miles, sandwiches in pockets, and climb the surrounding mountains. "Rob is teaching me mountain climbing," Margareta wrote to me. "He goes ahead and I follow, keeping my eyes on his stockings, never higher. It's a rule for mountain climbing."

They were so very happy, so truly free in their way of life in spite of the bleak cottage with no heat, no water, fires to be built each morning, and the wood to be gathered as well. Margareta used to go out with a basket on her back, the strap

177

about her forehead in Indian style. Yet she has weathered the winter there, she and Karin, with a visit from Rob's mother.

Margareta made happy home-comings for Rob with Swedish cooking as a treat and the sweet soups of Sweden. Such strength to make a home in such conditions, alone and in War--such self-denial and such singleness of purpose. Where is the reward?

Margareta, my dear, you deserved better than you have received. My bewilderment is as great as yours.

And still June, 1941.

I was shopping on the High Street, Bideford, one morning, when large posters in the windows of Chope's, the drapers, attracted my attention.

"Buy a Spitfire!"

Life-size photographic cut-outs of a smiling R.A.F. Pilot stood about the display. By the shop entrance was a small table with a collecting box and an open ledger upon its top. Passers-by were dropping contributions into the box and then signing their names in the ledger. A pleasant-faced woman with a brisk manner, presiding at a table, thanked each person with a sincerity that somehow touched me.

"Buy a Spitfire." I re-read the sign.

The contributions now being collected were to buy more Spitfires in memory of young Cobber (Edward) Kain, a New Zealander. He had been killed over France just a year ago, in June 1940, on the very day of his leave to return to England to be married.

I tho't of Pete, and wished I had put more in the collecting box and turned to do so, when suddenly a fleeting expression on the face of the charming woman by the table struck a light within me.

"Mrs. Kain," I said. "You <u>are</u> Mrs. Kain, aren't you?"
She was.

As a result, Mrs. Kain came out to "Springfield" the next day for tea. She brought pictures of Cobber (she called him "Eddie") and of Cobber's fiancee (an English girl), and an enlargement of a photo of Mrs. Kain and Cobber's sister leaving Buckingham Palace where they had received Cobber's D.S.C. It was to attend the ceremony of presentation of this decoration to Cobber that his Mother and Sister had been flown here from their home in Wellington, New Zealand.

Cobber was killed shortly before they landed. One of those wartime tragedies that seem somehow doubly hard to bear--like that of Pete and Alix. So near--and yet so far--the promised, hoped for meeting of loved ones. (Mrs. Kain had remained in England to help with the war effort.)

The Fourth of July, 1941
Falmouth, Cornwall
Evening.

Such a thrill! Our stars and stripes flying beside the Union Jack all up and down the High Street! English speaking people should stick together. People of common heritage should be united. We feel this very strongly, Dick and I. And we found much in Falmouth to strengthen our belief.

Dick has been giving "talks" here and there on American Government, with some highlights on our non-belligerent aid to Britain, etc. The talks help the English People to understand the How and the Why of our actions

179

nowadays; that our sympathies are with England, but that we are a very large Nation peopled by a very large and varied Public and governed by a system that is truly impelled by the People. And the American People, as a whole, are not yet ready to enter this War. They have no desire to. Who can blame them? But I believe that they will do so eventually--hating War as much as the English do, loving Liberty too much to let it be strangled, believing in the rights of Man, willing to die for all this, as the English do, but still not sure that this War is their War, America's. The Atlantic Ocean is a barrier in more ways than one.

We like Falmouth. The palm trees bordering the streets and drives lend an exotic touch to this old English seaport. Colonel (Col. Harry Gamble, Retired) and Mrs. Gamble have come along with us. We think of them as our first Instow friends. They are dears, and we hope they are enjoying it all as much as we. It was a lovely drive down to Falmouth from Instow, through South Devon into Cornwall, via Launceston with its Old Castle on the hill, then through Indian Queen and Bodmin and across the wild moor with its clay pools of bright blue water and its carpet of heather spiked with tall poles against enemy plane landings. Jagged, towering heaps of white slag from abandoned tin mines broke up the long horizon line. There is talk of reopening some of these tin mines. Malaya is an extra long way off nowadays, when measured in terms of enemy submarines and dive-bombers.

The Mayor and Aldermen of Falmouth gave us a dinner. Then we were escorted in state to the Guild Hall, where the Gambles and I were seated to the right of the platform in a boxed-in bench very much like the front pews (and as hard) in the Old Meeting Houses at home in New

England. (No doubt these old English ceremonial seats had been the inspiration for the New England pews.) The place was packed. Very gratifying. So was the applause, the foot stamping particularly. Here are a friendly people.

After Dick's speech, and the Vote of Thanks, we all-- the Mayor, the Aldermen and their wives, Col. and Mrs. Gamble, Dick and I--went on to the Town Hall. There, in the Mayor's Parlor, sherry was served and we drank to Anglo-American friendship. As though the hospitality of the Town and its people were not enough we (Dick and I) were given tangible proof, talisman for the future a pair of lovely silver spoons with the Falmouth coat-of-arms in pale blue enamel. The sincerity of the little speeches made there in that old room, the Mayor's Parlor, touched us greatly. Friendly cables of greeting were exchanged between Falmouth, England, and Falmouth, Massachusetts, U.S.A. For years our parents, Dick's and mine, had had summer homes at North Falmouth, Mass. What strange coincidence, or plot, has set me and my husband down here in Falmouth, England, this Fourth of July, 1941?

From the Mayor's Parlor we were escorted through the public rooms with their old paintings of former dignitaries. The high, stone window ledges were gay with big pink and blue hydrangeas. Mrs. Gamble and I admired them. Whereupon we were each presented with a plant--did we blush!--and learned that the Mayor, who grew the hydrangeas (he is a Nurseryman), had done landscape gardening for the King (George VI) when he was Duke of York. He, the Mayor, took us into his office and proudly showed us correspondence signed, "Albert, R." -- the letters in longhand, informal and genial.

"A fine man," said the Mayor. "No flourishes--just signs himself 'Albert, R.' We've got a good King."

The consensus of the British people I am sure.

July 5, 1941.

Gunfire in the very early morning. A convoy, going out in the gray light before dawn, must have sighted something. In the harbor lies the burned and battered H.M.S. "Registan." While she was picking up survivors on May 27th following the naval action against the "Bismarck," the Luftwaffe dive-bombed H.M.S. "Registan." Although the Luftwaffe knew that Germans were being rescued and that many Germans were already aboard H.M.S. "Registan," these facts seemed to mean nothing. The Luftwaffe dive-bombed the Hell out of H.M.S. "Registan," and 400 Germans were killed, or rather roasted, in the resultant fires, along with most of the crew of the "Registan." Joe Divers was one of her Officers, one of the survivors, Martha knows Joe well. She met him when he was 1st Officer on the Queen Mary the time Martha and I went home for a visit in the summer of 1938, and she has seen Joe off and on ever since. I'm sure Joe never pictured that particular bit of Hell--the divebombing of H.M.S. "Registan" (The "Registan" had limped into Falmouth Harbor on May 29th, later was salvaged, then went into action, and was torpedoed and sunk in 1943. Joe, in time, became Captain Divers of H.M.S. Queen Mary.) --in his horoscope. That might be "horrorscope".

Strange and awful things happen nowadays. Makes me remember an experience of Terry's (Lieut. J.P. Tulloch, R.N.R.). Terry, now on a destroyer, formerly had an M.T.B. (Motor Torpedo Boat.) Navy youngsters are put in command of these fast little boats with a big kick, and very shortly these Navy youngsters become the "Baby-faced killers" some journalist wrote of so enthusiastically a while ago. Their youth is certainly out of all proportion to their deeds.

To return to Terry. Out in the English Channel one day Terry sighted 3 German Airmen in an inflated dinghy and buzzed off to their rescue. As his M.T.B. rushed nearer Terry and his crew were horrified to see two of the Germans push the third into the channel, and then systematically and vigorously set about drowning the man.

Terry shouted and hooted and waved his arms. But the two busy Germans paid no attention. They had finished their job as the M.T.B. drew alongside the dinghy.

"Good God!" said Terry. "Why did you do it?"

But the Germans only shrugged their shoulders and glowered.

The Vicar of a little country church, there by the sea, could speak German. He got the German Airmen's story after they were brought ashore.

It seems that the third German was a member of the Gestapo, and had been sent along on recent flights over England to sit behind the two German pilots and hold a revolver at their backs!

This episode, without names, was printed in the

183

newspapers--to the edification of the British Public. Morale in the Luftwaffe must be low! It was some time later that we learned from Terry that it was he and his M.T.B. that were concerned in that news item.

December 7, 1941.

Pearl Harbor!

One doesn't need to expand on those two words. They stand large and black and flame-red in the sequence of World War II, particularly to American minds. But I think that the British--and we Americans here in England--accepted the treacherous Jap attack as though it were another devastating air-raid, but an air-raid with three distinct differences from those already experienced. I. This attack was distant. II. It brought in another enemy to fight. III. It gave us another ally to stand with us. There was horror, and relief, in a strange blending of emotions among the people here in England.

"The States are in it now!"

"The Americans will fight with us again!"

It was like a blood transfusion to a very ill man. New life surged into the fighting spirit of the British. They had never felt licked, but they had felt tired and alone. Now there was a good friend standing with them, and the strength of that friend, America.

1942. Another year of War
"Springfield" Instow

Ugh!

This living in the country!

Mud is coming in, on boots and shoes and paws, through all the doors onto all the rugs. Pig perfume, from the house of Napoleaon and Josephine up the back garden, coming in all the windows and vanquishing the flowers in the "vahzes." Vegetatables, heavy with fresh black earth and quite unshorn of outer leaves, roots, etc., heaped on the kitchen table. Cinders and coal dust from the hot water heater camouflaging the furniture and mantelpiece in the Staff room. Rabbits, quite newly dead, offered at the door by village lads. Chicken in full dress--and I don't mean "dressed"--to be plucked by Mrs. Pedler, who "operates" in the kitchen sink under hot water so that a glutinous mass of wet feathers rises to her elblows. Milk, unpasteurized, and delivered in bottles with nicked and jagged mouths. A larder, 15 feet and 2 doors from the kitchen, with black slate shelves like a morgue, where cook prefers to park the joint, the fish, the butter, rather than in the Fridge (our contribution to "Springfield', brought from London,) which stands conveniently in the kitchen. (Any ice-box is called a "Fridge", as Fridgidare was the first type ice-box to be used in England. And any vacuum cleaner is called a Hoover, for a similar reason. "Madame, should I Hoover the carpets?" But our vacuum cleaner is out of use for the duration. The carpets are "done" on hands and knees with a dustpan and brush.) An overflow pipe from the second floor bath, that trickles water down the outside of the house.

185

The "extras" that one acquires through living in the country, English country, are fearful and wonderful!

Our London flat was never like this. To think that I ever complained of the fresh soot each morning on the window sills, and unkempt look of mattresses on the dining-room floor (our air raid shelter), the unwrapped bread, piled in hand carts and pawed over by the baker's boy, the queues for fish. Here we live by the sea, and for days there is only chopped skate to be had and whiskered, red gurnet and bowls of laver, a gummy seaweed-like mass of marine life that the Devonians love when fried in blobs.

My! After that list of depressants you would think we didn't like it here. We love it! Any experience--and this living in Instow is an experience--where kindness, friendliness and a measure of security may be found is never really blighted by such mundane things as inconvenience and discomfort.

Also, I remind myself, not a Blitz!

Hardly a siren.

And the view we have!

And the lovely flowers, growing everywhere. No "barrow blossoms," trying to look genteel in tin cans as they are hawked about the London streets.

And the green fields astir with sheep, shadowed by companies of rocks and starlings.

And a sentinel pine upon the lawn.

And the sea--whose tides reflect the mutability of Time, the grandeur of Eternity.

186

I have come full circle in my thoughts.
This living in the country!
Lovely!
Lovely!

The Merry (?) Month of May, 1942

Margareta and little Karin were with us from October, 1941, to April, 1942. Penelope and Karin were like two kittens together. And Margareta was as another daughter in the house. Poor darling, I had hoped to make things easier for her and, instead, the maids were "called up" one after another and Margareta helped in every sort of way in addition to taking care of Karin. Perhaps to be so very, very busy was a slight help in itself. I hope so.

Mrs. D'Almaine, Bob's mother, and Margareta's mother-in-law, came for a visit while Margareta was here. Dorothy was in bed at the time with flue and a bad ear-ache from a cold caught in the draughty Services' Canteen where she and Alix do several shifts a week. Martha had been sleeping on a mattress in Dorothy's room, as no one can get a nurse nowadays. The girls and I were in a dazed condition from incessant vegetable scrubbing, cooking, cleaning and washing-up.

Now I had never met Mrs. D'Almaine. But she hadn't been in the house an hour before it seemed that she had always been there, that we had always known her. Mrs. D'Almaine is a Sister (Registered Nurse) and nursed all through the last war. She took over Dorothy at once, and climbed the two flights of stairs from the kitchen all day long with trays, hot drinks and hot bottles. She also helped with the cooking. No guest ever received so much to do! No guest ever gave so much of herself unstintingly. You couldn't say she had a wonderful time. Yet, in recalling that visit, I remember that she laughed a lot, always finding something to joke about. As a member of the W.V.S. (Women's Voluntary Service) she has been working in a British restaurant in Oxford. Her visit to the "Cotton Canteen" couldn't have been much of a change.

I have since had a card from her saying that she tho't she'd try another form of war work. She was tired of food, which is not to be wondered at! But, upon application to the local Ministry of Labor she had been offered a Baker's "round."

"I can drive a car," writes D'Alie (she is now that to us), "but I doubt my capacities to hop in and out of baker's vans with heavy baskets of heavier bread. Besides, it's food again."

Always finding a laugh to put heart into others. Yet her own heart so full because of dear Bob. A brave woman. There are many, many like her in England these days.

With Appledore (refitting and repair depot for the Royal Navy) just across our tiny bay, a flotilla of small ships up the river, landing operations along the beach with square-jawed leviathans that spew men and tanks upon the sands, a Hospital Ship at anchor in the middle of our view, we have not lost touch with the War. Also, there are the mines. They explode with startling detonations that shake the window frames. Some of the sea mines are washed up in storms, one such batch blasting roofs and windows nearby. Land mines are tested and tried out on the open beaches at the entrance to our bay. Some of the planted mines along the coast have been trod upon by unwary visitors who miss the signs. There have been fatalities, most sadly; among them a young couple--a sergeant on leave, with his fiancee down from London. Walking on the beach they failed to see the sign at the foot of a mined cliff and proceeded to climb. A guard fired his gun in warning. But it is thought that the crashing waves overlapped the sound. At any rate the young couple kept on climbing--to their deaths.

The golf course is ringed with barbed-wire and surrounded by mines. Straying sheep are blown up with unsettling results upon the golfers' play. There is gun practice on the Front. There are convoys of tanks and guns and R.A.F. lorries and Red Cross ambulances on the narrow winding roads. The Bideford Hospital and its Staff (Alix and Martha are V.A.D's there) are pushed to the limit with Service Cases. For the cliffs and beaches of the West Coast of England are used as battle training ground, and the accidents run from flesh wounds to broken necks. Also, of course, there are the "sea incidents." A torpedoed ship produces dozens of burn cases. We are near the Bristol channel, with Lundy Island to be seen on a fine day, and the waters thereabouts and the air make good hunting for the Royal Navy and R.A.F. Coastal Command. Several very dead Nazis have been washed up on the beaches. No, we are not out of the War here.

Early on (as the English say) in this year a young British Navy Lieutenant returned home to Northam across the bay, Lt. Douglas Lambert, R.N. of the submarine "Regent". He became a frequent caller in our home, and a most interesting one. Upon his first appearance he wore the

189

greatcoat of a Yugoslav officer over his R.N. uniform. This quite intrigued us. So did his explanation. We recognized his story as that which had appeared in the newspapers some months earlier.

Lt. Lambert's submarine had been ordered to a Yugoslavian port to take off the British Minister and his staff. Things did not proceed according to plan. The submarine negotiated the tricky waters, mine fields and all, and entered the Yugoslavian harbor, but the proper signals and Mr. Ronald Campbell, the British Minister were not forthcoming. The Germans had occupied the region. Yugoslavia had signed an Armistice, and the Italians were in charge.

After much dickering and parleying--and all the time in extreme peril--it was finally arranged that Lt. Lambert be sent ashore to look for Mr. Campbell. An Italian Army officer boarded the submarine as hostage. But, while Douglas was ashore, Italian aircraft suddenly swirled out of the sky and dive-bombed the submarine. There was nothing for it but to leave, taking the Italian hostage along and trusting Lt. Lambert to make out as best he could.

Months later an exchange of hostages brought Douglas Lambert home to Northam, still wearing the Yugoslavian Officer's greatcoat that he had worn through his internment.

"The dive-bombing was done by Germans in Italian aircraft!"

And now Lt. Douglas Lambert was back in England awaiting fresh orders.

When Douglas left, after that first evening call at "Springfield" he was wearing the greatcoat of a Lieutenant in the royal Navy and doubly proud to do so. Margareta had

190

given him Rob's coat.

In the evenings an armored train shuttles up and down the railroad line along the coast at the foot of our hill. It looks incongruous against the soft and peaceful sunsets, the pale green or early twilight.

Major H (His name must be kept secret for fear of reprisals.) - is C.O. He comes in of a late evening now and then for a cup of tea and a chat. Sometimes a brother officer is with him. They are both fed up with "training" (no pun intended) and long for action.

"To keel a Cherman--many Chermans!"

How they envy the young Polish lads in the R.A.F. For Major H- was of the Polish Army and fought in Warsaw at the dreadful beginning of this War. Escaping from that city after its fall, he left his wife and children in their country home. And never a word since has he had. He broods. Who wouldn't? And has a fine hate stored up against the day when he again will fight the Germans.

"It will come--that day. Nefer fear, nefer fear."

And his brother officer, K--, who can speak but little English nods his head vociferously and glowers, and tears well in his eyes. "I keel--I keel--Oh, I keel!" And he clenches and unclenches his hands.

He is the sole survivor of a family of six. The Germans lined up his father, mother, two brothers, a sister and himself in the courtyard of their home in Warsaw. Then shot them.

"Bang! Bang! Bang! So, I fall!"

And Major H--explains that K--, wounded, fell to the

191

ground and feigned death.   Later that night K--scaled the courtyard wall.

There is no forgetting in the eyes of either Major H-- or K--. there is only one purpose in their lives.

Such scenes as they have witnessed must curdle one's innermost being. I should be sick--sick--all the rest of my life. And my soul and heart would have shriveled into hard cancerous knots of hate.

Make certain that the Victims of this War and their Liberators sit side by side at the Peace Table. (When Major H-- and K-- were transferred, Major H-- presented me with a book of Polish songs as a farewell gift. The music I can cope with, but the words are quite unintelligible. However, the friendly appreciation that came along with the book, that I can completely understand.)

In spells we have a Staff.   That is; Cook, House-Parlormaid and Housemaid. Here, in England, domestic help is paid very little by American Standards. In the States one pays for a cook what here one pays for a more than adequate Staff (Remember the date!). In a sprawling house with nine bedrooms--and having a voluntary commitment (from our hearts) to both the British and American Red Cross to put up active convalescent Officers or just Officers on leave--either from the British Forces or the American Services--we are dependent on some help other than Alix, Martha and myself.

But suddenly there's a "call-up" and Ruby, the House-maid, departs for the W.A.A.F.'s (Women's Auxiliary Air Force). This is more of a calamity than it appears. For now

Cook wants to know who'll do the vegetables? Freda the House-parlormaid, says it's not her job. What about her hands for serving at table? And what about the ironing? Is she taking that over? But that's really the Housemaid's job!

"It's not my place, M'am."

That prim and precise and often final expression is heard externally nowadays. And the replacements one acquires through the local Domestic Bureaus!!! Oh!

There was Rachel, for instance. "The Smasher," we called her. As House-Parlormaid for several months, her intentions were of the best. But she went about like a whirlwind, and with the same devastation.

At one time I had a pair of country girls called up at the same time. They left my employment together. Four pair of hose went with them! Since these were new hose sent from home as a gift and preserved for the future, in jam jars à la instructions from the Clothing Board, their loss was a definite calamity. Hose here are rationed. Also, the fit and wearing quality of English wartime hose is something one cannot discuss with calm.

But, in spite of the domestic "misfits," I also have my share of "treasures" who create a real loss to my household when the War transfers them, in necessary turn, to factory, field, or Force.

Fortunately the girls and I as Americans, can do 'most anything. We are domestic Jills-of-all-trades. But now we miss the American household gadgets! Oh, my oh, my!

Still the Merry Month of May, 1942

I feel pushed around and rather lost in the shuffle nowadays. But I wouldn't have it otherwise. The American Eagle Club (Members are American -- who enlisted in R.A.F. via Canada -- before U.S.A. entered War - Dick is one of the founders), and the American Red Cross send us boys on leave who want to spend their precious respite from battle in a home with a friendly atmosphere, which is about all that we can offer save for the lovely country hereabouts and a bit of riding and fishing. But this appears to be enough, for the young officers arrive very tired--wanting sleep, mostly, in a bed with sheets. And they lie in the sun, when there is any. Fortunately we have had some gorgeous golden spells. Then we have tea out on the lawn, and the grass is flattened by lilos and cushions all in a good cause. With Penny and the two dogs. and upon occasion one or two horses, the front lawn of the house is never quiet. I can look out my bedroom window almost any afternoon as I change for tea and discover one, two or three uniforms that were not there the last time I looked. If it's the first of the week--O.K. there will be "marg" enough for bread or scones, with jam (rationed). If it's the end of the week, we must do something with cheese (also rationed). But tea there is--always. The men bring their ration cards--a real bonus.

The heat of the day has caused my mind to boil, and out of the stew of memories--like taking a rabbit from a hat--I pick one of our visits to London during the past year. It was just about a year ago (mid-May, 1941) and there had been more raids, one of them particularly heavy with H.E.'s (high explosives) and incendiaries. Hartley Davies had come into the Park Lane Hotel for dinner with Dick and me, and the raid of Saturday, May tenth, became a conversation piece. Hartley was sure that it was the worst that he had so far experienced and we quite agreed. (We had arrived a few days after this raid, but had read and heard of it. In the many later accounts of this particular raid, the night of May 10, 1941 is called "the Night of the Fire".) Only a miracle could have left St. Paul's still standing, its spire like the finger of God pointing to Heaven. For the ruins close about the Cathedral fan out into an immense area of destruction, mute testimony to a colossal raid.

Hartley and Betty Moss, a friend of Martha's, had been at the Savoy dancing that evening. Suddenly the sirens and bombs screamed simultaneously. No warning at all! Hartley spoke to us in such prideful terms of Betty's courage and aplomb throughout the raid that I took a good look at his face. What I saw made me remark later to Dick, "Hartley's in love with Betty. He's going to marry her. Wait and see."

Last month (On April 8th, 1942) Hartley and Betty were married in St. Geroge's, Hanover Square. We all went up to London for the wedding, and the reception following at Claridges. It was a lovely affair, a charming interlude where most of us forgot the War for a few hours.

But, that evening a year ago when I first felt this wedding to be possible, Dick, Hartley and I were discussing the War at dinner--as one does most of the time--and I happened to mention that I would very much like to have a look at the extraordinary night life crowding the Underground platforms. The raids were driving people to shelters again;

assorted crowds made up of transients, groups of neighbors, whole families, were practically <u>living</u> in the underground like rabbits in a warren. Neither Dick nor I had seen this typical sight of War-time London as we, ourselves, had never sheltered in the Underground. So now we, including Hartley, decided to tour the platform shelters by the simple expedient of taking the Underground from Green Park Station (Piccadilly) to the Bank Station ("The City"). I shall never forget the panorama of those grotesquely crowded platforms at each station as we progressed. When we got out at the Bank Station platform and stood among the conglomerate mass of human beings there, living their particular private lives in such utter publicity--why, the scene just didn't seem real!

Four tiers of bunks--mere slats or springs between iron piping--stretched the length of the Underground station platform. There before us was a community of families preparing for the night. And I really mean preparing, for some of the girls were putting their hair in curlers or creaming their faces, and youngsters were being toddled back from the "conveniences," mug in hand, towels flapping. Those people lucky enough to be near a light were reading. Women and men sat about talking, or rather, shouting because of the trains--and, if one could have heard such a homely sound as a snore in that cacophony of noise, I am sure that there were many in all keys. For some people were already abed and asleep, wrapped in grubby, parti-colored blankets. Others were rolled up in quilts on the hard, concrete flooring. A young couple lay beneath an eiderdown nose to nose, the young man's breath stirring the stray curls on his beloved's brow. A youth <u>leant</u> against the wall deep in a book. "Poems of . . ." was all that I could see. Young love and poetry--the sturdy will to live--and resignation

196

of the tough sort--it was all there before me. I shall never forget it.

We went up from the Bank Station platform (Dick, Hartley, and I) through the long tunnel, itself as crowded as the platform, that led to the stairs beneath the streets of "The City" ("The City" is the financial district of London, as "Wall Street" is of New York.) of London. As we came up and out into those self-same streets, nearby the Mansion House where the Lord Mayor lives, the ugly, black crater left by the H.E. bomb yawned almost at our feet. There was a bit of a fog in the air, so the tempered moonlight seemed to fall in winding sheets about the buildings.

The three of us stood, hesitant and silent, staring at that roped off, gaping space. Here was where an H.E. had made a direct hit--through to a large public shelter. Here was where many defenseless men, women and children had been killed, injured, buried alive. Here was the Mark of the Beast. And not the only Mark. And not the last--alas.

Dick's Dutch agent, Hans D . . . (Name omitted in fear of reprisals.) of Amsterdam, had escaped to England. It was primarily to see him that Dick had come to London on this particular trip last May. So Hans came into the Park Lane Hotel, and we talked far into the evening. He had so much bottled up inside him of terrible experiences and worse sights that he looked acutely ill, as though poisoned by something, as indeed he was. By the Nazis! I will give the highlights of what he had to say.

Hans and his wife were in Rotterdam when the Germans bombed it.

"Hell on earth!" said Hans. "I went into the streets afterwards trying to help. There were bodies all 'round. Two women leaning against a house had blood running down their faces. Their clothes were torn. They tried to call me. But when they opened their mouths they couldn't speak. Only more blood ran out of their mouths. When I touched them they just collapsed in a heap--stone dead. I seem to see <u>them</u> mostly when I think of Rotterdam.

Then there were the parachutists! They came down all over the place. The men and boys were popping them off like birds. Ping! The Nazis would double up like they had a stomach-ache. By god! I liked doing that! So did everyone who had a gun.

My wife and I were put in concentration camps--one camp after another. We saw terrible things. The worst was when the Gestapo took a crowd of Jews from our camp and herded them into a church. All the women and children were just pushed and stuffed into that church 'till there was no more room. Then the Gestapo shut the doors. The men and boys were then made to dig a huge grave before the front door. When the grave was ready the Gestapo went around to the back door and drove the women and children out the front door into it, and pushed them in with their bayonets. The men were forced to shovel earth over the people. They struggled terribly. There was a lot of shooting. And when the grave was filled the Gestapo shot all the men and boys. And the earth went like this for hours." Hans moved his hands in slow undulations. "We could see it from the camp!"

That had happened months ago. But the sweat came

out of his brow and his hands shook as he lit a cigarette. "Can I ever forget?"

Eventually Hans and his wife escaped. They <u>walked</u> over the Pyrenees. Eight months of walking and hiding and bribing themselves out of tight places with cigarettes and money. They had started with $40,000, but when they arrived in Lisbon where they could get a ship to England, they were down to but a few hundred.

There they became separated. It was understood that, accommodations for only one of them being available, Mrs. D. . . was simply going ahead of her husband. He was to follow on the next ship to England. But through some unexplained error Mrs. D. . . had been sent to Jamaica! There she still was, but in custody for "undeclared monies."

"Like a woman," said Hans, shrugging his shoulders, "she hid the bit of extra ($100 bill) instead of declaring it. She was afraid of having it taken away."

He made two fans of his thin fingers.

"Put the bill in her compact, behind the mirror. Of course she was searched, and of course they found the money! Now she wants to join me. How?"

He looked at Dick. His brown eyes were as pleading as a spaniel's.

"Will you help me, Mr. Cotton?"

The matter was discussed at length. Help for Mrs. D..could come only from the States where Dick was going in a few months on another mission. Hans, himself, would accept a small loan--" just a little for now"--but he turned down the job Dick offered. He wanted to fight with the Dutch, of course.

A university graduate with years of business experience, he later went to sea as a radio operator on a Dutch war vessel.

Any way to get at the Nazis! And some months later his wife joined him in England, by way of the States. (We have a very precious but sad momento of this family tragedy. After the war Hans and his wife returned to Holland. Hans went to his parents' home. It stood intact. But his parents were gone--first into a Concentration Camp, then into the Ovens. How does one live with such a memory!)

At the foot of his parent's garden Hans found a certain spot, and dug up the family silver and treasures hidden there. Among them was a very unusual and beautiful reproduction in Dutch silver of a castle.

The back of this fabulous ornament (which is 8 1/4" x 4" and stands 3" high) is formed by eight peaked turrets, linked. These turrets represent the facade of a castle upon which there are three balconies. And jutting from each turret is a flagpole with a flag which flies--it really moves. There are 7 entrances with human figures before each.

Before the facade of the castle is a moat with waves 'whereon are two sailboats with men at the helms.

There are two drawbridges which work up and down--one at either end of the moat. On one drawbridge there is a gate-tender by a wheel--on the other is a coach crossing to the castle.

On a 1" wide roadway before the moat is a second coach, complete with two horses, coachman and two footmen. There were also an outrider and several pedestrians.

To believe this object of art you must see it. It is a miracle of Dutch artisanship in silver. My husband had always admired it when in Hans' parents' home. Hans gave it to Dick. We treasure it for more reasons than one.

July 17, 1942.

Well! I have to pinch myself and say, "Is it you, still you, Peg Cotton? Or is it the Queen who has been riding in a procession this afternoon through streets lined with a flag-waving and cheering populace?" For I feel exceedingly grand in that particular sense. Instead, no doubt (in reverse), the Queen after one of her public appearances or state visits,--say to a war factory,--pinches herself upon her return to the palace and says, "Is it you, Ma'm? Or is it the blonde warworker who was so clever with that oily punch-machine at the factory this afternoon? For I feel exceedingly weary and my head buzzes from the factory clatter."

I think I have an emotional hangover this evening from a potent mixture of pride and patriotism. Dick and I were among the honored guests of "The Mayor, Alderman and Burgesses of the Borough of Barnstaple. . . . on the occasion of the presentation to His Excellency the Hon. John G. Winant, Ambassador of the United States of America to the Court of St. James, of the Honorary Freedom of the Borough at the Guild Hall, Barnstaple, on Friday the 17th, July, 1942 at 3 p.m." We consequently feel positively historic, almost legendary in fact. "The Cottons were of the party. Mr. and Mrs. Richards W. Cotton of Boston, Mass., U.S.A. sat in the row behind the Burgesses at the Guildhall." the whole affair to me, and I think to Dick also, will be unforgettable. And perhaps one day I shall quaveringly relate to my great-grandchild, "There we were--your great-grandfather and I--riding in Lady Astor's car. And your great-aunt Martha stood among the people by the roadside and waved an American flag among all the British ones."

And indeed it was so.

Martha said to me later, "Mother, I never thought I'd stand on the kerb and wave a flag as you and Daddy rode by."

Well, neither did I. And, of course, the flag-waving was for Mr. and Mrs. Winanat, and Dick and I were really at the very tail end of the procession, in the last car in fact. But still we were there, and feeling as puffed up and high as barrage balloons. Although I don't suppose I should assume that Dick felt like a barrage balloon just because I did.

It had showered in the morning and the streets of Barnstaple were wet. Later the sun turned the wet streets into shining mirrors. reflecting the animated and happy scenes. I know that Mr. and Mrs. Winant were happy and touched by their welcome in that one thousand year old town of Barnstaple, North Devon, where young and old turned out to welcome them.

Mr. Winant said, "Thank you for your welcome to Mrs. Winant and me, and I would like to say we were especially grateful to the children. I do not think there could be any happier welcome even at the gates of Heaven."

The scene at the old Guild Hall above the Market was a blending of Tradition and the Present. In the Speakers' balcony were Mr. and Mrs. Winant, the Mayor of Barnstaple and the many Lord Mayors and Mayoresses (Lady Astor is Mayoress of Plymouth, South Devon.) of Devon, their colorful robes and chains of office positively regal to us Americans. About the long table in the center of the Guild Hall, whereon reposed "the famous Gold and Silver Plate of the Corporation," were ranged the Aldermen and Burgesses, the latter in blue robes and enormous blue velvet berets similar to the one that Henry VIII wears in the Hogarth painting. The gathering of civil guests

202

was well sprinkled with the Khaki, the Blue, and the Grey Blue of the various services. Gold braid and decorations made small bright patterns in the tapestry thus presented, its border a mingling of American and British flags against the walls. The whole scene reminded me of an historic picture such as "The first American Congress," wherein stands one of my ancestors, Elbridge T. Gerry. I felt a warm glow within me, and it is still there this evening.

When Mr. Winant rose to speak, a low lock of black hair lending shadow to deep set eyes already shadowed by heavy brows, his friendly smile illuminating an otherwise sober and thoughtful face, there was a burst of applause. Then an expectant hush fell over the Guild Hall.

I am sure that I was not the only person present who saw a likeness to Lincoln in our Ambassador to the Court of St. James. That likeness has been remarked often. And, like Lincoln, John Gilbert Winant has the Humanities and Freedom for All deeply rooted in his heart. He also has the courage to expound these doctrines, and the knowledge and experience to promote their growth.

"We cannot afford to tolerate large scale unemployment, malnutrition and bad housing conditions . . . Out of the event of the recent past there should emerge a heightened consciousness of the meaning and value of Freedom, and the realization that Freedom in its best sense cannot survive without the fullest cooperation between those who value it in all parts of the world. Civilization can only be placed on an enduring basis when its benefits are extended fully to all communities and to all peoples within each community."

"Hear, hear," from the audience, in enthusiastic repetition.

After the speeches a short reception was held in the mayor's Parlor. Dick and I had a chat with Lady Astor. She is a forthright and dynamic person. Although a Virginian by birth, there are no languid attitudes of the proverbial Southern Belle about her. Upon learning that we came from Boston, Massachusetts, Lady Astor threw her head up in a challenging manner. "Ha!" she said, "Another Damn-Yank!" Shot out her right arm in the gesture of a sword thrust, and gave Dick a good poke in the chest. Needless to say, after that vigorous introduction our conversation became quite spirited.

As we all progressed from the Guild Hall to Broadgate House (now a nursery for bombed-out children financed by the people of Barnstable, Massachusetts, and which Mrs. Winant "opened"), from there to Queen Anne's Walk by the River Taw, and thence to the ancient Penrose Alms-houses, I felt that Mrs. Winant appreciated Lady Astor's lively approach and greetings to the various welcoming committees. Mrs. Winant could thus relax into her own particular quiet charm and sweetness that require few words. She has an almost spiritual smile, although often plagued by (and perhaps because of) the devastating twinges of Tic Doloreux. And there is a certain little-girl quality in her face, beneath the Burns-Jones hats she chooses.

At tea in Bromley's Cafe later, as two regimental Bands vied with each other, Martha remarked to me, "Look at Mrs. Winant's feet, Mother." We were seated at the neighboring table with the Deputy Mayor, Mr. Oliver, and his daughter, Mrs. Hughes.

I looked.

Mrs. Winant's feet, in their sophisticated, high heeled shoes, were rolled over on their outer edges, sole to sole, in little-girl fashion.

I smiled. "I expect she's very, very tired."

Hilda Dravers (Now the wife of Colonel R.S. Hawkins, R.A.), a friend of Martha's visiting us, was at the celebration, also, and the two girls wanted to meet Mr. and Mrs. Winant. So Dick took them over and introduced them.

"And do you know what Mr. Winant said to me, Mother? When he shook hands with me he said, 'I am very glad to know you. Your father has been a good friend to me.' Isn't that wonderful?"

He, John Gilbert Winant, would find sincerity and scope in any help or service rendered him no matter how small that help or service and he would not forget it.

My heart and mind are happily full this evening. I have acquired a very lovely memory for the future.

July 19th, 1942.
Blandford, Dorsetshire.

Speech Day at Bryanston School.

It has been a perfect summer's day with sun and haze. Dorset is a lovely county. The old town of Blandford, on one side of the river, with Bryanston School (formerly the home of the Duke of Portland) on the opposite bank, presents a rural setting of Peace and Beauty. Indeed, it is hard to believe that there is a War--that it is the 3rd year of War in fact! The rolling lawns of Bryanston, the playing fields, the boathouse among the willows, the long drives darkened by tall arching trees, all seem so serene. Yet, there is an enormous Army Camp close by the school. And some of the "Military" have even encroached upon the school grounds. A Searchlight Battery is set up on the Cricket Pitch and lines of Army lorries crowd the grass verge along the entrance drive. There are craters beside the playing fields where bombs have whistled down at night, too close for comfort.

There is Beauty.
But there is not Peace.
Bryanston School is an English Public School; we would call it a (private) Boarding School. In spite of petrol rationing and wartime travel quite a few parents were present. The gym was packed at speech time.

I was much impressed by the speech of Mr. Tharold Coade, the Headmaster. Just a few lines from it: ---"Here at this school we try to cultivate responsiveness as the basis of education------close contact with others of his own age trains a boy by experience---a far better teacher than precept.-----his social conscience is trained to take responsibility appropriate to his age---a boy, while living here at school, should become aware that, while his roots are in the past, he is living out in the present a community life which he hopes and believes to see perpetuated in the future.----"

There was sincerity and vision in the address, and definite planning to make that vision a success. Mr. Coade meets the harsh realism of today with a sure touch. If boys must go to war let them be trained, give them a chance to understand and cope with the danger and dangerous mechanics of War. The 554th Squadron of the Air Training Corps has been formed at Bryanston School. Many of the senior boys are now in uniform. Gerry is one of them. I found my eyes misting over at the Review of the Squadron, the final event of Speech Day. When the boys snapped by, arms swinging in the British fashion, eyes right, their faces set in unboyish severity, it did something to my heart. I didn't like it. Neither did a lot of other mothers, I could see, but we are all terribly proud just the same.

And we all shall pray at night, over and over again, "Dear God, please, please end this dreadful war. Soon. Soon."

During the next few months I made several "speeches," (I don't know what else to call them), to "open" various Shows in aid of the many war charities, to give information on American Aid to Britain at one period, and later to explain and to promote Anglo-American friendship. I always found my audience responsive. This, I believe, arose from a true interest in America and Americans and not from a charitable feeling toward the one American who was there speaking to them. I shall always be grateful for the kindness and friendliness extended to me at such times.

The very first time I spoke was on Thanksgiving Day, 1940, before the Girls Club in Bideford, and the young people were so keen to learn of America--of American Youth and the American Way of Life that I just kept on talking and passing around American magazines and newspapers (and did the English girls' eyes pop at the Sunday edition of the New York Times!) and answering questions, as it was most informal, until I had to be told to stop! It was past blackout hour. Thereafter I always inquired as to the length of speech desired.

Because I found pleasure in this service of friendship I dare to include here in this Journal some of the "speeches" or part thereof with explanatory notes on time and place--in the hope that the data thus presented may afford some interest to others.

I open a Garden Fete in Bideford for the Bideford Girls' Club.

We had absolutely no Staff (maids) at the time. The girls and I were running around from morning to night like the seven dwarfs, but not whistling while we worked. On this particular afternoon Alix was V.A.D.-ing at the Hospital and Martha was helping at the Clinic. So I arranged for a woman to come in and look after Penny. She was to arrive on the two o'clock bus from Bideford and I was to take the 2:30 bus from Instow into Bideford. The Fete was to be opened at three o'clock.

Everything went wrong, save for the fact that Penny slept at naptime, and continued to sleep as I hurriedly dressed for my "debut." At 2:15 I was out on the front lawn scanning the distant road for the lumbering double-decker that would bring my Relief on the Home Shift. Sister Anne had been no more anxious than I. It was hot, and I began to wilt.

With the wild idea of rushing next door to Mrs. Kerr, a neighbor who, because of past kindness, I knew would help me, I started down the drive and met the Relief at the gate.

"Thank Heaven!" I exclaimed. "Where have you been? Penny is still asleep, but should be up and out." With a parting, "You know what to do," I dashed for the 2:30 bus.

"Oh, my goodness, my goodness," I muttered like the

208

rabbit in ALICE IN WONDERLAND, looking at my watch every ten seconds. "Don't let me miss it. Don't let me miss it."

Wasted breath and worry. I stood for half an hour at the bus stop, at the foot of the hill, in a growing queue of restive people, among them a Salvation Army girl who had a sympathetic gleam in her eye for my very evident nervousness.

No doubt that old bus had broken down. They are always doing it now. The gas-producing trailers attached, to save petrol, are must unreliable. They give up entirely now and then. One often spends ages in a static bus in forced contemplation of the rural scene. Sometimes the gas trailers catch fire and then everyone gets out and waits for the replacement. I drew a most temperamental bus one day. It was when Doreen was visiting us. She and I were returning from market in Barnstaple, and suddenly for no apparent reason the darn bus commenced to go backwards! And refused to do otherwise absolutely. No doubt that was what the 2:30 bus from Barnstaple to Bideford was doing.

My speech kept milling about in my head and the words became so insistent that I furtively looked about myself. Had I said them aloud?

3 o'clock.

In desperation I ran across the road to the District Nurse's Cottage. "Please May I use your phone? The bus is late and I'm late, and I simply can't be late."

Perhaps Dick could come from the factory and fetch me. I 'phoned the Works.

"Mr. cotton is busy on a trunk (long distance) call."

"Oh, dear! It's most important."

"I'll see what I can do,"said the factory operator. "Will you wait?"

I waited. Then the moving shadow of the bus fell across the glass panels of the front door. Dropping the receiver to dangle on it's wire, I fled from the cottage screaming, "Stop! Oh, Stop!" But the bus had already stopped. The smiling Salvation Army girl held out a hand to pull me onto the rear platform.

I asked them to stop for you," she said. "I could see that you were most anxious to get this bus."

Christian discernment and a Christian act.

"You've no idea!" I gasped.

By the time I reached my destination I was not surprised to find a delegation of worried looking women, in garden party finery, half way down the road to meet me.

"The bus! The 2:30 bus never came! I had to take the 3 o'clock."

Still apologizing, I was ushered up a long drive and introduced to Prebendary Manning of the Parish Church in Bideford, who, in turn was to introduce me. He was most kind and understanding and had a sense of humor. The Fete was held on a broad lawn before the terrace of a rambling country house. So, grasping me firmly by one elbow, Prebendary Manning and I navigate the slippery grass slope in record time.

"How do I address you? Do I say Mr. Manning? Or do you have a title?

I wasn't sure what Prebendary was.

"Say Prebendary. Mr. Manning would be all right, but I am really Prebendary."

"Prebendary." I repeated. "Prebendary. I do hope I can manage it."

"You will," he laughed, and steered me to a vantage

point beneath some lovely trees.

There was a spatter of applause and I became so terrified that I prayed for an air raid. Any diversion!

"Now," said Prebendary Manning in a soothing voice. And then, facing the audience, he boomed out jovially "I am afraid we have something else for which to blame Hitler. There was no 2:30 bus for Mrs. Cotton. It broke down. Of course we wouldn't have buses with gas-trailers that break down if we had enough petrol and, of course, we would have enough petrol if it weren't for the War, and, of course, we wouldn't have a War if it weren't for Hitler. So I think we all agree that Hitler is to blame for Mrs. Cotton's delay in getting here this afternoon."

Everyone laughed. I managed my speech and the Fete was opened.

Don't ever tell me the English are standoffish. They are really most friendly. It is just that they express themselves differently. And, if you want to learn the temper of a people, live among them, don't just "stay awhile."

I had a lovely time that afternoon. Prebendary Manning and his very charming wife gave me tea, served at long tables on the upper terrace. Members of the Girls Club "waited." The scones, cakes, and buns were all home made. The atmosphere and spirit were like that of the May Breakfasts our Women's Clubs at home in the States used to give each year. A community and homely effort.

I have a theory that it is just because we Americans and English are truly so much alike that we don't agree--like a mother and daughter who, because they have similar characteristics, argue on many points. I really believe that if we (Americans and English) didn't speak the same language, we would get on better. When dealing with another language, one makes a greater effort to understand the people as well as the language.

Well, here is my little opening speech.

"Prebendary Manning, Ladies and Gentlemen. I feel very complimented and honored to be asked to open this Fete. A ceremony such as this is so decidedly English that for you to think of me, an American, to do it for you, is most friendly. It is heartwarming.

This Fete is primarily for young people and gotten up by them. That is right in keeping with the times we live in. for like Mrs. Roosevelt, I believe that young people are important people and have a great deal to contribute to our way of Life.

I do not like to say, 'It is their day', for it is not a happy day nor one of their choice--this War and all that goes with it. Some of the heaviest, and certainly the most active, part of this War falls on the youth of your country and mine. And the responsibility for a safe, secure and sane future depends on them. That is a large order.

Their health, their education, and their guidance (I refer to religion and ideals) must be the foremost concern of England and America after this War. Plans for such are even now being made, splendid plans. I expect to see them come true.

So I feel very happy to be here today because I think that real friendship prompted your thought of me, an American. And that just so surely as large and beautiful buildings rise from placing one brick upon another brick, just so surely will a great, lasting and understanding friendship between England and America rise from all the individual friendships now forming here and at home between You and Us.

We English speaking people are going to stick together--really stick together this time, like true friends, smoothing out the large difficulties, overlooking the small ones and finding a lot to like in each other: And build on that. We can.

And so, in the name of Friendship, I declare this Fete open."

Trite as it seems I meant every word of it. I find that sincerity usually is met with friendliness. I certainly felt it there at the Garden Fete in Bideford, August, 1942--and many, many times afterward.

"The English people are a friendly people." A good first sentence for a Primer on Anglo-American Relations.

By the time Dick called for me at six o'clock that afternoon on his way home from the factory, I felt I had acquired a host of friends. Also, I had two baskets of vegetables, herbs and flowers, a collection of oddments from the White Elephant Stall and a large box of buns and cakes sold after tea.

"Peg! Do you feel all right?" asked Dick as I climbed in the car.

"Well, I'm a bit tired." I answered. "Why? Do I look awful?"

"I thought there might be something wrong with your head!" came in caustic tones as we rolled out of the driveway.

"Whatever are you talking about! Did you hear my speech?", a dreadful possibility pushing itself into my mind.

"No. but whatever were you trying to do this afternoon at three o'clock?"

"Oh, that," I said, remembering the incomplete phone calls to the factory.

"Yes,--THAT--. I am interrupted in the midst of an important trunk call to be told that my wife wants me, at once, that Mrs. Cotton sounded frantic!"

"I was."

"So I call the house I get no answer. I ring three times. Then I get out the car and drive to 'Springfield.' I yell through all the rooms and find no one. I thought something must have happened to Penny. Then the house 'phone rings and the factory tells me they've located Mrs. Cotton at the Fete!"

My husband looked as though he had swallowed a toad.

"So I go back to the factory. You ought to be jailed for making me waste all that petrol!"

"It was Hitler's fault," I expostulated.

"Now I <u>know</u> there's something wrong with your head," groaned Dick.

So I told him of the bus that never appeared, of my frantic efforts to get him on the phone, and of what Prebendary Manning said when he introduced me.

"So you see, dear, you can blame it all on Hitler."

My patient and forbearing husband grinned. But somehow I don't think I really convinced him.

The last week of August, 1942, was a very full one: crammed with housework, principally cooking (for Ethel, the cook, was now in Dick's factory and quite content with an oily machine and long hours, also more money), several guests, a christening and another "speech." The weather was gorgeous, hot and scented. Kay and Bill Williams had come for a visit bringing their little 18 months old Vanessa and nursemaid.

Kay and Bill are sentimental over this part of Devon, for Bill used to tour the West Coast as a member of a cricket team and Kay and Bill spent their honeymoon along these shores. Now their little daughter was to be christened in the tiny picturesque old 12th century church of St. John's, Instow.

Speaking of Instow, the long shadow of coincidence again falls upon us. For Pete's grandparents once had a cottage here in Instow, and Dorothy used to bring Pete when he was very young for summer visits, wheeling him on the Front as we wheel Penny. Now Pete's grandparents lie in the old churchyard of St. John's. And Dorothy is here (with us) in Instow with her grandchild.

We have known Kay and Bill (Mr. and Mrs. Ralph Williams) ever since the summer of 1935. When we first came to England (To be explicit, Dick arrived in London in mid-December of 1934. I followed, with the children, in February, 1935.), in February of that year, we took a flat on Hamilton Terrace, St. John's Wood, London, and in the top flat of the adjacent house lived five young men--the four Wilson brothers (Chris, Dave, Horsey and Geoff) and Bill Williams. Chris was almost our first caller and remains one of our best friends, though it is a long time since we have seen him. He is now Major C.M. Wilson, Queen's Royal Regiment, and is in the Middle East as a Supply Officer.

I wish to digress a bit here.

I remember very well that first evening we met Chris and Bill. We Cottons were sitting in the drawing-room of our London flat--a bit homesick and a bit bored--when the doorbell rang that early Spring evening of 1935. Two young men were ushered in. I think every one of us had the same mental reaction. How very English! And why wouldn't they be,

215

goodness knows? The two young men were wearing white flannels, "Old Boys" ("Old Boys" is synonymous with our "Alumni" and "Old Girls" with Alumnae.) blazers, School ties and long white woolen scarves, wrapped about their necks like boa constrictors and reaching nearly to their plimsoles (sneakers). They had tennis racquets tucked under their arms, and shy but friendly grins shone on their faces. They introduced themselves--Chris doing the honors--and in the course of time Chris Wilson and Bill Williams became frequent and most welcome guests in our home.

Our friendship with them has been cemented by arguments for the young men had to learn to understand us Americans (if they ever have!), and we certainly had to learn the English viewpoint and also the customs of the country. For, When In Rome, do as the Romans do.

When we first arrived in London, Alix, Martha and Gerry used to walk about St. John's Wood, exploring. School for them was not to start until Fall. The children always had something strange, or funny, to report upon their return home: the "milk floats" that were nothing at all like ours (milk shakes with ice cream), but were rubber-tired dairy carts drawn by cobs; the barrows of flowers so cheap; the pearly Kings and Queens; the game of Cricket and it's odd terminology, a "googly," a "yorker," "silly point," "silly mid-on." But one day the girls were not amused. They had identical complaints and spoke them simultaneously as they came into the drawing-room.

"We are not going walking with Gerry anymore! Not in those clothes, anyway."

They indicated Gerry's brown corduroy knickers, plaid

lumber-jacket and tweed cap with dark distaste.

"He gets whistled at!"

You're too fussy," said Gerry imperturbably, and went out onto the balcony.

But I saw what the girls meant. As an American boy in America he was O.K., but as an American boy in England he was anything but posh!

I took Gerry down town the next day and bought him the typical long gray flannels and gray jacket and gray Eton cap of an English lad. He looked considerably toned down, but his spirits were still decidedly American. He missed the games of baseball and catch on the park at home with the gang. Life in the London flat can pall on a boy of ten. We got compaints now and then from sundry neighbors of a misdirected tennis ball or of the crash of an empty "Squash" (soft drink) bottle down the shaft of the tradesmen's lift. But then we didn't care for the crash, now and then, of another type of empty bottle on the gravel paths of our garden late at night-- or the early morning, very early morning shouts of someone who had forgotten his key.

One evening we had a most unwelcome visitor. Dick was out. I was reading in the drawing room alone, as the children were all in bed. The girls' room opened out of the drawing-room at one side, and the long triple window of their bedroom overlooked the garden, one floor below, where adjacent to the house ran a terrace with a low brick wall.

So suddenly and so silently did the girls' bedroom door open that, at first, I didn't believe what I only too clearly saw--a man in shirt sleeves carrying a bunch of roses, and obviously drunk. He came unsteadily to meet me and beyond him, in the now lighted bedroom, Alix and Martha sat huddled in their

217

respective eiderdowns, their eyes like luminous marbles.

"He came in the window, Mother!"

"And he's taken the roses out of the vase!"

"What do you want?", I demanded.

"You!" said the drunk.

He said it the way a ghost says, "Boo!" And I had the usual reaction. I was scared.

"If you don't get out of here at once I shall call the police!"

"Naughty, naughty," said the drunk and shook a heavy-headed rose in my face.

My instinctive bats at the flower were translated by the drunk into belligerence. He backed away, and I got behind him. It was then only a matter of seconds to propel him through the flat and out the front door.

In a way, I hoped Dick might be returning at that moment, and, in another way, I didn't. The drunk with his flourishing posies was not a sight to inspire the confidence of any husband. But later, I knew, we would laugh about it. We did.

That strange incident of the unknown drunk and our happy times with the Wilson boys and Bill Williams as our neighbors, seem a long time ago now and, when one figures that about half the time has been spent in a War, it seems even longer. Our flat on Hamilton Terrace and later the maisonette in Regency Lodge, on Avenue Road, London, seem a long way from "Springfield," Instow. The Wilson boys are scattered among the various Services and Bill Williams is a Quantitive Surveyor, building camps for the Army. He and Kay lost all their possessions in the Battle of Britain, but they are thankful

218

to be together.

Back to "Springfield."

It was lovely having them here at "Springfield." The christening of their little daughter on August 28th was a sweet party. The girls invited some young friends and, of course, our dear Gambles and the Rector and his wife, Rev. and Mrs. Robinson. Martha was Godmother and we all went to St. John's Church, including Penny. After the ceremony we returned here for the christening cake and rum punch, which even little Vanessa sampled.

It was a real hot day, most unusual. The air simmered. So, although the punch was iced, (our blessed American "fridge!") two of the guests felt it and had to sit down. To my horror, one was the Rector's wife. But both she and her husband laughed at my solicitude.

"I was tired to start with," said Mrs. Robinson, "and should have known better. But the punch was so lovely and cold. I am now going to be late for choir practice."

"She's really very wicked," laughed the Rector. "Next time I'll bring a wheelbarrow."

It was comforting to find such a sense of humor in the Rector, and his wife has a girlish enthusiasm for new people and new scenes.

While the Williamses were with us I was asked to "say a few words" about our American Red Cross at the first meeting in Bideford of "Relatives of Prisoners of War." The British Red Cross planned to open a Social Center in Bideford where friends and relatives might meet and exchange letters and news concerning Prisoners of War.

Mrs. Symmes, Commandant in the British Red Cross, runs a clinic (Duart House) in Bideford, for sick children, principally evacuees. The work is voluntary and a full time job. Mrs. Symmes' sister does the marketing and the cooking. The staff is quite inadequate and the clinic often overcrowded. Martha spends her mornings there at Duart. Her year's medical training comes in handy. There is always plenty to do, from a session in the office of correspondence and phone calls, to bed baths, "temps," and even delousing. The state some of these children are in when they arrive! But Martha loves it at the clinic. Formerly a V.A.D., Martha joined the British Red Cross and now wears its uniform.

Because we are Americans and because our English friends are truly grateful and wish to say thank you for the help which has come pouring across from America to bombed-out families here in England and to British Prisoners of War, Mrs. Symmes paid me the compliment of asking that I speak at the opening meeting of Relatives of Prisoners of War in Bideford. I couldn't refuse a person who does so much good for others and works so hard doing it.

Knowing that I stood proxy for all Americans I felt a deep responsibility, but I also felt again that very nice warm glow inside me.

"The English people are an appreciative people and they are gracious in their appreciation." The second sentence for a Primer on Anglo-American Relations.

As a child, I was brought up to believe that ingratitude is a cardinal sin, never to say thank you and to accept everything as one's due. There is no ingratitude here. There is gracious appreciation.

The day of the meeting opened like a full blown rose, into blue skies, sun, and that soft air peculiar to Devon--like a dewy kiss on one's face. Mr. Braddick, the Mayor of

Biddeford, had lent his lovely riverside home for the occasion. Martha and Kay accompanied me and, as we entered the long drawing-room, with its deep violet carpet from wall to wall and vases of mauve Michaelmas daisies and purple asters reflected in the enormous gilt mirror above the wide fireplace, Martha looked at me quizzically.

"I had no idea," I murmured.

"Very nice indeed, dear," said Martha with a grin and went off with Kay to find seats among the people already assembled.

I was wearing a violet suit and hat! It had seemed both summery and dignified, also it was my one costume. Now I wished I might become a modest violet and blush unseen-- under the grand piano perhaps.

But Mrs. Symmes appeared and took charge. Then Mrs. Chanter, Red Cross Commandant for North Devon, and the Countess Fortescue joined us. Finally His Worship, the Mayor. We were ready. At least I hoped I was. The Countess Fortescue opened the meeting. Mrs. Chanter gave a resume of the work done by the North Devon Detachment of the British Red Cross for Prisoners of War. Then it was my turn.

As I rose to speak I hoped that what I had to say would interest and perhaps comfort the many women present, those women who had someone near and dear a Prisoner of War. There in the front row with two young children was a blonde young woman whose husband had been captured before Dunkirk. I could see Mrs. Card, Manageress of Bromley's Cafe in Bideford, her husband taken prisoner a year ago. There was an elderly lady who, as next of kin, received the German printed form cards from a grandson. There was Lady Irwin-- her son-in-law a prisoner. Here, beside me, was Countess

Fortescue, her only son "missing," believed a Prisoner of War. (A year later I read in the newspapers that diligent investigation had proved the Earl of Fortescue's son and heir to have been killed in action.)

I need only tell these brave and patient women something of what America, through her Red Cross and Bundles for Britain, etc. was doing to help the British sons and husbands abroad and the British people here. I did not need to tell these same women that the help came from a people with full hearts and a belief in their British friends. My audience--in the understanding way of women--knew this. Here is my "speech."

"Lady Fortescue, Mrs. Chanter, Mr. Mayor, Ladies and Gentlemen.

This particular meeting of the North Devon Red Cross and its guests of today has a very special cause in view--your Prisoners of War. The Red Cross,--true to its complex role of Guardian Angel, Florence Nightingale and Lady Bountiful,-- plans a club room or meeting place where relatives of these prisoners of war may meet to exchange news and obtain information regarding the welfare and needs of their loved ones. This is a kindly thing to do. It is English.

When, during the Battle of Britain, your gallant 'Few' beat off the Luftwaffe and your people's courage and doggedness carried them through the destruction, destitution and death that followed you 'started something'--as we say at home. You lighted a bonfire, a beacon rather, of admiration and appreciation for you British throughout the States which, in spite of flickerings like Dunkirk and Tobruk, later roared into a conflagration that swept America from one seaboard to Another. 'Help Britain'--'Aid for Britain!' Became popular

222

slogans. And Help you have had, with our hearts tied up in all the Bundles for Britain, the Red Cross supplies, the ambulances, the mobile canteens, the cases of woolen comforts and books for your Service men, etc., which have come from us to you.

At this time there are over 400 different organizations in America sending aid to Britain and among them, the British War Relief Society of the U.S.A. spends at the rate of over $1,000,000 (£250,000) a month. At the beginning of the War one half million Red Cross volunteer women workers in the United States made surgical dressings. Hospital supplies, etc.-- What they make, and collect--are sent here as gifts from the American Red Cross to you, our English friends. This giving is a kindly thing to do. It is American.

The evacuation of your children from the cities at the beginning of the War stirred people everywhere. The homes of England and America opened wide their doors in hospitality and kindliness. It was an Anglo-American effort. A number of English youngsters were sent to the vicinity of Boston, Massachusetts, where I come from, and were housed temporarily at Wellesley college, which I formerly attended. A friend wrote to me at the time, "I have seen the English children at Wellesley. They are so sweet. We shall have more than enough real homes to welcome them'". An American mother taking an interest in other people's children who needed help and comfort.

May I use that for an analogy and say that the Red Cross is a Universal Mother taking an interest in many people's children who need help and comfort. The Red Cross certainly gives the unselfish service of a good mother, and it continually amazes me how far reaching that service can be.

The upkeep of transport and communication during this immense and far flung War is a miracle--nothing less. The way parcels and letters come and go--from here to Moscow--to the States--from America to England--to China--to anywhere. And there's a War! Well, this getting places, this getting things done, is English. It is American. It is Anglo-American.

So, efficiency such as this plus humanity--the kind helpfulness of people such as is embodied in the Red Cross, for instance--is going to win this War--and the Peace.

You see, you lighted a beacon of good will and kindliness. Shall we call it just a light? The Light. And say, 'May it become an everburning flame of friendship and goodwill between your country and mine.'

Thank You."

Then we all went out onto the terrace and had tea. In spite of their own particular sorrow because of the War, many of the women found something kind and gracious to say to me about my country's help for them and theirs.

Some of us went on, after tea, to a Garden Party raising funds for the Red Cross. Lady Irwin and her married daughter very kindly drove me there and on the way Mr. Churchill got into our conversation, as he usually does nowadays. Lady Irwin recalled one of his visits some years ago to their home.

"Winnie (as she called him) is very jolly and good company. Which is a fortunate thing. I remember the day when my daughter, very young indeed, had just graduated into knickers (panties). She was exceedingly proud of them. Mr. Churchill was expected that afternoon on a visit. When he arrived the child rushed out into the hall and flourished her skirts in great pride well above her knees. "Look!" she said. Winnie looked. and how Winnie laughed!"

We have a "bombed" cook. And what a bonus that is. The rationing is such a problem. But Bridget copes marvelously. She was cook in a Service Mens' Canteen in London until the place was bombed and Bridget landed in the hospital with back lacerations and burns. Upon recovery she was permitted to return to domestic service and, since her nerves had been a bit shattered, a post outside London was suggested.

Bridget is competent, willing and cheerful--we are lucky. Also, she knows what to do with the off-ration oddments (called "offals!") that we get from the butcher, and the strange (strange to us) fish we get at the fish mongers.

One morning Mr. Smallcorn (the butcher with whom we are registered) had an off-ration offering for us. Such is almost always an "unknown"--until the parcel is opened, at home. Martha went to fetch it. Walking back up the hill with the precious newspaper-wrapped parcel, she suddenly felt the "contents" slip from under her arm. The newspaper had become soggy at one place, and the "unknown" had escaped and was rolling down the hill. Martha flew after it. It was food.

Catching up with it she was appalled to see a bloody sheep's head leering at her--it's tongue lolling. Feeling that Mr. Smallcorn was not the type to play practical jokes, Martha hastily scooped the head into the tattered newspaper and went back up the hill to "Springfield."

In the kitchen she dumped the parcel into the black stone sink.

"Something hideous!" said Martha as Bridget, all interest, took a look. "Must be for the dogs."

"Ooh, niver!" exclaimed Bridget ecstatically. "'Tis a

225

luverly sheep's head."

"We don't eat such things." said Martha.

"Gist yer wait an' see, Miss Martha." Bridget grinned. "'twill give Penny her supper and make a tasty bit fer lunch--an' then the dogs kin hev it."

With two deft flicks of her thumbs Bridget flicked out the brains and doused them in salted water. Then she removed the tongue, washed it and put it aside. Lastly the head was eased into a kettle of boiling water.

Our staple for lunch that day was a slice, each, of toast spread with minced, cooked tongue. For supper Penny had poached brains on toast, along with her usual cube of cheese and lettuce leaves. The dogs had a treat--sheep's head soup poured over their bits and pieces, with a few bones to gnaw on. Thereafter, we always were deli ̗hted to receive--in our turn--a sheep's head from Mr. Smallcorn.

We are to keep no more pigs! I have delivered an ultimatum. Once upon a time a roast of pork--succulent, crusty and brown attended by fried apple rings--was my favorite roast. Not so now. There is something about the flesh of pigs that one has known by name and fed and in due course has had "removed and prepared" (professionally by the butcher and gardener), and then stored for months in the cellar, sedately apportioned in portions, among enormous brown earthen-ware tubs there--there is something about such pork that quite "puts me off," as the English say. I wouldn't claim exactly that I feel like a cannibal when eating home-raised pig, but my feelings were certainly similar. And there was the added distraction of having the "morgue" directly beneath one's feet, the dining room being over the cellar.

The first two pigs Dick bought were properly exclaimed over, just two cute little shoats. They were fed and back scratched and even named. Alix named them at lunch one day.

"Well, I've decided what to call the pigs," she said, just as Mrs. Waters wheeled the service trolley into the dining room. "Bill and Mabel."

Alix innocently contemplated her salad. The trolley took a skid and the hot dishes on its top clinked. I glanced at Mrs. Waters. She had a startled look.

"Now why was that?" I wondered aloud as Mrs. Waters left the room.

"Mabel is Mrs. Waters' name. Bill is Smale's (the gardener)," and Alix with a grin.

"Um-m," I murmured.

But Bill and Mabel the pigs remained even when later, much later, we were eating them.

"Wonder if this is Bill" someone would say when pork was served.

"Bet you this is Mabel--real sweet," at another meal.

Although we raised two more pigs, Napoleon and Josephine, I could never enjoy them when they appeared as roast pork. It gagged me. I loathed the sepulchrally draped brown tubs downstairs. They became too full of ghosts and clanked about whenever I dared venture into the cellar at night.

I'll buy my roast of pork, when I can get it, from a proper white marble slab in a proper butcher's shop with my proper meat ration after standing in a proper queue--thank you. (Dick thought that 2 pigs would give a great addition to our

227

scanty meat ration (2/'s worth (48 cents) a week per person.) So he had obtained a permit for same.)

At Christmas I had given Dick a Pointer Bitch. Dick had always wanted a Pointer. Now we had a place big enough for such a dog.

Tessa (she was already named) was white with brown spots and brown ears. She had very loving, questioning, big brown eyes and a nervous disposition that kept her dancing on her toes like a ballet dancer. She seemed to know that she was Dick's, and Dick's alone, for she quite adored him. In fact, Tess and Dick loved each other and she was always sitting on the right hand corner of the lawn, high above the road, at six o'clock each week day. I think she could hear the car three miles away as Dick left the factory in Bideford!

In April Tessa presented us with nine puppies, all beauties. Dick and I were in London at the time. We were having breakfast--the wonderful wartime one of fried potatoes with fried bread-in-skins (sausages)--when the telegram arrived. Alix had sent it the night before and it read, "Have been at it all day. Total 9. Love, Tessa."

Seven of the nine puppies were parceled out among friends. One all over brown puppy, named Trigger, was kept for Penny and one white puppy with a large circular brown spot on either flank, named Target, was kept for Gerry. But the cares of a family weighed too heavily on Tessa. She went a bit wild and took to hunting with Target along.

One evening Mr. Mist, the Constable, called Dick away

from dinner. He was gone quite a while.

As he came into the drawing-room later and sank into a chair I wondered what he had to tell us, he looked so stricken.

"Tessa is dead," he said.

"What!" It didn't make sense to me.

"She was shot."

Then we got the story. the previous night, a chap in the village had caught Tessa, Target with her, killing one of his chickens. The chickens run wild in a field so Tessa could hardly discriminate between the domestic and the wild article! However, the young man, without notifying us of Tessa's trespass, lay in wait for her the next morning. He shot her as she ran away, leaving another dead chicken as evidence. A lawyer said we had no case.

One day when we feel really <u>settled</u> in some place, Dick shall have another Tessa. But I doubt whether Tessa II will be quite the same. For Tessa the 1st, with her dancing ways and expressive devotion to Dick, was made of canine stardust and moonshine, loyalty and love.

We haven't had much luck with dogs, I'm afraid, for later I was to lose my little dachshund, Mitzi, the most human of creatures. She could understand every word and mood. She would play ball on her own, tossing the ball up with her nose, then catching it. She would play "find the ball" after we had hidden it.

"Go out of the room, Mitzi, and wait."

She would do so. Then, at the words "All right," she would come in scurrying, her claws slipping on the polished floor, and frantically nose under rugs, pillows, and magazines.

Her pet toy was a tiny wire hairpin.

"Want a hairpin, Mitzi?"

She would lie on her back on the rug and juggle the hairpin about with her paws, or push it around with her nose, nipping at the wire and worrying it.

One afternoon she met with an accident. Or, rather, one befell her. I had been entertaining a friend, Miss Eve Berry-Torr, at tea and she and I were in the drawing room chatting when the most frightful commotion started to shake the very house. A pounding of running feet in the hall and dining room, banging of doors, shouts, and piercing screams--canine ones.

Miss Berry-Torr and I dashed out into the hall. The focus of noise was in the dining room. There Martha and Cook were chasing Mitzi around the table, Mitzi alternately running in circles and rolling on her back, howling all the while. Before I could comprehend the situation Martha and Cook had seized the poor little dachs and, without ceremony, set her on the table (pink damask tea cloth, dishes and all) and Cook proceeded to rub Mitzi's back with a cake of margarine!

The doggie yells continued. Martha wept and expostulated. Cook shouted. "Twas the fat, Mum! Exploded, bowl and all, an' the poor dog c ught it!"

Too true. Mitzi had been in the kitchen while Martha was showing Cook how to make American doughnuts. The used fat had been poured into a warmed Pyrex bowl, the usual procedure. With no warming at all, as Martha and Cook were washing up, there was a loud crack and the hot fat sprayed onto the table and floor, falling in large burning dollops onto Mitzi's back as she scrambled from under the kitchen table. We have always thought that the resultant injuries weakened the nerves in her back.

Clever little Mitzi. When in London during the Battle of Britain I could always tell when an air-raid was imminent.

Mitzi would begin to rush about the flat in a haunted manner. A minute later the sirens would go. And how she hated the bombs, as we did. But she would sit quietly and patiently and wait for the "All clear," as we did.

Human little Mitzi. She eventually caught "a cold on the kidneys" and became paralyzed in her hind quarters. So Mr. Irwin, the Vet, put her to sleep in the study. Then Smale tucked her into a tiny plot in the rose garden where she formerly used to tear up and down the flagged walks.

Why does one keep on having dogs and getting fond of them? Even loving them.

September, 1942.

In September I spoke to another Meeting of Relatives of Prisoners of War, this time in Barnstaple. It was gratifying from two points of view, I think--mine and my audience's--for I could give really impressive statistics. I hoped this information might bolster the hope, patience and day-to-day courage that British women nurture within themselves, or rather, perhaps are nurtured by. For, that British women feed on something other than the eternal cabbage, sprouts, microscopic bit of rationed meat and drab wartime bread, I am convinced. They, the women of Britain, have such stature of soul and such endurance.

Here is my speech.

"Mrs. Symmes, Ladies and Gentlemen.

I have been asked to tell you a bit about the work our American Red Cross has been and is doing for you, our

English friends .... Figures, although satisfying, are not always illuminating. One needs the human, or intimate, touch to make things glow with a bit of warmth and light in this modern Dark Age of ours, this War. So I have a few stories to tell as well-- not exciting stories, just a common every day variety. Stories about everyday people who have wanted to spare a bit of their time, thought and heart for you, their neighbor in need. For, in spite of the Atlantic Ocean, we Americans have become your neighbors and, as such, take a deep interest in you and yours.

As some of you know there are over 400 voluntary organizations in America giving aid of some sort to Britain. A few of the more prominent ones are the American Red Cross, the British War Relief Society, Bundles for Britain, Anglo-American Ambulance Committee, the Civilian Committee for the Defense of British Homes.

The American Red Cross, by virtue of its seniority and the very nature of its work, is the best known but, even so, I doubt that the average Englishman and English woman realizes just how extensive the work of the American Red Cross has been, and is, here in England.

I have a report from the American Red Cross Headquarters in London, where I was most kindly and considerately furnished with figures and skeleton resumes of work already accomplished. I'll now quote portions of that report.

Before war came to Europe in Sept., 1939, the American Red Cross was a peacetime organization of 15,000,000 men, women, and children. War came. Immediately half a million Red Cross volunteer women workers in the United States took up their duties making warm garments, layettes, surgical dressings, etc. As the struggle

232

intensified the number of these women increased to a million, then to two million, ... For the relief program in Europe a special war fund raised £5,000,000 (25 million dollars). These funds, like all American Red Cross monies, were contributed by the American Public--citizens in cities and towns, villages and rural areas. The money was put right to work buying supplies.

This outpouring of supplies to feed, clothe and heal the civilian victims of the War was soon moving across the sea ... space in as many as 31 ships a week was provided.

The American Red Cross Committee in Great Britain was formed to advise on the actual needs and the best means of distribution. The Committee, with the American Ambassador as Honorary Chairman, includes American businessmen who live in London.......

Two agencies were selected to distribute the relief goods after arrival in the British Isles: The British Red Cross and the Women's Voluntary Services. The British Red Cross handled all medical supplies. The Women's Voluntary Services distributed garments, mobile canteens and all such items for civilian aid.

The supplies sent to Britain fall into over two thousand different categories and are divided into six groups. They include more than 6,000,000 articles of new clothing for civilian bomb victims; more than 150 ambulances, 150 mobile canteens, station wagons, trucks, motorcycles and vans for transporting clothing; hospital supplies ranging from mobile x-rays on three-ton lorries down to small surgical dressings.

The American Red Cross also established in this country, in collaboration with Harvard University, a fully equipped hospital, brought to this country in pre-fabricated sections and staffed by American Red Cross Nurses (comparable in training to your Nursing Sisters or State Registered Nurses.)

Cash grants were also made for such projects as the setting up of war nurseries and convalescent nurseries for children under five. 98 such nurseries were established with contributions by the American Red Cross amounting to about £75,000 ($375,000).

At the time of the attack on Pearl Harbor on Dec. 7th total aid to Britain stood at something between £6,000,000 and £7,000,000 (30 to 35 million dollars). Immediately came a promise that aid would continue despite the inevitable difficulties and the heavy call on its resources which the American Red Cross would have at home.

That promise has been kept today. Nine months after the attack on Pearl Harbor, The American Red Cross is able to announce that £8,500,000 ($42,500,000) has been spent on aid to the civilian population of Great Britain. End of report from American Red Cross Headquarters in London.

In addition to all this work and these gifts from the American Red Cross, the British War Relief Society, another large American organization sending you aid, spends at the rate of $1,000,000 or £200,000, per month on aid of various sorts for you and your people

After Dunkirk when arms were short and invasion was feared, the Civilian Committee for the Defense of British Homes was formed. My husband was one of the founders and has been very active on this committee ever since. The aim of this committee was to collect gifts of arms, ammunition, steel helmets, binoculars and stop-watches from Americans at home and to distribute these articles here in England to the Home

Guard, the factories and civilian defense in general.   The
scheme flourished. The arms, ammunition, etc. thus obtained
was to the tune of over £500,000 ($2,500,000). The broadcasts
from the B.B.C. by Dick and Mr. Priestly did indeed reap a
fine harvest. Their monetary value was far exceeded by the
desperate need for these vital arms and ammunition, as they
were quite unobtainable here at that time, as you so well know.

Many of the gifts of personal rifles and revolvers (and
there were thousands of these) had tags attached with the
owner's name and address and often some phrase of
encouragement such as "Keep your chin up," "Good Luck and
God bless you," etc.

There was a lady's small pearl-handled revolver in one
packing case. The owner was a New Yorker and she had
written on its tag, "Because I can't come along myself."
Kurtsinger, America's premier jockey, comparable to your
Gordon Richards, sent along his gold stop watch, a valued
souvenir of his racing career. One New York business-man
went out and bought 100 brand new rifles and 50,000 rounds
of ammunition and sent these along as his gift "to the brave
families of Britain." Mr. Hill, President of the First National
Bank of Boston, Massachusetts, where I come from, purchased
300 pairs of new binoculars and sent them over to Mr. Cotton
to distribute.   Just a few instances of personal gifts from
impulsive Americans among the many thousand gifts sent to
the Civilian Committee for the Defense of British Homes.

At the time Hess landed in Scotland the people of the
State of Georgia bought a rifle and ammunition and had it
flown over by bomber to MacLean, the Scotsman who capture
Hess. They reckoned a pitch-fork in a stout Scotsman's hands
had been adequate but a rifle would certainly be better and, you

never could tell; Goering or even Hitler might follow Hess' example one day!

A great friend of my husband, Mr. William Thomas of Cleveland, Ohio, corporation lawyer and Commodore of the Cleveland Yacht Club, instigated the raising of funds to buy a mobile canteen. Mr. Thomas and fellow yachtsmen sent this canteen to Mr. Cotton following the Battle of Britain, to be presented to the Royal Thames Yacht Club for use among the docks of London.

One morning during that period of terrible raids, the Battle of Britain, when thousands of your people were going through active Hell, my husband received a letter form a Mr. Bauer of Cleveland, Ohio, owner of a chain of grocery stores in the United States. Mr. Bauer wanted to know if Mr. Cotton could supply him with a list of 30 deserving English families and he, Mr. Bauer, would send them each gift packages of food every month for the duration. Mr. Cotton supplied the list of 30 families and Mr. Bauer has been supplying the gift packages ever since. You may be interested in Mr. Bauer's name--BAUER. It is German, but Mr. Bauer is one of the hundreds of thousands of good, loyal American citizens of German descent. Mr. Bauer wanted to show his gratitude to America and his sympathy for England.

One cold winter's day, some time ago, I had a most charming letter from a lady I have never met, a Mrs. Savage of Meriden, Connecticut. Her husband is Vice President of a large manufacturing company in America and a friend of my husband. Mrs. Savage wrote that she was sending a packing case of scarves, pullovers, and helmets that she and some of her friends had knitted. They wanted "the brave English lads on the sea" to have them. Would I be good enough to

236

distribute them? I loved doing it. And the "lads" receiving the articles wrote their thanks themselves to these American mothers, which was much appreciated. One of the youngsters, a Lieutenant in the Royal Navy, wrote me that he was most pleased and grateful for the woolens and that he and his crew had so enjoyed them for one bitter cold day and night! Then they lost everything, he and the entire crew of his Motor Torpedo Boat. Still they were all very grateful and would we think of them again? We did. Terry, the young Naval Lieutenant, has since progressed from M.T.B.'s to Destroyers and up to date has had 3 of his ships sunk under him; but Terry is still fighting fit and I just had an airgraph from him. He hopes to get leave to come home and get married.

A Mr. Burr of Chestnut Hill, a suburb of Boston, Mass., has just sent us two dozen new books to be distributed among the minesweepers. They will go to Lt. Vivian Bowyer, who is in command of a flotilla of minesweepers. Vivian gets bombed or machine-gunned almost every day, and at the same hour--the Germans are very methodical--but he arrived for a leave with us looking very fit and with a cheery grin.

One of the things that one is continually grateful for, and ever amazed at, is the courageous and steady outlook of the Youth and Men of Britain who never know what the next shell or bomb will bring! You, whose dear ones are Prisoners of War, can at least know that they, like their free brothers-in-arms, still have their chins up and their eyes steady.

There are American boys now in the fighting and among the Prisoners of War. They, too, have their chins up and their eyes steady. They're American. I am sure they are learning much from their English brothers-in-arms and giving much in return.

237

It is this exchange of the intangible things of life--like hope and encouragement and brotherly love--as well as the tangible gifts of money and supplies, that will make for the building of that truly better world that we talk about--and hope for--and pray for--when there is Peace again.

Thank you."

Then tea was served. And again, among these welcoming and friendly British women I felt a strong kinship.

At odd hours the intense whir and frightening zoom of planes distracts us here at "Springfield", as boys from the 'Drome "beat up" the house. I don't like it! The girls find such practice complimentary! They wave from the lawn and grin hospitably as Johnnie or Freddie or Death (that's a real nickname!) shoot down from the blue, streak across the garden--the roses on the trellis flattening beneath the rush of air--and then climb in quick, almost perpendicular arcs over the house, just missing the chimney pots.

The morning Johnnie Striebel (Capt. John Striebel, U.S.A.A., D.F.C.) streaked under the telephone wires hedge-hopped the lower garden fence and just crested the roof, I hung out of a window and shook my fist at him and yelled, "Don't you dare do that again!" As tho' he could hear me! I was so scared I was mad.

But later, when I learned that Johnny, a Fighter Pilot, had been returning from a tricky job and had felt so darn good at seeing "Springfield," that he just had to say "Hello"--why, I couldn't stay mad, of course. I felt grateful and amazed, as always, at the courage and endurance of these youngsters. To them, taking chances is like taking a drink or taking a walk, but to me--whether in an air-raid under enemy planes or under frolicking friendly ones--taking chances is still just taking chances.

Larry Murphy (Flight Lt. W.L. Murphy R.C.A.F.), rear gunner of a Halifax, who spent last Christmas with us is a Prisoner of War. For months he's been missing after a raid on Bremen. And, when we heard that, we remembered that Larry on his last leave had felt that his number was up. I've now had a letter from his Mother in Kingston, Ontario, telling us the news; that Larry is a P.O.W (Prisoner of War). We rejoice with her. Altho', in sad truth, to be a P.O.W. is no cause for rejoicing, save for the bare fact that the young man is alive. One hears too much nowadays to be happy about such a condition of that of P.O.W.

Gerry O'Brien of the U.S. Navy has been a P.O.W. since the very first months of this War. Martha received form cards, the official bits printed in German, assuring her that he, Gerry, is well--that they play football-or that they have an entertainment--or that he has grown a beard--and thanks so much for the cigarettes. That is all. The card comes addressed to "Miss Martha O'Brien, c/o Cotton." Which must intrigue the Postman! But Gerry can write only to a relative.

These thousands, hundreds of thousands, of Prisoners of War! These young men behind barbed wire! Their lives static; their hopes, ambitions, dreams, all feeding on loneliness, the loneliness that is found in crowds. May God send special legions of his Angels to watch over them.

239

December 8th, 1942.

Dick and I attended the Prize-Giving at the Barnstaple Girls' Grammar School at the end of Term. Mr. Oliver, Chairman of the Board of Governors, had asked Dick to speak on American Education, and had invited me to present the Prizes. But I was not informed of the fact that I was also expected to "say a few words" to the students. Dick nonchalantly advised me of this on the very eve of the affair.

"I just stand on the platform and present the prizes and shake hand with each girl. Is that all?" I asked Dick, after dinner on December 7th.

"Oh, well," he said, "after the prizes are given out you just say a few words to the girls. I am giving my talk afterwards."

"Say a few words!"

I knew what that meant. I felt a bit frantic. Think up something, write something, memorize something! And here it was 10 o'clock at night--and the next day at 2:15 p.m. I would be sitting on a platform and quaking inside.

I got out a paper and pencil. And, all of a sudden, there it was:--the anniversary of Pearl Harbor; and Christmas; and Britain and America. And I could always memorize easily--especially before sleeping. My Mother had taught me that (My Mother had been a concert Reader and had taught Elocution before she married), and I had used the method to advantage thru' Speech Days at school and Amateur Theatricals. It worked.

As I have said often, the English are our friends and

they have a keen interest in us and our way of life. Those young students of the Barnstable Girls' Grammar School (Quite different from the U.S. Grammar Schools, they are comparable to our High Schools save that the majority of pupils here in England pay tuition. A small minority attend on scholarships.), and their teachers and parents, were intensely and attentively interested in what Dick had to say on our system of Education--and that, for the majority, it was co-educational and free until the child entered a University. That even then, for the youngster without financial means, scholarships and provision for students to earn their way thro' a University made this higher education available to all. That this "working" of students in College or University:--Bookshops, Laundries, etc., waiting-on-table, and similar jobs,--creating no class distinction. In fact, often the most popular boys and girls were those who were "working their way through." Such a statement is always an eye-opener to the English, a class-conscious people.

Of course Dick worked in remarks on our government and on our Armed Services since, for sometime now, the American boys have been swarming over England--and he concluded with,

"If we, as Americans, and you, as Britishers, cannot get on without trouble, what hope have we of getting on with the rest of the World in the Peace to come?"

Dick does a thorough job in these talks of his. He's a good speaker--informal, informative, and interesting.

Now I supply the sentiment--being a woman. Or rather, being the kind of woman I am. You might say that Dick provides a feast for his audience--real nourishment for their minds--a proper meal, as it were. I offer only a bouquet for the center of the table--a posey of Pansies for thoughts, Forget-me-nots and Rosemary that we may always remember and think of the best in each People, and Hearts-ease for the suffering that has been and is to come in this War which we, Americans and British, now share.

What flower typifies Hope? Could it be the sturdy little English Daisy? The ubiquitous Dandelion might represent perseverance in adversity.

Well, anyway, here is my "Speech" at the Prize-Giving at the Barnstaple Girls' Grammar School, December 8th, 1942. The largest audience I had yet addressed was there--hundreds of faces in the big hall, all those faces turned to me. But, do you know, as I stepped to the front of the platform that afternoon, I felt no nervousness, no apprehension. Instead, I felt a wave of friendly interest surge up to meet me. It quite supported me.

I must confess that I forgot to "address" the platform dignitaries and my audience. I simply began to talk to the young people there.

"I am very happy to be here today. Mr. Cotton and I very much appreciate your tho't of us, Americans, to take part in this English School ceremony. It is such a friendly thought. And now, with the world in such a turmoil of bitterness and hate, one needs all the goodness and kindness possible. And friendship is just that. It is goodness and kindness.

England and America.

America and England.

Doesn't that sound solid, and strong and good? So we must no longer be simply friendly Nations--we must be Friends. True Friends.

There's a Peace coming--one day--when your Country

and my Country must work shoulder to shoulder; not as we are working at present, to make Arms--to fight--to destroy--even tho' it be Evil that we destroy--but to build and to keep on building--a Better World, with foundations of Honesty, Good will and Good Health--with Equality of Education and Opportunity--as our Ambassador, Mr. Winant, said when here in Barnstaple--and with the intangible something without which nothing truly lives--Ideals, things of the Spirit.

Each one of you girls--members of this Grammar School in Barnstaple, North Devon, whence so many American ancestors emigrated--each one of you shares, even now, the responsibilities of the coming Peace which, this time, must not fail.

"Peace--and Goodwill toward Men."

This is the time of year when our hearts are extra full of Hearth and Home, and all that means to each of us.   In America--from Christmas Eve to New Year's--lighted Christmas trees stand in the center of almost every city, town, and village.   And in the evening people gather about these lighted trees to sing carols in a spirit of neighborliness, friendliness and good will.   And on Christmas Eve--all that night long from dusk to dawn--lighted candles, or night lights, burn in the windows of many houses to guide the Christ Child to our homes.   This is a lovely sight.   Beautiful!--because it means so much.

There may be no lighted-windows in America this Christmas--as there have been no lighted windows here for some time.   But that Inner Light--our Spirits--cannot be dimmed. We free people have something within us that makes us strong. It is that strength which is going to win this War-- and the Peace.

So remember. It is friends, working together in Understanding, Trust, and Happiness, who create and build the finest things in this World. And you are our Friends. We are proud to be yours.

So let it be: --

England and America.

America and England."

As we left the School Hal! later a very enthusiastic young girl, in the brown tunic of the school uniform, shyly came up to me--offering an autograph book. Would I please write in it?

This was an enormous compliment--and I felt decidedly elated! My ego swelled. And then my Heart took over and I got things in the right perspective. I felt humble. The pretty young girl with the ginger hair, in asking for my autograph, was really saying "thank-you, and we British like you Americans, and we are grateful that you are now in this War with us." That was what her gesture meant.

"The British are an appreciative people. They are gracious in their appreciation."

For months Dick had talked of going to the States. "They want me to go to the States," or "They want to know how soon I can go to the States," or "They say I really must go to the States," in the usual cryptic way of men nowadays--men who are doing a job a bit on the hush-hush.

So, at last, on Dec. 30th, I saw Dick and Mr. Baker off at the Instow station. Mr. Baker had never been out of England and one would never have known that he contemplated a 3-to-5

244

day wartime journey by air to America. For Mr. Baker wore no hat and his long white scarf, wound and draped in English style, gave him a very casual appearance. But, perhaps--in view of the unpleasant trip to come--a casual approach was best.

Dick had never flown before--had never wanted to--and had always said he didn't think he'd like it. He didn't! But for more reasons than the one he had anticipated--that feeling of non-support in a limitless void.

The weather was atrocious--sleet and a high-wind. Dick and I had been invited to the New Year's Eve cocktail party at Miss O'Brien's, next door. I went alone. And nearly got blown away in the short space I was on the hill road. It even snowed a bit. Of course, I wondered if Dick was "aloft"-- and how was he doing.

My feelings were not too buoyed up at the party, either--as I had hoped they might be--because, for some reason known only to himself, a guest there related to me, in detailed length, his own first experience in a plane--plus the crash! How that man could have thought his information comforting to me under the circumstances which he knew full well--I have never understood. And I couldn't forget the story until I received Dick's cable several days later. "Arrived safely after uncomfortable trip. Love. Dick."

When I was at the cocktail party, that early evening of Dec. 31st, Dick had been in the Dunraven Arms, a small hotel set in the Irish countryside near the Earl of Dunraven's estate. The sleet storm had forced a stop-over on the passengers.

"No one was surprised!" said Dick later, upon his return, while telling us of his experiences.

The prospective passengers had put up at the Grand

Hotel in Bristol, England, the night of Dec. 30th and were to be called at 6 a.m. the next day when they would be driven to the airfield. They were waked at 4 a.m. instead.

"That was the beginning," said Dick.

Later, after all embarkation formula at the airfield, the passengers went aboard the plane--and waited. They waited half an hour. A passenger was late. An hour. The crew were stoic and resigned, but the passengers became decidedly irritable. It didn't help matters when the late passenger turned out to be the Princess Paul, returning to her children and husband (Prince Paul, formerly of Yugoslavia), interned in Africa. For the Princess Paul had her maid with her and the maid was cross-eyed. "My God, what a jinx!" And from then on everything went wrong.

The weather blew up a storm that was felt, not seen, as due to security regulations, the plane was blacked-out between England and Ireland and not simply for certain periods at the take-off and the landing, as usual.

"If you think it rains in England you should see Irish rain!" Said Dick. "And, my God, was it cold!"

For the stop-over, the Princess was driven to the Earl of Dunraven's to stay the night, but the rest of the passengers were escorted to the Dunraven Arms. There was only a peat fire in the lounge so they started to slowly freeze.

"Suddenly everyone thought of it's being New Year's Eve and we should do something about it. Max Milder (Warner Bros. Representative on the Continent) insisted upon champagne for all and the evening sort of went by. But, Boy! Was it cold! We wondered if the Princess was cozy and warm and what her cross-eyed maid was going to do to us the next day."

By morning the weather had lifted and the passengers were again driven to the plane--This time a seaplane. The Princess and her maid appeared on time. All were buckled into their seats. The motors roared. Faces became tense and expectant. And the plane taxied off across the bay--smack into a buoy! There was a loud crack! the plane settled on the water like a duck with a broken wing. Everyone looked at the cross-eyed maid and thought things!

A pontoon had been damaged and must be repaired. So the passengers were escorted back to the Dunraven Arms, after being unhappily informed that the wait might be for quite a while--maybe a day or so.

"This is wonderful fast travel by air!"

However, the delay was hours not days and the plane was not too far behind schedule in spite of bad weather when it finally put down on the jungle-fringed airfield in Bathhurst, Gambia, West Africa. There, the Governor of Gambia with a proper escort, awaited the Princess, who must emplane again to reach her husband and children--interned in Africa by the British and most correctly accorded full "honors" by those most correct of diplomats, the British. For the Princess Paul is the sister of the Duchess of Kent, and had been visiting her following the recent death of the Duke.

Blood is thicker than water. In this case, the flood water of Naziism--surging and black. Prince Paul sold out Yugoslavia to the Nazis. Remember?

"The best part of the trip was crossing the Atlantic," continued Dick. "Right up above the clouds. You never saw such beautiful colors! And such light! The sunset was indescribable!"

But the last lap of the trip--from Trinidad to New York-

-was pure Hell. At Trinidad they took on the crew of a torpedoed tanker--a lot of Italians whose superstition and excitability went completely haywire in the severe blizzard the plane ran into that January night.

"I awoke in the middle of the night because the plane was bumping. I had nearly hit the ceiling! I looked out the port side beside me and the plane seemed on fire. It was only "St. Elmo's fire," but it didn't make me feel too good.

We had run into a blizzard. And we all knew it, believe me! The little stewardess was a game kid. And was she busy! Most of the people were sick. I wasn't. I hate to think what you'd be like in a plane, Peg! (I'm the World's worst sailor.)

The Italians were sprawled or kneeling in the aisles, praying out loud and moaning. No one thought we'd ever get to New York."

Decidedly "an uncomfortable trip."

January 8th, 1943.

(Entry in my Diary)
"Today Anne Gamble and Lt. Anthony Melville-Ross R.N. were married in the little Instow Church. The reception was held here, at "Springfield."

Col. and Mrs. Gamble have 3 daughters, and they all were married within 18 months. So when Anne (the last) and

Tony wanted to marry, Mrs. Gamble felt decidedly floored.

"Another wedding!" she sighed--although truly happy for Anne "I've hardly recovered from Penelope's." (the middle daughter, now married to Dr. David Ebsworth of the R.A.F.)

One of the first things I heard of the Gambles after our arrival here in Instow was, "Col. and Mrs. Gamble have 3 beautiful daughters. " Now the youngest was to be married. My own two daughters, as well as I, love festivities of any sort. A wedding would be extra special. As Mrs. Gamble sighed the girls and I had only to look at each other.

"Dear Mrs. Gamble, would you consent to having Anne's wedding reception at Springfield?"

When the time arrived for this--Tony's leave--there was only 2-days' notice. So preparations sort of boiled. Mrs. Pedler came up ïrom the village and we "turned out" the lower rooms. Martha made the wedding cake--and it was super. Mrs. Johnson (a very dear friend of the Gamble's--and with whom I often enjoy Bridge and Tea of an afternoon) contributed sugar, raisins, and eggs. Such a gift must not be minimized. It meant saving and self-denial. Along with the cake's ingredients Mrs. Johnson furnished the recipe for the marzipan, without which no English, or Continental, wedding cake is complete. The marzipan recipe was a wartime one of semolina (I would like to know in how many different forms I have eaten semolina during this War!)--but it was a great success. As for the frosting, it was absolutely pre-war. We happened to have some icing sugar, sent to us from the States. At midnight, the day before the wedding, Alix and Martha were beating, pouring, beating that frosting. And the resultant thick white coating on the 3 tiered wedding cake was truly professional.

249

But, alas, there was a dearth of flowers. At the time there was a ban on the transport of flowers by rail. Flowers were non-essential and wartime trains were overburdened. However, the Cornish growers and those of the Scilly isles were getting around this snag by hiring men to cycle up to the big towns and cities--and even to London--in relays, with loads of fresh blooms. The cyclists asked and got enormous fees and the retail prices of flowers simply rocketed.

Gerry (on school holiday) and I went over to Barnstaple on the day before the wedding and had very little luck. However, after a round of the florists there, we felt enormously elated to have collected 12 large sprays of salmon pink gladioli, and 3 spikes of madonna lilies. That was all. But there would be flowers for Anne's wedding.

You couldn't have asked for a better mid-winter wedding day than that of January 8th, 1943. Bright sun smiled on the eternal green of the English countryside. These sudden warm Spring-like days in the midst of the dark chill English winters are like a tonic. In this case the brightness seemed like a good omen.

Smale borrowed strings of flags from the Sailing Club-- and looped them in rows of bright colored bunting above our drive and the hill road in Nautical salute. The girls made sandwiches and spread crackers. Mrs. Pedler polished the silver. I did the flowers. We were all pleased with ourselves when finished.

Col. Gamble had sent up lashings of rum. Rum punch is not only very good, but it is also very simple to serve. You make pitchers of the stuff and just pour it over lots of ice cubes in the punch bowl--and keep on adding punch, or ice, as needed. (I think we have the only "Fridge" (electric icebox) in

Instow. We brought it with us, and it has been more than twice blessed, many times.)

The piece de resistance, of course, was the wedding cake. It stood by itself on one of the buffets before a mirror. Two silver and gilt cherubs swung above it, and lighted white candles in candelabra stood on either side. Not only had we found a bridal-cake ornament, complete with bells, for the top of the cake, but a tiny submarine which "idled" on the upper tier of frosting in honor of Tony. He was just returned from a long spell of submarine duty--for which he was later to be decorated.

Well, we loved having Anne's wedding reception in our home. It made us feel almost like "family" with the Gambles-- of whom we are very fond. For the house was full of the Gamble's friends who made us feel as though we, too, had known them (the friends) a long time.

At the Church ceremony, where decorations of the green leaves and vines of winter made a prettier setting than one would have believed possible without flowers, Martha "stood-up" with Anne. In the English style Martha followed the bride down the aisle. I do like our American custom better where the Bride's attendant, or attendants (pages, flower girls, bridesmaids, and maid of honor) in that order of importance, precede the Bride. In spaced and slow moving procession they form a prelude to the entrance of the Bride, on her Father's arm. Thus the best is saved for the last. But in this case, Anne-- radiant in blue, as befits a Sailor's Bride--led the small procession down the stone-flagged aisle of the little old village church.

But Martha not only followed Anne down the aisle, she followed Anne as she left for her honeymoon! Anne and Tony

251

were traveling North to Scotland, stopping overnight at Bristol. Martha was going to Bristol to attend a Red Cross Officer's Training Course. And there was but the one train. So they all three left together after the reception, Martha discreetly waiting for the meager shower of rationed rice to cease before dashing for the car, herself. She felt decidedly "de trop" in her Red Cross uniform, in the bridal car bedecked with ribbons and old shoes.

And at Bristol, having reservations in the same Hotel, Anne and Tony entertained Martha at dinner that evening. Good sports, the young Melville-Rosses.

This same month, Jan. 1943, Gerry--still at school--injured his knee at Games. Falling on gravel--another boy having leapt on his back--the additional weight drove Gerry's knee into the fine sharp stones. His knee burst open. "Like a ripe tomato" Gerry said, when Martha and I went to visit him later in the school infirmary.

The surgeons predicted a stiff knee for some time, but were most hopeful about the "nerves". Although it was months before the knee was normal it did heal perfectly.

Gerry was sorry to leave Bryanston later at the end of Term. He had been very happy there. But there is a War and Gerry wanted to pull his weight. He now hoped to get into the U.S. Navy. However, none of the Services would have him because he is subject to "anti-philatic shock". He nearly died from this, swelling up like a blow-fish with one injection; his face distorted, the soles of his feet one inch thick and hard as boards with the poison thus germinated. There was a rack over him for weeks.

So, since Gerry could not get into uniform, he went into the factory--to remain there for the duration. Away from the sun all day--and being on the night shift at times--he has become weedy and pale. But sun and diet can, one day, change all that.

I think of those boys who suffer the loss of a limb, and even two limbs sometimes--the loss of their sight (most precious possession of all)--the loss of their own particular "look" because of facial injuries. These boys have become exposed to the pity of the World. But Heaven forbid that we ever offer it to them! For it is as though the privacy of their innermost selves had been invaded. They feel "stripped"-- because they have become vulnerable, in a way that they never were, or could have been, before.

Anyone can face and fight a tangible enemy. But the black depression caused by certain "final" wounds is a spell to be exorcised by each man, alone, and from within. I am not "preaching" nor do I claim that "Religion" helps these men. But I am convinced that God, or rather a belief in God--and I mean by that the particular conception of each individual of what constitutes Strength, Inner Strength--I believe that this Help defeats the intangible enemies of Depression, Hopelessness and Despair. Nor do I think that I am alone in this belief.

The spate of young men in uniform continues--young men bursting with health and good food, on leave before "being moved"--or young men tired, "jumpy," wanting sleep

253

and rest and to wander about the house and gardens.

"Gee, it's good to be in a home again!"

"My Mom sure will be glad to hear of this."

"I bought Mother one of those long silver skewers for a letter opener. She loves old things."

Boys on leave from Hell.

They go horse-back riding, or for long walks--and the charm of rolling Devon country and the many beautiful views from the many hills here about make magic in their tired selves.

Some of the boys are old friends, some are new friends, some arrive as strangers, sent to us by the American Red Cross--to become friends.

One morning Florence, our then House Parlormaid, (before her call-up for the Land Army) appeared as usual in my bedroom to pull the drapes.

"Ma'am," she said, "there's a young man downstairs. He says you are expecting him."

"Now?" I gasped.

"Yes, Ma-am. He was sitting on the steps when I unlocked the front door.--I've fed him," added Florence.

"Good Heavens, Florence! What time did he get here?"

"Says he's been traveling all night, Ma'am. He didn't like to ring the bell too early." Florence looked glum. "Looks like there's something the matter with him, Ma-am."

"It must be Lt. Wilkes," I said. "The wire read 'arriving about 7.' I thought it meant the evening, of course."

It was Lt. Wilkes--Gilbert Wilkes, whom, along with his brother Geoffry, we have known for several years. They are real "family" friends. Gilbert was just up from a bout with jaundice--and looked it. The girls and I thought he should never have been allowed to travel so soon! But "Rush them out--Rush others in"seems to be the motto of Army Hospitals.

About a week later I went down to breakfast to find a stranger at my board. If it weren't for the fact that nothing surprises me nowadays I might have remarked upon the fact. The stranger, my husband and Gerry were deep in some war discussion. My, "Good-morning, Everybody," brought them to their feet.

"Peg, Lt. Goldbaum," said Dick.

The young man bowed.

The three men sat down--and resumed their discussion. It was as though Lt.. Goldbaum had always been there. From Alix and Martha, I gleaned the information that Lt. Goldbaum had come from the American Red Cross in London.

"No, Mother. There's been no wire. A mistake somewhere, of course."

"Florence saw him sitting on the doorstep when she pulled the drawing-room drapes."

"What!--Another!"

"He's in pictures."

"No. A photographer--from Hollywood."

Lt. Peter Goldbaum and his parents had formerly lived in Germany. He had attended a German University. The Goldbaums were now naturalized Americans. Peter Goldbaum was in the U.S. Army--attached to the Victoria unit in London. The time was coming when Peter's knowledge of Germany, the German people, and Germany would be one of the numberless cogs in a relentless giant wheel of Defeat rolling over Nazidom.

Shortly before one of Dick's visits to Washington a young Lt. John Hilton R.C.A.F (Royal Canadian Air Force). came to us on leave. Johnny was Canadian and engaged to a

255

girl back home. He was a serious boy and thought and spoke often of the future when most of the lads lived only for the present. He wanted advice as to the best shop in which to buy a diamond ring!

"If I send an engagement ring home to my girl that will give me an anchor and something definite to fight for--and to go back-to."

We saw quite a bit of Johnny as he was kept in London on a job for some time.

Johnny became a Captain. And then Johnny went overseas. Someday we hope to see him again. In the meantime we have a continual reminder in the pretty Wedgewood salts and peppers he bought for me the day he went to Clovelly on his first leave with us. Also, we remember with laughter the incident of the blown fuses--and Johnny's "fixing" of them.

As often happens here in a rainstorm some of the lights went out one evening. Dick was in London, so Johnny volunteered to fix them--and was shown the fuse box in the pantry. The lights came on again and the young people continued their card game. I went up to bed to read. It is my wartime "escape act." There were no lights to be had in my bedroom! I lit the 2 candles on the mantelpiece and then called down the stairs to Johnny.

He obligingly went out to the fuse box and "fixed" the lights in my bedroom. But at the same time the drawing-room lights went off! There was much chat and advice--and Johnny went out to the fuse box again. This time the lights in the drawing-room came on and those in my bedroom went off! So I lit the candles again--and made more remarks over the stair rail as I went down the hall to my bath.

I was soaking in my rationed 5" of water, hoping that my bedroom lights would be O.K. as I had a good book--when complete darkness shut down over me like an enormous coal scuttle. I looked up at the transom in the door and there was no light in the hall. Feeling my slippery way to the door I opened it a crack and announced loudly and in no uncertain words that I had had enough of "light-fixing!" Was Johnny playing a game?

"Oh, Mother!" cried Martha from the darkened stairwell. "It's not Johnny's fault! It must be the rain. All the lights are off now. We're going to light some candles."

I finished my bath and dried by the touch system--and felt my way along the hall to my room. I could hear muffled voices and faint noises from the direction of the kitchen. No doubt the young people had a kettle on and were scrounging around for biscuits as well as candles.

For a short while, a very short while, I tried to read by candlelight. But the English drafts of an English country house made the flames flicker and the words wiggle. How did the people of those centuries before gas and electricity ever read, sew or study after dark? But at least they didn't have a fuse box to contend with! I gave up and went to sleep--to be awakened hours later by a blinding illumination. My bedroom lights were on--every one. Praise be! But if the Air Raid Warden was on our road at the moment we'd catch Hell and a heavy fine, as the window drapes were open.

"Poor Johnny," I thought as I hurriedly turned off the lights. "It couldn't have been his fault. It must have been the rain." Which was still coming down in good old Devonshire style.

At breakfast the next morning I was apologizing to

Johnny for my apparent brusqueness of the previous evening--
when Cook said that Smale wanted to see me.

Alas, during the electric capers of the fuse box, the
incubator full of eggs, had gone off! (The incubator was in the
cellar.)

"And the chicks ready to hatch in 3 days," mourned
Smale. "I don't know what Mr. Cotton will say!"

Poor Johnny. He looked stricken. It took a lot of
talking--and much good-natured banter from my husband later-
-to convince Johnny that no doubt the rainstorm was at fault.
Johnny, himself, finally had to laugh, and often spoke of the
episode later. "When Johnny fixed the lights" became a
household legend.

By strange coincidence we had a similar experience
recently when several American officers were here. Some of
the lights went out again and the boys volunteered to "fix"
them.

"No," I said laughing. "I once let a young Canadian
Officer fix them--and the incubator full of eggs went off and
we lost all the chickens. It really wasn't his fault. There was a
heavy rain storm. Still, I'll wait and call the electrician in the
morning. We aren't using the incubator now."

I called the electrician alright the next morning--but on
an emergency basis. Smale was in a state! The incubator was
full of eggs!

"It was to be a surprise for Mr. Cotton--when he comes
back from America."

It was a surprise for me, also, as I had not been told!
Although the electrician came at once--and the eggs were still a
bit warm--all the chicks were lost. Poor Smale. It was a
dreadful disappointment of course.

258

But how odd--to have two such similar incidents. Trouble with the lights--and the loss of all those chickens--just as when Johnny was here. And we had recalled that incident at the time. But had not, apparently, profited from it! Johnny had the laugh on us this time. (I must explain how we happened to have chickens and an incubator. Eggs are so strictly rationed (2 per month per person), and the dried eggs, although a veritable God-send, are not too plentiful. So Dick obtained a permit to keep fowls, but strictly on the basis that we obtain a certain number of "customers" for the eggs - people who were willing to get their rationed eggs from us. This we did. And everyone hopefully expected to get a few extra eggs. But alas, the fowl (although coddled by Smale) went on a strike at times. And those people who were obliged to do without any eggs were the Cottons, so we gave up the Hen and Egg Business.)

And so it went--young men on leave--in uneven lots. We loved it all--and them.

We had only one unhappy visit (or rather visitation!) from young men on leave. It was a bright Spring day and in the mid-afternoon. At the time I was alone--no Staff whatsoever save for Smale in the garden. The girls were at their respective war jobs. Dick was in Washington again. Gerry was at a movie in Bideford as he was on the night shift at the factory; he'd be home in an hour or so. And Penny was asleep upstairs in the nursery where I had settled her for her nap.

Anyway, I was in the drawing-room when two young

men appeared. I saw them walking up the drive. They were in mufti, just as some of the boys chose to be when on leave. They gave their names, but no rank, and said they had come from Chivener, an American Air Base slightly to the North of us. They had no luggage save a battery-radio and a flight bag. So I assumed their stay would be very short and was thankful for that under the circumstances.

I was not impressed with the appearance, speech and manner of the two young men. There seemed something spurious about the whole matter. But then you can't like everybody! So I told them to make themselves at home and announced that there'd be tea at 4 p.m. Wondering how I could manage two extra at tea, I went out to the kitchen. They must get their ration cards and leave-passes at once!

While I was rummaging in the larder, Martha arrived home early and came out to the kitchen. She looked very upset.

"Mother!" she said. "Who are those two oafs in the drawing room?"

"Oafs?" I said, with a sinking feeling. "They're on leave from Chivener. But I really can't take to them."

"Who could!" exploded Martha. "Do you know what they're doing?"

Of course I didn't.

"They're on the divan with their feet on the coffee table! They got two bottles of Daddy's liqueurs and they're drinking! When they saw me they said, "Hi, Babe!" Martha looked insulted. "How could you let them in, Mother!"

I really didn't know.

"I must have been daft," I said.

"Well, what are you going to do?"

"I'll have to think. Somehow get rid of them, of course. But we mustn't let them suspect. Take off your coat, dear, and do please see to Penny--time she was up. I'll go ahead with tea."

I was in the dining-room when Martha appeared, a finger on her lips. (Now to get to the cloak-room to hang up her coat Martha had had to go through the study. One of those eerie English arrangements.) Martha looked even more upset than before, and this time she <u>whispered</u> "Mother, I think those guys are A.W.O.L.! One of them was at my typewriter in the study and he's typing a card, looks like a leave-pass!

Now I was scared.

They must be got away! But how? Smale <u>might</u> manage to throw them out---but it was two against one. I decided to go down the hill to Colonel Harry Gamble who was head of Civil Defense in our area. I didn't dare to 'phone, for fear the young men might hear.

It was very windy and rather cool so I ran upstairs for a scarf and a cardigan. Upon my return to the lower hall, Martha and Smale came out of the study.

"Mrs. Cotton, those two chaps just took off with two shotguns."

"They must have sneaked off while Miss Martha and I were in the dining-room!"

"They're Daddy's guns, Mother! We've checked in the study. And Gerry's gone with them!"

"Chaps met him at the foot of the drive, Mrs. Cotton. I saw it all from the rose garden and come in t'speak t'you."

"I'm going to get Colonel Gamble. I'm sure he'll help."

"I'll go along up the hill, Mebbee I kin find 'em an' keep an eye on 'em." And Smale set off.

261

"I hate to leave you and Penny," I said to Martha.

"Oh, we'll be O.K. Mother. We'll have tea."

I flew down the drive.

Colonel Gamble agreed that no doubt the boys could be A.W.O.L. He phoned the Air Base and gave the boys' names-- which were for real. (How could they have expected to get away with this performance). And they were A.W.O.L. The Base would send a jeep and M.P.s for them. Colonel Gamble was to get a local unit and go after the boys and take them to Bideford, where they'd be held until the M.P.s from Chivener came for them.

So I returned to the house.

At the top of the drive I noticed that the two tall wooden gates to the stable yard were almost closed--not quite. As I passed I cau$_L$ht a glimpse of a jeep. Quick work, I thought--and then remembered two-way radios.

The house seemed deserted.

There was no one in the study, the drawing-room or the dining-room. So I went through the pantry and Staff-room into the kitchen, where I found Martha making tea. Penny was still asleep.

"Did you know there was a --," I began.

"Oh, yes," said Martha. "it's lying in wait in case those nuts come back here."

"Well, I'm going into the drawing-room and watch from the windows."

Unexpectedly soon I saw Colonel Gamble come walking up the drive. Now what? I wondered.

Colonel Gamble went into the stable yard. And then Colonel Gamble came into the house.

"Don't worry, Peg," he said. "Got the two A.W.O.L.s

The other jeep has them--dropped me off. I'll go home in the one here."

"But Gerry and Smale!"

"They're walking home--be here soon. They have the guns."

So I fetched a couple of drinks. Colonel Gamble had certainly earned his. Dear Harry, a friend in need!

But I couldn't help wishing that Gerry and Smale could have ridden home--in a jeep. But the Military is the Military.

Because Dick was abroad (in Washington again) I, as wife of the Director, was asked to open the Sports Club for British Rola, Ltd. The Company had taken over an old cinema, cleared it out, and now has a meeting place for the Workers; where there is floor space for dancing, whist drives, etc., a stage at one end, and, at the other, up a flight of steps, what was once the old projection room of the Cinema has been turned into a Bar, with a small balcony in front. This arrangement resembles the Bridge of a ship and gives the club a very sporting air.

Dorothy was visiting us at the time, so she accompanied me. And since Frank and Elsie entertained us both at dinner before the opening and then went along with us, I felt quite bolstered up. I "spoke" from the little balcony and almost began my "speech" with "Romeo, Romeo, wherefore art thou, Romeo?"--being a creature susceptible to suggestion.

Here is my "opener."

"Mr. Smith.

Ladies and Gentlemen.

How kind of you to ask me to open this Sports Club. I suppose I am proxy for my husband who is still in Washington--and wallowing in luxury, as we say out at the house, 2 eggs and bacon for breakfast, chickens whenever he wants them, all the fish of the sea, even a car, in spite of petrol rationing, in which to shuttle back and forth between the British Air Commission and the Pentagon, that huge new building that houses innumerable committees, covers acres of ground, and has miles of corridors, so that there are tricycles on each floor for inter-office communication. And Washington has only a dim-out, no blackout.

But, do you know, in spite of all that, I believe that Mr. Cotton misses us--me, the family, and his other family, British Rola. And I am sure that he would like to be right here with us all tonight.

This Sports Club is something that is right up his alley--if I may so speak. A place where people can get together in good fellowship, in fun, in competition of all sorts. For competition, no matter what kind, makes for progress of some kind, usually good. And we can do with a lot of that. for we are going places--you British and we Americans.

We make a good team.

We play well together. And, when we have to, we fight well together. And this particular show that we are in together--this Second World War--has drawn a record gate. Practically the whole World is watching us. And we're going to win! And one of the reasons for our Victory will be good sportsmanship.

We Americans think of you, our British Friends and Allies, as a nation of sportsmen--a people with a sporting spirit. That means Fair Play.

264

We admire that.

And we like to feel that we Americans understand that, too--and employ it.

So, let it be in the name of Fair Play--and good sportsmanship--that I declare this Sports Club open.

Thank-you."

I understand and appreciate fully what my husband always says of those men and women who make British Rola, Ltd. what it is--one of the most efficient factories in England. "The job depends on the men and women doing it and I'm lucky in the lot I've got. They're enthusiastic, hard-working and most of them efficient." (The Ministry of Labour's Engineering Magazine published an illustrated article on British Rola, Ltd.).

However, Dick often remarks on the unskilled labor that, because of the War, he's had to take and train. But there is always the other side of the picture. Most of the unskilled workers become skilled workers and help turn out "pumps" for the Air Force, so perfect that not one has ever been returned as faulty. A Wonderful record. And, as Dick says, "The Workers make the pumps."

Hundreds of Bideford people have entered the factory-- upsetting many a local business enterprise. The upsets were often considerable. So I think that the men of the Bideford Rotary Club, in inviting Dick to become a member, certainly showed forbearance and tolerance--for there's no doubt that Dick became a thorn, a pricking thorn, in many sides!

He complained of the low, almost non-existent, water pressure at certain hours. "What about raids?" he asked. "Or Incendiaries? Or just ordinary fires?"

He complained of the lack of bathing facilities for his

265

Workers. Many billets had no baths--even in houses built as late as 1929! There are no Public Baths in the town. The river is hardly suitable in mid-winter and, besides, sewage still drains into it! So Dick built showers in the factory Annex. Mind you, there are plenty of Bidefordians who want to change all this--the lack of up-to-dateness. But changes come slowly in England and extra slowly in Devon. (An English Scientist claims that there is some strange quality in the red soil of Devon that enters vegetables nurtured by this soil. And that the Devon character is formed from a diet of such vegetables!)

However, the War has quickened Public Interest in many things. The women, particularly--so it seems to me in my relations with the "Members of the Inner Wheel" (Comparable to our "Rotary-Anns.") in Bideford--want progress. As Mothers they are thinking of the children and their future.

At the moment, two "thormy" episodes connected with British Rola come to mind.

I went into one of the Drapers Shops to speak about a bill that I understood had been paid by Dick before he went to Washington. I had to see the Manager about the matter--and, in settling affairs, both the Manager and I got "a little hot under the collar", to use a New England expression. For it seemed that the second bill had been a mistake due to shortage of Staff.

"And why not!" expostulated the Manager. "With Mr. Cotton taking 30 of my girls into his factory!"

You would think that Dick had commandeered the Sales Staff! But he <u>had commandeered</u> certain houses for his workers--and that was another pricking thorn, of course.

However, there are roses as well on the British Rola "bush" that flourished in Bideford for the duration. Business in

266

town has boomed, social life has expanded, and the county (Devon) and the City (London) have become neighborly in thought and outlook.

Speaking of roses reminds me of one particular bloom, or "bloomer" rather, that sprouted so many thorns on the British Rola "bush" that Dick began to think he was harboring a hedgehog.

For some months we had had a housemaid at "Springfield" who was more trouble than help. Little rolls of dust became so prevalent and active that the cat began to get a complex about them--thought they were mice. The ironing, without benefit of mangle, was yet mangled. And at any hour of the day one could ask, "Where is Rose?" and be sure to find her in her bed-room, smoking or reading. Cook was nearly driven crazy. But nowadays one accepts what the Labour Exchange sends--and likes it--or does without.

Now that was another of Dick's complaints. For, eventually, Rose had to register for National Service, and the Labour Exchange sent her to British Rola. Dick refused to have her.

"She's lazy and incompetent and will never make a good operator. I ought to know--she was Housemaid at Springfield. If that girl comes into the factory she'll break something. I can't run the risk of having imported machines broken. Time is too important nowadays."

But Rose became an operator at British Rola, ltd.--and in a very short time broke one of the imported machines. That was a definite calamity--factory output was lowered while the machine was being repaired.

Still Rose remained. "She must be given her chance." although she had a guard, of course, on her machine and had been cautioned repeatedly about using it she "couldn't be bothered." The back of her right hand was badly roweled one day--and Rose became a patient at the Bideford Hospital for some time. All at British Rola's expense--coming under Welfare. A Miss Pollack (blond, helpful and efficient and known as Polly) is head of Welfare at British Rola. Rose became a problem indeed, for in due course, Rose returned to the factory. This time the trouble following Rose's return was of a more intimate nature--and, according to Rose, was hers alone and no one's else.

Dick came home one evening exceedingly disgruntled.

"It's that Rose again. She's going to have a baby. Polly is in a state--can't find out who's responsible. Rose says no one is. Says she "got it in Lavatory C!"

Well, the upshot of the matter was, that Rose continued at British Rola for some months and was then escorted to a "Home" in North Devon. Miss Pollack drove her there, by car, after collecting money and a layette for the girl. British Rola again taking the responsibility--because of Lavatory C, I suppose!

Somewhat later, I ran into Miss Pollack on the High Street in Bideford one day.

"How is Rose?" I inquired, wanting to know the final chapter in the Saga of Rose.

"It's a girl," said Miss Pollack. "And Rose has named her Angela!"

I had to smile. "I suppose that's the end of the affair."

"Oh no," said Miss Pollack with a sigh. "She's returning to the factory to earn money to support Angela."

"Dick will like that!" I exclaimed.

"Won't he--just!" grinned Miss Pollack.

In March, of course, another birthday caught up with me. In spite of the fact that Dick was still in the States it was a happy day. Dick had left me a gift (in Martha's charge) and had ordered flowers for me. Miss Ward (Dick's secretary) and a friend appeared in the morning with their arms full of the loveliest flowers. The red earth of Devon not only produces enormous cabbages , it produces the largest blooms I have ever seen! The cream colored single narcissi were like miniature parasols!

We decided to have some people in for drinks; must share all this beauty.

The drawing-room resembled a conservatory when the girls and I had finished. All those Devon flowers! Their color and their scent! Knowing how he loved flowers, I called Smale in to see the gorgeousness. And when I told him that Mr. Cotton had sent the flowers to me he said, "What! All that way?"

I don't know what we'd do without Smale. He's an excellent gardener and keeps an extensive lot of vegetable patches flourishing in rotation. Smale also tends the fowls (and took care of the pigs) and feeds the dogs and, on occasion, looks after Alix' horse when she's away. He also brings in the coal. And is almost always cheerful and pleasant.

But his Devon idioms sometime amuse us. When I ask him how his sore thumb was one morning, he answered, "'er is better." And when calling the dogs he says, "where be-e to, Tessa!--Where be-e to, Target!" And just before a very cold spell he will announce that there's going to be a "Black Wind" although there may be no wind, and white snow perhaps, instead of blackness.

I had two sisters from a nearby village, Gertie and Belle, at one time as domestics. They would come to me of an evening and ask, "Can us go out, Ma'am?" The Devon use of objective pronouns as subjects. Gertie, the House-parlormaid, would say, "Shall I lay-up now, Ma'am?" meaning shall I set the table. Penny loved placing the knives and forks and would ask, "Can I help Gertie lay-up?" Also Penny would now and then say, when asked where Gertie or Belle was, "Her is in the kitchen." We decided then that a Nannie, or Governess, was essential--although Gertie and Belle loved Penny and would play with her by the hour. I once looked out of the drawing-room window to see Gertie and Penny rolling over and over in the heliotrope like a couple of puppies!

Gertie was a bit child-like. Also, she would eat only certain things--mostly potatoes. Martha once spoke to Gertie about this. "It's not right for you, Gertie, to eat all that starch."

"But I'm not right, Miss Martha!" said Gertie. "When I was five I drank boiling water out of the tea-kettle spout. And I've never been right since." These sisters were as set in their ways as English customs and usage are. Houses still have "meat safes" (instead of "Fridges"). Meat safes are boxes of wire mesh with hinged doors--like bird cages to imprison very stout birds, such as vultures. Some of the meat nowadays tastes like vulture meat! There are domes of muslin, stretched on 2 crossed wires or reeds, to be placed over "remainders." We use these Domes in the larder. There are tubular earthen crocks, a third full of cold water, wherein milk bottles stand-- each in their own private well, as it were. Our "Fridge" does away with these, thank goodness.

All this reminds me of Mrs. Postlethwaite, an English

270

housekeeper I had--years ago--in the States. She used to tell me how "her people" kept milk fresh in a running stream or in big brown jars of water--and how there was a larder "up the tree" by the scullery door--but that a "dark, cool place down under" was better.

One summer's day Mrs. Postlethwaite went completely off her head. It might have been the heat. At any rate, she started throwing things, including cups and saucers. One cup crashed against the wall beside me and I 'phoned the doctor. Her son came later and took the poor soul away. Said she'd had "spells" before!

For months afterwards--in the Fall, when the cellar was in use again because of the furnace there--we kept finding butter, still intact in shop wrappings, and loaves of bread, wound in tea clothes, hidden in the most outlandish spots--even under the coal in the bin. Poor Mrs. Postlethwaite must have been thinking of that "dark, cool place down under."

The War!
This dreadful War!

It is in the newspapers (the casualty lists)--on the Radio (H.M.S. Barham hit)--in our conversation (John Russell has lost a leg)--in our minds and hearts (the conscious and unconscious prayers we offer.)

It is even in our stomachs. These sausages of bread or semolina. The bright yellow Bakery buns and cakes. What kind of flour produces this jaundiced look?

It gets in our hair (brittle and colorless) and under our skin (dry and taut.)

271

It feeds on Life--particularly Young Life.
It is Death.
Pete's Death.

Martha is now in Mr. Tomsett's factory at Woolacombe. She's very keen on the job in spite of long hours. She's in charge of the payroll and acts as sort of secretary and general factotum for Mr. Tomsett. She even makes him a rice pudding now and then which is baked in the belly of the iron stove in the office! She takes the 7:25 train from here to Woolacombe each morning--returning for dinner at 7:30 in the evening. Twice a week she wears her British Red Cross uniform. On those days, on her way back here after work she continues on past Instow to Bideford, arriving home from there on the last bus at 9:30 p.m. She's in charge of the British Red Cross Youth Classes at Bideford and loves it all. I think it is really too much for her--but most people work beyond their strength now, anyway, and Martha is young.

Hundreds of Americans have taken over Woolacombe sands and cliffs as training ground for an Assault Course. Their Headquarters are adjacent to Mr. Tomsett's (Mr. and Mrs. Reginald Tomsett soon became Tommy and Kit. They are dears.) factory, and the fields about are full of tanks, "ducks" and jeeps. The confusion and the explosive noises of almost constant maneuvers are turning Woolacombe into a nightmare for it's residents and evacuees.

In some ways there are compensations--the dances at Headquarters and the American boy-friends the English girls

272

now have. There are decidedly mixed opinions on these Anglo-American Relations! But again, the matter rests with the individual.

Martha has met a lot of nice young officers at Woolacombe. They take her and Alix to the dances--those fabulous dinner dances of an American Army H.Q. where the food is like ambrosia to a people so long on rations and sharply curtailed variety. They come over to Springfield--big, husky chaps with a real appreciation for a sing-song, a game of Bridge, a meal in a home, even though the meal is a distinctly wartime one. They come like the Greeks, bearing gifts--of tomato juice, candy, gum, cigarettes, and even a cake now and then. They remember Penny with special fruit drops and oranges. They talk of their homes--their parents--their wives-- their children--their girl friends. They exhibit snapshots of all these Human bits and pieces that make up the whole special "Heart Experience" of each man--the thing he's eventually going to fight for, Home and Family and his Right to enjoy these things in Independence and Peace.

All Devon swarms with Americans. The swaggering, boisterous antics of thousands of G.I.s bewilder the Devonians. In the Pubs the American soldier treats the English beer and "whiskey & soda" like soda-fountain or milk-bar drinks. That is, he drinks--all he wants-- without discrimination. He mixes drinks--and, in treating his English girl friend, he mixes her drinks! The result is not one to enhance the reputation of American young manhood. Windows are broken. Heads are broken. Hearts are broken.

The English, because they do not understand, look askance at the Americans' free and easy ways. To the G.I., no matter who the girl is, she becomes Millie, or Jane, or Babe, at once! There is no formality. The girl, to begin with, is uneasy when the American boy tightly links his arm in hers, as though they were very close friends. But in a very short time she accepts this as natural. She walks with nonchalance, hand-inhand, with her American boy-friend. She chews gum. She boasts of the candy and sugar (both strictly rationed here) that he gives her. She is more leg-conscious than she ever was--wearing sheer American stockings (from the P.X.). She thinks all Americans are millionaires--and would like to marry one--and go to live in that country where everything is done by Modern Magic.

I creep inwardly at the disillusion of some of these girls in the Future, for although American life is definitely more stream-lined for "better living," it also has it's decided drawbacks--many of them unfortunately: The crowded tenements, the isolated, un-modern farms; the extremes of temperature in the different seasons (although I must say that one usually knows what to expect and can dress for it!); the frantic hurry of the Big Cities; the mad scramble and fight for buses (we should learn to queue in orderliness and fairness); the rudeness of some (too many) Traffic Cops who think that bawling one out and swearing is a measure of their authority; the eternal race to make money; the too-wide-spread non-comprehension of how to use ones leisure.

Must we Americans always have the Largest, The Most, and The Best--no matter what? And don't tell me I'm an anglophile! (I hate that word--there's a sneer in it). I'm an American who has lived among the English long enough to do more than scratch the surface of their lives--and to feel able to look at My Country (God Bless It!) and My People (God Love

274

Them!) objectively. You should hear me toot the horn of America! I have deafened many a wary Britisher's ears extolling American ways and means. But an objective view makes for clearer vision. And so I say that America and Britain should <u>pool the best in each country</u>. We would thus come nearer to realizing a Utopia than any book or speech ever envisioned.

Almost always, alas, it is the small incidents brought about by small people that build up an adverse "blanket" opinion. For instance, the reckless driving here of American jeeps and motor-cycles along the narrow, twisting English roads. In Instow alone, we have 4 different smashed walls from accidents. The walls are private property. Their owners don't think much of Americans!

Frank Heaver's car was run into by an American Jeep. It's driver--in a tearing hurry, and on the wrong side of the road at that--hops out and goes up to Frank, who was ruefully looking at his damaged hood.

"Can't you get out of the way? Don't you know there's a War!"

Now Frank entertains the American boys in his Bideford home--where he and his wife now live because of the London blitzes, and where his parents also live because their house was burned by incendiaries. His wife's brother is a prisoner of War, under the Japs.

"Don't you know there's a War!"

That just about burned Frank up. But, in speaking of the incident, he said, "Of course he was only one among thousands of darn nice boys. But that kind of thing doesn't help a bit."

No, it doesn't.

But I feel gratified and proud when I see and hear of all the nice things, the decent things, that most of our American boys do here in England. And they love children. They will go out of their way to speak to a youngster. I was standing in a bus queue at Barnstaple one day when an American Jeep drove into the adjacent parking place and stopped. The driver slid down behind the wheel, dug a piece of gum out of a pocket, and commenced to chew. In a detached way he looked us over--a line of women with laden shopping baskets, and the usual lot of children, too young to be in school or left at home alone.

As though someone had pulled a few strings, the young man suddenly straightened up, reached over into the back of the jeep, and then climbed out. Both hands were full of candy and gum. He went down the long queue, giving every child (even those in their Mother's arms) a share of the sweets.

"Hi, Buddy!" or "Here, young lady!" he'd say--and grin shyly when the women thanked him.

"Shucks! It's nothin', M'am."

He went back to the jeep. And was asleep before our bus appeared. But the queue buzzed with happy appreciation. And the corners of the little children's mouths now turned up, rather than down, as they busily chewed and chewed.

I rather think that gum has come to stay here, in England--in more ways than one. You should hear what the Staffs of Hotels, Pubs, and Snack bars have to say about the small, gray, adhesive ornaments they now scrape from under chair seats and table edges. It may be that American boys look on those wads of chewed gum as some sort of legal tender for the strange souvenirs they "pick-up" here and there.

The strangest souvenir I know of was that removed

from a coach on the Ilfracombe-Barnstaple train one afternoon. Martha was returning from Tommy's factory in Woolacombe (which is the next stop to Ilfracombe on the R.R. Line) and, when her coach was shunted off at Barnstaple onto the single track running to Fremington, Instow, Bideford and Torrington, she found herself quite alone. But the Conductor and the Guard (Brakeman) soon joined her, and, apparently being in a chatty frame of mind, commenced to discuss "The Americans"--thinking Martha was English as she was wearing her British Red Cross uniform.

The average American soldier seemed to be a cross between a feeble-minded pup and a predatory wolf--with a mania for thieving!

"The things they take!" said the conductor. "Why, the other afternoon, when the train got into Ilfracombe, the W.C. (Toilet.) was missing from one of the lavatories. Quite gone-- just a hole in the floor! There was only American troops in that coach--train full of 'em!--new lot."

"Mebbe they put it out through the lav window," suggested the Guard.

"Then it's in a field some 'eres along the Permanent Way (Track.), snorted the conductor.

Where, no doubt, it is a great source of wonder and interest to the cows and sheep.

Or, perhaps, the Devon Pixies, thinking it a Magic Ring, dance upon it of moonlit nights.

In August Dick went off to Washington again, after only 2 months here, in England, upon return from his first trip. I drove to Poole on the South Coast with him, where we had lunch with Kay and Bill Williams (who were in Wimbourne at the time) before the plane took off. The B.O.A.C. plane looked like a toy to me as it sat complacently on the surface of the bay--"riding" a bit, veering with the wind.

All the long drive back to Instow it rained. And, where the road skirted the sea, low heavy saffron clouds seemed about to blanket the waters. I thought of the "toy" plane, with Dick in it, nosing up into that stuff and zipping along blindly. Which just shows that I, myself, have never flown!

Well, Dick made a quick crossing--by the Northern route to Botwood, Newfoundland. And the rest of the family, left here at Instow, settled down to routine again.

Alix took a job as Liaison Officer (Red Cross) at Fremington Hospital--one of the many such American Hospitals scattered about the British Isles. A group of one-story buildings, looking more like barracks than anything else, upon inspection they reveal efficient and modern hospital Wards, Operating Theaters, Kitchens, Staff-rooms, etc. A beautiful old mansion on the grounds serves as quarters for the Doctors, Nurses, and Red Cross personnel.

Alix likes the job and makes our eyes pop and our mouths water with accounts of the food to be had there. According to Alix our countrymen and women--although far from home--are stuffed with the most wonderful stuff! Tomato juice--orange juice--quarts! Chicken all the time. (We almost pray over our fowls here--just to get an egg! As for eating them--the fowls! It would be killing the goose that laid the golden egg!) One and a half pounds of meat a day per man! (Our whole family ration is less than that a week!) And ice-cream--always ice-cream--the manufacture of which is now forbidden to the English. As for the American Coffee--it is

278

really coffee, pure coffee, not coffee essence.

Come September Bideford held a large Agricultural Show in the Pannier market--a Red Cross Victory Show, where there were exhibits of fruits, vegetables, flowers, rabbits, fowls and canary birds. Smale had many entries from the gardens of "Springfield". For weeks he had collected, sorted, and finally washed and polished potatoes, carrots, leeks, onions, apples, etc. The evening before the show he and Mrs. Pedler worked in the game-room, wrapping each individual vegetable or fruit in newspaper--ready for the Carrier in the morning. A lot of hard work, time and infinite patience went into Smale's exhibit. He deserved all the prizes that he was to receive.

The proceeds of the Show were to go to the Red Cross. So representatives of North Devon Red Cross were present, among them Mrs. Symmes. The Mayor and Members of Bideford Council attended and Officers of the Agricultural Society. It was quite a party. We, the Allies, were doing well in Italy, and the word Victory on the posters (Red Cross Victory Show) looked good to us all.

I had been invited to open the show. Not since I was a child and used to go to the Food Fairs in Mechanics Hall, Boston, Mass with my mother, had I attended such an affair. Upon arrival, the long trestle tables of vegetables and fruit--the vases of flowers--the cages of birds and rabbits--all brought a nostalgic lump into my throat. I seemed a long way from home!

279

But I wasn't given much time to reminisce. People had collected and the clock said 3 p.m. I was helped up onto a table--as there was no platform--and the Mayor introduced me. The word Victory in the poster had given me the "heart" of my speech. Here it is.

"Mr. Mayor,
Ladies and Gentlemen.

I am only too glad to come here today to open this Red Cross Victory Show. One can never do enough for such an unselfish organization as the Red Cross.

The addition of Victory--Red Cross <u>Victory</u> Show--is a happy idea. We have tho't Victory, we have felt Victory, but now we can see Victory.

You people of Bideford--and 'round about--have put on many such good shows of all kinds, for all the different branches of work involved in this War. You are to be congratulated--and one day thanked--by my people as well as yours for the splendid support you have given the Total War Effort and for the fine spirit that seems to flourish in the community amongst you people.

It is the people of a country that is that country's Heart--it's Soul--it's very Life. Knowing you people--the people of England, the people of Britain, the people of the Empire--one has felt Victory in this War for your country and mine to be a foregone conclusion. You do well to call this Show a Red Cross <u>Victory</u> Show.

Victory is an inspiring word. Let me spell if for you.
Victory.

V--is for Verity--An Englishman's word is as good as his bond.

I--is for Ideals that nourish the soul--and bolster the

heart--and turn men into supermen, working the miracles of the Battle of Britain, the retreat from Dunkirk, the capture of Sicily, and now the Beginning of the End--in Italy.

C--is for Courage,--the heart of a Lion.

C--is for Courtesy--"Honi soit qui mal y pense."

C--is for Crusade--This World-wide Crusade, wherein each Allied Service Man becomes a modern Knight.

T--is for Truth--founded on Honesty.

T--is for Trust--whereon the weak may lean.

T--is for Tenacity--of the bulldog-brand that never knows when it's licked.

O--is a symbol--a circle--an unbroken line signifying unity. "United we Stand."

R--is for the Right--The Right of Mankind to live in Peace, Security, and Neighborliness, under the Creed, "Do unto others as ye would be done by."

And Y--is for You--without which Victory can not be completed.

That spells Victory.

And now I declare this Red Cross Victory Show open.

Thank-you."

Then Mr. Ellis (Councilman) thanked me, and the Mayor's little granddaughter presented me with a lovely bouquet of lilies, carnations and scabius. I was then escorted down the various aisles of produce and poultry where I was embarrassed to find so many cards reading, "1st (or 2nd) prize--So & So--entered by Mrs. Cotton." There was a great deal of interest shown in Smale's "Assortment"--as the vegetables in that group were American, yellow hooked-neck summer squash, sweet green peppers, yellow tomatoes and a Hubbard squash--all quite unknown to the majority of people present.

For the "Assortment" Smale got a special prize. Smale was so good about experimenting with seeds from America!

At another large Agricultural Show held soon after this, Smale did even better. He won so many prizes that he was awarded the Cup. It is the custom here to give your Gardener a "gift" for his efforts, so that he and his pals may gather at some Pub, or Inn, and drink to his successes. This is called "Filling the Cup." So on that evening Smale, in high feather, after presenting me with all the colored prize-cards (which almost made a "grand slam" in exhibits) went down to the New Inn on the front, where the Cup was put to proper use.

I couldn't help thinking that those cards should have read,--"First Prize--So & So--Entered by W. Smale." For Smale had done all the work. It was his Show--not mine.

For some time we had been trying to engage a Nannie for Penny--Alix and Martha being in War jobs, and I up to my neck in the house and it's problems, not to mention the "visitors" now and then. but, so far, only a succession of Temporaries had been available. They were each adequate in their own way but, being just what they were--Temporaries-- the arrangement was not good for Penny. All that chopping and changing!

But at last, one afternoon, I went down to the Station to meet a Miss R-, sent by a well-known London Agency. Her credentials had been good and so I had engaged her. Miss R-, herself, had written me a few days after, asking would I like a good Cook, as she could bring one with her. I wired "yes" at once! Because of call-ups, we now had no one to help in the house at all--only Mrs. Pedler who came for a couple of hours in the morning. A Nannie, plus a Cook, seemed too good to be true.

It was!   For when the London train pulled in that afternoon the only "unclaimed" person was a hatless woman about 40 with a vast amount of luggage.

"At least she's thinking of staying!" I said to myself and went forward to meet her.

"Are you Miss R-?"

She was.

"If you'll show me which is your luggage I'll have it put in the car"--the one taxi to be had.

"There--and there--and there!" she said, pointing to the various cases strewn along the platform.   "I couldn't lose it!"-- in an exasperated voice, pushing back her straggling ginger hair.   "I tried all the way from Waterloo.   But I couldn't lose it!"

"Merciful Heaven!" I tho't.   "Something is quite wrong somewhere."

But I saw no alternative at the moment but to fetch her up to the house.

Trying not to notice the driver's consternation at the four cases, 1 hat box and 1 burst parcel, I also tried not to notice his increasing edification as the car climbed the hill road to "Springfield."   For Miss R- <u>sang</u> most of the way--with a word upon the scenery tucked in here and there.

The car no sooner stopped before the front door than Miss R-was out like a flash.   Running to the lawn overlooking our long view, she dramatically clasped her hands above her heart and chanted (no other word will do) "Beautiful--It is

Beautiful--It is Beautiful!"

Well, it really is--the view from our lawn. But my sentiments couldn't coincide at the moment. I went to fetch Smale. All that luggage! I couldn't get over it. Neither could Smale. But he took it up to her room, next to the Nursery.

Penny was visiting with a little friend for the afternoon, luckily. But Gerry (waiting for a Labour Permit in order to go into the factory) and Jimmy Johnson, (Lt. R.N.) came back from tennis to join me and Miss R- for tea. She insisted on holding my dachshund, Moxi, in her lap and feeding him--although I said we didn't permit it at table--and jumped up several times to gaze out the large window overlooking the Torridge River.

"My, what a big river!" she commented. "Is there a big wave here?"

Thinking she meant something like the Bore on the Severn, I said, "No. It is a tidal river--but any bathing is done from the sea front.

"Do you ever put the child in the sea?"

"Penny only paddles.--Do come and finish your tea, Miss R-."

She jumped about so and spoke so coyly to the boys that, on one of her sorties to the window, Gerry and Jimmy rolled their eyes at me and tapped their foreheads significantly.

"Oh, dear!" I tho't. "Is she really?"

After tea I followed Miss R--to her room. The 4 cases were down the middle of the floor--in a zig-zag line like stepping-stones. That was not Smale's arrangement, I was sure.

"Miss R-", I said. "If you will unpack these cases Smale can take them up to the box-room."

I still thought she might be just tired and "nervy"--or one of those rather wearing creatures who have too much energy and jump about and speak explosively.

"No, thank you," said Miss R-.

"Well, shall I have Smale stack them in the corner? You'll fall over them if they're left on the floor like that."

"Oh, no!--no!" trilled Miss R-. She "lilted" her words, with a continuously rising inflection. "Oh, no!--No!--See!"

And she proceeded to skip back and forth over the cases--down the line.

I fled--out to the garden, and Smale.

"Noo.--It don't luke right," he said. "Fur fair."

As Alix was late returning from the hospital, and thinking that normal treatment would produce normal actions, I introduced Penny to Miss R-and let her bathe her. Martha would be changing in her room and could listen. So I started dinner and took Penny's supper tray up to the Nursery. I couldn't resist a peek in the bathroom to see how things were going. What I saw sent me flying in to Martha.

"She's crazy as a loon!" I gasped. "What do you think she's doing?"

Miss R-, attired in a brown suede jacket and wool scarf--evidently donned for the occasion--was alternately stooping over the tub, filling a large bath sponge and then, rising, with arms outstretched, squeezing the spongeful of water over Penny, who sat in the bath with her mouth open--a dazed expression, like that of a hypnotized bird, on her face turned up to Miss R-.

Martha went in and took over.

The next morning Alix and I (Martha and Gerry had left early) awaited Miss R- and Penny at breakfast. Alix had stopped in at Miss R-'s room the evening before and all had seemed well. But now neither Miss R- nor Penny appeared.

"You'd better run up, Alix. I don't like it."

"Neither do I. And at this rate I'll miss my bus." Alix was due at the Hospital by 9 o'clock.

In a few minutes Alix appeared--with Penny, dressed.

"That woman! You must get rid of her, Mother! Penny was running around the Nursery in her pajamas. Miss R- hadn't done a thing! I knocked on her door--and when she didn't answer I opened it. She wasn't even dressed, herself! I said breakfast was on and why hadn't she dressed Penny--and guess what she said? 'Dress her yourself. What'd you have a child for if you can't dress it?'--That woman's crazy, Mother!"

Alix gulped her breakfast and flew for the 8:30 bus. Penny and I were left--with Miss R-.

What a day!

I sent Penny out to her sandbox and awaited miss R-. over an extra cup of coffee. Eventually the dining-room door opened and Miss R-, in a very girlish jumper and skirt of bright green, wearing plimsols (sneakers) on her feet, slipped in like a ghost.

"Good morning, Miss R-", I greeted her. "Did you sleep well?"

No answer.

Miss R- never even looked at me. She tripped over to the trolley and poured herself a cup of milk.

"There is tea or coffee, if you prefer, Miss R-".

No answer.

Miss R- helped herself to a piece of cold toast and went over to the window behind me, cup in hand.

"Is there a Miss R- here? Or is it I that is not present?"

I said to myself. "Maybe I'm a ghost."

"What a lovely lot of water!" Suddenly and loudly. "Is there a big wave here?"

"That's Miss R-all right! She's really here with you at Springfield," prodded my mind.

"I would love to put Penny in the sea," added Miss R-.

Now I was scared.

"Miss R-, if you have finished, will you please go out on the lawn with Penny. I have things to do here."

Smale was in the rock garden there and could keep an eye on her.

Mrs. Pedler would be arriving soon. I must think what to do. Obviously Miss R-. must go. But I couldn't simply turn her loose!

In my spasmodic observations from the front windows I noticed that Miss R- and Penny sat, side by side, almost immovable, at the top of the stone steps into the rock garden. This went on for some time. So I went out to them.

Miss R- was wearing a heavy tweed coat, buttoned up to her throat, but she had removed Penny's jumper. The air had a tang in it.

"Miss R-, I think Penny should have her jumper on."

Miss R- cast her eyes up to the sky and spread her hands out, palms up.

"It's not raining!" she trilled. "It rained in the night--but it's not raining now!"

"And I think Penny should be running about--playing some game--rather than sitting here all morning."

Miss R- looked scandalized.

"Children shouldn't run!" she warbled in High C. "Children's legs are not made to walk on!--They should sit."

I retreated into the house--hastily.

"Mrs. Pedler!" I related what Miss R. had said. "Do go out in a few minutes and ask the same questions. Se what Miss R-. says."

Mrs. Pedler did so. And returned with a broad grin. Miss R-., in answer to Mrs. Pedler's suggestions about the jumper and Penny's playing bout, had repeated the identical words she had "sung" to me!

"Course she's not right," commented Mrs. Pedler. "But hi don't think she'll 'urt Penny."

However, we kept Penny with us the rest of the morning. And Miss R-. went off for a walk.

Gerry was home for lunch. I had settled Penny for her nap--and Miss R-. was in her room. I rang the luncheon gong and Gerry and I sat down.

No Miss R-.

"Ring the gong again, Gerry.--Good and loud."

He did.

Still no Miss R-.

"I'll go up," said Gerry.

He came back laughing. "She says she's had lunch!"

"She couldn't have! There's no place here you can get lunch--except the Marine Hotel, and you have to order it ahead there."

"Well, that's what she said. And she's reading a Peter Rabbit book!"

I went upstairs.

She was reading a Peter Rabbit book!

"Miss R-., lunch is getting cold. Will you please come down?"

"No, thank you very much. I've had my lunch."

"Where?"

Miss R-. rolled her eyes up to the ceiling and swept her arms out in an explanatory gesture.

"On the Estate of Springfield!" she caroled.

That settled it! Now I knew how I was going to get rid of Miss R-.

Back downstairs I went.

"Gerry, you listen for Penny. I'm going next door to 'phone for the Doctor, so Miss R-. won't hear me."

It was arranged that the Doctor (Dr. Martin Littlewood of Bideford) drop in for tea so that Miss R-, unsuspecting, would be herself for observation.

I dressed Penny and had Gerry take her and her milk ration (each child takes it's own share of milk along for tea nowadays--the ration is so meager!) to young Mrs. Arbuthnot, who had kindly said "yes" when I 'phoned for the favor, where she (Penny) could play with little Georgina Arbuthnot for the afternoon. Part of the problem was solved.

And then Miss R-. disappeared!

However, the Doctor arrived as planned, and we had tea. But no Miss R-. appeared.

"If she isn't back by 6 o'clock we'll have to have a search," said the Doctor.

But at 5:45 we heard Miss R-. come in and go upstairs.

"See if she'll come down for a cup of tea," said the Doctor.

But Miss R-. refused. She was tidying the Nursery and wouldn't even look at me as she answered. "No, thank you. Can't you see I'm busy! I've had tea--in a Cafe. And, I'm very sorry, but none of the shops had any of things you asked me to get."

What an imagination!

The Doctor and I then arranged that we both should go up to Miss R-.'s room--ostensibly to get some sheets and pillow cases from the linen cupboard which was there.

"My wife would like to borrow some linen, Miss R-." said the Doctor as I introduced him. "The Laundry calls only every fortnight now-a-days and we are having guests."

I left him with her. She was chatting about some Hospital she'd been in.

In less than 10 minutes the Doctor came downstairs. "quite off," he said brusquely. "We must get her away."

"Tonight?"

"Well, no. There are certain formalities. Keep the child away from her--but try to have everything appear normal. Get one of the young Navy Doctors to stay the night. I'll go home and make some telephone calls. Can you get in touch with her family?"

"I might find an address among her things," I assented.

"Good."

And away went the Doctor.

When Alix returned, in time to settle Penny, she suggested to Miss R-. that they exchange rooms as Miss R-'s room and the Nursery were on a small private hall off the main bedroom hall, by the bath. Alix wished to be near Penny.

Miss R-. was insulted!

What! Leave her own room? It was the first time she had ever gone on a visit and been asked to move at once!

"No, I shall stay here," she said.

In the evening a young American Doctor from the Hospital Ship came up for coffee. We had it in the dining-room, as Miss R-. had condescended to dine with us and was

290

still there when the young Officer arrived. As Miss R-. left the table later he raised his eyebrows.

"I'll sleep in the Nursery with Penny," he said.

Well, to shorten this account, Miss R-. disappeared again!

But at 10 o'clock there was a knocking at the front door. Martha answered it.

"Well, I never!" said Martha in a low voice, coming back into the drawing-room and shutting the door after her. "Yes, it was Miss R-. She had a basket with her. I asked her where she'd been and she said, 'We've been black-berrying. But it got too dark for Penny to see the berries! So we came home.' Penny's asleep upstairs of course!"

It seemed as though Miss R-. would never go to bed that evening. The one time I looked in on her she was praying by her bed--fully clothed. Poor soul. I did feel sorry for her. But she refused all friendly overtures.

At last we all were settled for the night--which passed uneventfully, save that Penny woke once and wanted to know what that man was doing in her room! Fortunately, Martha heard--and quieted her.

In the morning Miss R-., as before, was not at breakfast. Instead, she slipped down the stairs and out--in a negligee! But, since she seemed to have the instincts of a Homing Pigeon, we let her go, and got on with the business of her removal.

On the hall table lay a post card addressed to a Mrs. S-. at a small hotel in London. The card read, "It is lovely here. There is a big river. There is a puppy too. I play with it. E.R."

Martha had remained home for the day to help--but Alix had had to report at the hospital. Martha 'phoned the

London Agency and told them of Miss R-.'s alarming "Qualifications," and learned that she had a sister but no one knew her name or address.

So then Martha got through to the address on the post card. Mrs. S-. had left, leaving no forwarding address but the Hotel <u>thought</u> she came from "X" in Sussex. By mid-afternoon, much before the Doctor called, Mrs. S-. was located. And we heard a strange tale!

Mrs. S-. was Miss R-'s sister. But there was another sister who had been "certified" for 15 years! And Mrs. S-. had been trying to get Miss R-. certified for a long time! She had been "put away" several times--but, in each case, eventually discharged in Mrs. S-'s care.

For years Miss R-. had been taking posts (positions), getting complained of, cared for by Mrs. S-., only to escape again, disappearing into another post, to again be complained of as "peculiar" or "eccentric." But no employer would prefer charges--or whatever you call the process of getting an irrational person put in proper custody. Mrs. S-. was very grateful to us for pressing the matter. Perhaps now Miss R-. would be properly taken care of! She (Mrs. S-.) would bear all expenses, of course.

Why Mrs. S-. had never been able to trace her sister on these "escapades" of hers we simply couldn't understand. A woman of Miss R-.'s appearance, with her "singing" voice, and all that luggage--3 more cases had come by a later train, and still later another burst parcel of clothes appeared by post--should have been easy to locate! Also, I couldn't help thinking of all the children who, at various periods, had been under Miss R-.'s care.

The Doctor, when he arrived, was not only interested in

Miss R-.'s "history"--he was relieved. "That makes it easy," he said.

"Then you can take her away this afternoon, Doctor?"

"No. I'm sorry. there are still formalities. But I'll call for her tomorrow. Have her things ready by 3 o'clock."

No need to relate the following events. They were much as those of the previous day and night, save that Miss R-. stuck more to her room and either prayed or read the Peter Rabbit book.

Thankful as I was to see her go off the next afternoon, I felt very sad. She must have been such a nice young person once upon a time. You could still see that. Something had gone very wrong somewhere--sometime. The unknown tragedies in some people's lives!

The "low-ceiling" created by the heavy, moist Devon climate, depresses me--and Martha. The rest of the family feel quite well when here. But every so often--to me and Martha-- there comes a point when we feel we must get out of this Turkish Bath! It is not that it is so warm always--for it can be terribly cold in winter, a damp cold--but the atmosphere here seems to steam (like a Turkish Bath), with white vapors that lie on the fields or boil up into nebulous clouds of sticky warmth. There is a heaviness in the air which becomes like a leaden weight on one's head. The Devonians call their climate "relaxing". To me it is impossible!

Only in late Fall or Winter mornings, or when there is a heavy frost, do I feel energetic. Then the countryside sparks and the air is as exhilarating as a tonic. I am reminded of home--where the static in the wintry cold air draws sparks when one brushes one's hair, or when people's hands touch after scuffing across a heavy carpet. I feel that this "electric" quality in the air of America produces the representative energetic and talkative American.

Martha and I used to escape to London now and then. But her job in Tommy's factory curtails these trips nowadays. However, in early December I went up to town to meet Dick. M.A.P. (Ministry of Aircraft Production) had notified me of his impending arrival from the States. I checked in at the Park Lane Hotel on Piccadilly as usual--our wartime "home-away-from-home"--to find a message from M.A.P. reading, "Delay. No further news." I waited until after tea and then called M.A.P.

"I can give you no news, Madame. Security reasons."

Of course. I shouldn't have asked. But I kept thinking of that first trip of Dick's and the terrible storm. And it was winter again.

I went for a walk in Green Park.

Upon my return to the Hotel there was still no message for me at the Desk. But, as I entered my room, there, on one of the beds, I saw a florist's parcel--several dozen carnations and a card, the personal card of Mr. Carlton Dyer, an associate of Dick's at M.A.P. The flowers quite terrified me! I was sure that something had happened--something dreadful.

Shaking, I 'phoned M.A.P. again.

"I can tell you nothing, Madame."

But my agitation drew the additional, "I will call you at once, Madame, when I have news."

I couldn't move. My knees shook, even as I sat beside the 'phone. I waited.

At long last the 'phone bell!

I shall never forget those few seconds between the ring of the 'phone and the pleasant voice of the young woman as I lifted the receiver. What message would she have for me?

"Mr. Cotton is in England, Madame. That is all for now."

I was so relieved I wept. And then rang for a vase for the flowers.

"Wait 'till I see Mr. Dyer! Scaring me like that!"

Eventually I got the message that Dick would be arriving at Victoria Station that evening. And that "Two Observers from Washington" would be with him. I transferred to a suite, left the door ajar, and proceeded to wait. The waiting I've done in this War! I had decided against meeting Dick at Victoria as wartime trains are often so very late.

At last the lift gates clicked for the "steenth" time. I heard Dick's voice. Rushing into the corridor I saw him, in familiar camels' hair coat (Because of what Dick was doing for Britain's Ministry of Aircraft Production, he had--as U.S. Lt. Commander in the Naval Reserve--gone to Lord Beaverbrook some time ago feeling that the time would come when he'd be called up. Lord Beaverbrook immediately called President Roosevelt on the 'phone and received permission for Dick to remain attached to M.A.P. Dick likes to say he was a Lend-Lease Loan!), accompanied by a U.S. Army Colonel and a U.S. Navy Commander--the "Observers from Washington." They all looked absolutely fagged!

There had been several unpleasant episodes on the trip. After leaving Bermuda, when about 1/3 of the way across the Atlantic, the plane had lost a propeller, and the Pilot was forced to turn back. Then, on the second sortie over the Ocean, one of

295

the plane's motors had conked out. Where-upon 1800 gals. of petrol had had to be dumped, and the plane once more returned to Bermuda. The third crossing was successful--in another plane! But, when coming in to land--at Poole--there was a fog. The Pilot had had to circle and circle, until a momentary break in the fog showed a patch of water below. Down they would glide--only to have the engines suddenly roar again, and the plane zoom sharply up! More circles--more glides--more zooms.

"It began to get on our nerves," said Dick.

"Very nasty!" agreed the Colonel.

"We've already decided to return by sea," announced the Commander.

Mr. Dyer appeared later and I berated him for the scare he had given me with those flowers. He laughed. "The flowers were for you. When I send Dick any floral offering it will be a large cabbage--the biggest one I can get!"

Dick and I saw quite a bit of the "Observers" during their two weeks' stay. Although they were being rushed off their feet, both day and night, by Army, Navy and R.A.F., they yet found time to see a bit of London, with us, under black-out conditions. The Germans even put over a few sporadic raids-- so that the Sirens, A.A. fire, the new rocket guns in Hyde Park, and some bombs could be "observed."

I was amused by Commander X's description of their trip to Dover. Shelling of the town was frequent at the time. But both Commander X and Colonel Y were far more impressed with the damp cold of England and the paucity of heat indoors.

"We got into bed with all our clothes on--coats, boots, and all! Ye Gods, were we cold! The shells coming over didn't mean a thing--and some were uncomfortably close. We were too busy trying to get warm. What a climate! And you can't even get warm indoors."

We knew all about that. What with the coal cuts and a water shortage and so many things rationed, one just can't be comfortable nowadays. But, whereas we had endured such deprivations for years, the "Observers" had leaped from bombless Washington to bombed London--from luxury to strict rationing--from comfort to a decided discomfort--and from safety to a "spot of bother", as the Englishman, in his casual English way, speaks of a situation where all Hell may, and does, break loose at any moment.

But always Comm. X. and Col Y. were impressed--as all our countrymen and women in the various Services are upon arrival here--with the British spirit of "chin-up" and "carry-on". If Comm. X. and Col. Y. had felt any discouragement over the War situation before leaving the States I am sure that they returned with the conviction that--hard as the job may be, the hazards great and seemingly insurmountable--none the less that Victory lies at the end of the road, that war-torn road of Destruction and Death along which American men now travel with their English brothers-in-arms.

January, 1944.
Another year of War is past. Another Christmas--and a houseful, as usual. Another New Year's Eve Party--this time at the American Officer's mess in Woolacombe. Such nice

boys! Doc, Gordon, Nip, Mac, Pix (Doc-Dr. Chester Albright, Major U.S. Army, Gordon-Lt. Col. Gordon Cauble, U.S. Army-later Brigadier General, Nip-Lt. Col. Reginald B. Page, U.S. Army-retired, Mac-Lt. Col. Macwhorter, U.S. Army-killed, Pix-Col. Alan G. Pixton, U.S. Army-later Brigadier General). We all had a wonderful time! There was a big Christmas tree in the dance hall--and plenty to eat and drink. Only the fact that these young officers are here on an Assault Course--training for the Invasion--recalled the War at the moment. They laughed--and danced--and laughed--and drank--and laughed. We all did. Yet each man there knew that 1944 was The Year for him--that when D-Day comes 'round the numbers will begin to go up. Will his be one of them? On the sands of some French beach will he say, "This is It!"

Happy New Year!

February - 1944.

In the same month we had 2 "surprise packages" among the usual guests. Terry (Lt. T. Tullock, R.N., a New Zealander and friend of Pete's.) came down on leave after a long spell in the Mediterranean with the Royal Navy, and Richard King,--just landed in England from the States,--arrived for a short visit. Rich, now Capt. King, U.S. Army, is the son of our very good friends, Mr. and Mrs. E.H. King of Newtonville, near Boston, Mass. Dick and I and the Kings used to play bridge together, gossip and drink coffee together, go to Cape Cod together on holiday. It was wonderful hearing their son, Rich's voice on the phone. Some one from home!

He came to us for 3 days--just as Terry arrived. And

later the 2 boys went up to London with Dick and Alix. How Rich longed for an air-raid! And the very night of the day he left London there was one. Was he disgusted! While in town Alix dragged him about to see the "ruins"--and up into the Dome of St. Paul's for the wonderful view--and around to the Horseguards and Westminster Abbey and Buckingham Palace, etc. They went to Grosvenor House for dinner/dancing,--and to tea on Piccadilly,--and down Bond St. for souvenirs--and along Oxford St. for the crowds,--etc. Rich loved every bit of it. But most of all he loved the West Country where we are, at "Springfield." He fell in love with the English countryside--it's eternal green. He had come straight from snow and ice--a white New England Winter. He loved the thatched cottages--the high hedges--the Pubs--the little old stone churches--the Wineries, where whiskey may be bought in noggins.

"I could stay forever!" said Rich.

American hyperbole, of course. But we understood it--for we have felt the same. The land here casts a spell. The beauty of the country almost blinds one to the discomforts found here--not quite. We shiver in Winter--in spite of the green grass with it's illusion of eternal Spring or Summer. There are times, nowadays, when we would swap our gorgeous view for a gorgeous steak--or just two fried eggs and an honest rasher of bacon--or even a mass of porridge, provided it had real cream and lots of sugar on it! These mirages in the barren desert of War rationing!

Having trouble with the water pipes one day we inveigled a plumber out here. He made a quaint discovery. After ripping up most of the floor in Martha's room and a good part of the upper hall he located a portion of piping wherein there was another pipe--fully 3 feet long! How this pipe--and bright brass at that--ever got inside the larger one, and how long it had been there, the plumber had no idea. But he didn't seem surprised.

The vagaries of English plumbing are manifold. There are pipes on the outside of houses, where they freeze in severe winters, and there are outlets, for the overflow of baths, projecting from the outer walls like small fountains!

When the children and I arrived in London, England-- just arrived in fact--Martha came down with chicken pox. So, since she and Alix shared a bedroom, the Heavers most kindly had Alix to stay with them in Wimbledon. She promptly took a bath. It was afternoon--and, following a family custom, she read in the tub with the taps open and nicely regulated, keeping the bath temperature at perfection.

A sudden commotion inside and outside the house interrupted here. There was a loud knocking on the bathroom door and, in very firm tones, Frank wanted to know what Alix was doing! Water from the overflow pipe was spouting in foamy suds from the side of the house above the drive. The grocer's boy had been drenched! Would Alix be so good as to shut off the water and get on with her bath.

That was our first acquaintance with these "overflow pipes." We had already met with the English ventilation system for bathrooms--a 6-inch square grillwork, high up in the wall, and quite open to the outer air, chill breezes, damp and all. We had promptly pasted thick brown paper over the "ventilator" in the wall of the bath at our London flat. But the "overflow pipe" we had not heard of until then. Sure enough though--upon investigation--there it was, sticking out of our flat wall above the Tradesmen's entrance. There had been no complaints. Probably because, as a family, we usually bathe at night when Tradesman aren't around.

The "overflow pipes" here, at "Springfield," are out of business "for the duration." Water is rationed. We must keep the bath water below 5 inches. I read in the papers some while ago that the baths in Buckingham Palace have "plimsol lines" painted at the 5 inch mark. The Royal Family shares this War with it's People.

I was grumbling one day to Cook because the very last spoonful of some jam had not been scraped thoroughly from the pot into the serving dish for tea. Jam is rationed.

"Why don't you put the jam pot on the table, Madame? Even the Queen eats straight from the jam pot these days," she said.

I wouldn't be surprised.

End of February, 1944.

Things have moved a bit thick and fast these past few weeks. I don't pretend to recount the War--it's active waging in all theaters but, being with us always, in some phase or another, and it's conditions imposed upon us, it gets into this Journal, of course. It's shadow spreads over all England. The children--and even the animals feel it. The food problem, alone, gives so many headaches--and so many heartaches, because we must deny the children, and the sick, so much that they need. The overworked Doctors can not even put a patient on a diet nowadays--too many things are quite unobtainable.

But the rationing is fair--very fair. For instance, there is no chance of using all one's weekly food coupons for meat--or for any other rationed articles of food. That would create shortages. Here we have 2 oz.'s of butter a week per person-- and no more. We have 1s. 2d. (24 cents) worth of meat a week per person--and beyond that may buy only offals (dreadful word!) such as liver, kidneys, and hearts--if you can get them. Or sausages that are 60% bread or semolina, and are so highly seasoned that I hate to think what may be thus camouflaged within them.

Speaking of sausages, one day when we had toad-in-the-hole for lunch (sausages in yorkshire pudding) I was appalled at the color of the "toads." They were quite black.

"What ever can be in these?" I said as I dished out the servings. "Looks like gunpowder."

The explosive sounds--accompanied by wild-eyed clutchings for glasses of water--that simultaneously followed the first mouthfuls of the main luncheon dish seemed to corroborate my thoughts.

Gunpowder, indeed.

The family being speechless at the moment, I sampled one of the black sausages, myself.

"Pepper!" I gasped between gulps of water. "Black Pepper!"

The sausages, being off the ration, had been purchased by Alix at a butcher shop other than the one where we were registered. Upon complaint the next day we learned that the Butcher's Boy had been sacked.

"I near lost my customers," groaned the Butcher. "What a mort o' pepper that boy must 'ave used!"

I'll say so.

The middle of February, Dick was scheduled for another trip to Washington. This time he planned to take me and Alix with him. It seemed a good idea after what Alix had been through. We would be gone a couple of months--so the problems of passports, visas, clothes, etc. kept us busy for some time. Since we would be sharply curtailed as to finances while in the States, we had to take with us all essential clothing. That meant lots of luggage, as winter clothes are bulky. And, because most American homes and hotels are very warm in spite of the cold outdoors, we would need lighter frocks there than here where one dresses indoors almost as warmly as when outdoors. As a consequence, when Alix, Dick, and I set off from the Instow Station we had a batch of cases and one trunk between us, including a large roll of steamer rugs wrapped around magazines for the voyage. We looked as though we were planning to be gone a year! As a matter of fact Dick was away 6 months. But Alix and I were back in Instow in a fort night!

There had been some controversy over Alix' Exit Visa due to her English marriage. But at last, the very day before we left Instow, we were notified that it was coming through. So off we went. At the Park Lane Hotel a message awaited Alix from the Home Office--a gloomy message. If Mrs. Dean would contract to remain in the States for the duration, she could go. But a return visa would not be forthcoming until after the War.

What a bombshell! This definitely was an unexpected, last-minute blow to our plans. Dick worked frantically. Sir

303

Robert Renwick interceded.   But the Home Office was adamant.

Of course it was because of coming D-Day and it's closely woven plans--but I knew nothing of that at the time. However, travel of all sorts had been suddenly clamped down on. A week earlier and we might have made it.

Well, I couldn't leave Alix. It didn't seem fair. Just a bare 24 hours and I could have "done something"--taken Penny along, for instance, and then she and Alix could both have remained in the States for the duration. But the "boat train" was leaving in a few hours.

Dick was glued to the 'phone in our Hotel bedroom. He sat on one bed and I on the other--the 'phone on the bedside table between us. It was late evening, and Sir Robert and Lady Renwick had been in for dinner with us. They had been kind and very sympathetic--but nothing further could be done. Dick could only call "So-and-So"--and "So-and-So"--and hope for the best. This Dick was doing. But it soon became evident that Alix and I were not going to the states.

Dick put down the receiver with a very final click.

"I can do no more, dear," he said.

"It's just as well I'm not going," I answered a bit tearfully. "I'd worry all the time over there with the rest of the family here--raids and everything.   The change was more important for Alix."

"It's a damn shame!" Dick snorted. "How'd you like to go to Edinburgh?"

This was not so crazy as it seems.   Dick and I had planned a short trip to Edinburgh in the Autumn of 1939, after the children returned to school.   We had never been to Scotland. But the War had upset that trip. So I knew what

Dick really meant--that he was terribly sorry that I was done out of this trip, and so how about an alternative?

"Do you want to go to Edinburgh?" he repeated.

"Without you?" I wailed. "And in this damned war! What would I be doing in Edinburgh!"

Well, instead of a trip to Edinburgh, I settled for 2 weeks in London. I simply couldn't go right back to Instow with all that luggage--after having farewelled all my friends there!

"But, mind you, Peg, you're then to stay out of London 'till I return." (Dick knew of the threatened Robots--but he didn't mention that fact to me at the time, of course. It was hush-hush information.)

I thought him a bit fussy. We had been through too many air-raids for him to get a complex about them at this late date. But I agreed.

So Alix and I, with rather mechanical smiles, waved Dick off as his taxi left for Euston Station and the Glasgow train. The Night Porter took away most of our luggage for storage, and Alix and I took up where we had nearly left off--in London, dear shabby London.

"We'll rush about, shopping and seeing people," I said to Alix. And to myself, "We won't have time to think of being disappointed. There'll be distractions."

There were distractions, all right. After a spell of comparative calm the Germans began raiding London again. it was like old times. And how!

Alix and I were at the Plaza Cinema one evening--in lower Regent Street--when "Air Raid Warning" was flashed on the screen. We decided to try for the Park Lane Hotel before the German planes got through to London. I don't like

Cinemas in the air-raid. All those closely packed people with only a roof above for protection!

But, as we came out into the street, the guns to the South of London were already tearing the night sky into ribbons of deadly white light. We dashed around the corner onto Piccadilly for a bus. Good old London buses! They always carry-on.

As our bus trundled along Piccadilly, making it's stops as sedately as though it were a star-lit night of Peace, I looked at the faces about me in the intermittent gun flashes. Calm, collected passengers paying their fares to a busy young conductress who unfalteringly made change, pushing the tiny, shaded, blue light bulb, on a trolley above her, along the aisle as she progressed. All the other lights were off. What a people! I thought.

Just as Alix and I alighted at our bus stop before the Park Lane Hotel the guns across Green Park opposite opened up. The terrifying salvos sent us flying across Piccadilly, heedless of the traffic. Not only was there shrapnel coming down, but enemy planes must be overhead. Pushing through the revolving entrance door and into the lighted lounge was like stepping from one world into another. There sat men and women nonchalantly chatting, drinking coffee, cocktails, beer-- the little waitresses bustling about. The dining-room was full, the writing-room in use. Save for those "extra" people, who had patently come in from the street for shelter, and were standing about in groups along the wall, the scene was normal. I never failed to find this interesting--this classic acceptance of an air-raid as a nuisance.

People looked bored or irritated--never excited or frightened.

That evening was but the beginning, a prelude to a series of Night Raids--short raids, but very sharp ones. The H.E.'s (High Explosive Bombs) then dropped upon London and her outskirts, seemed to have matured along with the war. They burst wherever they hit with an explosive overripeness and rottenness that spread DEATH, in capital letters, among the people once again.

But the days were perfect--sunny, clear, just cold enough to feel bracing. We would go shopping, or out for lunch, and even to a Cinema, with the fair certainty that, if there was going to be a raid, it wouldn't start until evening. People are strange creatures, indeed. Neither Alix nor I had thought of curtailing our visit. Alix stayed one week, as she had planned--while I remained on for another, Elsie and Frank Heaver coming up to town to join me.

The night before Alix left there was an extra sharp raid about 11 p.m.--a favorite hour with the Nazis. Alix and a young British Army Captain had come up-stairs to keep me company. I was reading in bed.

"George (a war reporter) has been up on the roof, Mother, and he counted 7 fires--out Hampstead way."

"Been popping in a bit closer tonight," said the young officer. "But I think we're driving them off now, Mrs. Cotton."

We certainly were trying to by the sound. My bed was vibrating from the rocket guns in Hyde Park.

"It's just as well you're going back tomorrow, Alix," I said. "You should be with Penny."

"Well, you ought to go back too, Mother. Daddy wouldn't like this at all--with him away."

But I have a weakness for London to the point of being quite witless. Since I wasn't likely to return for a while I was going to get my 2 weeks' worth out of the city--raids or no.

Certain highlights of that particular February week in London with the Heavers will remain permanently painted on my memory screen. There was the night Frank Champion (young British Pilot, who, at the time, was shuttling back and forth between England and Egypt) came in to dinner with me. None of us had seen Frank for almost 2 years. Martha used to go dancing with him when he lived in London. He had been on ships with Pete. Dick and I knew his parents. Frank was one of my boys. It was good to see him again. He looked fit. Yet about a year ago he had broken his back in a crash in Africa. The resiliency of youth.

The Heavers dined with us and we all had a great old gossip. We also had a great old raid--and at about the usual time. Frank Champion had left, and the Heavers and I were having a good night chat upstairs in our suite when the raid started. Frank put out the lights and pulled open the drapes at one of the windows.

"Going to be a good show," he said and sort of sniffed, like an old war horse.

The sky was a smoky yellow, streaked by weaving searchlights with gun flashes breaking up the pattern. It didn't seem like night, that we looked out into from the Hotel window--neither was it twilight, nor daylight. It was a peculiar light, a light that seemed to have body and a hidden threatening power. Personally I recoiled from it--and was half-way across the room when the first really near bomb struck with an explosion so sharp that it sounded more like an oversize clap of thunder than an exploding bomb.

"Whew! That must have hit the Hotel somewhere!"

308

ejaculated Frank. "Sounded like it got the end of the wing,"--
which projected to the left of the windows.

"Do let's go downstairs!" I said. "We'll have 2 more
floors over us there!"

Frank, and even Elsie, seemed reluctant to leave the
window. But we did go down to the writing-room--to find it
full, of course. Although it was a sharp raid it was a short one.
and we were able to go up to bed very soon. But I had only
just crawled between the sheets when the darn Siren went
again. This often happens--and is most annoying! We all
hurriedly dressed and went below again. When you may have
to rush out into the street at a moment's--or second's--notice 'tis
best to be clothed and in your right mind. I could be clothed--
but I wasn't sure about a "right mind."

There must be a Fireman somewhere in my Family Tree
for a raid always keys me up. Often after the All Clear, we
went up on the Hotel roof to count the fires--I counted 11 fires
about us one night--and the ring of manacing flame had a
terrible beauty as it shot up in gigantic tongues of hot lights
into the brooding dome of night. And later, when in bed, the
windows open again, the smell of smoke would seep into my
dozing senses like a narcotic--and I would sleep, in spite of
recent pandemonium and the resultant destruction and death
throughout the city. Are we savages at heart?

The night one of the H.E. bombs fell in the Horse
Guard's Parade at the southern end of St. James park, and the
windows in the Admiralty and Whitehall and along the Mall
were blown in, and the Treasury set on fire, that evening I went
out, with Frank, onto the pavement by the Piccadilly entrance
to the Hotel and watched the crackling fountains of white flame
pour up behind the trees across Green Park. The sky on either

side was red from terrible fires.

As Frank and I took in the scene about us, I could well understand the strange fascination that brought groups of American Red Cross Girls (quartered in the Park Lane) out to see the show. But Frank grumbled at their "cluttering up the place." As an Englishman it was his country, his city, and therefore his show. He didn't say this but that was what he meant--I thought. For many English resent what they call "The American Invasion."

There are several reasons for this resentment. In the first place, American Service men and women receive much higher pay than the British. Therefore, the English girls gravitate to the Americans with their free spending ways--and many an English Service man thus loses his girl. Also, the food in the American messes seems luxurious to the point of pampering; by comparison with that of the British Forces, the Americans are spoiled. And of course, the American P-X's offer so many ariticles either rationed in England or downright unobtainable. American nylons, alone, are fabulous bait. All this is common knowledge but, in many cases, it promotes differences rather than understanding between the English and the Americans. I expect all this will come out in the wash-- Anglo-American Laundry, Ltd.!

In the 13 days I remained in London there were 13 raids in the last 9 days. On the evening of the 12th, bombs fell so close to the Park Lane Hotel that 128 windows were blown in. The Heavers and I were in the Writing-room, as usual, when a near bomb splintered the window boards. The roller shades flapped in the blast. Men in uniform went down on the floor. But many people, including myself, jumped up--which is bad form under such circumstances.

There was a surge to the air-raid shelter in the basement. Formerly the Hotel ballroom, the shelter looked like a 3rd rate cafe, with the piano shrouded in baize for the duration, the chandeliers lowered from the ceiling and encased in burlap, and small tables about the place with lanterns, or candles, on them, a few bracket lights on the walls. Mr. Plaster, Advertising Agent for British films, was seated at a wall table, reading. We joined him. He was living in the Park Lane Hotel, standing his turn at Fire Watch on the roof, attending to his business through the week, and spending the weekends with his wife at their villa on Saunton Sands the other side of Barnstaple--quite near us at Instow.

"I always come down here now," said Mr. Plaster. "Best air-raid shelter in town since the American Army reinforced it. (2 floors of the Hotel have been taken over by the U.S. Army.) Had my windows blown in one night, and sounds like they've just gone again."

"And no wonder," grunted Frank. "With all the American Army vehicles about Mayfair we make a fine target! All those big white stars painted on them!"

Bang! Crash!

A bomb to the left of us.

Bang! Crash!

"I'm going back tomorrow," I said. "At this rate I'll be staying just one night too long! The children ought to have one parent with them in this War."

"Don't tell me you think you'll be getting out of the War in Instow, Mrs. Cotton!" laughed Mr. Plaster.

"Well, it's not London," I answered.

"No, but look what happened to me a while ago. Machine-gunned by the Nazis in broad daylight! One of your

311

Assault Courses was holding maneuvers on Saunton Sands and I had a bunch of Brass Hats and Staff at the Villa. We were on the Terrace, having some drinks, and watching the show. All of a sudden I spotted a plane coming in from the Bristol Channel. 'That's a Nazi plane!' I yelled.

'Nonsense!' said the General beside me. But the plane tore right at us. The General took one peek through his binoculars and went flat behind the Terrace Wall. We all did! That Nazi plane ripped right into the boys--killed 2 or 3-- wounded several. Shot up my garage, put bullets through the car windscreen and scared the daylight out of my pup. She was asleep in the car. Didn't find her for 3 days--miles away from the house! You might as well stay here, Mrs. Cotton."

After the All Clear the four of us went out to reconnoiter. A couple of bombs seemed to have fallen near Dick's London Office and I wanted to see what damage had been done. Several side streets, leading from Piccadilly down to St. James Square, were sprinkled with the shattered glass of many blasted windows. The Ritz had miraculously escaped. Down St. James Street we picked our way towards the fire engines and the crowds already assembled. But Elsie and I had to give up. Evening sandals are poor protection on a crystal carpet of glass.

"Maybe I could carry you?" said Mr. Plaster facetiously.

I refused. Supposing Mr. plaster slipped (with me) on all that jagged glass! It might not be our feet that would be cut, and we'd be eating off the mantelpiece for weeks. We all returned to the Hotel.

"Now remember, Mrs. Cotton," admonished Mr. Plaster as he bade us goodnight. "You'll not be getting out of the War if you go back to Devon tomorrow!"

Well, there didn't seem to be a War in London the next morning--unless you concentrated on the damage done. It was a beautiful sunny day.

"That's the trouble, of course," said Elsie. "Everything can seem so normal in daylight."

But I decided to leave on the afternoon train. I would be cutting my 2 weeks visit short by only one day. And, who knows, that very night, might be The Night for the Park Lane Hotel. I wasn't going to tempt Providence--or the Nazis.

So I took a bus to Kensington for a last errand--and was horrified to find practically every window gone from Princes' Gate to Knightsbridge to Kensington High Street. The Albert Hall was eyeless, roofs on adjacent buildings were "pitted." The flats facing Hyde Park and Kensington Gardens were riddled with black gaping apertures where shining glass would otherwise reflect the morning sun. The only block of flats that twinkled and blinked in the February sunshine was that at Ia, Queens Gate, where the Martens lived.

"What a freak bit of luck," I thought as my bus rolled past. "But they certainly deserve it."

Major Frazer Martens, the eldest son, is a Jap P.O.W.-- has been so ever since Singapore. Two very short messages are all that the Martens have received from him. Now a ghastly silence has prevailed for months. No news at all. Yet the Martens continue to hope, in the face of bleak despair bred from the horrible accounts of suffering among the Jap P.O.W.s. The third son, F/O (Flying Officer). Arthur Martens,-- "Tubby" to family and friends--was lost on operations over Germany. Pilot of a bomber, he was reported missing--later "presumed killed."

I recalled Mrs. Martens' courageous decision to remain in London and keep a home for her boys to come back to. The home is still there. So are Mr. and Mrs. Martens and their 2 daughters, both of whom are in War work, both standing their turn at Fire Watching.

Indomitable courage. Fealty to the Family.

These are the ties that bind a nation into a close-knit band of heroes and heroines who, defending their Country's freedom and way of life by the simple expedient of living as best they may in the midst of shortages, discomforts, and dire peril, yet help to fight--and win--this War. Should you call the Martens heroes and heroines they would be as deprecating as the English (the Martens are Canadians).

"What else would you have us do? We must support the boys."

I took the 2:30 train home from Waterloo Station that afternoon. And, when Gerry and Smale met me at the Instow Station, I fairly tumbled out of my compartment onto the platform. The reaction had set in.

"My! Am I thankful to be home again!"

The following week I had tea with the Gambles. Peggy, their eldest daughter, (Mrs. Jack Foote) and her small son, Dickie, were there. They had been bombed-out in those February raids on London. Living in a top-floor flat near Kensington High street, Peggy,--with Dickie in her arms--had but just reached the basement floor when a close-falling bomb blew in the windows, damaged the roof, shook plaster from the walls and ceilings, and made a frightful mess of the place. It had been a narrow escape.

So Peggy salvaged what goods she could and took the earliest possible train to Instow, where her parents met her.

"You've no idea how I felt," said Mrs. Gamble to me. "There was my daughter, sitting on a case in the luggage-van, holding Dickie on her lap, cases, bundles, pram beside her. All the way from London like that! It made me feel terrible--as though she were a refugee. Poor Dear!"

I understood perfectly.

"To think that my daughter should have been driven from her home--that she should have had to suffer such indignities--that England and her way of life have come to such a pass that her People are hounded by death and destruction!"

That was what Mrs. Gamble meant.

Judy and little Margo are here. We had them come down--just after my return from London--to get out of the raids. Judy is from Springfield, Mass. Married to an Englishman, Lt. Stanley E. Beverley, R.N., who is stationed at the Admiralty in London, Judy has endured practically all the London air-raids. She broke her ankle running for a bus in the black-out, and Margo (Margaret Ellen Carey Beverley), now 10 months old, was born in an air-raid. It was high time that Margo and her Mother had a break.

We are a houseful (I think I've said that before!), but a happy one. Rich King is here again for a few days. When he learned that there were already 12 people in the house and that

315

he would make a 13th he was all for leaving at once. But I persuaded him that 13 was a lucky number. Dick and I were married on the 13th, a Friday! Then Stan came down for 48 hrs. leave. So every bed, and cot, in the place is occupied.

Spring in Devon is on the bloom. The daffies are everywhere. I tell Rich, everytime he extols the beauties of nature here--which is often!--that he hasn't seen anything yet. he should be here in May and June--the rose season.

In the evenings, and sometime at tea, if it rains and is very cold, we light the drawing-room fire. It's cheerful crackle produces an answering cheerful chatter amongst us all. Stan entertains us with stories of people and incidents, past and present. He has an endless fund of such. His knowledge of English and American History would make a successful platform lecturer of him! He could certainly qualify as a guide about London--and he is always ready and willing to talk to Americans and to show them about. What is more, he offers them the hospitality of his flat in town. He and Judy are always putting up some one.

As though housework, cooking, bringing up Margo, queuing for rations, fish, and vegetables, collecting Margo's orange juice from the Clinic, drying wash in the bathroom, taking a lift down to the basement whenever the sirens go, sleeping on the floor in a friend's flat downstairs when Stan is on night duty--as though that were not enough to do, Judy shares her hectic, busy, but cheerful, life with innumerable young men and women in the various Services who find it impossible, or too expensive, to get accommodation in London on a short-notice leave.

"Stan is always bringing someone home," says Judy. "I

316

don't see how you cope with it all, Peg. I find it very difficult at time."

But neither Judy and Stan, nor I and my family, would have it otherwise. We all get very tired, but, also, we all get a great satisfaction and a great pleasure out of this "being together," this "sharing," this communal experience of living, through the war, like one big family.

Rich King is intrigued by the names hereabout--"Pine-Coffin" on a memorial shaft by the Bideford Bridge,--"Gabriel and Sons," the stone cutters, who fashion and inscribe gravestones and monuments,--and the prevalence of hyphenated names, Churchill-Longman, Pollard-Loseley, Hill-Climo, Berry-Torr, Critchley-Salmonson, Champion-deCrepigny, etc. To an American, such names have an Old World flavor. We find them more English than the English.

"If you are interested in names," said Stan one evening, "listen to these. I can vouch for them. I've seen them.

"Shove and Tidy--Sweeps." (Chimney Sweeps). That sign is in Rochester Row, Westminster. Perfect, isn't it? And in Oxted, Surrey, there's a concern named "Smellie and Humms'. Can't remember what they are--but I remember the names well--who wouldn't?' And there's a London Pub--on Seven Sisters' Rd., I think--called 'The World Turned Upside Down.' That's appropriate enough!"

"When I was in the Personnel Office of Peter Jones," added Judy, "I thought I'd never get used to the names of the people working there with me! There was a Miss Parrot, a Miss Beer, and a Miss Herring, a Mrs. Blitz, and a Mr. Rainbow."

Which reminded me of Mrs. "Urn." We had been

cookless (as usual) for weeks when, one day, Mrs. Pedler spoke to me of a friend, a Mrs. "Urn," who would be willing to come to me as a daily cook. So Mrs. "Urn" was engaged and a few days later I told Mrs. Pedler how pleased I was.

"But what an odd name," I said. "Urn. Mrs. Urn." (It made me think of "Pine-Coffin" and "Gabriel & Sons.") I didn't think I'd like the name, myself. (Mrs. Urn.) "How do you spell it, Mrs. Pedler?"

"Hache Hee arr en hee," replied Mrs. Pedler.

"Oh! You mean Herne, Mrs. Pedler!" I exclaimed. "Why don't you pronounce it that way?"

"I do," said Mrs. Pedler. "Urn."

Persistent people, the English.

Easter Sunday, 1944

The little church looked very, very lovely this morning--bursting with people and flowers, mostly daffodils. It was like sitting in a garden enclosed by high stone walls--the orifices crowded with blooms. But, in spite of all this loveliness, rather unlovely thoughts fluttered about in my mind.

The Easter offering is a personal one. It goes to the Rector as a slight gift--very slight in some cases. There are so many poor and overcrowded districts--small, quite unrenumerative parishes, slums, dock areas, etc.--where the Churches system of "Trial and Denial" places it's servants.

However, the poverty of the people and their dour surroundings become both a challenge to the Rector and a source of spiritual inspiration. Years as Shepherd of such a flock is an experience productive of great tolerance, a certain austerity, and a wide humor. But one can't help wondering

318

why such "proving grounds" as poor and overcrowded districts are necessary--why they must exist at all! Perhaps the fact that you cannot build an edifice without money, but that you can build a soul without financial aid, has something to do with the matter.

It has always seemed to me so unfair as to be almost unchristian that so many, many men (and women) in the service of the Lord should be so poorly paid. And, as though that were not enough in itself (this paucity of independence, for that is what an inadequate salary often means, unfortunately) the additional matter of the Easter Offering (Will it be of substantial help?) is aggravated by the fact that a certain percent of the offering is deducted by the Government according to taxation laws here.

This is a very muddled world, indeed, and to straighten it out will take a bit of doing--when this War is finally over. There will be not only the rubble of blitzed buildings to clear up, the evacuated people to re-place into their homes, and the countless homes to build anew, but there will be the ruins of hundreds--thousands--of broken War marriages.

(I know personally of a few, and have heard much of many, alas.

1) A young woman, not yet thirty and with a ten year old son, had not seen her husband, save on infrequent leaves, for over two years. Because of the air-raids she was living in unattractive rented quarters away outside London, her former home. The loneliness was unbearable, the discipline of a father lacking for the

boy. The young wife took up with a gigolo type, a chap unfit for any of the forces, but employed in a wartime job nearby. One late afternoon the son returned from the cinema to "catch" his mother and the gigolo. The boy ran away. The mother attempted to drown herself in the bathtub.

2) Once a happy and united family, the P---s became almost extinct as such. The elder of two sons was killed. The younger son--having promised to look after his brother's wife and two children should just such a tragedy occur--married his brother's widow. This upset Mrs. P----and her husband. And cumulative war worries caused a fatal heart attack for Mr. P----. In time to come Mrs. P-----committed suicide.

3) A young flying officer fell in love with a lonesome young wife (with one child) and spends all his leaves with her. She plans a divorce--and the Flying Officer and she will marry.

This latter sort of thing is rampant--but rarely with the steadying outcome of marriage, alas. Loneliness, loneliness for the women; "today we live, tomorrow we may die" for the men. Promiscuity is an insidious disease produced by the War.

4) I had a young American Officer (a bachelor) ask my advice on a very personal problem. His younger brother had been killed, leaving a wife and child. The younger brother had asked the older to help in such

case--and a promise had been given. "I am very fond of her," the American Officer said. "I might even learn to love her." the only advice I could offer was for him to keep in touch with the young widow by correspondence, but with no slightest suggestion of what he had in mind--a possible marriage with her. The promise to his younger brother would thus be kept, and time might well offer the right solution. I never heard the result of this matter, but have often thougt of it--and remember the Officer's final remarks. "I'm going to pray over this. For, if I can, I will do it--if she wants it. But, after the War, I, too may not make it back home, of course." He did make it back home, and after a year he married his brother's widow.)

Can they be rebuilt? And the establishment of a decent and adequate way of life for all must be accomplished. More than mere financial aid is needed here. The Church must produce a few so-called modern miracles to tempt the modern world--and to convince it. Spiritual help is needed also. But so long as money remains a factor in this commercial minded world--whether the commodity be soles or souls--money must be reckoned with, for vast rehabilitation requires vast sums. One's mind and heart are puzzled indeed.

Not only has mankind asked the ultimate sacrifice of it's Youth but--when there is Peace again--this same Youth is going to be asked to solve some staggering problems. Are we, of another generation, going to be able to help?

Dick is still in Washington. How I miss him--and at

times need him! There's the day Gerry tried to enlist in the British Army. He still longs to get into uniform and Dick has tried to arrange this while in the States. Dick even went to see Surgeon General Parran. But, no! For Gerry absolutely could not be given an anti-tetanus shot--it might kill him. (To this day Gerry wears one of those medical bracelets reading, "Subject to anti-philactic shock. Specifically horse serum.")

So, as I said, Gerry is in the factory. Right now he is on the night shift, which enables him to get out into the sunshine and fresh air of the days. One day he did not appear for lunch as usual. I asked Smale if he' knew were Gerry was.

"Didn't you know, Mrs. Cotton?" said Smale.

"Know what?" I asked.

"He went to Plymouth to enlist."

"Enlist?" I repeated stupidly.

"Yes. In the British Army."

I flew to the 'phone and called Washington. Luckily Dick was in his office. He called Nip in Woolacombe.

Soon Nip called me. He had contacted the proper authorities in Plymouth. I was not to worry. Gerry had been turned down because of subjectivity to anti-philactic shock. He'd be home soon.

Was I grateful! Not only might Gerry have had an Anti-tetanus shot but he would have lost his American citizenship if Sworn into the British Army.

April 17th, 1944

This has been Animal week at Springfield! We began with a love-sick cow! Martha (having the day off) and I were playing Bridge here on Tuesday with Elsie Heaver and May Bauer. It was a perfect Spring day--too nice to sit indoors, really. But we had the windows open, and the pale young green of trees and grass was reflected in the mirrors so that, along with the view from the windows, we seemed to be sitting in the garden.

The banks of purple aubretia and spikes of yellow wallflowers were poetically decorative. Spring burgeoned. And the voice of Spring was heard in the land. Strident and plaintive moos, long drawn out, continually interrupted our game.

"Where is that cow!"

"What's the matter with her?"

"Spring," said Elsie laconically.

The bovine yodeling went on, at intervals, for over an hour. An echo seemed to come from the hill behind the house.

"Must be 2 cows," said Elsie.

And then one of them appeared. She charged up the drive-way and took a few "dervish-turns" as Moxi, my dachshund, flew at her.

"Good Heavens! She'll get in the garden!" Martha dashed out the door, the rest of us following.

The cow crashed on, up the bank, along the flagged walks, into the rose arbor. Moxie was having a high old time. The mooing cow was feeling frustrated. She went about in circles.

A well-aimed rock, thrown by Martha, sent her leaping--like her ancestress who jumped over the moon--over the hedge and back to the drive, where Moxie exuberantly finished the chase--out into the road.

We resumed our Bridge.

"Well, one cow is not so bad as the eight sheep we had one afternoon," I remarked.

"We had 14 cows in our garden last year!" said Elsie. "We had to get the farmer and his dog to drive them out. The dog did almost as much damage as the cows--it dashed about so, breaking down the plants. And you should have seen the lawn afterwards! Pitted with holes 3 inches deep!"

The next morning, Wednesday, I was dressing for the London train when the doorbell range. Expecting the Postman, Alix answered it. Five minutes later she was in my room, an over-sized and gangling black Labrador pup in her arms.

"Aubrey (Naval Lt. friend of Alix) gave him to me. He's off--Aubrey is. Right away! He wants me to have Bass."

"What!"

"Bass. Aubrey named him Bass because he likes beer. Isn't he cute?" Alix was charmed.

I was not! We'd had pups before--11 at one time, 13 at another--litters of our 2 Pointers. I would as soon house a swarm of locusts! But I had to catch the train, and left.

Bass remained 6 days. The removal of half of the baize from the Staff room door, one third destruction of front door mat, the ruinous chewing of fringe on best chair in drawing-room--not to mention the unmentionables about the house-- added up to an eviction quota when I returned from London.

A young Airman had come back with me for a 48 hr.'s leave with us, and, when he left, Bass went with him. Not only is there more scope for such a pup on a large airfield but, if transported in a Bomber and dropped by parachute over Germany, his sabotage efforts would be tremendous. They might shorten the war.

The hen entered the picture the last day that Bass was

with us--a short and sharp visitation by one of our Rhode Island Reds in the kitchen and Staff room at tea time. Bass in pursuit, plus Moxie's efforts, made a tidy mess (can one say that?) of the rubbish bin, vegetable racks, and the elegant (?) basin of "green leavings" that accumulate for Smale, to feed the fowls.

I like the picturesque in country living. But too much of anything is too much

Then came the black-bird. It flew down the chimney in the drawing-room Friday morning, after breakfast. It brought all the soot with it! You never saw such a mess. Getting the bird out of the room didn't help matters. Soot everywhere-- thick, like black snow, on the mantelpiece, hearth, and rug-- thin, like a dingey film, everywhere else. Practically the whole room had to be washed!

The Sweep is coming next week. But it will be like "locking the barn door after the horse has been stolen."

That was Animal-Week at Springfield.

August 23rd, 1944.

Spent the afternoon out with Dolly Gamble, and, upon return, sighted 2 American Army Captains in the drawing-room (through the windows). So I circumvented same and went upstairs to wash and tidy up--being frowsty. Returning downstairs, I met Meda (Miss Marie Flack, Penny's governess) and Penny in the hall, back from tea on the beach. Meda looked very elated and the gilt tops of 2 champagne bottles stuck out of her knitting bag.

"Paris est liberè! Madame!"

325

I had not heard the news on the radio so felt a bit stunned.

"Madame! Paris est liberè!"

Such a luminous smile on Meda's face and tears in her eyes.

"I thought to myself," continued Meda, "we must have something in the house with which to celebrate--and here it is."

She patted the 2 bottles of champagne.

"Where ever did you get those, Meda?" I asked. "They're scarce as hen's teeth nowadays."

"From Mrs. King (wife of Mr. King, owner of hotel), at the Marine Hotel."

Meda clasped her hands in a devout attitude and again exclaimed, "Paris est liberè!"

I kissed her on each cheek--French style. And it was arranged that Meda come down to the study for the 9 o'clock news and we would then open the champagne and drink to Paris and the brave French people.

The 2 American Captains were taking Alix and Judy out to dinner, so Martha and I had cocktails with them before they left, in the drawing-room. We toasted Paris and her new Freedom. A cocktail was sent up on Meda's tray at dinner and Bridget, the cook, was presented with one, which she carefully parked on the dresser in the Staff-room.

"Later, Ma-am, if you don't mind," she grinned. "I'll get the dinner through safely first."

At 9 o'clock, seated in the study, glasses of Meda's champagne in readiness--Martha, Gerry, Meda and I listened to the broadcast of the liberation of Paris. It was very stirring. And, when the Marseillaise was played, we stood up and drank to our French Ally. Emotion, as well as the stinging bubbles of

326

champagne, choked us. I think I am right in saying that the four of us had the same thought: --Freedom!-- how glorious is Freedom! This--the liberation of Paris--is the real Beginning-of-the-End of the War. There is nothing to stop us now. Let us say with the French,

"Allons, Enfants de la Patrie,
Le jour de Gloire est arrive."

Meda came to us in May. For ages I had experimented with Nannies and governesses for Penny--with varying results, all unsatisfactory. Finally, Meda (Miss Marie Flack) was engaged--sight unseen--by post. And when she walked in the front door, fresh and trim after the long ride from London, I took one good look at her face and said to myself, "This is the one." And I haven't changed my mind.

Meda went to Paris when a young woman to take up a post as Governess. She remained 30 years. She was with the Renaults for some time, and was with the Dupuys family at their Chateau in the Gironda Valley when the Germans interned her.

When I engaged Meda she had been repatriated to England for only eight months--after 3 1/2 years in an Internment Camp at Vittel. (Later, a film, "2,000 Women," was made, based on the experiences and life of the women at this camp.)

Among the many incidents Meda has recounted to us of her internment the following ones stand out particularly.

1) When taken from the Chateau, with no notice at all, the Germans allowed Meda but one small case of necessities. She was crowded into a train with many other women, and left for 48 hours without food.

327

2) At Besançon en route to Vittel, boiled grass was served for Christmas dinner.

3) Without the Red Cross parcels the prisoners would have fared very, very ill, indeed. They might have died. They had inadequate bedding and clothes. (Meda wears a costume (suit) made from cloth sent to the camp by the American Red Cross.)

4) There was barter and exchange of the contents of Red Cross parcels among the women Internes at Vittel-- cigarettes and coffee having the highest exchange value. Cakes and puddings were concocted with pounded and pulverized crackers as their principal ingredient. There was even such a birthday cake upon one occasion.

5) A horrible odor would sometimes pollute the air-- from the direction of large clouds of smoke seen at some distance from the camp. Inquiry brought the answer, "They are burning the corpses of consumptives." But black rumor distorted this sentence into hideous stories of "extermination." (Which, God knows (or the Devil!), is only too true in the Concentration Camps.)

6) Some of the women became decidedly "odd" in captivity--and a few went completely mental and had to be shut up.

Among Meda's interesting recollections of the years in France before all this horror is the visit of the King of Spain when she was with the Renaults at their Herqueville Chateau. As souvenir of that event, Meda has a very ornate trinket box (you now have this box, Penny)--the top is original Lalique. The box once contained chocolates, and had been a gift to her and her charge (young Jean Louis Renault) from the Spanish

King upon his departure from Herqueville Chateau.

And later, when Meda was with the Dupuys family, Laval was often entertained at dinner. Meda imitates him--tucking a serviette beneath her chin and "spitting" as she speaks, her mouth full, her lips puffed out. "Faugh! He is no gentleman."

For some while, before the Germans descended upon Legonzac Chateau, home of the Dupuys, the sign "Consulate de Paraguay," put up by the Ministre de Paraguay, had kept the Chateau, and its inmates, unmolested. The Germans had wished to commandeer the Chateau as Headquarters, so the Ministre de Paraguay, then a guest of the Dupuys, had conceived the plan of transforming Legonzac Chateau into "Consulate de Paraguay." and for some months the plan had worked, the family Dupuys and their menage enjoying immunity for that time. But eventually, and suddenly, the Germans had swooped upon the Chateau. Monsieur Dupuys left for Vichy, leaving Madame Dupuys and the child. (Meda did not see them again.) And Meda was interned.

Her one idea now is to return to France--not only to recover her personal possessions, if they can be traced, but to see, once again, that family to whom she was so much attached that, given the opportunity early on in that War to leave and return to England, she refused. She chose to remain with the Dupuys family, to share their discomforts and terror--and, later, to be imprisoned.

Shortly after Meda's arrival in our midst I found her writing letters one evening in her room, in such a sad frame of mind that it was noticeable. I asked what was the matter. Could I do anything?

It seemed that the International Red Cross had notified

her of a balance of 2,500 Fr.s, which Meda had saved from the 300 Fr.s paid monthly by the Red Cross to each internee. Upon repatriation, after transit through Germany to Sweden-- whence the Internees were embarked for England in the "Empress of Russia"--the Swiss Legation had given each Internee £ 1 ($5.00) for "expenses" on the trip. This £ 1 was a gift from the British Government. Now Meda was writing the Red Cross to tell them to keep this sum as a small thank-offering for all that the Red Cross had done for her.

"Without those parcels we would not have lived, Madame," said Meda.

That is true gratitude.

And now Meda, having lost everything, is starting anew to earn her living.

That is courage.

And she intends, one day, to return to France, to Paris, and to her friends there.

That is faith. (Two years after the War, Meda did return to Paris to become governess to the Dupuys' two grandchildren. Whenever in Paris, Dick and I would see her. But she was frail, contracted tuberculosis and went into a convent for nursing care. There she died. Dear Meda! We'll never forget her.)

April 26, 1944.

Heavenly day. Celestial evening. The best part of the 24 hours nowadays is from 6 p.m. to 10 p.m.

The English countryside reminds me of the nursery rhyme,

330

"There was a little girl
And she had a little curl
And it hung in the middle of her forehead.
And when she was good
She was very, very good
But when she was bad she was horrid."

England can be so very beautiful, so very alluring, so poetic. On an evening such as this, for instance, when clarity of air and the unique light of early evening gives a translucence to an otherwise very earthy and country-fied, though lovely, landscape--at such a time England is "very, very, good." But when it rains and rains, or mists, or simply glowers, with a penetrating chill that bites the marrow--as happens far too often and goes on and on for days and days--why then England is definitely "horrid."

Mr. Longhurst (Journalist, and broadcaster at the B.B.C.) came up this evening to return a book. he asked me if I thought that we, America and England, were the Lost Tribes of Israel? I said I'd heard something about it, vaguely.

"Well, why didn't the Germans invade after the Battle of Britain? And remember Dunkirk? We certainly seem favored by the Lord. We could be the Chosen People, couldn't we?" said Mr. Longhurst.

Hardly, it seems to me! We don't deserve any such special dispensation of Grace.

And, as for being the Lost Tribe of Israel--Israelites-- aren't all Israelites Jews? I've often wondered about that. I shall take it up with the Rector one day.

April 28th, 1944.

I read in the Daily Telegraph this a.m. that the Nazis plan to flood Holland. Among the areas "condemned to be flooded--or already under water--is Haarlem-meer Polder" and the Hague, where the Reurs family are now living (at Wassenaar on the outskirts). Or are they? Surely the Dutch people have been evacuated! Another horrible experience for our dear friends.

The Neue Zeucher Zeiting says "Inundation with sea water would mean a catastrophe lasting decades during which even grass wouldn't grow."

I remember the late summer of 1929 when Dick and I visited the Reurs family in Noordwyke. We drove there from the Hague--through Leyden, Katwyke, and Haarlem. The countryside was like a patchwork quilt with it's flowering squares of pink and yellow and green and mauve--the canals, with their silver threads of water lacing the pattern. Like exclamation points the windmills emphasized the flatness of the country.

Such a friendly country--a bit on the fairy-tale side in looks, but solidly human with Dutch hospitality and love-of-life. I can hardly believe that the Nazi have "drowned" a part of this. Or rather, let me say, I can hardly picture this for, there is no shadow of a doubt, the Nazis are capable of such a deed.

Alas, quite probably, a part of lovely Holland lies beneath the waters--as the fabled town of Atlantis does. One may not hear the tinkle of submerged Church bells there, in Holland, as reminder, but Dutch memory and love will hold the drowned land in fief until free Holland reclaims it for her own. May it be soon.

332

The era of the Robots, the flying Bombs, the Doodle-Bugs, Those Things--is upon us. These horrible and fantastic weapons are what Dick must have anticipated when he asked that we all stay out of London while he was away this trip. The Fly-Bombs come in across the South and East coasts as the piloted planes did but lower, at a higher speed, with rare deviation from course--like a shot out of a gun. Fighter Pilots and A.A. guns are now up against a new equation. As Mr. Churchill says, to shoot down a Flying-Bomb is like trying to shoot down a projectile. But he is confident there is an answer to the problem. So is Ted, a young Polish Flying Officer. "Give us a bit of time to learn their tricks," he says, "and we'll soon stop them."

Ted has been fighting German planes ever since the Battle of Britain. He's what you call a specialist at this job. But how he keeps his health and his nerves through an apparently everlasting series of bouts with Death, I simply can not fathom. When here with us, he is ever cheerful, boyish, and interested in the present. The future is something he can take care of later. Now he lives. (Shortly after D-Day Ted was killed. To have fought so long, so gallantly--and then to die! What cosmic force, or Divine Purpose, apportions each and all their moment of departure from this World?)

The populace of London, it's outskirts, the districts along the Thames to it's outlet into the sea, and that part of England labeled "The South" by the newspapers--the people in such areas once more live in fear of imminent death. But now

333

there is an added horror. That of a feeling of defenselessness--which produces a near panic in many places. There is a tremendous exodus from the target areas. Women and children crowd the big Railway Terminals. People newly arrived here in the country, in search of sanctuary, tell of masses of people awaiting trains, of their being kept in the Underground until train time and then, herded on the station platforms, of having to fling themselves upon the concrete at the dreaded warning. People pray. Children cry. It is hideous!

The Fly-Bombs, traveling at terrific speed, make a frightening sound--a loud whirring and throbbing--that is heard as the bomb approaches, and as it passes over and on--to suddenly dive, and strike with an explosion that spreads <u>wider</u> devastation than that produced by the H.E. bombs dropped from piloted aircraft. So long as the awesome vibrant chug-chug, chug-chug of the Fly-Bomb is heard, one lives, but when it dives straight down (and there is no warning nor escape) one dies.

Judy and Margo are therefore here again with us. The Beverley's flat, at Eton Place, is near some Marshaling yards (freight yards) which have always been a target. Since the noise of the Doodle-Bugs (as Judy calls them) is similar to the revving up of an automobile motor, the sound is lost in traffic, and the poor Londoners--even with a last minute Siren warning--are caught in the streets, their homes, their beds, and most particularly, at meal times in small family groups or in an assemblage of diners at restaurants or hotels.

Judy says that one of the Doodle-Bugs flew so low above their flat (they are on the top floor) that the walls shivered and creaked. "I thought we were for it that time--but it crashed near Mill Hill"--a district that is getting it pretty badly and where Peggy Gamble Foote is now staying with her husband. It looks as though she and little Dickie will soon be back in Instow again.

Eve Stackpole, Mrs. Gamble's niece, is having a rest down here at the moment. The Ministry of Information (in Russell Square) where she is a secretary, is in a Fly-Bomb "belt", which has taken a lot of punishment. Eve was in the greengrocer's on Tottenham Court Rd. during her lunch hour, when (with no slightest warning) there was a dreadful explosion and crash. The big glass window of the shop burst into dozens of small sharp projectiles--the floor heaved beneath Eve's feet. Automatically she ran out onto the pavement where a friend had been waiting for her. Miraculously, there her friend still stood, dazed, but untouched, in the midst of a sad mess of humanity, paving blocks, glass and oddments of vegetables, parcels, hats, etc. Rescue Squads were already on the job--and ambulances appeared as if by magic.

This kind of Incident (That word "Incident!" Understatement for sure. Always a horrible bit of bombing and it's results!) befalls the people day and night--haphazardly, but often. "Those Things," as the imperturbable Londoner, still in town, speaks of the Fly-Bombs--"Those Things" are worse than raids. We don't like them at all!" Classic British understatement.

Alix, when in London for a week-end, happened to be in a Chemist's shop (Drugstore) as one of the Fly-Bombs passed directly overhead. Alix was speaking to the Clerk when the young woman suddenly raised her head--listened--and exclaimed, "Here comes one of "Those Things!" She ducked behind the counter. Alix ducked also.

335

"It sounded like a flying bus," recounted Alix. "And when it hit, a couple of streets over, bottles came down off the shelves."

"It's trying to make out whether you really hear a Doodle-Bug, or whether it's a motor in traffic that wears you out so," says Judy. "The cars going by Eton Place rev-up for the hill. So I was always expecting a bomb. It was awful!"

I'm sure of it.

"Springfield"
Instow.
June 6th, 1944, "D"-Day

It is on! The Invasion of the Continent!

What comes out of the radio is frightening enough, but what goes on--there above and on the English Channel, and against the beaches of France--must be so terrible as to beggar description. The vast numbers of Allied ships planes, men, and weight of armor must be a concentration of the very essence of War--so powerful that never has it's like been known before.

Will this Invasion be successful?

If the Power of Prayer is of any avail--and if Faith can indeed move mountains--then the myriads of prayers rising from the burdened loving hearts of those who wait at home in Faith (and fear) must ride the other like spiritual cohorts, their unseen strength--flung into this Battle of the Invasion--the final winning Factor of an Allied Victory. We shall see.

Like the lull before the storm there was a quiet spell of warm and golden weather before D-Day. Here, in Instow, the young people sun-bathed on the lawn. Penny and Margo ran about in singlets. Hot sun steeped our senses into a brow of well-being and contentment that our minds subconsciously chilled into apprehensive waiting and acceptance of the inevitable.

We were on the eve of something--the Invasion of the Continent most probably. The gay and friendly American officers of the Assault Courses had been "dropping in" at odd times for little visits. They were "moving on." Something was in the air and the calm presaged a whirlwind. We felt it in our bones. Our skin prickled with it. But we could ask no questions. We waited, like the rest of the World.

I shall always remember a certain lovely summer afternoon just before D-Day. Gordon called in at "Springfield." His jeep came noisily up the winding drive and swung smartly into the corner by the rose garden. Gordon and two fellow officers jumped out.

I was in the drawing-room, writing--all the windows wide open. The girls and the two children, plus a couple of British Naval Officers from the front, were sprawled about the lawn on lilos and rugs. The dogs beneath the hydrangea bushes were puffing in and out like bellows. All were half drugged with sun and drowsy Devon air.

The advent of the U.S. Army changed all that! There were shouted greetings, laughter, and a surge from the lawn to the jeep. The American officers trooped into the house, hot, dusty and thirsty--to emerge in a few minutes--washed, and stripped to the waist for sun-bathing. The girls mixed a pitcherful of iced orange (synthetic) squash and took it, with

337

glasses and a plate of home-made cookies, out to the lawn. And for two hours the young people sat and lay about on the grass, their laughter and noisy conversation belying the fact that this happy and peaceful interlude might well be the last for certain of the boys there--American and British.

Nothing was said of the matter--but we all knew that Gordon and his friends were "on their way," that when they left later and their jeep headed South, they were likely to keep on going in that direction--eventually to land on the other side of the Channel. (Gordon was badly wounded at St. Lo, sent back to an American hospital out-side Cheltenham where Martha visited him, and then flown to the States, to be presented with the Bronze Medal.)

Dave (Lt. Col. David Talley, U.S. Army) is here for the night. An officer in "Signals" he saw part of the Invasion and is now here on a quick job, off again tomorrow. So we have been privileged to hear interesting and exciting accounts of the Invasion from an eye-witness. I asked Colonel Gamble to come up for a drink with us. As a retired Colonel of World War I, he would thoroughly appreciate the opportunity of talking to a Colonel active in World War II.

Dave had so much to tell us--we sat enthralled. His stories padded out the newspaper and radio accounts into more graphic and detailed pictures of the Invasion. Dave saw Gordon on the eve of D-Day--in one of the "cages" where Officers and men of the Invasion forces were concentrated in isolation and preparedness those last pregnant hours of waiting. "He (Gordon) was on his toes and ready to go," said Dave.

And in the thick of it now! thought I.

Already the wounded are streaming back. Quick transport and new drugs are working miracles.

"I watched German prisoners coming ashore at a South Coast Port," continued Dave. "They look marvelous--very well out-fitted, giants in health and strength. We're up against a tremendous force of perfectly trained men in the pink of condition. It's going to be hard going. But, "Dave added, "don't let it worry you. Everything's going according to plan."

Which sounded darn familiar! But also sounded very reassuring, the way Dave said it. His voice was triumphant and his eyes sparkled. Battle sure does something to a man. "The Light of Battle in His Eyes" is no mean statement--it is a fact. And I saw a reflection of this light in Colonel Gamble's eyes as he listened to Dave.

About three weeks later I received a letter from Nip, in which he wrote that the boys from Woolacombe had all come through the Invasion O.K., (which seemed miraculous considering all that had happened!) and that he had seen Gordon.

Nip also wrote, "Congratulate him (my husband) for me on the good job. We here can very definitely feel the effects of the good procurement work that's been done by him and others like him."

That will make Dick feel good. For he has worked hard (and is still working) in Washington, as Controller of Signals Equipment for the British Air Commission, and would give much to be in the Big Show himself. To feel that he had forwarded our successes in any way will mean a lot, I know. (Dick and Sir Richard Feary accomplished miracles in procurement for D-Day!)

339

June 13, 1944

Found an Invasion Bug--at least, it was armored and looked like a baby tank--when making my bed this a.m. Crawling things make me crawl. And the English do not believe in screens at windows and doors.

Our first experience of this was the summer of 1936 when, for a few weeks, we took a cottage at Earnley, Sussex--on the South coast near Chichester. It was altogether charming there. The cottage was modern, there were lovely gardens, and by walking through two pastures, tenanted by curious cows, we could bathe from a long sand beach. Dick drove down from London every week-end, and we all got fat and brown--I, like a trout, speckled.

But the insects, the bugs, the flying creatures! At breakfast and at teas, when the jam or marmalade was on the tables, flying armies of wasps would zoom through the open unscreened windows and do battle over the jam pots--diving into them and often getting fatally stuck there. The children and any young men guests would flail the wasps with their knives, beheading the creatures neatly and then brushing them off onto the floor. This daily--and deadly--performance was a bit wearing and I, for one, couldn't feel quite the same about the jam and marmalade. We tried a lure, putting saucers of honey on the window sills at mealtimes and it was partially successful, but one still had to fend off the buzzing pests, and the beheading went on all summer.

Now, I love to read in bed. It is my escape act (I think I've said that before too) and a good book will make me forget temporarily, many things. But spiders the size of a quarter prancing along the picture molding of my room at night, or

340

being playful on their "home-spun" thread over my bed, are more distracting than any plot. I used to go and wake Alix-- who would then sleepily grab the broom handle I thrust into her hands and stumble to the slaughter. She was always efficient. One swipe with the broom and one less spider. And she always made the same remark. "Oh, for goodness sake, Mother, can't you ever do it!" Not if I could help it.

Here, at "Springfield," we have the same trouble. Lots of insects and no screens. I was stung on the throat by a wasp when in the kitchen one afternoon. And, while sitting at my dressing table one evening, a wasp dropped from the electric light shade above me on to the back of my neck. My reflexes did the wrong thing. I made a grab at the wasp--and was stung. My yells so startled Dick that he burned a large hole in the mantelpiece (over the bedroom fireplace) with a dropped cigarette--and Alix rushed into the room.

"Heavens, Daddy!" she exclaimed. "Are you beating Mother again?" Then, as a proper V.A.D., she put a dressing of Boracic Acid paste on the sting.

Why not have screens instead of all this bother?

And I hate ear-wigs! They have horns and they bite. And I simply creep inwardly when I find one parading on my wash basin, or on my desk, or even in my bed. As for the flies! But now one hardly notices them. In England they are apparently not considered purveyors of disease. They flock in friendly fashion wherever they desire--principally where there is food. The large umbrella-like shade of the indirect light above our dining table wears a constant crawling halo of flies. I am almost immune to the sight. But not quite. I still long for screens.

Speaking of insects, I had a farm girl named Letty here

341

as domestic for a while--and her preparation, or rather nonpreparation of vegetables was unique. We, the family, were always finding surprises in the food. It was a simple matter to shake the lettuce flies off the salad leaves--a fairly simple matter to remove a boiled white slug now and then from green spinach--but a rather tricky job to comb out the small cooked creatures which often inhabited the boiled cabbage when it came to table.

Our biggest "surprise," though, appeared the time that Letty seemed to be under the impression that she was serving bouillabaisse. Although I am sure she never even heard of it! A concoction of cauliflower, milky fluid, and enormous snails, plus their shells, arrived before me to serve one noon. (I had ordered creamed cauliflower; it was to be our main dish.)

My first reaction, and the family's was to send it back to the kitchen. But there wasn't much else for lunch. Also, to hurt Letty's feeling was unthinkable, as we'd been months without any 'help' and Letty, plus her failings, came in handy for washing dishes, pans and floors. So we picked out the snails and ate the cauliflower.

I do not think the Devonians eat snails--but I may be mistaken. If they do, it is consistent with English cooking that the shells be served also and then discharged at table. And the plums and cherries of English "flans" and tarts must be pitted when eaten, as this process is omitted in their preparation. Many, many times I have nearly broken a tooth on a pit! As an American I am accustomed to eating my fruit tarts and pies without first indulging in a mine-sweeping operation with my fork and spoon in English style.

As regards the snails, I have eaten them--in Paris. But the garden specie of Devon is something else. Penny brings them into the house Spring mornings--cradled in large grape leaves, the snails rampant, their horns waving before them. The creatures seem like miniature dragons. I couldn't eat a dragon. Neither could the rest of the family.

Autumn, 1944
71 Portland Place,
London

When Dick returned from Washington in July he announced that a flat in London would be necessary, as his main office must now be in town. That suited me fine. A place of our own in London again! No more Hotels there! Although the Park Lane Hotel on Piccadilly has been like another home--during the War anyway, whenever any of us were in London.

Leaving Alix to run "Springfield," I sat out on a week of flathunting, Martha along as blood-hound to track down elusive agents and their still more elusive prospects. Martha could leave her Red Cross job easier than Alix could leave her hospital job.

It took more than one week. It took many! To find an unoccupied furnished flat in London was like finding the proverbial needle in a haystack. One had first to contact an agent who had a flat to rent! Such a person seemed extinct in the Autumn of 1944 A.D.

There were Agents who had occupied flats to show-- flats full of American officers who, sharing the rent, acquired extravagant living quarters at extravagant rentals. The Agents, seeming to think it well that we at least keep in mind the idea

343

of renting a flat, would send us to view these American-occupied premises.

"There is always the chance, Madame, that the officers will vacate. When they do, they go quickly! If you like to put your name on our list we could notify you."

But upon such decision, Martha and I discovered that we were by no means first on said list. The matter seemed a bit hopeless.

Martha, however, using blood-hound tactics, following every sign and trail that advertisements, recommendations from friends, and mere hearsay, offered--and with the aid of a sort of Flat Porter's Underground Movement--tramped the Squares and Streets of Central London, scanning the lists in flat lobbies, chatting with Porters and Concierges, and at least narrowing our search by the elimination of such flats as were occupied on long leases. And, wherever Martha went, she was just one minute later than a contingent of American officers! It looked as though we had some sort of military campaign to contend with as well.

But, at last, Martha's unflagging efforts were rewarded and we acquired a very comfortable furnished flat at 71 Portland Place, W.I. The very day that Martha and I went together to view the place and to count the beds, etc. (for we had to furnish "linen & plate")--no sooner had we unlocked the front door, then, like rabbits out of a hat, two American Army captains appeared on the steps behind us.

"Is this flat for rent?" they chorused.

"It is rented," I said.

"To us," added Martha, like an Amen.

We like our flat and we like the location. One can walk down wide and dignified Portland Place to busy Oxford Circus, cross over to Regent Street and then on down to Piccadilly Circus. Or one can turn the right hand corner by our front door and go down Devonshire Street to Harley Street, left along its sadly bomb-scarred length of Doctor's, Dentist's and Specialist's offices into Cavendish Square, whence it is but a step to Oxford Street with D.H. Evans, Marshal Snelgrove's (new Bond Street opposite), Selfridges, the Marble Arch, etc.

Seventy-one Portland Place, being situated at the upper end of that short, broad thorough fare, is but a few minutes walk from Regent's Park, and not far from Madame Tussauds and Baker Street, where Dorothy lives in Dorset House. At the lower end of Portland Place are clustered the B.B.C. (British Broadcasting Corporation), the Langham Hotel (where we attended Enny Reurs' and Charled Gray's wedding reception some five years and several thousand bombs ago), All Souls Church (with its truncated spire) and Queen's Hall (what there is left of it!). And along Portland Place itself, stand the Turkish and Chinese Embassies, the Headquarters of U.N.R.R.A. (United Nations Rehabilitations & Relief Association), the offices of the British Council, and the Interim Treasury Committee for Polish Questions, etc., etc. Just a few doors away from Portland Place, on Weymouth Street, is the Consulaat General der Nederlanden, and on Cavendish Street the Swedish Legation. Diagonally across from our flat and to the right is the American Forces headquarters. Above it's entrance flies the Stars and Stripes. My heart salutes it each morning.

And everywhere--opposite my bedroom windows on Devonshire Street, and to the right and to the left of us on Portland Place, and "all about the town"--are the blackened and eyeless shells of bombed buildings. Most of these ruins are

345

"dated," having been caused by piloted bombers in the era before we left London for Instow. But there are also the newly devastated sites where the fantastic Fly-Bombs have landed. However, these snorting, chugging missiles seem on the wane. Rarely do we get a Fly-bomb warning nowadays. but when we do, instead of Anti-Aircraft Fire, we have a spell of "listening." for so long as the Alert prevails there is danger that the dreaded chug-chug of the "doodle-bug" (Fly-Bomb) may be heard coming in one's own direction. Then one must be on the qui vive in order to flop flat upon the floor or pavement should that ominous sound, once heard, suddenly cease. For then the bombs dive--straight down. Waiting for a Fly-Bomb is not nice!

But now there is something also "on the loose" against Britain. Something that is far more worrying--the Rocket Bomb or V-2 (Vengeance-20 as it is called) (the Fly-Bomb is V-1). We experienced this new menace some time ago when first in town to look for a flat. Strange and unaccountable explosions occurred now and then on the outskirts of London. Their impact could be felt for several miles. Londoners were puzzled, and rightly apprehensive.

In the early summer a young Lieutenant in the U.S. A.A.F. had come down on leave to "Springfield" just after the mysterious explosion out at Kew, one of the first such. Dick was still in the States and I was getting bored with the country and longing to go up to town for a while. In fact, I already had been up for a few days with Martha and Gerry, to visit a couple of Specialists, as Martha had fibrosis and Gerry a diet deficiency. This beautiful War! It was my first visit to London since the advent of the Fly-Bombs and the children and I found them erratic, to say the least. But at the moment the Fly-

346

Bombs seemed to have fallen off a bit. So I asked Jerry, the young Lieutenant, what he thought about the matter. How about my going up to town again? What were the "heavy explosions" the newspapers now spoke of once in a while?

"They're the new Rocket Bombs," he said, "I wouldn't go to London now if I were you, Mrs. Cotton. Those Rockets are too unpredictable. You don't ever hear them coming. they just land. And do they make a mess!"

Well, from Jerry, we learned that the V-2 was "long as a telegraph pole," that there was absolutely no warning of and no protection against it, that it traveled faster than sound, the whistling of it's transit through the air being heard after the explosion when it landed--that two explosions where heard, the terrific one of the Warhead as the Rocked landed, and a much lesser one as the Rocket mechanism exploded. The V-2 was like a colossal bolt of lightening and a gigantic clap of thunder, all in one. It came out of the sky, with no warning at all--but it was not from heaven! It was the work of the Devil, the Anti-Christ, Adolf Hitler!

"The Rockets are falling short of London, but I'd stay out of there just the same, Mrs. Cotton," reiterated Jerry.

But, by the time Dick returned from the States, so many V-2's had fallen on England that the people were adopting a fatalistic attitude about them--as one does toward lightening, either it hits you or it doesn't. No truer words were ever spoken than "You can get used to anything," (I've said that before, too!) for we have definitely gotten used to having bombs thrown at us. There is no other way to explain our acceptance, since the Battle of Britain, of the bombs dropped from piloted aircraft, the pilotless Fly-Bomb (V-1's) and now the Rockets (V-2's). We endure them all--we hate them all--but we try to ignore them all, to the point of disdaining to allow these V-2's to disrupt our lives.

Martha, regretfully resigning from the British Red Cross (she had risen to the rank of Commandant, one of the youngest) but anxious to get into the uniform of her own country, joined the American Red Cross and went to work at their Headquarters in Grosvenor Square, London. So she and Dick live in our flat at 71 Portland Place, Dick spending the weekends at Springfield. Whenever we feel like a few days in London, Alix and I are never deterred by the V-2's, but come up to the flat for a visit. I suppose that, subconsciously, we just aren't going to let the Nazis scare us.

I am familiar with the ground now being fought over. We, the family, have traveled through a good bit of it--that part of Western Europe where the American and British Armies are thrusting inland, slowly but surely, and, alas, with heavy casualties--among them Col. E. Warfield, C.O. of the U.S. 116th Infantry, and young Lt. Edward Tucker of the same. The 116th Infantry has been terribly shot up--because it has advanced into some of the hottest spots of enemy concentration. The Officers of this outfit undoubtedly knew-- months before D-Day--the specific part that they and their men were to play in the Invasion of the Continent, and some of these Officers even may have "felt" just how far (and no further) they were to go, themselves. Such premonitions are often realized by some people in this War.

For some time before D-Day the 116th Infantry was stationed at Launceston, Cornwall. Alix and Martha attended some of the dances there as the guests of Lt. Tucker and Capt. Scott. Eddie (Lt. Tucker) spent several leaves at "Springfield," and whenever he came to see us, in addition to his Emergency Cards, he always brought some otherwise unobtainable delicacy; a tin of tomato juice, or salted peanuts, or Nabisco wafers, or soap--and always some candy for Penny. He was thinking of his own small child and young wife at home, I know. He often spoke of them. "Wonder when I'll see them again?"

Eddie was killed on D-Day plus ten.

As I read the newspaper accounts of how the Battle in the West progresses, I look at the pictured ruins of certain Continental towns. How well I remember these charming, historic places. And now they are shells--lifeless and empty, most of their former inhabitants (those who have survived) driven hither and thither over the countryside by the whirlwind of war. And the same whirlwind has swept through the innermost beings of these driven people, leaving a great emptiness of Spirit, a vast vacuum of Mind and Soul.

There will be need of a U.N.R.R.S., after this War-- "United National Rehabilitation and Relief for Souls."

Last May, shortly before D-Day, as the young American Officers of the Assault Training Course at Woolacombe commenced "moving on," Nip brought a Lt. Col. Holmes to call. Nip reckoned that, since Lt. Col. Holmes was moving in to Woolacombe, he would like to meet a family of Americans, people from home, and that we, people away from home, would like to meet another countryman. We appreciated this, for we were going to miss Nip and Pix and Doc and Mac. (Mac was killed.)

Unfortunately, Lt. Col. Holmes was "moved on" himself, quite soon. However, we soon acquired three very good friends among the Officers of what turned out to be the 18th Replacement Depot, stationed at Woolacombe for some months. The three particular officers are Lt. Col. Lorin Solon, Commanding Officer, Lt. Co. Henry Settle, Executive Officer, and Lt. Col. Robert Castle in charge of Training. Martha, at that time still in Tommy's factory at Woolacombe, played bridge now and then of an evening with Henry and Bob, and on the Saturday nights that the Officers' mess held dinner dances, she and Alix had very gay times there.

On Sunday afternoon, Lorin and Henry and Bob would come over to "Springfield" for tea. Then the dining table would be extended to it's full length and Meda and Penny would join us. Sitting at one end of the long table, with all the tea paraphernalia in front of me, I used to feel like the Madame of a Pensione, Premiere Classe. I liked it--the rattle of china, the gabble of voices, the laughter of people forgetting the War for a little time.

Whenever these three officers came to "Springfield," they always came together. They were always good company. And they always had a way of arriving with a flourish of cheery greetings and largesse of cigarettes, oranges, candy and colossal chocolate cakes. "God knows what the cook thinks of my appetite!" Lorin used to say ruefully.

I called them The Three Musketeers. They are somewhere on the Continent now--close behind the combat units--and undoubtedly mad as Hatters that they, the Three

Musketeers, are not mixing it, <u>Hand</u> to <u>Hand</u>, with the Germans!

December, 1944.

Tony has arrived in England. What a wonderful Christmas present for Dorothy. And now they will <u>both</u> be with us for Christmas.

Tony was wounded February 6th, when in the Arakan jungle, by a Jap grenade. The humerus of his left arm was badly shattered. To quote from Dorothy's letter, giving particulars: "Tony lost his glasses" (Fancy accepting such a near-sighted man for active fighting, anyway! Tony is a Lieut. in command of a field Battery), "and with broken arm he crawled through the jungle to a first aid post where his arm was set and he was put in an ambulance. Owing to conditions the journey took about 24 hours instead of 6 or 8, and the arm swelled and went black. The native driver of the ambulance stopped the car and ran away as they were being pursued by the Japs. Eventually a British driver reached them and drove them in to safety, but they only escaped by a few minutes. The Japs arrived almost at once.

Some of Tony's men were in a Field Hospital near the Camp in the Jungle, and the Japs overran it and bayoneted all the men in bed, and shot the Doctors and Nurses, etc. One doctor escaped to tell the tales, as he smeared himself with blood and lay absolutely still under a bed and was thought to be dead.

There was an operation on Tony's arm after the ambulance journey, and at last the stretcher cases were all packed into the river steamer heading for the Indian Frontier. This steamer was the target for dive-bombing by a Jap plane, and many men, alongside Tony on the deck, were blown to pieces. He could not move as he was weighed down by 60 lbs. of plaster, and he says he was shaking with fright and could do nothing but smoke cigarettes.

After a frightful journey they got to Bareilly, and into Hospital where he had another operation, and after some months there, was moved to Poona General Hospital where the final tendon operation was performed. While in the hospital all these months Tony studied Hindustani and took an exam in it-- he was so bored with the mental inactivity!"

Naturally, Dorothy is to be congratulated on Tony's escape from Death. Tony has been spared to her. It is a blessing. But every Mother knows that the hurt from the loss of one child (Pete) is never mitigated by any sort of good fortune--even the sparing of another child (Tony). The heart's wound never heals. It is merely glazed over, with that secret sorrow and strength that passes all understanding.

---

71 Portland Place
London

Early 1945.
I seem to shuttle back and forth between town and country nowadays. A couple of weeks at "Springfield" and then a fortnight in London at our flat. I love this varied, active

life.

We had a happy Christmas at "Springfield"--Dorothy and Tony joining us for the holidays--and on Boxing Day we gave a cocktail party there. In England, December 26th, the day after Christmas, is called Boxing Day. This is observed as a holiday, also, so that people in shops, factories, etc. get at least 2 free days over Christmas. I think this is an excellent idea. We Americans could do with a day for recovery after Christmas!

Although Boxing Day, as such, has been going on for years and years and years in England, I have never yet been able to find anyone here who can tell me <u>exactly why</u> the day after Christmas is called Boxing Day. "It just always has been!" people say. The most frequent explanation, and the one that makes the most sense--although none of my informants can swear to this explanation--is that boxing Day has something to do with the fact that at Christmas the Postman, the Coalman, the various Tradesmen's "Boys," the Dustman, etc., receive money gifts that are known as Christmas Boxes. In assembling these gifts for disbursement one says, "Now what shall we give to so-- and --so for his Christmas Box?"

As I wrote, on this past boxing Day, December 26th, 1944, we held a cocktail party at "Springfield." It was likely to be our last such (the War going so well) before leaving England--and we very much wanted to let our friends in Instow know that we had very much enjoyed our stay among them and that we were very much going to miss them all when we left! So we made the party as festive as we could--and it was a lovely "do", if I may so. Dorothy and Tony were with us for the holidays, and Nip blew in from the continent that very afternoon at tea-time. Between 5 and 8 o'clock that evening a good part of Instow climbed the hill to "Springfield" and, for 3 hours, the air in the candle-lit drawing-room and dining-room seemed to quiver visibly with the gay and friendly chatter of people who knew and liked each other. I looked at all those kind English friends of ours and thought "What a happy occasion they have made of this party--for us Americans to remember!

Mrs. Russell was the first guest to arrive. As we stood before the open fire in the drawing-room, making small talk over glasses of sherry, Mrs. Russell suddenly said, "Have you been able to buy any toilet paper, Mrs. Cotton? I haven't. There doesn't seem to be a roll, or packet, in all of Devon!"

Within a few months of the declaration of War people began to think of laying in a few stores of those commodities which, in time, were likely to become scarce. My grocer in London recommended tinned goods, sugar, candles, soap and toilet paper. The latter article made us smile.

"I remember the last War very well, Madame," he admonished me. "And there wasn't even a telephone directory to be had!"

So I ordered several dozen rolls of T.P.,--and kept them intact until the summer of 1944, when I found it necessary to gradually deplete the lot.

Until an article becomes very scarce, and later quite unobtainable, one rarely attaches a full value to it. Before the summer of 1944 T.P., was no particular problem, and certainly one never spoke of it in ordinary conversation. T.P. was one of those things found only upon household lists, or in the shelves of Grocer's and Chemist's Shops, or quite unobtrusively displayed in its proper habitat in homes, Hotels, R.R. Stations, etc. T.P. was an enchanting blessing that one accepted without thought or thanks. But suddenly, in mid-1944, the British public became "T.P.--conscious" and began to realize how very unappreciative it had been of T.P.'s important contribution to the Nation's comfort and morale.

At first the shortage of T.P. merely meant searching from shop to shop. When I was fortunate enough to locate a few rolls the Clerk would brusquely say, "Only 2 rolls to a customer, Maddam!" and would plunk the 2 rolls down upon the counter with an expression that seemed to infer that I had just tried to bribe her into selling me the Crown Jewels! Well, so far as I am concerned, I had just purchased 2 Kohinoor diamonds and, being very pleased with the purchase, had no qualms whatever about putting them, unwrapped, (wrapping being forbidden, anyway) into my open-meshed shopping bag and allowing the World and sundry to see the spoils of my day's shopping! After a week in London, plus several miles of pavement pounding, I would triumphantly return to Instow with 6 or 8 rolls of T.P. As a supply for "Springfield", they never lasted long!

Meda has a nephew who deals in such paper commodities. Once in a while she had been able to obtain a few of these for me. I exclaim over their arrival, by post, as tho' the parcel contained 6 pairs of nylon hose (practically non-existent in wartime). I am overcome with gratitude.

All odd bits of paper--from the very rare white tissue to the anemic and thin wartime brown appear used for necessary wrappings--all such paper I cut into suitable squares. The happy advent of oranges in the shops, at very, very rare intervals, has a twofold value: --the vitamin C within the fruit, and the crinkly squares of tissue wrapped about each piece.

Alas! After a period of scarcity, there arrived a time

when no one--your Best Friend, a government Official, or "so--and--So" in a certain road--knew where one single solitary roll, or packet, of T.P. might be bought. There wasn't even a Black market in T.P.! Things were very bad.

This state of affairs went on for months. Inquiry at Chemists' Shops would produce a blank look. "None at all, Madame." Quite probably there were very limited stocks "under the counter" which were kept for old customers--just as many choice articles, "in short supply," are kept during this War!

In desperation, I bought blocks of notepaper, lined or otherwise. Stationers would sell only one block to a customer! That necessitated each member of a family buying a block in rotation. The system smacked of the illegal--as tho' one were trying to "get away with something." Also, it was a nuisance.

One week-end Dick arrived at "Springfield" with a present for me. It was an oblong parcel, done up very tidily, and he handed it to me with a flourish at tea-time.

"Present for you!" he said.

Excitedly I unwrapped the "present," and discovered 6 rolls of T.P. I was thrilled!

But I didn't ask Dick where he had gotten those 6 rolls. I didn't dare. I was afraid he might have stolen them!

Shortly after my conversation on boxing Day with Mrs. Russell, anent the special paper shortage, I came up here to the flat in London, to stay a couple of weeks with Dick and Martha. Ian Sinclair, First Officer in the P.& O. (Peninsular and Orient Line), was having a spot of leave, so he came in for dinner with us one evening. The men and I were having drinks and chatting in the drawing-room when Martha breezed in from Red Cross H.Q.'s.

"Look!" she said, and jubilantly flourished 3 rolls of T.P. "Got'em at the P.X. (Post Exchange)!"**

"Lovely!" I said.

Ian chuckled. "Once in a while I take Mother one from the Ship's Stores. And she thinks it's lovely, too!"

"Bet you can't guess what Joe gave me the other day?" continued Martha.

We certainly could.

"T.P.!"

Joe comes in 3 mornings a week to clean the flat. Joe is a member of Civil Defense, Light Rescue, and, at present, on Night Duty. He arrives straight from his post, takes off his Uniform jacket and heavy shoes, dons a blue and white striped apron and house slippers, and proceeds to do a thorough job for 4 hours. Since Martha and Dick are away all day Joe buys the bread, pays the milk bill, and sees that the Laundry leaves on time. He also valets for us. Joe is very versatile.

One morning, as I was writing letters, Joe brought me a large, dark blue, knitted bed slipper.

"Would you like me to do any of these for you, Ma'am?" he asked. "I knit them. Seems foolish just <u>sitting</u> at night, waiting for incidents. These V-2's aren't like the old raids. Don't keep us on the run. So I knit. First pair I did was for my nephew--got 4 toes cut off in a train accident, coming on leave. Couldn't get a shoe on when he began to walk in Hospital. So I got some unrationed carpet yarn and knit him a pair of these. Then the other men in the ward wanted some. So now I have quite a business. Done over 130 pair already! Wouldn't you like a pair, Ma'am?" His round face beamed with good will.

You can see that Joe is not only a person who likes to keep busy, but Joe is one of those people who can always find time to do the "extras" that help. Dick has a favorite saying, "If there is anything extra to be done, find me a busy man."

"The other night, when I got home," continued Martha, "I found 2 rolls of T.P. on the hall table, and a note from Joe. He'd written, "Miss Martha, you overpaid me 2 shillings (50 cents). The toilet rolls were 1/10 (one shilling, ten-pence or 44 cents). Could you call it square, Miss Martha?"

More chuckles from Ian. We all laughed.

T.P. has certainly risen in the world. It has become the fashionable bon-mot of conversation. Not because people think up "T.P. stories"--this isn't necessary, as there are so many anecdotal true experiences--but because T.P., or rather the lack of it, is an ever present problem that refuses to remain in one's subconscious. And, like so many things brought about by the War, the T.P. shortage is not only very aggravating but, also, often very funny. People laugh a lot over it. Which is all to the good this sixth--and, let us hope, the last--year of the War.

These weeks following Christmas have seen an improvement in the T.P. situation. You might even say that the T.P. situation has stabilized. But we are still morbidly over-careful about keeping at least 3 rolls "to the good" on the household shelves. War continually teaches, "Preparedness Pays."

The first V-2 (Rocket Bomb) to land in the West End of London fell on the Red Lion, a Public House (pub) in Duke

Street,--off Oxford Street--and just across from a side entrance of Selfridge's. Dick was reading in bed at the time--in the Park Lane Hotel, as we had not yet moved into our flat at 71 Portland Place--and anyone knowing London can appreciate what he heard and felt when that Rocket came down!

The newspaper accounts were very short and couched in the usual vague phrases, like this: "A V-2 recently landed in a shopping district in the south of England. A Public House received a direct hit and adjacent buildings are damaged. There were some casualties. A taxicab, containing 3 sailors and a woman, was blown by blast into the large display window of a shop. The sailors and cab driver were killed. The woman has not been accounted for yet." Having become adept at expanding such meager descriptions into full and graphic accounts, we know that the above "Incident" had been a nasty one. And, upon learning from Dick just where the "Incident" had occurred, we felt that it was even nastier because the Nazis seemed to have London's range at last.

Even so, Alix and Martha came up to town to clean the flat for occupancy (impossible to get a char (Char: "charlady," or cleaning woman)at the time) and to settle-in our own few belongings such as linen, china, and kitchen utensils. The flat had a 6 months accumulation of London dust and soot! By evening the girls were usually too weary to go out but, when they did spend a late evening dancing, they noticed that the then fairly distant explosions occurred most often between midnight and dawn. They spoke of the Nazi's apparent method in their madness to Sydney, the Flat Porter, one day. Sydney is in Civil Defense, Heavy Rescue, and has been continuously in the "front line" of the bombing of London.

"It's just like the Doodle-bugs," he said. "They mostly

came at <u>meal</u> times at first. You sort of <u>know when</u> to expect them. These <u>Rockets</u> mostly come at <u>night</u>--after 10 o'clock to morning. That's why there weren't more killed in the Red Lion--past closing time. Awful mess though! I was on that job. Terrible time getting out the people--<u>and</u> the bodies. And then that taxi, blasted into Selfridge's window across the street. We got the bodies of two sailors and parts of a woman. Found her arms one place, her head another, and one hand all by itself. But we couldn't find the torso! You can't take an incomplete body to the morgue. It's got to be a whole one. Doesn't matter whether it's <u>all</u> the <u>same</u> body, or not. Any rate, we had a proper hunt for this woman's torso. Never located it 'til the taxi was lifted out the window. It was underneath the wreckage! Very nasty Incident."

Between this unpleasant story and the sight of the extensive damage done by that particular V-2--which can be seen any day by any shopper--I feel uneasy, to say the least, whenever I (in London) sense, or faintly hear, the muffled explosion of a V-2 landing several miles away. Any time-- night or day--the Nazis may land another right on the West End, right on 71 Portland Place! I counted 4 such distant and dulled explosions one night between 11 p.m. and 7 a.m. It was not reassuring. During the day I can sort of brazen it out--the sunlight and the crowds of people putting a safe and sane look upon things. Even when an infrequent <u>daytime</u> explosion can be heard on the outskirts of London, the hustle and bustle of people about me somehow negates that threat.

It is late at night that I sense that Frightful horror of a deadly missile, against which one has absolutely no protection. I lie in bed--unuttered prayers in a continuous stream, milling 'round and 'round within my subconscious mind, and wait for the next explosion. Hammersmith seemed to be the target at one time. Two V-2's fell in the very same spot there--the Reservoir. Their impact traveled along subterraneously, so that at the flat one sensed rather than felt that "something" had happened.

For the very reason that one can do nothing about the V-2's, one pushes them into the subconscious and tries to forget them. So I always come up to London when I feel like it. I always go about in normal fashion during the day. I always go out to dinner or to the theater or cinema, with Dick and friends. I always sleep, at night. I always am a bit crazy, I guess! But I have plenty of company.

There are two schools of thought concerning the V-1's and the V-2's--both of which are coming over nowadays. There are those people who prefer the V-1's, because you sometimes get a warning and can take cover of a sort--and there are those people who prefer the V-2's because, since one gets no warning at all for them and one can't do anything about the darn things, anyway, one might as well forget them. Dick belongs to the first group. Martha to the second. The two of them have friendly arguments about the things. I am sort of on the fence. I can't feel any real preference for either--but I am inclined to lean to Martha's side of the argument. At least you won't know when a V-2 hits you!

At breakfast here one morning, Martha and Dick were talking of a V-1 that had passed over both Dick's office and American Red Cross Headquarters the day before.

"If you can hear something coming you can get ready to duck it!" said Dick.

"I don't like the waiting for the things!" said Martha. "When that Doodle-Bug came over the office we were all sitting tight on our chairs--just waiting for the darn thing, and listening. And then hearing it going over us, not knowing whether it was going to conk out on us, or not! Poor little Joyce (an 18 yr. old English girl employed in the office. She and her family were bombed-out by a V-1 some months ago) was shaking all over. Now she'd rather have the V-2's any day! So would I."

But the strain is ever with us--whether V-1's or V-2's--and the progress of the Allied Armies on the Continent is watched with impatience and prayer. The allied Armies, themselves, are taking terrible punishment from the Fly-Bombs and Rockets, along with all the other dread weapons of War that are being hurled at them by the enemy. We are asking miracles of our fighting Men!--that they destroy the Rocket sites; that they destroy the Men who make them; that they destroy the power of Evil behind these men.

Yet the men of the Allied Armies are doing just that! We, here in Britain, along with the rest of the World, watch the brilliant strategy, the sure strength and thrusting power of the Allied Armies as they roll in a tidal wave of inevitable Victory across Western Europe. We swell with pride over their progress. We weep over their casualties. We wait. We pray. We feel sure.

In the middle of January Terry was married. We all--save Gerry--attended the wedding. It was bitter cold. There was frost as thick as ice on the pavements, and some snow fell during the ceremony held in the Savoy Chapel at noon. But the sun came out later as the Bride and Groom left the Hotel

Mayfair, after the reception. Since--when Terry's leave was up--he no doubt would be off to the Pacific, bright sunshine on his Wedding Day seemed a happy omen.

The cold spell continued. We nearly froze here in the flat. Many people really have suffered from the wintry-like conditions. There has been discomfort enough, in normal weather, because of the meager coal ration. Now lack of transport curtailed even that. From the storage "dumps" about London women fetched coal in prams--children carried it in shopping bags--men from the Forces (Services) became temporary coal-heavers--Army lorries were pressed into service.

There was more snow than many a Londoner had seen for many years. Trains were held up, or so slowed that some runs were taking twice and three times as long as usual. I decided not to try to return to "Springfield" for a while, and 'phoned the house. Gerry was ski-ing! Winter had certainly come to Devon. Roads were snowed under. Rail and bus transport was almost at a standstill. Food was short in some homes. Many workers couldn't get to the factory--Gerry among them.

And then, as suddenly as the winter had descended, a spurious Spring bloomed everywhere. The weather turned balmy overnight. Streets ran with water from melting snow, rivers became raging torrents, and the poor Farmers, especially, didn't know with which they'd rather contend, snowdrifts or floods. "And you say you like snow!" Our English friends would ironically remark.

The first day of February I went shopping. There was nothing unusual in that. But, the day being such a perfect Spring day for so early in the year, imprinted everything I did and everywhere I went indelibly on my mind in golden ink, distilled from sunshine. I had ordered a book from Foyle's on the Charring Cross Road, so I set out to walk there.

Down Portland Place I went, sniffing the soft air, and thinking how unaccountable English weather was, and no wonder that we called our particular part of the States New England. For we have just such days--following on just such winter weather as had vanished in the night. Turning left at Oxford Street, to Tottenham Court Road, then right--and on down Charring Cross Road to Foyles, the world-known storehouse of books. I call it a storehouse because it has the air of a warehouse, rather than a book-shop, being so large, so musty with years, so crowded with books--shelf upon shelf to the ceiling. My book, on order of 4 months, was not available (paper shortage)--so I decided on lunch, and, being in the vicinity, headed for the Chinese Restaurant in Glass House Street.

From Foyle's I crossed Cambridge Circus, where the posters of "Gay Rosalinda" on the Palace Theater proclaimed a London success, which we had seen just recently. The glass of the enormous canopy before the theater entrance was gone. Only a skeleton of steel ribs projected above the pavement, like a "de-materialized" umbrella. A bombing souvenir.

Then right, into Shaftsbury Avenue--a slice of London with it's own particular color. Crowds of British soldiers, American G.I.'s, Aussies, Canadians--their girls in startling hair-dos copied from the French--moved in Kaleidoscopic procession with the civilian population. There was a leisurely air about the people--a savoring of the warm Spring day.

Past the Trocadero Restaurant and Rainbow Corner (U.S. Services' Club run by American Red Cross) to Piccadilly Circus, where the conical wooden "hide-out" of its Eros fountain projected above the human and mechanical merry-go-round that dizzily and constantly turned about this hub of London. I stood there for a moment, now at the corner of Glass House Street. Like the Cafe de la Paris, in Paris, where, it is said, "All the World passes by," I felt that Piccadilly circus was well entitled to the same distinction. The place boiled with the People of many Nations.

From out the opposite side of the Circus ran the Haymarket--and from the left Coventry Street curved to my right. All names that mean London--each separate part, yet always London. Beyond Regent Street--yet also out of the Circus and to the right, like another spoke in the wheel of London--the "posh" straight line of Piccadilly commenced it's march past Fortnun & Mason's, Bond Street, The Berkley, The Ritz, Green Park, The Park Lane Hotel, Park Lane, itself--to the Jagger War Memorial at Hyde Park Corner, opposite the entrance to St. George's Hospital.

Other scenes quite out of sight clicked in rotation thru' my mind. Beyond St. George's Hospital sprawled Knightbridge, with Harrods, like a snobbish Duchess, rising above the lesser shops. Sweeping to the right, and back, like this -- my mind's eye followed the "pictures" through Hyde Park--where Rotten Row now wears a deserted and forlorn appearance, where a line of parked, red London Transport Busses, adjacent to Park Lane, cock a snoot at their Elegancies. The Dorchester and Grosvenor House--on to Marble Arch, the Cumberland Hotel, the Mount Royal--right down Oxford

365

Street, past Selfridges, the "Big-Shop--without-a-name."

Between Oxford Street and Piccadilly lay that squarish chunk of the West End where "Office" life and "Flat" life and "Night" life rub elbows; where the U.S. Embassy matches it's dignity with that of Claridges; where the gold braid of Rank competes with the flat white of the helmets and gaiters of U.S. Military Police; where Ladies (real and not-so-real) lend color and romance (also real and not-so-real) to that portion of Wartime living compressed within this cube of the Largest-City-in-the-World.

Scattered throughout my walk were the sad, but "graceful," ruins of bomb-damaged churches, the eyeless facades of shops and flats, the bomb-craters, the open spaces above the foundations of homes now completely gone.

Dear shabby London, war-scarred and sorely tried--but dauntless, a symbol of the integrity of a People.

I saw all this in the one moment that I stood upon the corner of Regent and Glass House Streets that Spring-like day of February 1st, 1945. And I felt identified with the Pageant of Life spread there before me. Turning into Glass House Street, I entered the narrow doorway of the Chinese Restaurant and went up the carpeted stairs to the First Floor Dining-Room. I was very, very hungry. Spring, and the People, and the "Pictures" had concocted a potent aperitif.

February, 1945

Back at "Springfield"
While I was in London Bill Williams 'phoned--the

evening of Jan. 31st. He was in Plymouth, on a new job for the Army, and desperately wanted to get Kay and Vanessa away from Whitstable where they were staying with Kay's Mother. Both the V-1's and the V-2's were prevalent in that vicinity. But Bill, so far, hadn't even found a room in Plymouth! Would I have Kay and Vanessa at "Springfield" until he could find accommodation?

"Gladly!"

So Kay and little Vanessa are now at "Springfield" with us for awhile. We are enjoying them--and Penny and Vanessa are most happy together.

Both Kay and Vanessa were exhausted when they arrived. No wonder.

Over 8 hours traveling is hard on a Mother and young child. Kay's Mother, whose home is in Canterbury, has been bombed-out twice--once by the "ordinary" bombs and later by the V-1's. So she had taken a small place in Whitstable, on the Kentish Coast. This doesn't seem to be a much better location so far as bombs go--or, rather, so far as they come! The V-2's are landing about there, also, Shortly before Kay and Vanessa left Whitstable one of the Rockets landed in the town, when Kay and Vanessa were shopping. Where there had been apparent peace and stability, suddenly there was explosion and upheaval. Kay and Vanessa saw a bit of their immediate world disintegrate before their eyes. The glass in the large shop they had just left showered into the street, which the two of them had but just crossed! The tinkling rain of crystal seemed to go on forever. Actually all was over in a few seconds.

This Incident--on top of all the other raids and bombs they had experienced--plus another V-2 near them at 4 a.m. of the very day they left Whitstable to come to us, had been too

367

much for little Vanessa. The evening of their arrival here there was rain and a high wind. During dinner screams from Vanessa sent Kay up the stairs several times. The rattle of rain against the window panes was too reminiscent of the rattle of falling glass. Vanessa was afraid the windows were going to fall in on her! A night light helped that. But later, a shower of hail down the chimney into the bedroom fireplace became another problem--until Kay hit on the happy idea that Father Christmas was dropping little pebbles down the chimney to amuse Vanessa!

"Just as a sort of joke on his way back home after all his Christmas journeys." So Vanessa finally went to sleep. And after 3 nights the child had forgotten all her fears. Such is the resiliency of Youth. (That, too, I have said before! But it is most apt.)

In addition to the actual War, itself--the waging of War by the Armed Forces, with all the hardships, dangers, the casualty lists that such a mad performance entails--there is the strange life of the civilian here in England, a life of privation, rationing, bombing, queuing, and the difficult, difficult problem of finding a place to live! The daily life of Kay, Bill and Vanessa has become unsettled, to put it mildly. Sporadically they have lived with Kay's Mother. But now a married sister and her children are there. Bombed-out themselves, they need a refuge. The house at Whitstable is crowded! So Bill is frantically trying to find a place of some sort--any sort--for his little family.

"All these years we've paid out thousands of pounds for rent. We don't own a stick of furniture. All ours lost in the early Blitzes. But, of course, we are lucky!" says Kay. Quite true. Everything is merely a matter of comparison nowadays.

The other evening Kay and I laughed so at an illustration in one of the American magazines (sent from home) that we actually became a bit hysterical. We were curled up on the divan by the drawing-room fire, having a "read"--which really meant "looking through these magazines and commenting on the illustrations and articles therein". They seemed positively fantastic by comparison with our daily lives. Suddenly we saw a picture of a hat--and began to scream with laughter.

Bill had come up from Plymouth for "over Sunday" and he, Dick and Gerry were in the Study listening to the News. They all rushed in to see what the matter was!

Kay and I were almost speechless. So I handed over the magazine, open at the illustration, and managed to gasp, "Look at that, will you!"

The 3 men looked.

What they say was a page of new hats for women.

The 3 men gaped.

1.   "What's so funny about those?"
2.   "Seen funnier ones on you!"
3.   "What's the joke?"

So Kay and I explained--a bit breathlessly.

The gorgeous colored illustrations of food and clothes in American magazines always hit us 2 ways--and hard. Food and clothes are rationed here, and most of the articles are quite unobtainable. So such pictures annoy us. They really hurt. Yet the food and clothes thus pictured look so "super" to us war-starved females here that we derive a certain spiritual, or imaginative, satisfaction from merely looking at these illustrations. The pictures fascinate us!

But there was one illustration this evening that not only hit me hard, it nearly knocked me out! It was a photograph of a young woman wearing a very high white turban--And the caption beneath read--"B;s high white turban is important!"

That nearly finished me off! With all that is going on over here, not to mention what is going on on the Continent (and in the East)--all the devastation! That Titanic Fighting, with men dying by the thousands!--For some fashion writer to say that hat (tho' I wouldn't call it that!) was important quite stunned me.

Why the darn white had only lacked a handle! Then it really might become important.

I had shown the picture of said white hat to Kay. And we both laughed like anything. Then, suddenly, we both had the same idea. "Pot de chambre!" We screamed. Tears ran down our faces. It was a synthetic laughter--the kind that "something funny" touches off, but that one's "sub-conscious" expands into hysteria, because of some tragedy or heartbreak that is concurrently stirred into being.

"And people are dying for a World that produces something like that!"

"Fancy! People are dying for a hat!"

"God in Heaven! Are we all mad?"

Hysterics hit us again. Kay and I simply howled. And then the three men rushed in.

After our explanation the men still looked a bit puzzled. Having, all their lives, endured or ignored millinery monstrosities atop their respective females' heads, the men were a little slow in getting the significance of Kay's and my reaction to this particular millinery monstrosity pictured in that American magazine. That they finally did comprehend is symbolic of the charity of man.

"Yes," they agreed, as Kay and I abruptly sobered up. "Yes! We see what you mean--now."

And the three men, sober themselves, went back to the News.

I have never forgotten that hat. I never shall. It will be a reminder to me to help keep the Peace--when it arrives. For proportion and perspective in life, or rather living, will be even more important in peace than in war. It will be difficult to find and keep and use a true perspective in everything we do--when there is Peace again. But we must do this. I pray we can.

---

71 Portland Place

London

On Monday, the 26th of February, Dick and Mr. Anderson (who is a Director and Secretary of British Rola) drove up to London from "Springfield". I begged a ride and came along. I love "going places"--who doesn't--and the trains are often so crowded nowadays that the carriages have the look of dilapidated Arks, full of Humans rather than animals. At the Big Stations there are long wide queues of people for hours before train time. And, when the crowds are allowed through the gates and turned loose on the platform, there is a sort of stampede towards the carriages for seats, standing room, or just floor space for one's 2 feet, the rest of one's self being automatically supported by pressure from one's fellow travelers.

In compartments formerly labeled as accommodating 6

371

persons (3 seats to each side) there are now signs announcing that 8 persons (4 to a side) may be accommodated there. This is a fantasy of the British Board of Transport--that a mere 8 persons be accommodated in one compartment. I have shared such a compartment with 12, or more, people. And have made mental note that, if I could unhinge my feet, and tuck them in under the seat, why then, at least one more traveler might avail his, or her, self of the luxury of that sardine-box-on-wheels. I say box rather than tin or can, because most British Railway Carriages are of wood.

However, one does not complain. We "have been cautioned,"--to use a British phrase. "Is your Journey Really Necessary?" ask the porters in R.R. Stations. And so since Dick's journey to London on Feb. 26th was really necessary and did not involve a train trip, I simply couldn't resist the opportunity of combining pleasure with a clear conscience! We left Instow at 10 a.m. and arrived in London about 5 p.m. Not bad, for those narrow, winding roads. During the drive I jotted down a few notes on the countryside, places, and people. The jottings being rather haphazard and uneven in style seem expressive of that long 6 to 7 hour ride. So here are the jottings and a leisurely expansion of them after my return to "Springfield."

Jotting No. 1. **Break a Snake's Back**

The meandering up-hill, down-dale and around corners of Devon and Somerset roads always thrill my sense of appreciation with the soft beauty and rustic charm revealed along their way. Familiar as these scenes have become, I never tire of them. And I never fail to remark to Dick, "I wish we could show all this to the folks back home!" You must see it to believe it.

372

Jotting No. 2. **On roadside: Pussies, catkins, purple
        beech buds, "flags" of sedges.**

The brave new pennants of an early English Spring
were flying everywhere. These tentative blooms presaged a
fresh life stirring. Could it be an omen that the end of a Reign
of Death approached--that the War was truly on the wane?

Jotting No. 3. **A large Jackdaw and Stonehenge.**

Perched on a thorn bush by the road across Salisbury
Plain, the somber bird cast a predatory eye upon us as we
rolled past. The atavistic granite slabs of Stonehenge pointed
like fingers to a blue Heaven. "Look upwards, not down," they
seemed to indicate. But the teetering Jackdaw cast impudent
aspersions upon such things as ideals and aspirations. In the
wide free spaces of Salisbury Plain this little black and white
feathered creature became an oracle.

"Spring is here, my fine Fat-heads of the Human Race.
Be lulled into a false security. Forget that Salisbury Plain has
been--and still is--a Training Ground for Men and Machines
that they may indulge in that most enormous of enormities, a
War, even though it be a Defense. Stumble into the Future, you
Demi-Gods, and there make the same mistakes."

No! No!

Jotting No. 4. **Pete and Nether Avon.**

Pete trained here--high above Salisbury Plain--to
become a Pilot in the Fleet Air Arm. He won his Wings at
Nether Avon. And he and Alix lived for months in small
comfortless digs at Fighledean, nearby.

The air above Salisbury Plain was thick with the beat of
seen and unseen Wings.

The jackdaw turned into a Dove of Peace--and flew

373

away, into the Sun. "Make it come true," my heart beseeched. "Peace in a shining World." That is the only fitting memorial to the Dead of this War--Peace, a Lasting Peace!

Statues and granite shafts and plaques are but pricking reminders that eventually find the hide of the people too thick to longer feel the pricks. The future generations will sigh and say, "How sad." And then mayhap make the same mistakes;-- an isolating apathy, a hectic prosperity, a quick belligerence, another War. Then more statues, granite shafts and bronze plaques as memorials. The cult and practice of "Love thy Neighbor" and "Do unto others as ye would be done by" might breed something with more life in it than graven stone.

Is all this just Women's talk? Or can we really make a dream come true--create a lasting Peace?

For miles and miles over the wash-boardy roads (from Tanks) of Salisbury Plain I tried to solve the problem. And my husband continually croaked, "You can't change human nature." I began to think that the Jackdaw had returned!

Jotting Number 5.   **Micheldover and Tony.**

Leaving Salisbury Plain we by-passed Micheldover, a small community North of Winchester. I recalled that Tony once finished his school holidays there, helping with the Harvest. Within a week of the declaration of War, it was. "Way back in Sept., 1939. Since then Tony has been in the Burma Campaign and was wounded while in the Arakan , and is now back in England, fairly fit and ready for new posting.

For over 5 years Father Time and the gaunt Man-With-The-Scythe and the Three Parcae (the Fates) have been chopping up our lives in an indiscriminate manner. I simply can not find a pattern in all this!

374

Jotting Number 6.   **No U.S. Army Vehicles to be washed here!**

This was on a large sign by a water-splash in a small country town.

"Well, I never!" I commented.

"Probably don't want the stream blocked up with chewing gum," said Mr. Anderson laconically.

Jotting No. 7. **Cemetery urn at Andover.**

As we drove thru' Andover and passed "The Star and Garter," where Dick, Wing Commander Smith and I had stopped for lunch one last summer's day on a return trip from London to "Springfield," I vividly remembered my search for a sandbucket for Penny to use on the beach at Instow. Sandbuckets had been quite unobtainable, not even London yielding one. So on that summer's day, while awaiting a second sitting at lunch at the Inn, I had strolled through the town, looking in windows and shops and inquiring of clerks.

On the pavement outside an Ironmonger's door was a cluster of small dark green metal buckets. I went into the shop and asked for one. The proprietor, with sober mien and muted words, placed one on the counter, unfolded two short wire "legs" from the bottom of the bucket and demonstrated their use.

"Three and six (90 cents) Madame," he said.

Surprise must have shown in my face for he hurriedly added, "This is very well made, Madame. It will last a long time."

The proprietor had thought me incredulous at the price. Actually I was appalled to learn that I had purchased a cemetery urn for flowers!

But the urn did last a long time. the two "legs" were

removed, and soldered to the upper rim into one handle. As a sandbucket it was super. Penny was thrilled.

Jotting No. 8. **Only English Meat Served.**

We had been looking for a likely place to lunch, and remarked on the frequency of this notice beneath the signs of many Inns and Cafes. "Only English Meat Served." I must be of a suspicious nature, for the sign did not attract me. Although we have been almost "spammed" to death, I would rather have this American meat than Cambridge steaks, for instance. The explanation is a bit involved--but here it is.

At "Springfield", once a week, a lump of horse meat is delivered by the Carrier. The meat is for the dogs. There are daily advertisements in newspapers of "Horse meat for sale"-- and once I was amused by the entry "Bombed cows for sale." I am sure that often and unwittingly, I have eaten horse (the tender, juicy tournadeaux of French Restaurants.) Still, I abhor the thought. So the sign, "Only English Meat Served," made me wonder, "Is it possible that the thousands of Jeeps now leaping about England have made the faithful horses redundant?" Also, I have <u>heard</u> that the sturdy wild ponies that roam over Exmoor are captured and sent off by the lorryful to Cambridge. Hence my aversion to Cambridge steaks, which are minced meat cakes (hamburgers).

Whenever possible I like to know <u>what</u> I am eating, even though it doesn't have to be something I like! For I remember Kathleen Marlow laughing about a particular chicken casserole that she consumed one evening in Soho. Kathleen remarked that the chicken somehow seemed not quite real, by virtue of the ominous fact that a vertebrae of some sort lurked amid the gravy and vegetables.

And, if you please, in less than a fortnight later I read in

376

the paper of the forced closing of 3 or 4 small restaurants in Soho. Cat skeletons had been disinterred from their back gardens!

Therefore, in spite of the fact that the signs, "Only English Meat Served," were undoubtedly genuine advertisements for the best English beef--which is, indeed, the best--we continued on to an Inn that we had patronized before, "The Bear" at Wincanton. We were not disappointed in our lunch there, for it materialized exactly as we had expected--gravy soup, bread with postage--stamp-sized margarine, very thin slice of roast beef, yorkshire pudding, boiled potatoes (roast potatoes, or pan-fried, being reserved for Residents, since rationed fat is thus used) slabs of marrow, apple tart, coffee. And, of course, beer. On the tables stood flower arrangements of some dried shrub with which I am not familiar. The blooms looked like fuzzy yellow and orange moth balls attached to brown twigs.

But the meal and the decoration were consistent with the standard of British Trust Houses--the Best Obtainable at the Price. Consider the season, the stringent rationing, the shortage of Staff, the 6th year of War, a tired People, a depleted Country. Yet we were provided for! We ate. We drank. We were renewed--as the countryside about us was so being.

Jotting No. 9. The Cricketers.

Here we stopped for tea, tho' we might well have pushed on to London. But, somehow, in England, along about 4 p.m. one gets a frightful craving, an insistent yearning, that is both hunger and a thirst. Tea is the only satisfaction. So tea we had--at the "Cricketers."

You have only to see such a representative English Inn as this, "The Cricketers," to realize that the rock foundation upon which the British people stand is Tradition. I have been in and out of countless such Inns, and they all share the same characteristics;--cleanliness, polished floors and shining brass, a certain austerity (even before the War,) a lounge where small tables invite chat and cheer, a bar for "warming-up," a dining room where white table cloths (now darned and stained, but clean) hang in uniform drapery nearly to the floor, where bouquets of flowers in season enliven the white expense, where maids (now inadequate in number because of "call ups") in cap and uniform (mended and patched,) correct in black stockings (over-darned) serve "Elevenses," three meals, afternoon tea, etc., each day.

And so--after tea--on to London and 71 Portland Place. The 200-plus mile road from Instow had taken almost 7 hours.!

---

71 Portland Place
London.

A Polish woman committed suicide on our very doorstep today! Joe came in this morning to announce breathlessly, "A young woman has fallen out of a top floor window!" My heart turning over, I rushed to the front window in the drawing-room. There on the pavement lay a blanket-shrouded figure, and a crowd had already collected.

"How did it happen, Joe?"

"Mrs. Sydney (The Porter's wife) had just put your daughter (Alix, up for a visit) in a cab. She'd just driven off, when this woman hit the area railing and bounced smack onto the pavement beside Mrs. Sydney. She's in an awful state-- Mrs. Sydney is!"

Mrs. Sydney is expecting another child shortly. Poor soul! I hurriedly poured a glass of brandy, snatched the fresh flowers Alix had fetched from "Springfield" out of their vases, and ran down to the Porter's flat in the basement. Mrs. Sydney was tearful, but fairly composed. I expect the raids and the V-1's and the V-2's have made her a bit stoical. But what a shock, on a sunny, cheerful day, to suddenly confront the body of a woman hurtling to sure death! Mrs. Sydney could only repeat, "And there she was! Nothing could stop her! She's dead! Quite dead!"

After the ambulance had come and gone, Joe learned that the woman was Polish--that she lost her husband in this War--and that her only child, a son now 18 years, has just been called-up. Her loneliness, the material deprivations of the War, the mental havoc wrought by raids and personal worries proved too much for her. She had locked the door of her room, left a note on the desk--and jumped.

It was one way out, I suppose. But I couldn't help thinking of the son. Just a boy, really, If he is spared--and returns to London--where now is there a home, and, more important, parental love awaiting him?

Loneliness has created loneliness.

The price of certain foods off the ration is scandalous! 4 Scallops--10/--($2.50). These are deep-sea scallops. Minced and dressed with a sauce made of tinned milk and baked in the shell, one scallop serves one person, meagerly.

Chicory Hearts--1/6--(35 cents). Chicory in England is what we know as endive in America. Chopped up for salad,

379

chicory enhances meals when there are no tomatoes, no cucumbers, no nothing--almost.

Radishes--1/6--(35 cents).   They look bright and cheerful and are something else to chew on.

Carrots, of all things, are exceedingly scarce right now. I have paid 2/6 (65 cents) a bunch for these here in London to take back to Penny. The severe winter and some sort of blight has ruined the carrot crop!

I recently saw some large green sweet peppers in a Piccadilly window. "Lovely!" I thought. "I'll stuff one apiece for dinner; any bits of food will do. I walked out of the shop as fast as I went in! The peppers were 5/-- ($1.25) each!

Mushrooms--1/4 lb. 4/-- ($1.00).   That makes mushrooms 16/-- ($4.00) a pound. What a price mushrooms on toast for lunch?

As for fresh fruit, there are not-too-wonderful apples, at various seasons, at not-too-wonderful prices.   Native strawberries in their short season are gold-plated.

But the high price, here in England, of certain fruits has always astonished us, even before the War!--and even at that time allowing for their necessary importation or the extravagance of glass-house culture here.   As Americans, accustomed to a wide variety of fruit the year-round with a sliding scale of seasonal prices, we were stunned, upon our arrival in London, to find

Peaches -- from 2/6 (65 cents) to 5/ ($1.25) apiece!

A small melon -- 10/ ($2.50)!

Grapes -- anywhere from 7/6 ($1.98) to £1 ($5.00) and even 30/ ($7.50) a bunch!

Now non-existent during the War of course.

From such indications of the high price of living here,

one wonders how the average British family even exists. And yet, now, because of the rationing, hundreds of thousands of British families are eating better than they ever did before! Those families whose meager incomes permitted only the meagerest of diets--before the War--now have milk and butter (once considered luxuries) where before they had merely tea and margarine. And the bottled concentrated orange juice (This orange juice is made here, from the residue of oranges already processed in The States for tinned concentrated orange juice for the American Troops. The residue is brought here in British Ships upon their return from delivering young Britishers to The States for training there as Pilots for the R.A.F. One has to stand in a queue once a week to obtain the rationed small bottle of said orange juice allowed each child under 5 years.) At a controlled price for children under 5 years (and for expectant Mothers) it is a veritable miracle maker. I can see that certain British children are better off than they were before the War-- their health is better because of better food. For rationing has evened up the distribution and consumption of vital foods.

But the quality of such foods is sadly short. And, after 5 years of such conditions, the British people show it. Their faces are tired and lined. Upon arrival back in England, after each trip to The States, Dick's sensibilities are recurrently shocked. "The first thing that hits me upon landing here," he says, "is the tired, drawn look upon the faces of the people, and the overall shabbiness of things. It hurts." No doubt people's skin suffers from what our American Magazine Advertisements call "Tissue Starvation" (lack of vitamins.) Hair turns gray quicker, through lack of iron (liver, treacle, fresh greens, the year round, etc.) Rheumatism is on the rampage (lack of fats and calcium.)

The children, and people under 40 and even 45, can one day renew their strength and beauty when there is more food--fruit, milk, meats, fats--freedom from wartime worries and the threat of death at any hour. But the older generation will need a new Lease-on-Life as well. That lease will not be forthcoming.

March, 1945

The air raids have started up again--small ones, in a hit-or-miss fashion. The Germans are having a last fling. The planes come in over the East Coast--a bomb here, and a bomb there, and a burst of machine gun bullets upon some defenseless place or people. Definitely nuisance raids.

Penelope Gamble Ebsworth is at Sleaford, near Lincoln. Her husband, Dr. David Ebsworth, is anesthetist at the R.A.F. Hospital there. Penelope wrote her Mother that, upon returning from a dance one evening, a sudden swooping plane scattered the people from lorries and cycles into the ditches and under the hedges. No one was hurt. But the spat-spat of bullets about one is an experience not easily forgotten. One of those nightmarish, almost unbelievable episodes that so many British people will recall all their lives in a mixture of bewilderment and thanksgiving. Did this--or that--really happen to me! And yet I live!

Of course the V-1's and V-2's are still coming over, and London still seems the target. But the hit-or-miss raids are not at all nice either. I was in a London bus one morning about 11 o'clock, when an untidy and fairly toothless woman of about thirty-five sat down beside me. From her breath I could have told the time! She had been indulging in an "eleven"--this time beer, not tea or coffee--and was consequently in a chatty mood.

"Lor!" she exclaimed. "I move me Auld Mither out to t' country 'count of' these V-bombs--and now t'ruddy Nazis are pushin' <u>planes</u> over again an' droppin' <u>old-fashion</u> bombs. Right were we Mither is! I'm bringing' her back t'week-end. Kinda ridic'lous to be thinkin' <u>London</u> a <u>safe</u> spot! Now ain't it?"

I agreed.

Kay is back from the Continent. A member of the Canadian F.A.N.Y. (First Aid Nursing Yeomanry) Catharine Mackintosh has paid her way all through this War--a volunteer in every respect, furnishing her own uniform, paying her own passage here from Canada, financing herself on her infrequent leaves. For a certain number of weeks, when attached to the British Red Cross, she received 30/ ($7.50) a week, and a similar sum for a period on the continent. But that is all. Kay's effort has been practically 100% her own, and she entered the War at it's beginning. Now back in England on a short leave, she is with us at the flat. She has been a member of our family circle for some time--a very welcome member. One of the nice things about this War is the addition to our family group of a number of young men and women whom we definitely consider more than friends; in speaking of them Dick and I use the expression, "he, or she, is one of the Family." One of the family is now back with us in London.

For the first 6 weeks that Kay was on the Continent (she went over last Autumn) she was under canvas--a damp and chill experience. When the Winter set in the girls were billeted in a convent near Brussels. This habitation offered little increase in comfort. There was absolutely no heat. Women and men find this the worst of the many discomforts.

No hot water, therefore no recovery from chill in a hot bath. The one warm bath a week furnished at the Convent is considered an Act of Grace.

"But we've gotten used to roughing it," says Kay. "What we can't get used to is having the Nuns collect all our garbage and use it to feed hungry children! Our hearts are blitzed." Children--the Innocent of the War. And, of course, the Innocent suffer.

Georgia, one of our American Clubmobile girls, returned for a 48 hour leave this month. She has even more uncomfortable digs on the continent. For Georgia is in Germany, and her billet is a barren room lit by stars, or shells-- as only a bit of roof remains--and is ventilated through bombed windows and walls by the icy winds of winter. The entrance to this "Lodging" is a hole through a pile of rubble. Georgia exhibits snapshots of her "house." She--along with many other American Red Cross Clubmobile girls--is in Germany, close behind the American Army, often right up with the Army, and subject to Army rules and the dangers of that Army. American Red Cross girls have been wounded, killed, and taken prisoner.

Martha enjoys her Saturday afternoon Clubmobile trips out to the U.S. Hospital at St. Albans--a change from the office in Grosvenor Square. The girls serve 3,000 doughnuts and hundreds of mugs of coffee each Saturday to the boys out there.

"Part of it's fun," says Martha. "You're assigned one of the men to carry the heavy tray of doughnuts, and then you start walking--thru' Ward after Ward. You get whistled at and the men act like kids. It makes you feel good--because they feel good. But the bad cases make you feel awful; they never complain. All the grouses come from convalescents."

Yes, I know. My Mother always said that she knew when one of us children was on the mend, after an illness. When we became cross, she stopped worrying; we had begun to get well.

Terrible Incident at Smithfield!

V-2. Bad casualties.

At the worst possible time--when the Market was in full swing--a V-2 landed in the street there.

Smithfield Market is in the East Central district of London. People, produce, stalls and adjacent buildings were blasted to a shambles.

Two American Red Cross girls were there, to buy supplies for the Canteen at Headquarters. The girls were just getting out of their car when the V-2 landed. They are both in Hospital, and very badly off. One of the girls has broken ribs, broken arms, and burns. The other girl is so extensively and deeply burned that she is on the danger list.

The act of destruction and death took a few seconds.

The rescue of victims took a few days.

The billeting of the homeless will take a few weeks.
The healing of the injured will take an indefinite time.
The clearing of the bombed and burned site will take months.
The rebuilding will take years.
The dead are dead.
And this--the Smithfield Incident--is but one of many such incidents.

Writing of the Smithfield Incident recalls the V-2 that landed one Sunday morning as we were at breakfast in the flat. It was one of those clear, sunny days that make a mock of the imminent threat from Rockets. Unheralded Death from such blue skies seemed fantastic and improbable. But, as Dick, the girls (Alix comes up to London every so often for a weekend.) and I sat and chatted over a last cup of coffee, a sharp and loud explosion jarred us. The immensity of it was staggering.

"Golly! That was a near one!"

And we tried to figure out just where that particular V-2 had come down. It couldn't have been far away, we know.

That afternoon Col. Bigelow, U.S. Army, came to tea. He was on leave from the Continent and staying in the Cumberland Hotel at Marble Arch--about 6 streets to the west of Portland Place. That V-2 had come down at Marble Arch-- mercifully in open ground between the Rocket-gun sites (at the Park Lane end of Hyde Park) and that well known spot occupied by Soap-box Orators at the Park Gates opposite the Marble Arch. There had been but one casualty, a Salvation

Army Worker in a canteen. But there had been a lot of blast damage to the property on Oxford Street just across from where the V-2 landed--the Regal Cinema, the Cumberland Hotel and the Mount Royal, a block of flats.

Col. Bigelow was in his room at the Cumberland, awaiting breakfast to be brought up to him, when, to use his own words, "All of a sudden there was a terrible commotion." The understatement of an Army man. For there had been a vast bit of destruction from blast--windows shattered, walls pitted, doors warped.

"Luckily my room was at the back of the Hotel," continued Col. Bigelow. "Of course I never thought to see my breakfast."

And here is where the classic "view-of-the-War by Americans-in-England" is once again presented to you. It is not the dangers and the privations that loom in their experiences of the War here--it is the English people, their courage and morale. For Col. Bigelow said, "In less than 10 minutes after the explosion a maid appeared with my breakfast tray! She was a bit white and shaky, but all she said was, 'Here is your breakfast, Sir. I'm afraid it's a bit dusty. The ceiling's down in the Kitchen, in spots.'--Those British!" And then with a broad grin, he added, "I'm glad I'm returning to the Continent tomorrow where it's safer!" Which made us all laugh.

Later, one of the V-2's landed at Primrose Hill, just the other side of Regents park from us. Stan Beverley was in the courtyard of Eton Place (the Beverley's block of flats), settling Margo in her pram, when the Rocket hit. Stan threw himself across Margo, as the windows behind him rattled and shed a few panes. Another "near one" for the Beverleys. (And a "near one" for 71 Portland Place was the very last V-2 to land in London. A direct hit on an A.R.P. Post, two streets over. The full Personnel had just left. There was only a skeleton staff on duty--5 in all. They were killed, of course. But it might have been far worse. Blast from the particular rocket that caused <u>that</u> Incident blew in the entrance door of our flat and threw Martha out of her chair in the drawingroom onto the floor. Freak blast--for not a window was broken.)

One "contacts" this War through one's own experiences or those of friends. Otherwise, these terrifying years have become a monstrous Serial to be followed in newspapers, even the radio, from books, and the conversation of people. One can only pray that this historic conglomeration of foul deeds and heroic adventure, of bloodshed and sacrifice, resolves into the correct ending--as approved by the Hayes Office--retribution and Justice, wherever they belong.

April 1st, 1945
Back to "Springfield."
Easter Sunday.

Easter, <u>and</u> April Fool's Day. The pattern of the World today. Belief and Superstition. Right and Rite.

Martha and Yvonne arrived Saturday morning in time for breakfast. They had left London on the 1 a.m. train from Waterloo, and had sat up all night. At breakfast the girls debated the question, "Whether, or not, a heatless compartment (on the train) with drafts is preferable to a heated compartment with fuzzy air?" the latter had been their lot on Friday night.

The cold compartment won. In spite of numbed feet one does sleep, and the awakening is free of that stewed and over-cooked condition of brain that a night in an airless and heated compartment produces. Minor complications, such as drunks who sing, snorers, and people who, even in sleep, shift about continuously, are, of course, discounted.

Friday night, however, there was an "innovation," a chap with artificial legs, poor darling. He kept Yvonne awake most of the night. Wedged beside her, the poor man eternally crossed and uncrossed his legs. With the aid of both hands he would heave one leg over the other, jolting Yvonne from partial sleep--attendant creaks, like rusty hinges, disturbing the solidity of warm air and sleepers' breath surrounding them. "but I truly did feel sorry for him!" said Yvonne.

Yvonne and Martha have a scant 2 days here. But there will be renewal in those 48 hours away from London. It is really a sort of embarkation leave for Yvonne (Yvonne Berger-Soler, former schoolmate of Martha's in the States). She is a Red Cross Clubmobile girl, and is now awaiting orders for the Continent.

Today is Easter. Another Easter Sunday--the 6th of this War! Again the Churches are packed with people, flowers, song, prayer and memory. And again the promise of Resurrection is offered as solace for the mass Crucifixion of Humanity in this hideous War.

Still April, 1945
"Springfield."
The death of President Roosevelt on April 12th was

such a shock to the Public, highly keyed up by the mounting tension in news from the Continent with it's intimation of an early end to the War, that the bleak announcement of President Roosevelt's death taxed the overworked mental and emotional gear of the people here to the point of near collapse. The British felt as though they were dealt a body-blow.

I wonder if Americans in America quite realize the depth of feeling here, in England, for Roosevelt. He was looked upon as nothing less than a Savior of this country. The adjectives applied to Roosevelt in English speech and writing have been close to hyperbole, but prompted by an honesty and sincerity of feeling that may well become a monument to Roosevelt's statesmanship. One can read all this in the newspapers, and hear it all on the radio and at memorial services, etc. Such appreciation is commensurate with Roosevelt's high position in the world and his contribution to that World.

But the experience of personally receiving--upon Roosevelt's death--condolences from friends and acquaintances in the form of sympathetic remarks, telephone calls and letters has been a revelation. For there has been an intimate quality in these individual expressions of sympathy that has placed such appreciation beyond that of ordinary (or extraordinary) Public acclaim. To the British people President Roosevelt was not a Figurehead, a Demi-God on a pedestal--he was an earnest, idealistic man, a friend, "the greatest friend that Britain ever had."

My family and I have felt extremely touched by all this spontaneous sympathy extended to us--on our loss, as Americans, of "a great American." Letters from boys in the British Forces have come to us with such earnest and friendly condolence as to make us feel this public loss as a very personal one. A former parlormaid, now in the Land Army, wrote to me, "Dear Madam, I send you my deep sympathy on the loss of a great man." Friends have taken me by the hand and, with real sorrow in their eyes, have said, "What a loss for You! And Britain has lost a great friend. We will never forget him."

I am a Republican. I never voted for Roosevelt, although my husband did--to the consternation of his family and mine. I have disagreed with much in the political, diplomatic and economic policies of Roosevelt. But I <u>have</u> <u>understood</u> and <u>been proud of</u> the President's interest in and friendship for Britain, and have felt that there was a true personal friendship between Roosevelt and Churchill that served as touchstone in that larger relationship. Anglo-American friendship. Also, I admire the idealism that promulgated the four Freedoms.

Out of the ill-assorted ingredients--Power Politics, Secret Treaties, Tolerance and Intolerance, Isolationism, "Aid for Britain," Imperialism, Gratitude to America, etc., all boiling in the retort of World War II--out of this strange formula has come a bit of pure gold, Friendship, the friendship of many British for Americans, and vice versa. We can use this proven friendship between England and America as an investment in the future close Anglo-American Relationship for "The greater good of the greater number" in each country.

My realistic husband tells me I am chasing rainbows. I remind him that rainbows lead to pots of gold.

"Humph!" said Dick. "What you mean and I mean by gold are 2 different things. Mind you, I understand and approve what you mean--but it's hardly compatible with the facts of life."

I wonder.

Granted that aspirations and ideals--such as the Four Freedoms, for instance--and their application will produce many a headache for the World. But, if the proof of the pudding is in the eating, certainly a heavy mixture of high taxes, controls, strikes and unemployment is going to bring on an attack of acute indigestion, which a dose of material prosperity (should we get it) will not entirely dispel.

As any good physician will tell you--the patient, himself, must want to get well. "Mind over matter" is no idle phrase. The World must want a true bill of health and be willing to cooperate in obtaining it. But a batch of "isms"-- Communism, Isolationism, Socialism, etc.--chosen, like a batch of patent medicines, more for individual taste than healing purpose, is enough to turn the poor old World into a proper hypochondriac with no hope of full recovery.

Is it possible that World War II is a strong enough emetic to rid the World of certain poisonous ideologies? In any case, there will be a long period of convalescence, during which there will be great danger of a relapse. A tonic will be needed to put the World upon it's feet again. How about a few vitamins?

Vit. A -- Accord

Vit. B -- Brotherliness

Vit. C -- Christianity

Vit. D -- Decency

Vit. E -- Enterprise. The latter must be taken with discretion. An overdose might bring on "Cartel-isis," or even "Aggression-Fever" which, in virulent form, can become Fatal.

We were all interested and amused at lunch one day by a story that Dick told us. A Mrs. D. had come into his office at the factory that morning to return some shot guns which, some time ago, had been presented to her by the Civilian Committee for the Defense of British Homes. Mrs. D. is a crack shot, and she had been engaged in a very odd, but very necessary, War Job. The killing of Falcons! Let me explain.

In the transmission of messages between the Continent and England, and from Airmen forced down at sea, Carrier Pigeons have been vitally important in the War. Their route often followed the Devon coast, where high and rocky cliffs rise sheer from the sea. These cliffs are honey-combed in spots with caves, before which sharp ledges jut above the sea like shelves. The inaccessibility of these caves has been a screen to strange deeds.

For some time there had been a considerable loss of urgent messages due to the fact that numbers of carrier pigeons failed to get through to their bases. Investigation traced the stoppage to certain spots on the West Coast, here in Devon. And it was discovered that Falcons were swooping out from caves in the rocky, wooded cliffs, in the Blitzkreig on Carrier Pigeons winging their way home. Only liquidation of the Falcons would eliminate the strange and fatal menace to a small, but oh, so vital branch of warfare.

Mrs. D. was deputized to destroy the Falcons. The guns and ammunition used in this particular job of Home Defense were American--from among the thousands such sent by America to Great Britain at the time of her dire need for arms. The Civilian Committee for the Defense of British Homes--of which my husband was a founder--was responsible for the collection and disbursement of this voluntary American aid. Upon arrival in this country, cases of weapons and ammunition were delivered to the British Rola factory (here in Bideford) where Martha and volunteer helpers sorted the contents. Then, upon an appeal for weapons, Dick and the Committee would draw upon this stock, and distribute the weapons wherever necessary.

Many and varied were the uses to which these weapons have been put during this War. But their use against the Falcons on the Devon coast is, probably, one of the oddest. "Give us the tools and we will finish the job." Mrs. D had been given the tools, and she had finished the job. One is stretching no point when one again uses the expression--an Anglo-American effort.

April 29, 1945.

Food for the Dutch!
Headlines in this morning's papers.

I see the hardy and brave Dutch people standing four-square upon the land of Holland: the floods at their backs; the ruins of Rotterdam before them; their arms uplifted to a shower of food parcels descending like Manna from Heaven.

I think of Elijah and the Ravens.

I picture the Reurs family rushing from their house into the street--to garner tins of cocoa, spam, K-Rations!

I hear jubilant cries of denied happiness and frustrated salvation now freely shouted aloud in streets which once were silent beneath Fear and the Shadow of Death that stalked abroad in Nazi uniform.

I am punch-drunk upon these pictures of my

394

imagination. And I feel that the Dutch must be the same in their realization that Deliverance at last is shining bright before them.

Food for the Dutch
Another Liberation!
The Allies have been winning the War for some time. They are now ending it.
Food for the Dutch!
Bombs for the Germans! Should I say Nazis?--Yes.
Retribution and Justice.

An eye for an eye, a tooth for a tooth. My mind is in a maze. For what of these phrases: Turn the other cheek; Forgive thine enemy; That He gave His only begotten Son. My heart has always pondered such. And now--? That price the death of countless sons?

Food for the Dutch!

'Tis but the beginning of an Era when Mankind (particularly the Victors in this most horrible of Wars, for Victory is a heady wine) must find somewhere within himself a greater, surer strength than that begot of Power and assumed Virtue. Might and Right can win Wars. But soon there will be a Peace to be won. If we can win that, we not only will have won the last War, but we will have ended War.

Bio-Chemists and Scientists tell us that Man may be resolved into a chemical formula. Be that as it may, up to date this formula has produced some rather fatal explosions indicating a flaw somewhere in the equation. Of course, there is an answer to the problem. We shall have to try again.

I have a feeling that the right formula for Man, or mankind--the formula that will produce a lasting Peace--is so obvious and requires so simple a change in what we already

395

know of ourselves, that we quite overlook it in the complexities we have conjured up, clung to, and promoted, from one generation to another. I am inclined to think that those people, my husband among them, who offer remarks such as, "Now is the time to return to the soil," "The Simple Life is the Fullest," "Contented people are usually those with but a small share of worldly goods," etc.,--people who offer such remarks as implication that Man has been on quite the wrong track for a very long time, are people who "have something." But just what that is, I don't know. Perhaps you, who read this journal, can say.

April 30th, 1945.
Written on the train
traveling up to London.

Tomorrow is May 1st--May Day--Freedom Day--the day when parades of men and women used to tramp the streets, fly banners and sing. I am not a Communist. I use this simile and expression (Freedom Day) as representative of Spirit and Crusade thru'out the World and mark merely a coincidence of data, May 1st--and the imminence of Freedom on the Continent as coincident with Freedom Day. Could be--and this idea is entirely my own--that the Russians have made an enormous bid to synchronize Victory and the end of the War in Europe (international events) with celebrations of National importance. But that is their affair.

Be that as it may--not only tomorrow but every day, is Freedom day! For men and women still march to the call of Freedom--whether in battle to the accompaniment of

396

destruction and death--or on the Home Front, harassed by rationing and controls and bombs--or in the Underground Movements, ever in the shadow of death--or behind barbed wire in Concentration and P.O.W. Camps, beset with cruelty, starvation and loneliness. For, no matter what the locale, Man, himself, is free--in proportion to his spirit and his faith.

I have been reading the newspapers. My pulse is racing in answer to the headlines. Stupendous sentences are flung into the public consciousness: "Himmler wishes to Surrender unconditionally. But not to Russia!" "Hitler is Dead of a hemorrhage!" "Goering is shot;" "Himmler Surrenders to the Big Three;" "Hitler is Dead." The large black letters seem capped with doom, as stands a Judge when passing sentence on a man condemned to death.

Retribution and Justice.

Mussolini has received this--in violence and ignominy. How else should it be meted out to such as he?

"Hitler is Dead." If this be true, then Hitler has escaped that which every tyrant and dictator dreads--a public stripping of his power, an exposé of the man, himself--quite naked and small and evil, shorn of the camouflage of pomp, ritual and seductive speech. But whether Hitler is dead, or no, there remains a vast heritage of foul ideology that has blackened the minds of untold numbers of the German race. How shall we deal with the perversion of a People?

Retribution and Justice.

A while ago a young American Colonel told us this story. It illustrates one method--against one category of perverts.

Nazi S.S. men and the Gestapo have been running true to form. Once bullies, in defeat they have become cowards, and, in a bid for clemency, have been giving themselves up, quite naked!   It seems that the sight of an S.S. or Gestapo uniform is not being taken prisoner.

"And, at that, death is too good for them!" said the young Colonel.   "Anyway, these S.S. Nazis finally figured their uniform was against them. As if that were all! We began to get batches of naked Nazis, giving themselves up with wild yarns about being stripped of their clothes and driven into our hands, etc. We didn't fall for this very long! The boys got busy on a hunt for uniforms. They were found all right! Hidden, or buried. We count the uniforms and count the Naxis. Then we shoot a Nazi for every uniform. Sometimes the boys do a little fancy work with bayonets. We aren't getting so many naked Nazis now--wanting to be taken prisoner! They fight. And we fight. And we finish them off. that's the only way to stop a Nazi being a Nazi!"

Methods of the S.S. men and the Gestapo are not unknown!   Here is another story about them.   A young American Doctor we know was in charge of a Hospital train, full of wounded just back from the Continent. Among them was a young U.S. Army Sergeant--shot through the arm, the leg, and the chest, but slated for recovery. Here is the story of the Gestapo and the young American Sergeant.

A. U.S. Army Captain, a Lieutenant, and this young Sergeant were captured and sent before S.S. men at H.Q. of the enemy sector involved.   The Nazis wanted information concerning the U.S. Army unit to which the Captain, Lieutenant and Sergeant had been attached.   This the 3 Americans refused to divulge. So the Gestapo took over.

First, the Capt. was escorted before the Gestapo interrogators.

"If you refuse to give us the name and present location of your unit we will shoot you," said the Nazis.

The Captain refused.

So he was shot.

"The Kid (Sgt.) and the Lieutenant were in the next room and heard it all," related Doc.

"Then the Lieutenant was taken in to the Gestapo officials. They pointed to the dead Captain on the floor and said, 'If you don't tell us the name and location of your unit we will shoot you."

But the Lieutenant said, "No."

So the Lieutenant was shot.

And the Kid heard that, too," continued Doc.

"Then it was the Sergeant's turn, and the Nazis took him into the Gestapo. There were the Captain and the Lieutenant lying dead on the floor. 'Those Nazis don't understand psychology,' the Kid says to me. 'What they'd done just made me madder. They pointed to the Captain an' the Lieutenant an' they said, "You see what happens to people who don't do what we want? But we're going to give you 3 chances.

The Kid figured the Gestapo thought he might weaken. And, besides, he was the only one now who could tell them what they wanted. They weren't going to be too hasty!

So the Gestapo said, 'The first time you refuse to give us information we will shoot you thru' the arm. If you refuse again, we will shoot you through the leg. But, if you refuse a third time we will kill you.'"

Well, the Gestapo asked the Kid would he give them the name and location of his unit. And the Kid said, 'No.' So they shot him thro' the arm. Then they asked him again. And still the Kid wouldn't give. So the Gestapos shot him through the leg--and the Kid fell down. This, the Kid says, gave the Nazis an unfair advantage. They yelled at him like he was dead already and couldn't hear. 'This is your last chance!"

And here," said Doc, bringing the story to a climax. "Here is the darndest coincidence! Just like a play or film! The Gestapos yell, 'Are you going to tell?' And the Kid screams, "Hell! No!' when there's a terrible commotion outside and the Gestapos look scared. The Kid says they were so scared they couldn't shoot straight! Then they ran out one door, just as part of the American Army burst in the other."

'There I was on the floor with the other 2 guys,' says the Kid. 'But I was lucky. I wasn't dead. I only rated a trip to Hospital over here.'

Says he's going back," ended Doc. "The Captain and the Lieutenant are 2 important reasons."

I sure do like that story--some parts of it.

And now the War--the War in Europe--is ending

This morning of April 30, 1945, I look from the train windows upon the green English land as it slides past in a continuous strip of pictures, as though spun out upon a film, "Spring is Here Again." As Commentator on this Film of Nature my mind remarks, "What an artistic housewife is Mrs. Earth. How gaily she sets her bouquets of flowering fruit trees about the open green drawing-room of England on a brisk Spring day." But the headlines, blatant in the newspapers held before the intent faces of my fellow travelers, tweak my subconscious into wakefulness. Here, at the near end of the War, I am in the same puzzled state of mind as I was in the War's beginning.

"Lawks-a-mercy! Can this be I?"

Over 5 years of War have passed. Yet here am I, riding

in a train to London, where I shall join Martha and Dick at the Flat for a week or so. I shall shop, and "visit" with friends and see some shows. Excluding the tragic casualties of this War--and the bombed areas here, in England--life is fairly normal again. Or is it?

I look upon the green and peaceful countryside. My fellow travelers sit and read the papers. There is an apparently normal, everyday look about the scenes, without and within the train, that makes one marvel that 5 years (and more) of War have really beat upon this Country and it's People. Have we dreamed a dreadful nightmare?

Alas, No!

Tear away the gauze of that apparent normalcy. What are the everyday <u>realities</u>? And what do they reveal? As seen here on the London train.

Reality No. 1. **The newspapers.**

For years these have been but 2 scant sheets of paper. Paper makes munitions. Yet these rationed newspapers have carried-on throughout the War. Only where a severe Blitz has temporarily stopped printing or circulation has this Voice-of-the-People failed to present its' messages,--heartening or heart-rending--every day, so surely as that day would dawn. The rationed newspaper is one of the War's realities--and also one of the stabilities in our wartime lives, and doubly so this morning with such hopeful news.

Reality No. II. **The trains.**

Stripped of comfort and entirely lacking in heat. Today, in the Spring, the lack of heat is hardly noticed, but on a Winter's day, a long journey in an unheated compartment can become so acutely uncomfortable as to be a small bit of suffering. Another of the War's realities. Yet, also, one of the stabilities in this War. Because, although travel accommodation is cheerless and so rationed as to heat and comfort that no slight bit of either is offered, there still is travel accommodation. The trains carry-on.

Reality No. III. **The dress of fellow travelers.**

This has one consistency--an overall drabness that emphasizes the bleakness of wartime life in England. A pair of colorful knitted gloves (2 coupons if bought readymade, 1 coupon for the wool alone) a cheerful scarf (1 or 2 coupons, depending on the size,) a gay hat (unrationed, but very expensive,) a jaunty tie (2 coupons)--these accessories make a brave show at keeping up appearances. Shirt collars are apt to be worn--especially if already once turned; men's shirts take 8 coupons apiece! An inch of bare leg showing below the trouser hem of a crossed leg proclaims 2 wartime measures; no cuffs on men's trousers, and the horrible short "bobby-sox" that now masquerade as men's hose, here, in England. Another reality of this War. Yet, also, another of it's stabilities. One still can buy clothes.

Reality No. IV. **The pale, lined faces of the people.**

The children alone, offer a picture of health because of the concentrated bottled orange juice and the slight extra ration of milk allowed to youngsters under 5 years of age. (A great pity that these 2 necessities for proper growth could not be extended to 7 years of age). This reality of War--the pinched, or the puffy look (varying with individual metabolism) upon the people's shadowed faces--is produced by a diet unhealthily heavy in starch, frighteningly short on fats, sugar and meat and almost completely lacking in vital fruit juices. Only 1/2 pint of milk every other day! The reduced <u>food values</u> of the wartime diet here present a reality of this War that is not, alas, a <u>true</u>

stability. The wartime diet is stable only to that degree of life which such stringent rationing produces. The people here are tired--tired and worn, and half-starved. Make no mistake about this. Altho' the English people have had enough to eat in quantity, throughout this War, the quality (nutritional value) of food has been so reduced that the average diet here has undermined the people's vitality. Physically speaking, of course--for the English Heart is as stout as it ever was.

Reality No. V. **There are no Restaurant Cars--no amenities for refreshment.**

Travelers who wish to eat must carry a packet of sandwiches. Often these lunches are accompanied by a thermos of hot tea--and sometimes a bottle of beer, or even a bottle of whiskey and water (already mixed.) Odd bits of paper are the wrappings for these snacks. The infrequent serviette that appears, when spread upon the traveler's lap, is frayed and thin, It's shabbiness punctuated by frankly undarned holes. Another reality in this War--the poor appurtenances to living. In the hotels and restaurants one gets no serviette. But even these portions are now nonexistent. In some hotels one can not even be sure of sheets on the beds. Often there are no pillow slips--the lower sheet is drawn over the unembellished pillow of striped ticking. And, of course, one always carries towels and soap when traveling. These two appurtenances can never be counted on nowadays unless "in hand." These are definite realities of War. And the only stability found in rationed food and rationed comfort is that the food and the minimum of comfort (such a minimum as to resolve into discomfort!)--the only stability found in these harsh realities is that they have never ceased to be. At least we eat--and we can keep clean--to a degree.

403

Reality No. VI. **Reminders of War.**

Outside the train, here and there upon the lovely landscape stand stark reminders of War--A.A. (Anti-Aircraft) gun emplacements, Airfields, Army Camps, Emergency Hospitals, Black-houses, bombed buildings. These are such commonplace sights that they seem almost indigenous to their surroundings.

Thus, in the train, traveling up to London this morning of April 30th, 1945, I can read much of the topical history of World War II in the limited scenes about me. And the final chapter--yet to come--is forecast in the morning papers by the prophetic headings, "Himmler Surrenders--Hitler is Dead." the end of the European War, at least, is imminent.

In enumerating the Realities of War--to be found directly about me as I write,--I might mention the lack of drinking water on the trains. But this would be only a half-truth. It is quite true that one can not get a drink of water, unless one supplies oneself with such in thermos or bottle. But this inability to obtain a drink--a simple drink of water to quench one's thirst--while traveling on an English train, existed before the war. I can not vouch for every train--but I have traveled about quite a bit and, unless there were Restaurant or sleeping cars attached, I have never been able to get a drink of water while traveling by rail, here, in England.

This, at first, seemed almost uncivilized to me. But after some time in England, I came to the conclusion that the English when thirsty think in terms of tea, not water. That, no doubt, accounts for the absence of water-coolers in trains--and the sparse number of public drinking fountains, among which there is an unfortunate preponderance of old-fashioned germ-purveying cups-on-chains. Tea is what the Englishman drinks--consistently and in quantity as we Americans drink water.

This 8:30 a.m. train from Instow to London makes 2 "long" stops--Exeter Central, and Salisbury. At these stations practically every compartment door bangs open--and figures, male and female, leap out upon the platform and hurriedly zigzag thru' the traffic of people and Porters milling about there. The platform tea-trolley or the Station buffet is the objective of this race. The prize-----mugs of hot tea.

The return from this sortie for refreshment is like a triumphal procession. With a large white china mug of steaming tea in either hand, or a mug of tea in one hand and a couple of saffron colored buns in the other, the returning contingent surges back in groups--one eye on the slopping tea, the other on the open door of a particular compartment, both ears cocked for the Guard's whistle. At it's shrill screech there is a frantic dash of late stragglers. Cups in hand they leap into the nearest open door on the train. Bang--clap--bang--clap! the doors are slammed to and latched, all along the heavy 10 to 15 carriages now clanking with the slight "slip-back" as the brakes are taken off.

Outside on the station platform there is that flat aftermath when a train pulls out--a blank look, in spite of movement and people, in spite of emotion and fluttering hands among those left behind. The place, as such--Salisbury, for instance--has ceased to exist. We are on our way to other places and other people.

But inside, here in the compartment, is a fresh stir, a lively bit of chat, a stimulus in the air. Tea! Opposite me sit 4 people--with 4 mugs of tea. 2 of the people cuddle the mugs in both hands, as though the mugs were brandy inhalers. But

405

each of the 4 faces above those 4 mugs of tea have the serene, concentrated expression of the connoisseur of fine wine. Tea! It satisfies and stimulates. Yes, this "tea business" is another reality of War found here upon the London train.

Reality No. VII. **Tea.**

In spite of rationing, there is always <u>tea</u>--to soothe, to stimulate, to stabilize one's nerves, whatever the need. A good cup of tea! One of the realities of this War--and definitely one of the stabilities.

Now 4 empty white china mugs repose upon the floor beneath the opposite seats, one mug sedately placed beneath each of the 4 travelers. A prick of ribald humor tickles my risibilities. It is fortunate that those 4 men opposite have no idea of the indelicacy of a certain female American mind! Yet I warrant each man has a good sense of humor.

Reality No. VIII. **Humor.**

No matter what the locale, the circumstances, or the people--one can almost always find something to smile about. A sense of humor is a strong bit of armor against the knocks and hurtful thrusts of daily life in wartime. Humor is a real stability these unsettled days. And the British people have kept themselves going on many a laugh. The sense of humor has been the key note to their sanity, which has persevered throughout the restrictions, dangers, and tragedies of World War II as experienced in England.

May 8th, 1945,
" Springfield"
Instow.
V-E Day! Victory in Europe!

Some people are crazy with joy. They act as tho the end of the <u>entire</u> War had arrived. There are celebrations everywhere. But the majority of people with whom I talk are sober faced, have heavy hearts, and wonder how much longer it will be before the <u>Japs</u> are beaten. I think I am quite right in saying that it is the minority who are celebrating V-E Day.

By strange and happy coincidences, I received a letter this morning from Enny Reurs Gray. (Before the War we attended Enny's wedding in London. She married a young Englishman, Charles Gray.) Her family (in Holland) are safe and well. That is joyful news indeed on V-E Day. And it was Enny's husband (Charles Gray, attached to a British Intelligence Corps) who, at the liberation of Rotterdam, located the Reurs family there and walked into their house--to find Mr. Reurs at his desk, writing to his daughter Enny! What a dramatic re-union! Charles and his father-in-law had last met in London, before the War. And then Mrs. Reurs--and Kitty-- and Johnny--came in, one after the other, from various errands in the town. Enny quotes Charles as saying that everyone went a little crazy. It is not to be wondered at.

Knowing Mrs. Reurs--and her fear and hatred of the "Nazzias" and her long ago prediction of this War--the Occupation of Holland by the Nazis must have been a most terrible experience. For months Johnny was hidden beneath the floor boards of a friend's house--to keep him from a German labor gang or, worse still, the German Army. Kitty belonged to the Underground Movement. And an Aunt,

407

evacuated with her children from Rotterdam to the country, has aided several downed R.A.F. to escape. I refer to Enny's letter again. They (her Aunt's family) have not been molested, being so far out of the country quite away from things. "But Aunt Mok has gotten very thin," Enny writes. "Imagine Aunt Mok thin! And now, with the Canadians swarming about, she is in a flap because her eldest girl has fallen in love with one."

All the young people have been celebrating. The Canadians give parties everywhere. Rotterdam is wild with joy. The Canadians laugh and say that the Battles before the liberation of Rotterdam were terrific--but that the Battle of Rotterdam was the most terrific of all! I assume that the Dutch people, in their wild enthusiasm and joy at liberation, nearly finished off the Canadians! I get the impression that Rotterdam was rocked to its foundations by the jubilant antics of a people almost insane with happiness. The "Saga of the Reurs Family in world War II" has come to a happy ending.

I wish that it were true of all.

Some weeks later Mrs. Reurs (Her name is Katerina-- called Kato--then, as a diminutive, "To." Along with other friends I call her "To." Pronounced like "Toe.") wrote me. And it was wonderful to hear from her again! She wrote that the recent events were hard to believe after the past war years. "The Nazzias" (as Mrs. Reurs calls them) took her Father's house, put him and his brother of 91 out upon the streets with only the clothes on their backs, one blanket and one small case of necessities apiece. She heard nothing from her Father--a man in his eighties--until after the liberation of Rotterdam. He is well, but very feeble. The brother of 91, Mrs. Reurs' Uncle, had died of starvation! Food has been a most awful problem. When the dykes were breached she felt it was, indeed, the end.

As for clothes--they have been able to buy none for several years. "Do not throw anything away," she wrote. (I'd never think of it! We are wearing clothes bought in the States before the War. Shoes, too!) "Anything at all, no matter how darned or patched, would be welcome here." They consider themselves lucky to be alive--and together. After the bombing of Rotterdam they had gone to Wassanaar, outside the Hague. But, after the Rocket sites had been built there and the terrible Rockets, themselves, were being fired off so near their house, they returned to Rotterdam. And only just in time. A Rocket turned back and badly damaged the house in Wassanaar. They might well have been killed. And now what a wonderful thing to have Charles, their own daughter's husband, come to them as liberator and bring them food as well as good news. "If I had known that Enny was in so many raids over there in England, those Rockets and all--and was alone, with Charles away--it would have been too much to bear. I should then really have lost my mind."

May 9th, 1945 - Evening.

"Springfield"

Instow.

V-E Day, plus one. Dick had promised Penny that she should go to London the minute the bombs stopped falling. So Alix, Penny and Meda left this morning on the 8:30 train. I 'phoned the flat this evening to see if they had arrived safely.

The papers--and the Radio--have told of immense, and almost impassable, crowds in the London streets, and that there are no taxis to be had at all, and that even buses have stopped running. I wondered how Alix was going to manage the luggage--or even get to the flat.

Dick answered the 'phone. And, upon inquiry, I could almost see his broad grin by wire, as he replied.

"Oh, they're fine. They're all here. I sent a hirecar to Waterloo for them." I might have known!

"And how does Penny like London?"

Dick chuckled. "She says there's too many people!"

Of course. The countryside here has been her world for 4 years.

"If it's quiet enough tomorrow Alix and Meda are taking Penny to the Zoo. She wants to see the 'enqueerium'".

Not bad--that word. I feel as tho' I inhabited an 'enqueerium', myself, some days.

May 10th, 1945.

Larry 'phoned this morning!

Alix and Martha are both at the flat, so I took the call. I nearly fell over, when I heard that familiar voice. "Flying Officer" (Officer in R.C.A.F. - Royal Canadian Air Force) Murphy calling." Larry was in Bournmouth--just back from Stalag Luft III. Yes, he was O.K. Where were the girls? I told him and gave him the 'phone number and address. He's going up to London tomorrow. Such excitement!

After Larry was reported missing--from a raid over

410

Bremen--his mother never once gave up hope. She and I have corresponded through this war. And Larry's Mother always wrote, "I still feel that Larry will turn up. He's a prisoner, I think." And she proved to be right. but it was many, many months before she received that message. Yet she persisted in her belief that Larry was alright. "He can take care of himself," she wrote. "Somehow I can not feel that he is dead. He's going to get out of this, I know."

And so he had.

Week-end of May 20th, 1945.

We have been celebrating Martha's birthday. She was lucky enough to get a short week-end and came down from London Friday, on the late train with Dick. As a family, we seem to attract strange incidents. Martha got locked in the W.C. on the train! She was there a good half hour before she managed to get the attention of a Guard. And the corridors were lined as usual with troops! But the poor old train rattles and bangs so that a few more rattles and bangs were not noticed.

At last, the Guard heard Martha. But he and a couple of soldiers couldn't open the "lav" door. So the train Fireman was fetched. And at last Martha was freed.

"And do you know what the Fireman said when he burst the door in?" recounted Martha. "He actually said, 'Whatever were you doing' in there, anyway!"

It was funny.

Larry--and Brack--are also with us for the week-end.

Ten days in England have made them look quite fit. But, knowing Larry, he seems thoughtful and is certainly quieter. Brack arrived from London first--on Friday afternoon. I had gone into the dining-room to "lay-up" the table for tea. And there, coming in from the Butler's pantry, was a curly-headed young man in blue tweed sports jacket and gray flannels. I had never seen him before.

"Who are you!" I exclaimed.

I was expecting Larry--and a friend of his whom I had never met--on the usual London train due at 4:12 p.m. But it was not yet 4 o'clock. "This is no R.C.A.F. Officer," I thought.

But I was wrong.

"I'm Brack, Ma'am. Brakenbury is the name. But they call me Brack."

"Yes?"

"I rang the front doorbell--quite a few times. Then I went around to the kitchen. And the door was open--and no one there--so I came in. I'm sorry to upset you. Ma'am. You see, Larry's coming on the next train, like we planned, But I --"

"Oh, you're Larry's friend!"

The young man's engaging grin grew even broader. Brack and I retired to the drawing-room to catch up on things. And I learned that he and Larry had been at Stalag Luft III together. When Larry was shot down over Breman he had managed to escape--and had kept under cover for 3 months! With the aid of the Underground Larry got as far as the Spanish Border before he was caught.

"Very tough on Spud (Larry is well over 6 feet!)," said Brack. "And it wasn't too nice at Camp either." And then, in the deprecating way most boys speak of their prison experiences, "But then it wasn't too bad."

412

I knew, of course, that Stalag Luft III was the Camp from which the 50 young Airmen had escaped by way of a miraculous tunneling job. And that those 50 young men were caught--handed over to the Gestapo--and shot, in defiance of the Geneva Conventions. (March, 1944).

"The Nazis told all the fellows why they were being shot," said Brack. "Said it was to be an example. Ought to stop the escapes. Of course it didn't."

Later we gleaned quite a bit from Larry and Brack concerning life at Stalag Luft III. The mainstay of their existence had been the Red Cross parcels. (All ex-P.O.W.'s say this.) The boys used to concoct strange "puddings" from the articles within. But these "puddings" helped, in a small way, to fill the voids left by the very scant daily ration of bread, soup and vegetables furnished by the Nazis.

The boys had to do their own cooking. In groups of 6 or 8 they were assigned to a certain half-hour in the day when they might use the stove. The half-hour varied. So some days Larry and Brack would eat in the early morning--and some days not until 10 o'clock at night.

"You can get awfully hungry by that time," say Larry. "We had meat about twice a year! And only 2 slices of bread a day. Black Bread. Very tough and hard. We used to pound and crumble it up and make a sort of pudding out of it. The Nazis gave us 1 teaspoon of margarine and 1 teaspoon of jam every other day. We used these in cooking. The vegetables we got were mostly rutabaga--sometimes cabbage. That was all. Except the cup of soup each day. What soup!"

Yes, there had been lots of "unpleasantness" at the

413

Camp. There was the time some Canadians were being questioned and they wouldn't give the right answers, so the Nazis pulled their toe nails off--one by one. Larry, himself, had been beaten up several times. Had had 6 teeth knocked out. And had been in solitary.

When the Camp was finally liberated they were all taken to Lubeck and put in a compound there to await orders. And a British guard was put around the place.

"Brack and I didn't think much of that!" said Larry. We couldn't feel liberated with <u>any</u> guard around. So we left."

Just like that--apparently!

Anyway, Larry and Brack set off in the <u>direction</u> of England--intending to get there somehow, and soon. Things were very lively. Streams of War vehicles along the roads-- troops-Germans giving themselves up--"Displaced persons" swarming about--liberated P.O.W.'s making their way to Allied units, looking for "direction."

"All you had to say was 'Ex-P.O.W.'s'--and there'd be no questions asked. You'd get almost anything you asked for. We were treated well in every Mess we stopped at. We'd just say 'Ex-P.O.W.'s" Larry spread his arms in a wide gesture of largesse. "And they'd give us the place, it was wonderful!"

As the boys made their way along the crowded roads they decided that some sort of transport was needed. They weren't going to get very far walking. So at the next cross roads Larry went up to the soldier on traffic duty there.

"I asked him could we get a lift somewhere--maybe get a car?" I'd seen Allied Officers driving German cars, and wondered what our chances were. The chap was real helpful. 'Just ask any Nazi,' he says. But I haven't a gun, I tell him. 'Oh, they'll do anything you say,' he says.

So Brack and I set off. And pretty soon we saw a snappy looking Lagonda coming along the road. In it were 2 Nazi Officers and their girl friends, and the back was piled with luggage. They were getting out of things--they thought! I stepped into the road and put up my hand. And the car stopped."

Larry still looked surprised.

"So I went up and asked the Nazi who was driving for his papers. He handed them over--and I pretended to check them. Then I ordered the Nazis out. They didn't like it--but they got out. And the girls. And the luggage was dumped in the ditch. Oh, I asked them for their guns and got those too. Then Brack and I told them to go to H.Q. "That way" we said, and sent them off towards the compound."

Fantastic! But also logical. The Nazis are licked. They take orders now.

"But just outside one town a lorryful of soldiers swung out to pass us and got into a soft shoulder. The whole lot of them were blown to pieces! That was enough for me. We might be blown up, too, with mines in the shoulders! So I headed for the next airfield. And there, ready to take off for England, was a Dakota! Full of Ex-P.O.W.'s. So I went up to the Commandant and asked could Brack and I go aboard? He said no--we hadn't been deloused, etc.! But I took him to one side and asked him how about trading 2 seats in that Dakota for a nice German sports car. I pointed out the Lagonda, and told him the story. So Brack and I were in England in just a few hours!"

As Larry's Mother says, he can take care of himself!

415

Sunday we all went to church.

Shortly after breakfast Martha found Penny (now 5 years old) very vigorously carpet-sweeping the dining-room rug. She was pulling the chairs in and out from under the table and walloping the sweeper back and forth.

"Whatever are you doing, Penny?" "You don't need to do that!"

"I like to," answered Penny.

"But it's hard work for you, dear!" expostulated Martha.

"No, it isn't Auntie Mit," Penny replied. "But it's a Hell of a life!"

"What did you say!" Martha was startled, to say the least.

Penny repeated the phrase.

"You mustn't say that, Penny! That is no talk for a young lady. Do you understand?"

"Yes, Auntie Mit."

"You won't say it again?"

"No, Auntie Mit."

"Do you still want to clean the dining-room rug?"

'Oh yes Auntie Mit," says Penny enthusiastically, and begins to whang the carpet sweeper about the rug. "But it is a Hell of a Life just the same!"

Meda took over. Penny was deprived of her sweets for 2 days. And we all expiated the sin at church.

We knew that the Rector's brother was a Chaplain to the R.A.F. and had been a P.O. W. at Stalag Luft III. Both Larry and Brack remembered the Chaplain. So the Rector and his wife came over Sunday evening to meet the boys. And we all had a drink to celebrate their safe return home.

Still May, 1945.
71 Portland Place
London.

After their leave at "Springfield" Larry and Brack went back to Bournmouth where they were "on draft" to return home, and I came up to London again, with Martha and Dick. for a while. Gladys, the Rector's wife, came along for a visit with us. And while she was here, Larry appeared for a quick week-end, to say "Good-bye."

At breakfast, one morning, he explained to Gladys how it was that he and one other member of the crew were the only survivors when his Bomber went down near Breman.

"There was flak--and there were Nazi Fighters with cannon. We never did know what hit us! But all of a sudden the plane seemed to explode--all to pieces! I came to, up there in the air, just in time to pull the rip-cord of my 'chute. Horse-shoe 'round my neck!"

Larry signed gustily, still astonished at the miraculous escape.

"Horse-shoe 'round your neck?" Pop-eyed, Gladys leaned across the table. "However did it get there!"

We laughed so hard that it was some time before Gladys got a proper explanation of that slang expression or, strictly speaking, idiom. And then she laughed, too.

Of course our American slang and idioms are as familiar to us and as completely understood, as the puns, so indigent to speech and writing in England, are appreciated and comprehended by the English. Puns are continually used here in cartoons, newspaper headings and advertisements. And we Americans are sometimes as puzzled by the English puns and their application as the English are puzzled by our slang. Yet we managed to laugh with--not at each other. There's a world of difference.

July, 1945.
71 Portland Place,
London.

Anti-climax has hit us hard here, in England. Although only the <u>European</u> War has ended, the people expected drastic and immediate improvements in their way of life. The Bombs and Rockets have stopped. Thank God--and the Allies--for that! But, after the first wave of relief--during which every one gulped great draughts of freedom-from-bomb-fear, and got a bit drunk on it and thought everything was going to be rosy and bright at once!--after this little spree over Victory-in-Europe, the people are now feeling let down. Reality is catching up with us again.

There are still the Japs to lick. The War goes on in the East. Casualty lists continue to pour in. Rationing is tight--tighter than ever, with only 1 oz. of lard instead of 2 per week. Distribution of food is uneven. Queues are longer. "Points" don't go so far. More articles hibernate beneath the counters. "Only 1 lb. to a customer" is heard everywhere. It doesn't matter that I have 7 people to feed. "Only 1 lb. to a customer!" is the answer to my plea for more. And yet my neighbor in the queue (for tomatoes, say) is quite possibly a business woman living along. <u>She</u> will <u>feast</u> on her 1 lb. of tomatoes! I must find another green-grocer and queue another fifteen minutes to 1/2 hour for a second lb. of tomatoes--or divide the 1 lb. I have into minute shares among the members of my household. Which is what I usually do. There are only so many shopping hours in a day--and I have only 2 legs.

Oh, to be a centipede these queuesome days! However, there'ld be that many more legs and feet to ache--and that many more shoes to wear out! And, since I can not wear English shoes, that would be a problem. Some of my American shoes have been half-soled several times.

Shoes are a dreadful problem for the English, poor dears. Most of the shoes here, except the outrageously expensive, are of terrible stuff--even if you are lucky enough to be able to buy a pair, at 7 coupons per pair. Shoe-shop windows are full of shoes. But there are never any of the right size--inside the shops! I know people who every morning systematically telephone certain shoe-shops, one after the other, from a list of shops which have promised them that "the new quota" would be in any day! This telephoning takes time. But it's better than queuing, as many poor souls do for <u>hours</u>--only to be disappointed.

Things of this sort--the increased queuing, and the eternal "short supply," and the tightening up on things rather than the expected easing of restrictions and rations--at first sent a good portion of the populace into a flat spin. But most of them are now pulling out of this. And everyone is trying to. However, the feeling of anti-climax is so great that everywhere one hears these remarks. "I think we miss having the War <u>here</u>--the air-raids, the bombs, the rockets (V-I's and V-II's).

419

There seems nothing to keep up for now! I think we miss the War on the Continent. The European War furnished an excitement and an incentive that bolstered morale to high endurance. The War in the Pacific has not the same effect; it's too far away.

If this aftermath of the European War is so hard to bear, what will it be like when the Jap War is over--and V-J Day breaks upon us? Dick makes only the gloomiest of predictions. He says that the 2 years following the end of World War II will be more difficult and harder to bear, in England, than the War years, themselves. He's been right in his predictions most of the time. So I don't feel too happy.

One afternoon, following luncheon with a friend at the Park Lane Hotel on Piccadilly, I was standing on the pavement before the Hotel entrance waiting for the Doorman to get me a taxi, when two very well-dressed middle-aged gentlemen came along and stood beside me. They seemed to be in a hurry. So, when the Doorman had procured me a taxi, I was not surprised to have him ask me if I minded dropping the aforesaid gentlemen at the American Embassy, as I could easily pass it on my way to Portland Place. I assented with pleasure. One often shares a taxi nowadays.

I noticed, whenever we passed a bombed site, and particularly as we swung around Grosvenor Square by the ruined corner of Upper Brook Street, that my 2 elegant companions craned from the taxi windows. The men were clothed almost identically in gray flannel suits, freshly pressed, and immaculate white shirts with soft collars. They wore gray "felts" tipped over their smooth, unlined faces. One gentlemen wore eyeglasses, and I remarked the earpieces--they were attached at eyebrow level, very new and snappy! Ties--"High, wide, and handsome"--lighted up their ensembles. And an aura of sleek well-fedness and super-health surrounded them.

As the taxi slid in to the kerb at 1 Grosvenor Square I blurted out (I couldn't help it!), "You are Americans, aren't you?"

They nodded.

"I thought so!" I crowed. "No Englishman could look so grand after 6 years of war!"

They seemed a bit taken aback, but said they supposed things hadn't been very nice here.

"They certainly haven't!" I answered.

"Oh?"

"I'm an American, too--from Boston, Massachusetts. Been here through it all."

They didn't seem too impressed, but rather dazed, instead. I suppose that I was rude. However, I refused to let them pay their share of the fare--and drove off in a slightly uppish frame of mind. Of course, I had no business to resent their sleek, prosperous and well-stuffed appearance. It was perfectly normal for them. But, to me, their supergrandeur was a bit of salt in a wound.

No doubt those 2 Film Magnates--for I'm sure that's what they were!--no doubt they say, if they ever recall the episode, "Funny thing. One afternoon in London we shared a cab with an American woman. Been there all through the War. Must have been pretty well touched by it. Our clothes annoyed her!"

421

They certainly did.

August 2nd, 1945.
71 Portland Place,
London.

It is Dick's birthday. Just yesterday he arrived back from a very quick trip to the States--in time for his birthday, as he had promised. We've been very quiet this year--no celebration, just dinner at the Berkeley, Martha, Dick and I; the rest of the family are in Instow. But dining-out is a celebration in itself. One eats fairly well at the War-time controlled price of 5/ - ($1.25), although there is a cover charge over and above this. Quantity and quality are on the thin side, but there are several courses and the menus manage to be diverse. At the price it is really a bit of magic, food availability being what it is.

Later in the evening, back here in the flat, a fruit cake, with a few tiny candles stuck in it's glazed top. And a bottle of German Champagne--a present to Martha from Henry (Col. Henry Settle, U.S. Army), who was recently on leave--put a bit of fizz into our spirits. We have talked late, and most of the conversation has been of plans for our return home. I am of two minds about the matter:--(1) I want to see "my folks" and friends in America again; but (2) I shall miss England and our friends here. And I like London--oh, so much!

I once asked Dick what particular thing it is about London that so holds us? London is the Largest city in the World (At the time it was.). One can be very lonely in London. London can be sophisticated, in top-hat and long-frock manner. Following a code of formality and correctness, centuries old. The war years have substituted a tin-hat for the top-hat--and uniforms or short frocks for the gracious dresses of sweeping hems. But the sophistication, the formal correctness, has remained--to a degree. Yet, also, London has the intimate air of a huge and sprawling village. The many parks and squares--the informal pubs--the chatty cabbies--the ubiquitous Cockneys--the "mateyness" of the crowds, "Hi Chum!" One can feel an earthiness and a solidity beneath the many faceted surface of life in London. How is this accomplished? And why do I like living in London?

Dick says it is the tempo of life here. In spite of the fact that the city is overcrowded with people, that it's streets are teaming with traffic (even under petrol rationing), that the urgency of War has heightened it's pulse--yet the tempo of life here, in London, is more leisurely than that of comparable great cities in other countries. One can savor a specific Old World aroma in the air of London, War or no War.

Now life in New York, for instance, has a frenetic quality. There the very air vibrates with urgency. The wind in the street whispers "Hurry-Hurry!" And the people and traffic seem as though driven by that wind. Intense Work and Intense Play inoculate the people with a spurious elation, which in turn breeds restlessness. New York is a stimulant. The tempo of life there is uneven and staccato.

Paris is like a voluble, shoulder-shrugging Woman-of-

the World who has a bit of gamin in her make-up.   One
moment she is elegant and chic, with a polish of "dignité et
politesse," and then, suddenly, she rolls her eyes and shakes
her hips. And you put your tongue in your cheek and say "A-
ah! Now we see the true Paris." The tempo of life there
quickens into a dizzy whirl. Paris is fun.

But I still like living in London.

No doubt the fact that my ancestors were English has
much to do with my feeling at home here, in England among
the English. Dick feels the same and for the same reason.

August 9th, 1945.
71 Portland Place,'
London.

Yesterday, August 8th, was officially V-J (Victory-
Japan) Day--and London proceeded to take itself apart and
throw bits and pieces about in a frenzy of exaltation. But I
noticed one very particular thing about the crowds in the
streets. The majority of the people celebrating were young--
people with a future before them, an active future. Those of
middle age, and beyond, were in the minority, and neither their
faces nor their spirits seemed alight with quite the same intense
joy and exuberance that otherwise flared through-out the
celebrating crowds.

This being an historic occasion of great importance--the
end of World War II--Martha, Kay Macintosh (who is with us
again) and I set out about 9 o'clock last night to see what we
could see.   Dick considered himself better off in the flat.
"You'll only get stepped on and pushed around," he said, "And

I have the radio." The noises, alone, of Victory quite satisfied him. And he could see the flood-lighting from our windows. But the girls and I were curious. We wanted to see Piccadilly Circus, jam-packed with yelling people! We wanted to walk through the milling, surging masses of men and women who sang and danced in the streets as well as on the pavements! We had a desire to be pushed about by this happy throng--to yell a bit ourselves--and certainly to feel and share in whatever it was outside here (in the streets of London the night of V-J Day, 1945) upon which thousands of people were getting quite drunk! It wasn't just ozone, or even "Liquid refreshment," we knew.

So the girls donned their uniforms. Thus attired, they were less likely to be shoved about and mauled by hoodlums. I put on some very old shoes, sandals really, and the 3 of us set out--Martha on one side of me, Kay on the other, our arms linked. We swung right, along down Portland Place, the street as bright as though painted with moonlight, from the floodlighting on the B.B.C. The building loomed like a gigantic silver-frosted cake, it's sides festooned with the flags of every Ally. An enormous Union Jack, high on it's mast, sprouted from the top and waved triumphantly above the city. Over the entrance, flanked by the yellow flag of China on one side, by the red and white emblem of the U.S.S.R. on the other, the Stars and Stripes unfurled it's scroll of Victory.

I adore words--similes, synonyms, antonyms, etc.--the sound and the sense of them. I love comparisons. And so my mind automatically remarked that the Union Jack resembled a "tic-tac-toe" or a crossword puzzle (not always solvable)--that the Chinese Flag was appropriately representative of a yellow race--and that the Soviet Flag certainly went all out for labor,

425

communal labor, with everyone sharing everything, even tools, the one hammer and the one sickle! In my arrogance of nationality--patriotism, if you will--I saw my own country's flag as a bar of triumphal music, "Oh, say can you see!"

We went on--the girls and I--to Oxford Circus, and across into Regent Street, where we arrived within the "block" of V-J celebrations. It was a block alright--almost a solid one. It was reminiscent of the nights of the Old King's (King George V.) Jubilee, in 1935, when traffic was diverted from the central streets of London and the people danced and sang there as on a village green. (We had seen and shared in that celebration, also.) There was dancing and singing in the same streets last night--but the temper of the people was quite different. A decade has passed, with 6 years of War and all it's horrors. Last night it was not thankfulness for the good things of life--enjoyed through 25 years reign of a beloved King--which put a madness into the people and packed them in crowds before Buckingham Palace to shout, "We want the King!" It was thankfulness for release from fear, privation, devastation and death--and an urge to express their loyalty and appreciation to a Sovereign, and his Queen, who had shared all this with them, the British people.

Dodging the fire-crackers that spurted suddenly here and there above our heads or landed underfoot in terrifying explosion, the 3 of us traversed Regent Street to Piccadilly Circus. The place was a seething cauldron of humanity--with heads bobbing like dumplings in a stew, the spirals of smoke from firecrackers adding realism to the simile. At intervals the iridescent arc of a rocket (Peace-Time!) cut the night above. Along the kerbs stood fire-engines and ambulances--just in case. A frieze of tolerant London Bobbies enclosed the whole.

Martha, Kay and I worked our way up against the cement and stone of Swan and Edgar's large shop on the North side of Piccadilly Circus. Following along it's walls, we made the curve from Regent Street around into Piccadilly, and headed for Buckingham Palace.

It was slow work. The human traffic in the streets was like a river. One must breast the current of youth, arms linked, 4 to 8 deep, surging in waves over the macadam--or cut across the shoals of singing groups, knots of slightly "lit" men and women, and the inevitable tangle of lovers. But eventually we passed the Ritz, and ducked into Green Park. Here scattered bonfires bloomed hotly--indiscriminately fed by chairs and benches--their pagan crackle assenting the strange, unleashed exaltation of a shouting throng of people temporarily crazed by Peace-At-Last. Ahead of us through the trees we glimpsed an unforgettable scene--masses of people pouring along the Mall, and congregating about and swarming over the Queen Victoria Memorial in the Circle before the Palace Gates. A blaze of floodlighting beat upon, encircled and caught up this living historic picture into a globe of glory.

We hurried on across Green Park, squeezed through the narrow iron-lace gates into the Mall and The Circle, and joined the singing crowd. "Land of Hope and glory" shook the sound waves. And presently a chant arose. "We want the King! We want the King!"

A snake-dance of bereted Tank Corps men wove hardily in and out of the close-packed throng. Children rode aloft on uniformed shoulders. The tops of the high, ornamental Park Gates through which we had just emerged, crawled with people. A woman in pink knickers (there was no mistaking them!) clung precariously half-way up one of the archways.

Jeers and catcalls couldn't shake her loose.

Suddenly there was a hush. Then scattered voices, "I think they're coming out now. --Look, the King is coming out! And the Queen, God Bless her! --They're coming out!" The individual voices merged into one great roar of acclaim. "We want the King! We want the King!"

I found myself shouting the same, my eyes glued to the long balcony above the Palace entrance.

A shifting of lights along the glass doors at the rear of the balcony, then moving figures, and the King and Queen appeared at the flag-draped railing. The King wore a naval uniform. Bare-headed he stood, lifted his right hand in an informal salute, and smiled a very serious smile. The Queen was regal in white fox and diamonds, her diamond tiara, put away "for the duration," once more resplendent in her hair. She waved. Her Majesty has a most individual little wave of the hand--an upward, rather spiraling motion, that lends a certain naiveté to this royal gesture. It has charm and evokes affection.

Everyone waved in answer. And "God Save the King" poured into the soft night air from thousands of singng throats.

That moment of exaltation was the only moment of true celebration for the Peace, on V-J Day, so far as I was concerned. All along I had been trying to feel festive, goading myself with the thoughts, "The War is over. It is Peace at last." But heavier thoughts continually overrode these phrases. "Pete is gone. And Rob. And thousands like them. What is there to rejoice over?" But, for that moment, I shared the light-heartedness and hope of the people close about me. It was an historic moment--and I felt the impact of it.

As the King and Queen re-entered the Palace the crowd

428

commenced to recede. A large wedge of determined people headed for one of the narrow gateways into Green Park. The girls and I were separated. Helpless to do more than fend off a prodding elbow, a flailing arm, I was lifted from my feet and carried along like a twig in a log-jam, my ribs terrifyingly crushed inward towards my spine. I thought that they were going to meet--and crunch!

As the solid mass of single-minded humanity moved slowly toward the narrow opening ahead, I groaned aloud. How could this tangled lot of pushing people ever thin out enough to get through that narrow space? Being quite helpless, I waited--and was borne along, inches from the ground, up to the very gate. Then, in a quick and twisting motion, I was heaved between the non-resilient pillars--and deposited upon a gravel path, the crowd dispersing over the grass of Green Park.

"Talk about the eye of the needle!" I gasped as Martha and Kay appeared.

A bit disheveled, but still hardy, we set out to walk all the way back to the flat. Across Piccadilly we dodged, through groups of merry-makers, endangered by careening overburdened open cars--then down Clarges Street into Curzon, across Berkeley Square, up Hay Hill, and left via the arc of Grafton Street into Bond Street along whose famous and now bomb-scarred length we trudged to Oxford Street. A bit slowly now, because of me (was I weary!), we navigated the short streets, Cavendish Square, and more short streets--back into Portland Place, at last.

The multi-colored flags on the B.B. C. now seemed a bit faded, in spite of the floodlights. The girls and I were silent. We just kept walking. 1-2-3, 1-2-3. My pre-war sandals wobbled on my definitely war-time feet. In the ruins of the bombed buildings about us I could see sad ghosts who mocked the lights of peace.

Finally Martha fitted the key into the lock of the front door at 71 Portland Place. The 3 of us--Martha, Kay and I all solemnly said, "Well, I wouldn't have missed it for anything." But, without inquiring into the matter I knew that the girls were thinking just what I was.

"Whatever has it all been about? All this laughter--this gaiety--this yelling--this celebration of Peace--this madness in the London streets tonight--after such a War, such a terrible, terrible War--after so many casualties, so many deaths--the death of Pete."

September, 1945.
Back to "Springfield"

And so World War II has ended--the shooting War, that is. But what U.N.R.R.A. (United Nations Rehabilitation and Relief Association), chooses to call rehabilitation looks like another colossal struggle for everyone, everywhere. Conditions on the Continent are beyond words, of course-- deplorably bad and sad. But conditions here in England are certainly not cheerful. They are most depressing. Unless one has lived here, throughout the War, as an ordinary housewife, with the daily problems of feeding, clothing, and keeping well one's family (not to mention keeping them alive during the raids!)--managing all this in spite of the drastic rationing of food, clothes and coal--unless one has experienced such a life one can have absolutely no conception of what the people of England have endured and still face, for the rationing of food and clothes goes on and coal is scarcer than ever.

Then there are the returning prisoners of War. Many of them present an unhappy problem--their health, their mental state. Those men who, under the Japs, suffered a starvation diet of maggoty rice have receding lower jaws; the whole contour of the face is strangely changed, the upper teeth and lips prominently shelf-like. Certainly such physical changes can be rectified in time, but bodily scars from terrible beatings will never go away, nor crippled limbs. And the inner scars from a life of privation and torture with all it's attendant conditions and scenes (amputation of a limb by hacksaw, with no anesthetic, for instance)--these unforgettable experiences will never completely fade away.

The handful of men left from the several thousand Jap driven Allied captives who built the Bangkok-Moulmein Railroad are, apparently, in the worst condition. That they have survived at all is a miracle. Major Frazer Martens is one of these survivors. Re-united, at last, with his wife and 2 small children, I imagine England seems like Heaven to him.

The people here--those people so smugly catalogued as "the back-bone of a nation"--these people need all the help they can get. They have deprived themselves, as a Nation, to the ultimate limit. Everyone here has been--and is--strictly rationed. Yet, in spite of this fact, there are countless numbers of people who wish to sacrifice a bit of their meager rations to the starving people in Europe. Doctors here say, "No." The vitality of the British people can be lowered no more, not even by one sixteenth of an ounce of any ration.

431

Here are a few items of that strict rationing for almost six years of war.

Butter -- 2 oz's. per week per person.

Lard -- formerly 2 oz's., now 1 oz. per week per person.

Meat -- 1/3 - (24 cents) per week per person.

Milk -- 2 1/2 pts. milk per week per person.

Bacon -- 2 slices per week per person.

Jam -- 1 lb. per month per person.

Eggs - 2 per month per person.

Of course there are certain foods off the ration. But they are by no means always procurable. Take fish for instance. Fishing boats have converted into mine sweepers, and there are still minefields. I have seen and been in queues that have stretched from the counter, within the shop, outside along the pavement for quite some distance. I have watched the fishmonger's supply of fish--such as it was--diminish in varying lots to customers, until there has been no more and I have been turned away, empty-handed, as those British housewives left standing with me have been.

In addition to the rationing there is the "point" system-- coupons which may be used for certain foods, tinned and packaged, or by the pound. Here are a few examples of the articles "on points."

1 tin salmon	12 points
1 tin span (small)	17 points
1 tin spam (large)	54 points
1 tin sardines	2 points
1 tin vegetables	4 points
1 tin baked beans	4 points

At 20 points a month per person (used to be 24) one is rather stymied for meals now and then--certainly balanced ones. I gaze at the fabulous advertisements for fabulous food in some American magazine (fetched by Dick from the States) and groan. Then I flip the magazine together, heave it on the floor, jump up and down on it--and go out to the grocer's and return with two tins of baked beans. These on toast, with a batch of boiled cabbage, will do nicely for lunch. We have eaten this type of menu for weeks and months and years. It's not only your tummy that blows up--your mind sort of explodes.

And the business of keeping clean! With 1 coupon for 3 ozs. of soapflakes, 1 coupon for 1 toilet size cake of soap and 2 coupons for 1 bath cake, a cake of soap is used until it becomes a fragile, transparent leaf--which, in turn, maliciously vanishes into thin air.

Clothes and household linens also are rationed. No wonder Americans arriving in England remark how shabby everything is--how dowdy the people.

24 clothing coupons for 8 months per adult; children receive more. I'll mention only a few items, but these will give you a very good idea of the problem which British families (we along with them) have been and still are facing.

Women:	Skirt	7 coupons
	Pullover	6 coupons
	Wool Frock	11 coupons
	Suit	18 coupons
	Shoes	5 coupons per pair.
	Panties	2 coupons per pair.
	Nightgown	6 coupons
Men:	Shoes	9 coupons
	Shirt	8 coupons

433

```
Suit            26 coupons
(no cuffs allowed on trousers)
Pajamas          6 coupons
Coat            20 coupons
```

And petrol rationing continues. This has been most frustrating, of course. People have felt rooted--tethered might be a better word--in one place most of the time. Little trips, an impromptu visit to a relative or friend, or just transportation on a stormy day (where buses are far from the house) have had to be foregone all these War years--the small, precious ration of petrol hoarded for "the necessary," perhaps some unforeseen emergency.

I have been lucky with trips. Because Dick's business has been crucial to the war effort and takes him about England he is given the necessary petrol--and sometimes I have gone with him. These safaris into scenes other than the immediate have given me an enormous lift now and then--and certainly a deeper appreciation of how thwarted some people have felt-- how deprived--for they simply have not been able to do what they have so longed to do--move about freely.

So now, with the War ended at last and the years-long threat of imminent death and destruction from bombing removed, the rationing (all kinds) has become more aggravating than ever. Many people feel that they have earned a success from at least the harsh structures of a pinched daily living. But the British are realists; they'll carry-on (that over-worked wartime word!).

A Small Homily

The English people speak our language, we speak theirs. We Americans have many common bonds with the English. But somehow through the past years, and even during these recent dreadful years of World War II--when England and America once more fought side by side--some of these bonds have become rather stretched and brittle. We can not afford to have them break. I am not speaking in terms of Treaties or Alliances--nor even of Governments, Politics, Big Business, "Isma," etc., etc., etc.

I speak of Living, just ordinary day to day Living--Life in general--for the average human being. So can we not concentrate on what, for some reason, are too often considered the lesser things in life--contented and "homely" daily Living. Education more applicable to life as it must how be lived, and above all Tolerance--tolerance between Man and Man, Country and Country, with Friendship arising from that tolerance?

Peace has arrived. Or has it?

At any rate, the Future has become Today.

The tapestry of Life must be woven anew. The Past is over and done with. Let us apply ourselves to the present, and use all it's potentialities with Strength (moral), with Justice (God grant it to us,) and with Humanity (for all)--our Minds and Hearts as monitors. I can not think that Pete has died in vain. And he is only one among the legions of young men who died that we might live.

Little Penelope Marianne (for whom this journal was written,) you are possessed of a golden heritage--one that your

435

Daddy left you, an inheritance of Freedom. Spend this inheritance with care and forethought, sharing it in generosity and kindness, for it has been paid for with the dearest of currency--Life, the life of Lieutenant Peter Nelson Dean, R.N.,F.A.A. (Royal Navy, Fleet Air Arm).

"Greater love hath no man than that he lay down his life for another."

"Springfield"
Instow
North Devon
England
September, 1945.

Epilogue

Park Avenue
New York, N.Y.
U.S.A.

With World War II over, Dick must return to the States, establish an office in New York and find a home for us there, or at least a pied-a-terre. At first we all expected to sail together, the whole family, including Meda who had agreed to a year in America with us while we got settled. Sir Stafford Cripps (Chancellor of the Exchequer) was making a very big effort to get sailing accommodations for us. But, alas, only those people who could prove vital necessity were considered for transportation.

So in November Dick flew off to New York, after making arrangements for inventory and packers at "Springfield" so that all would be in readiness when a ship did become available. But the Cottons left England in installments; Gerry and Dick's secretary, Violet Ward (a young English-woman,) got a Swedish ship in mid-December, and in early January Alix and Penny and Meda flew to New York. Martha and I were left holding the bag.

For weeks Sir Stafford Cripps, true to his promise to Dick, tried to obtain passage to the States for Martha and me-- on a ship, the doctors having said "No," to planes for me. Almost six years of War, plus it's deprivations, dietary and otherwise, had put me into a spin. I spent much time in bed at Portland Place, and much money in Harley street for "shots" and pills. Some sort of After-the-War Thing! Many people had it, particularly the women. A feeling of deep frustration, a decided let-down after the keyed-up activity of the War, and

437

some depression. This last was compounded of 1, the seemingly useless slaughter (young men in the fighting and civilians in the bombing) and 2, the residue of War which was everywhere: The hospitals jam-packed with wounded, some never to live real lives again; the heaps of rubble, the gaping craters in the streets, the scarred buildings; the broken homes (broken by bombs or broken by death;) the realization that Peace could work no miracles.

But at last Martha and I received notice of a tentative sailing date. The longed for news did two things for me: At once I felt wonderful, my heart bursting with the joy of going home to the Sates; yet I felt a strange niggling in this joyous heart of mine. For I was going to leave England, my home-away-from-home for over eleven years (almost six of them in a war) and I was going to leave a host of dear friends who must carry on in the aftermath of one of the most dreadful of Wars.

But my true home was America. And my husband, my son, my elder daughter and my grand-daughter awaited me there. So Martha and I set about the necessary preparations to sail.

We gave up 71 Portland Place and returned to "Springfield". The inventory men and the packers came down from London, and everything "Cotton" was finally shipped off, save for necessary clothes. Then we had a last few days at "Springfield" to farewell (a bit tearfully) our dear North Devon friends. Finally we went up to London, this time to the Park Lane Hotel, to await our ship.

But some good friends, Doris and George Laimbeer (Americans,) invited us to stay with them in their house in Bayswater. Martha and I thrilled, of course, and grateful. George is European manager for General Foods and remained in London throughout the War, while Doris and the two boys, plus Nannie, returned to the States for the duration. Now the Laimbeer family is re-united and Doris is coping with the rationing and the drabness of English post-war life. Yet, in spite of this, the Laimbeers made Martha and me feel very much at home.

A good bit of our time was spent with friends and chat, tea and drinks--true Laimbeer hospitality. Judy and Stan Beverley popped in often! But finally I received a definite date to sail--from Cardiff, Wales, of all places!

It was an overcast damp day in late February that Martha and I drove to Paddington Station. Stan, staunch and loyal friend, met us there. He was going with us, all the way to Berry Docks, Cardiff--and see us onto the ship. And a mercy that he did.

Upon arrival at Berry Docks we had to walk from the station to our ship. Stan carried the heaviest cases, Martha the balance, and I managed (two on each arm) an assortment of bags (three string and one weird oil-cloth affair.) I resembled a donkey with pannier baskets--and I felt like one! And when I saw our ship I behaved like one. I balked.

The ship was a Liberty ship, in from France after delivering a cargo of coal (during the War she'd been a Gun Carrier.), and she rode quite atop the water, having no ballast. From the dockside her dingy gray structure rose as a cliff, a high one. There was no gangway. But from the dock, slanted up alongside the ship to an open deck, ran a companion-ladder of open steps with a rope rail on the outer side, no hand support along the ship. And the darn thing swayed. I was appalled to learn that I was supposed to ascend that!

Stan went up first. Then I. Then Martha. Stan, being

navy, simply skimmed up the ladder and disappeared into the ship. By concentrating on footwork, inching my left hand up the rope, and staving myself off from the ship with the right, I made it to the tiny platform at the top before the open upper deck. There I froze--on the last step, the panniers swinging.

"Mother!" said Martha from behind.

I seemed atop Mt. Everest. I don't like heights.

"Just step up onto the platform, Mother!"

And be plummeted under the single rope barrier there-- down into the murky water of Berry Dock? Not I! I stood-- and swayed--and hung on--and prayed.

And at that strategic second Stan appeared on the deck and pulled me up and into the ship.

Now I was in a dark, low-ceilinged cave, with a lamp or two on the walls. Papers checked, Martha and I (and Stan, bless him) were escorted to our quarters on the starboard side. We were to share a small cabin which normally served as the ship's Sick Bay. There were two bunks, one atop the other, with a port hole beside each--a narrow settee along the opposite (inner) wall--and, miracle of miracles, a basin with two faucets. Hot and cold? A few clothes hooks were on the wall to the right of the basin, and in that corner was a narrow cupboard.

The larger cases were stowed under the lower bunk, the others were simply placed on the floor in a pyramid against the after wall, while the bags were thrown, like pillows, onto the settee. Then Stan took us on a tour of the ship.

We learned much.

1.   The ship never before had taken passengers-- just cargo, guns.

2. The crewmen's quarters, two very narrow cabins with six bunks each (three to a side and supported by metal-piping fixtures) were to accommodate the eight male passengers.

3. On the portside two small cabins (given up by ship's officers who would go in with the male passengers) were allotted, one each, to two young women; one a young secretary from our Legation in Oslo, going home on leave; the other an English war bride, going to join her husband in the States, where she had never been and where he had preceded her by several months.

4. The Officers' Mess was to be our dining salon. Along the fore-side of the Mess was a leather-covered banquette with port holes above. There were four or five tables with several chairs apiece. Each article of furniture bolted to the floor. It all seemed a bit bleak.

5. The toilet facilities both fascinated and repelled. On the port-side, in a compartment, were several showers, their stalls without doors. On the starboard side, and almost opposite to our cabin was a door labeled W.C. In this compartment also were there several stalls. There was no lock on the door into the corridor. H-mm, I thought.

By then Stan had to leave to catch a train back to London. We watched him down the ladder onto the dock, where he turned to wave to us before going to the station. I don't know how Martha felt, but I was conscious of a rock in my tummy, a pebble in my throat and a mist before my eyes.

When out in the Bristol Channel the ship hove-to, to take on water--Cardiff Port Authority having refused ballast otherwise. The first two days I spent in my bunk, the lower; I am the world's worst sailor. I had with me an enormous assortment of pills--a regular battery from my good Harley Street doctors. In amazement and appreciation I arose on the third day, and thereafter was ambulatory and otherwise--as you will see.

The trip home became a trip to remember in more ways than one. In the first place a Liberty Ship is not an Ocean Liner, and in the second place her Captain and crew were very young, the only man over thirty being the Purser who was thirty-one. In the beginning, as a grandmother, I harbored a few doubts. But not for long. Ship, Captain, and Crew proved wonderful--and in some rather sticky situations and a terrible storm.

Early on, the young warbride became a bit of a problem, poor darling. A combination of fear of the sea and the unknown country ahead, plus a touch of claustrophobia, put her into real hysteria about once a day. On occasion the Captain would call on Martha for help. Sometimes talk would calm down the girl, sometimes pills, but a couple of times it had to be a "shot" for she had become very violent. Once she threw Martha on the deck and sat on her. The Captain considered radioing the Queen Elizabeth (at the time fairly near us) to take the girl off--she was in such a state. And one day she locked herself in her cabin and began screaming. The Captain had a crewman break open the door. Then the two men held her while Martha gave her a hypo (The first Martha (not being licensed) had ever administered in spite of her hospital work.). But no matter how she'd been during the day, the warbride would appear for dinner and the evening--prettily dressed and made-up, smiling and gay. Amazing!

As the dowager on the ship I observed rather than shared the activities of the days and evenings, save for bridge after dinner with the Captain whenever he was free. At that hour the Officer's Mess buzzed with chat and laughter. Everyone was so friendly.

During the day I spent a great deal of time in my cabin, lying on the settee, reading. I would have "callers," among them members of the crew who would invariably talk of home and family and exhibit snapshots of same. All through the War I saw young men carry these talismans of Faith and Love--particularly the Americans--and I always appreciated their wanting to share their bits of family life so dear to them.

About mid-way of our trip the wind blew up and the seas rose. The Captain announced that a storm was predicted and that he was changing course to evade it. We were to head toward the Azores. Since this would mean a bit of a delay no one was thrilled of course. And, alas, the storm overtook us.

The ship rolled forty-five degrees which, I was informed, was just about the limit for safety. I would sit on my settee, my back to the wall, my feet braced, and hang on as the ship dipped over--over to starboard, ever nearer to the raging sea. There--at forty-five degrees--the ship would hold, in seeming hesitation. Then, suddenly, as though having made up her mind, she would give a gigantic shudder, and roll back up--and over to the portside, where I would be reversed with her and as though on my back. This went on for two days and nights. Many things happened.

The stoves could not be used so we had cold food, which really didn't bother us, having other things to think about. Painting of the deck had been going on--Martha and the secretary helping--so there were opened paint cans which overturned into dark green rivers. Duckboards were put over these--and of course the ropes were up--so we could get about. The racks were on the tables. But the shenanigans of the ship, particularly the pitching, would send rolls, vegetables, etc. across the tables, from plate to opposite plate and back again. One never quite knew whose peas and carrots one was eating.

During the tumbling of the ship someone tumbled--hard--against the W.C. door and stove it in, making a large jagged hole. This hole was then covered over with paper. After that I felt even less happy about the W.C. But we were all in the same boat--Ha!--so it didn't seem to matter.

All at once, late in the second afternoon, the ship quit rolling--it seemed completely stopped, and in a fairly calm ocean--everything on an even keel. I breathed a sigh of relief. But not for long.

The Captain appeared in my cabin doorway. He looked a bit pale and haggard after so much loss of sleep--and his feeling of responsibility for the passengers, in addition to ship and crew, lay very heavy on him. Fine young man. I thought to cheer him up as I said, "You've done a super job, Captain, taking us through that awful storm."

"But I haven't, " he said.

"Oh?" showing my ignorance. "We're in the eye of the storm. Now we must get out of it."

"All that over again!" I couldn't believe it.

"Yes," the Captain said and heaved a huge sigh. "Won't be easy."

It wasn't. But this time the rolls didn't seem so deep, and although our waste basket and a batch of oranges hopped about our cabin like rabbits, this storm (or second installment?) seemed a shadow of the other. And two funny things happened.

All through that voyage, no matter what, my breakfast tray arrived--intact. (Martha evidently having sold me as a semi-invalid, I was fetched a breakfast tray every morning. The food! The food! Ambrosia from the Gods after wartime menus.) A long arm--up about five feet six inches from the deck--would suddenly sprout through my cabin doorway, a laden tray poised at tip of arm. Depending on the ship's roll, arm and tray would progress into my cabin--then retrogress-- then progress etc.--to be followed eventually by the young steward, in a sort of dance. He always made it (laden tray and all, not a drop spilled) to me (on the settee) where he placed said tray on the bed pillow I had ready on my lap. A bit of magic!

But one morning there was a variation to this Steward's Dance-of-the-Breakfast-Tray. It was during the storm and the ship was really reeling. I was ensconced on my settee as usual. In came the arm with tray. Then the steward did a waltz across the cabin--then back to me. The tray was plunked down, square on the pillow on my lap. "Bravo!" I said. And the steward grinned.

He set about making up the bunks as usual. Finished with mine, he stepped up on the lower bunk's rail to make up Martha's bunk. With each roll of the ship to starboard he would follow along, blanket or sheet in hand, over and across Martha's bunk for the tuck-in business on the further side. Now Martha had no bunk-board, so each night seven life-

445

jackets were stuffed under the outer edge of her mattress to keep her from falling out. This a.m. the ship gave a sort of dying, very deep roll to starboard and the steward headed over Martha's bunk. As the ship snapped up and back the steward did also. No bunk-board to grab onto! He flew through the air, backwards, across the cabin--and sat down smack! On my breakfast tray.

Not only was there tomato juice that morning but there was catsup for beans.

I got another breakfast and the steward another pair of pants.

The second contretemps was a matter of plumbing. Not fancying a shower while clutching the soap in one hand and the safety rail in the other (and having no third hand for the washing performance) I had evolved my own bath system. I would place two cases, one atop the other, before the hand basin in our cabin and, perched on these, I would make do with a sponge. Until heavy weather caught up with us it was O.K. But, alas, whether due to storm or no, one morning the basin became stopped up. Part of the water therein slapped in blobs from out each side of the basin as the ship rolled. But a good one quarter basinful remained. The drain had quit.

I spoke to the cabin steward about it and he said he'd send the ship's plumber. No plumber all that day.

The next morning--I again asked for the plumber. And again--no plumber.

So the next a.m.--feeling grubby as well as crabby--I grumbled when my breakfast tray arrived.

Where is the plumber you promised?" I asked. "The basin drain is useless!"

"Get him sure today, Ma'am," said the steward and

proceeded to make up the bunks while I proceeded to eat my breakfast.

As he came to take my tray I said, "If you don't get the plumber here today I shall speak to the Captain."

Without a word and quick as a wink, the steward picked up my fork--went over to the basin--and began poking at the drain.

Rattle, rattle of the fork on the drain. Grunts from the steward as he prodded.

Then suddenly a gush of water as the steward turned on both faucets.

"O.K. now Ma'am!" He returned the fork to my tray. "No speak to Captain," he said beamishly.

I couldn't have done it; I was speechless.

But at least I had had my breakfast.

One evening a group of us were having drinks with the Captain in his quarters, topside by the Bridge. We were now heading away from the Azores but it was still very warm. The port holes were open also the door out onto the Bridge Deck. With a nod from the Captain, Martha, the young secretary and I went out--to join the First Officer there.

Heavenly night! Beguiling sounds and sights. The rush of our silvered wake--swi-ish, swi-ish, swi-ish--was hypnotic. There, right above the sea, I stood entranced. In the deep blue of the domed night sky hung millions of enormous stars like Far Eastern lamps--so large, seemingly so near, in an aura of their own quite detached from the heavens, ready for plucking. I reached up a hand.

Just one, I thought. Just one to take home--to illuminate the rest of my life.

"Oh!" I said. "Oh!"

The immensity and limitlessness of sea and sky quite dwarfed our ship. And I certainly felt diminished--yet uplifted.

"Lucky you!" I said to the First Officer, meaning his opportunity to view such grandeur so often.

"Yes, Ma'am," he answered. But his viewing seemed limited--to the young secretary close beside him.

I recalled an item on the ship's grapevine. So, "Wonderful experience," I said. "Thank you very, very much." I poked Martha. She added her thanks to mine, and we returned to the Captain and the others.

Later, in our cabin, Martha said, "Did you have to be so obvious, Mother!"

"Well, I thought they were," I said. (And eventually the two young people did marry.)

At last!

We were only one night out from New York! After fourteen days at sea.

There was a very fresh breeze with a drizzle. But we nipped jauntily along through foam-capped rollers, with a bit of a bounce now and then. The Officer's Mess was full of happy and excited people. Martha and I were playing Bridge with the Captain and another Officer, the radio muttering an accompaniment.

All of a sudden we heard the announcement that a lion had escaped from the New York Zoo and was roaming Central Park. New Yorkers were perturbed. I couldn't help making the remark that we, too, had problems. "They ought to be out here. We have a Pride of Lions! All white-maned and roaring at us."

448

But during the night the wind died down and the rain stopped. The following day was sunny and cold. We were catching up with the U.S.A. The air was wonderful, a shot in the arm, and everyone became hopped-up with it. Impatience to land animated minds and bodies

But an inimical fog set in. The Pilot, due at six p.m. couldn't make it. So at dusk we anchored, somewhere off Coney Island. We could hear music and felt frustrated. However, at ten p.m. the fog lifted. Most of us went out on deck and stood enthralled by the bright lights on shore. Groaningly we watched the steady stream of HUGE American cars zooming by on the highway by the water--their lights and the street-lights in a tantalizing rainbow. There was the Promised Land!

I radioed Dick to hire a launch, or even a rowboat, to come out and get me and Martha. He didn't even deign to answer. And all this time I had believed the U.S.A. to be a land of miracles!

The next morning was golden and brilliant, capped with a blue sky. And a miracle did happen. After that stormy fourteen day crossing our gallant little Liberty Ship berthed in Brooklyn, New York, U.S.A.

On the bridge stood her young Captain, resplendent in his dark blue, gold-braided uniform, his cap set square in authority and accomplishment. He had told me that his young wife and baby son awaited him at the Hotel Commodore in New York. What a lode star!

The English warbride ranged the port rail. Gay in her tweed suit, her hair ordered, her lips smiling, her eyes a-spark, she searched the dock for her American bridegroom.

And pensive, in a deck chair, lay the young secretary

from Oslo--in no hurry to leave this ship. Planning her future?

Bunched at the gangway gate were the eight male passengers. Nothing now would keep them from their ultimate goals, and they would be the first to rush out from that hiatus in their lives--a fortnight at sea, suspended between two worlds.

Martha and I, strangely (yet not so strangely?) exalted by arrival at our native land after so long, peered into the shifting mass of people on the dock. At last we spotted Dick in the throng. He was the first on board.

We were home.